About the Editor

JOSÉ PEREIRA was born in Bombay, India, where he received a Ph.D. in Indian History and Culture from St. Xavier's College. During the past fifteen years, he has taught or studied at the University of Lisbon, the University of London (School of Oriental and African Studies and the Institute of Archaeology), and the American Institute of Indian Studies in Benares, where he was a Research Associate in the History of Indian Art.

Dr. Pereira, who speaks and/or reads some fifteen languages, is currently an associate professor of theology at Fordham University, where he teaches Sanskrit and lectures on the theology of religions—especially Hinduism, Jainism and Buddhism. In addition, he is a member of the Institute of Intercultural Research (Heidelberg) and the American Academy of Religion. He has published several books on cultural history and literary criticism, numerous articles for scholarly publications, as well as co-authored a number of works on traditional Indian music and cultural history.

In preparing *Hindu Theology: A Reader,* he has undertaken a task of major theological proportions—a single volume devoted to the great schools and archetypes of Hindu theology and their impact on Western thought. For every student of theology, as well as anyone interested in a readable compendium of Indic religious thought, this volume is indispensable.

Hindu Theology: A Reader

Edited with an Introduction and Notes
by

JOSÉ PEREIRA

IMAGE BOOKS

A Division of Doubleday & Company, Inc.

Garden City, New York

1976

Image Books Edition published November 1976

Library of Congress Cataloging in Publication Data
Main entry under title:

Hindu theology.

Includes index.
1. Hinduism—Addresses, essays, lectures.
2. Philosophy, Hindu—Addresses, essays, lectures.
I. Pereira, José.
BL1210.H47 294.5′2

ISBN: 0-385-09552-X
Library of Congress Catalog Card Number 76–2842

Printed in the United States of America
First Edition

TO MY PARENTS

ACKNOWLEDGMENTS

A work like this one cannot be accomplished without much help, which one owes to many more people than one can thank. I am grateful to them all, but I wish particularly to remember the following:

Miss Bhadra Akruvala of the Bharatiya Vidya Bhavan, Bombay; Mr. Anderson, Librarian, of the Bombay University Library; Fr. Thomas Berry of Fordham University, for permitting me to use his library; Mr. K. S. Damle of Ruparel College, Bombay; Mr. Ishvar Lal Kosambia of the Bharatiya Vidya Bhavan; Principal S. G. Mudgal of Ruparel College; Pandit R. S. Panchamukhi of Dharwar; Dr. D. M. Shanbhag of Karnatak University, Dharwar; Mr. A. K. Thakur of Ruparel College; Mr. K. K. A. Venkatachari, Director, Ananthacharya Research Institute, Bombay; and Mrs. Doris DeVito, New York, for typing my manuscript with great care.

And more especially Fr. Robert Gleason, S.J., former Chairman of the Department of Theology, Fordham University, for putting me in touch with Mr. John Delaney of Doubleday; to Mr. Delaney, Mr. Robert Heller and Miss Patricia Kossmann of Doubleday for their understanding of the problems involved in the compilation of a reader like the present one, and their helpful suggestions for solving many difficulties; to my wife, Angela, and the children, for spending the Christmas of 1974 by themselves, while I was visiting India in search of rare theological texts; to Professor Armando Menezes of Karnatak University, for much assistance and encouragement; to Professor Ewert Cousins, of Fordham University, through discussions with whom many of the problems of the Trichotomy were clarified; to my student Mrs. Gita Khurana, for procuring books by important theologians, who otherwise would not have been represented in this anthology; and to my student Professor Paul Murphy of the John Jay College of Criminal Justice, New York, without whose easing of my task in countless ways in the last critical stages of the work, and with considerable hardship to himself, this book might never have been completed.

CONTENTS

Acknowledgments 7
List of Schemes 15
Introduction 17

PART ONE: *AN OVERVIEW OF HINDU THEOLOGY*

The Significance of the Indic Religions for the West 21
The Contemporary Vogue in Oriental Faiths 30
Theology, the Architectonics of Religion 34
The Trichotomy, or the Three Basic Types of Theology 37
Hinduism's Dual Norm and Dual Aspect 40
The Evolution of Hindu Theology 42

PART TWO: *SELECTED WRITINGS*

THEOLOGIES OF DIFFERENCE

Preliminary Note 51

I. SANKHYA, or DISCRIMINATIONISM 53

1. Īśvara Kṛṣṇa, *The Sum of Sankhya Teaching, 56;* 2. Gauḍa Pāda the Sankhya, *Matter, Sole Cause, Selfless Servant of Spirit, 64;* 3. Vācaspati Miśra, *The Need for Theological Inquiry, 68;* 4. "Kapila," *Final Sum of Sankhya Doctrine, 70*

II. YOGA, or SELF-INTUITIONISM 77

5. Patañjali, *Principles of Yoga, 78;* 6. Vyāsa, *The Glorious Yogic State, 81*

III. RITUALISM, or MĪMĀMSĀ 84

7. Śabara, *The Nature of Religious Observance, 86;* 8. Kumārila Bhaṭṭa, *The Occult Virtue in Sacrifices, 89;*

9. Śālika Nātha Miśra, *Self-evidence of Revelation, 95;* 10. Pārtha Sārathi Miśra, *A Critical Inquiry into the Validity of Knowledge, 99*

IV. ATOMISM, or *VAIŚEṢIKA 105*

11. Praśasta Pāda, *The Creation and Dissolution of the Universe, 106*

V. LOGICISM, or *NYĀYA 108*

12. Vātsyāyana, *Liberation through Logic, 109;* 13. Uddyotakara, *Logic, the Light of the Sciences, 111;* 14. Udayana, *Vindication of Difference, 112;* 15. *Proofs of the Existence of God, 116*

VI. DUALIST VEDANTA, or *DVAITA VEDĀNTA 122*

16. Madhva, *The Foundations of Dualist Vedanta Theology, 124;* 17. Jaya Tīrtha, *Critique of Difference-in-Identity, 136;* 18. *Specifics, the Nuances Innate to Identity, 141;* 19. *The Limitlessness of God's Causality, 148;* 20. Vyāsa Rāya, *The Problem of Evil, 149;* 21. Vādi Rāja, *Finality of Madhva's Doctrine, 156;* 22. Vyāsa Rāmācārya, *The Inevitability of Dualism, 157;* 23. Vanamāli Miśra, *The Expressibility of God, 162*

VII. ŚAIVA ORTHODOXY, or *ŚAIVA SIDDHĀNTA 166*

24. Bhoja Deva, *The Sum of Śaiva Orthodox Theology, 168;* 25. Śrī Kumāra, *The Masculine–Feminine Polarity of the Universe, 175;* 26. Aghora Śiva, *God Not the World's Material Cause, 179*

THEOLOGIES OF IDENTITY OR NON-DIFFERENCE

Preliminary Note *185*

VIII–XIII. THE SIX NONDUALIST or *ADVAITA* SCHOOLS *188*

27. Gauḍa Pāda, *The Proclamation of Nondualism, 190;* 28. *The Epistemology of Illusion, 190;* 29. *The Causelessness of All Reality, 194;* 30. Śaṅkara, *The Vedic Law, 196;* 31. *Superposition, the Basis of Illusion, 199;* 32. Prakāśātman, *The Transmogrification of the Brahman, 201;* 33. Śrī Harṣa, *Critique of Difference, 206;* 34. Prakāśānanda, *Self-evidence of the Self, 209;* 35. Madhusūdana Sarasvatī, *The Category of the Inexplicable, 213*

THEOLOGIES OF DIFFERENCE-IN-IDENTITY

Preliminary Note *219*

XIV. SONIC ABSOLUTISM, or *ŚABDABRAHMAVĀDA* *223*

36. Bhartṛ Hari, *The Divinity of Language, 224;* 37. Hari Vṛṣabha, *OM, the Undisputed Center of All Thought, 237*

XV. ANCIENT VEDANTA, or *PURĀTANA VEDĀNTA* *239*

38. Bādarāyaṇa, *The Sum of Vedanta Theology, 240;* 39. *The Brahman's "Equivalent" Names, 242;* 40. Ṭaṅka, *Meditation on the Self, 247;* 41. *The Attainment of the Self, 247;* 42. Ṭaṅka and Dramiḍa, *God's Body, 248;* 43. Dramiḍa, *God's Power, 249;* 44. *God's Power and Compassion, 249;* 45. *God's Exalted Omnipotence, 250;* 46. *The Perfection of the Liberated, 250;* 47. Bodhāyana, *Connection of the Theologies of Ritual and the Brahman, 251;* 48. *Brahman the Light, 251;* 49, *The Mystical Honey Science, 251;* 50. Bhartṛ Prapañca. *Unity in Manifoldness, 252;* 51. *Duality and Nonduality, 252;* 52. *The Highest State, 252;* 53. *Identity of the Brahman and the Soul, 253;* 54. *Restoration of the Sense of All Being, 253;* 55. *Perspicacity, 254;* 56. *Mental Dispositions, 254;* 57. *Desires, 255;* 58. *The Form of Light, 255;* 59. *The Ever Seeing Self, 256;* 60. *Illuminating Knowledge, 257;* 61. *All Is Fire, 257;* 62. *A Conflux of Deities, 258;* 63. *Two Kinds of Liberation, 258;* 64. *Vision of Nonduality, 259*

XVI. CONDITIONED DIFFERENCE-IN-IDENTITY, or *AUPĀDHIKABHEDĀBHEDA* *260*

65. Bhāskara, *The Logic of Difference-in-Identity, 261;* 66. *Principles of Apophatic Theology, 265*

XVII. INDIVISIBLE NONDUALISM, or *AVIBHĀGĀDVAITA* *268*

67. Vijñāna Bhikṣu, *The Concord Among Orthodox Theologies, 269;* 68. *Joy Not the Essence of the Absolute, 276*

XVIII. QUALIFIED NONDUALISM, or *VIŚIṢṬĀDVAITA* *282*

69. Yāmuna, *The Vaiṣṇava Scriptures, the Pāñcarātra Corpus, Easy Summary of Revelation, 285;* 70. *Two Faultless Revelations: The Impersonal in the Vedas and the Personal in the Pāñcarātras, 285;* 71. *The Truthfulness*

of God in the Pāñcarātras, 286; 72. Rāmānuja, *Darkness the Body of God, 287;* 73. *The Transcendence and Accessibility of God, 288;* 74. Sudarśana Sūri, *Rāmānuja, Restorer of the Ancient Way, 290;* 75. Lokācārya, *The Nondualism, 291;* 76. Vedānta Deśika (and Śrī Nivāsa), *Theology: A Critical Science, 299*

XIX. INNATE DIFFERENCE-IN-IDENTITY, or *SVĀBHĀVIKABHEDĀBHEDA* *306*

77. Nimbārka, *Sum of the Theology of Innate Difference-in-Identity, 307;* 78. Śrī Nivāsa, *God, the One Object of Revelation, 308;* 79. Keśava Kāśmīrin, *Liberation: The Attainment of God's State, 310*

XX. PURE NONDUALISM, OR *ŚUDDHĀDVAITA* *315*

80. Vallabha, *Principles of the Theology of Pure Nondualism, 317;* 81. Jagannātha Paṇḍitarāja, *The Nature and Divinity of Aesthetic Emotion, 328;* 82. *Hari Rāya, The Motivelessness of Divine Play, 330*

XXI. INEFFABLE DIFFERENCE-IN-IDENTITY, or *ACINTYABHEDĀBHEDA* *335*

83. Rūpa Gosvāmī, *The Mystical Theology of Passion, 336;* 84. Jīva Gosvāmī, *The Delights of Kṛṣṇa, 340;* 85. Baladeva Vidyābhūṣaṇa, *The Knowledges of Majesty and Sweetness, 342*

XXII. MONIST PASTORALISM, or *LĀKULĪŚAPĀŚUPATA DARŚANA* *346*

86. Lakulīśa, *The Pastoral Way, 347;* 87. *Secret Virtue, Apparent Vice, 349;* 88. Kauṇḍinya, *Ashes, 349;* 89. *Nonviolence, 350;* 90. *The Universal Range of Knowledge, 351;* 91. *God's Glory in His Effects, 351;* 92. *God, One with his Effects, 351;* 93. *Joyfulness, 352;* 94. *Salvation through Opprobrium and Injury, 353;* 95. *Merit through Pretended Seduction, 355;* 96. *Life's Goal: Union with God, not Liberation, 355;* 97. *The Life of a Cow or Deer, 356*

XXIII. TRIADISM, or *TRIKA* *357*

98. Vasu Gupta, *The Śaiva Mysteries, 360;* 99. Somānanda, *The Śiva Nature of All Things, 364;* 100. Abhinava Gupta, *An All-inclusive Nondualism, 368;* 101. *Delight, the Agitation of Force, 369;* 102. *The Principles of Triadism,*

372; 103. Kṣema Rāja, *The Cosmic Vibrations of Divine Energy, 378;* 104. Maheśvarānanda, *Résumé of the Truths of Triadism, 381*

XXIV. ŚAIVA NONDUALISM, or *ŚIVĀDVAITA 389*

105. Śrī Kaṇṭha, *The Compassion and Pitilessness of Divine Terror, 389*

XXV. ENERGY-QUALIFIED NONDUALISM, or HERO-ŚAIVISM, or *ŚAKTIVIŚIṢṬĀDVAITA*, or *VĪRA-ŚAIVA DARŚANA 395*

106. Śrī Pati, *The Energic Fulmination, 396;* 107. Māyi Deva, *Categories of the Theology of Energy-Qualified Nondualism, 398;* 108. *Symbols and Energies, 401*

XXVI. ENERGICISM, or *ŚĀKTA DARŚANA 406*

109. Nīlakaṇṭha the Śākta, *The Goddess, the Supreme Divinty, 407*

PART THREE: *SCHEMES 409*

Notes *505*
Index *521*

LIST OF SCHEMES

1. Temple of Hindu Theology *411*
2. Cathedral of Catholic Theology *417*
3. Lotus of Indic Theologies *419*
4. Wheel of the Hindu Systems *421*
5. Rose Window of Catholic Theologies *425*
6. Lamp of the Vedanta *427*
7. Lotus Pool of Vaiṣṇava Theologies *431*
8. Trident Cluster of Śaiva Theologies *435*
9. Portal of the Vedanta Synthesis *439*
10. Shrine of Hindu Learning *443*
11. Fathers of Hindu Theology *447*
12. The Nyāya Syllogism *451*
13. Sankhya, or Discriminationism 1: Categories *453*
14. Sankhya, or Discriminationism 2: Evolution of the Universe *455*
15. Yoga or Self-Intuitionism: Categories *459*
16. Ritualism: Categories *463*
17. Atomism: Categories *465*
18. Logicism: Categories *467*
19. Dualist Vedanta: Categories *469*
20. Śaiva Orthodoxy: Gnostic School: Categories *471*
21. Śaiva Orthodoxy: Southern or Devotional School: Categories *473*
22. Nondualism 1: Categories *475*
23. Nondualism 2: Evolution of the Universe *477*
24. Ancient Vedanta: Categories *479*
25. Conditioned Difference-in-Identity: Categories *481*
26. Indivisible Nondualism 1: Categories *483*
27. Indivisible Nondualism 2: Evolution of the Universe *485*
28. Pāñcarātra Theology: Evolution of the Universe *487*
29. Qualified Nondualism: Categories *491*

30. Innate Difference-in-Identity: Categories *493*
31. Pure Nondualism: Categories *497*
32. Ineffable Difference-in-Identity: Categories *499*
33. Monist Pastoralism: Categories *501*
34. Triadism 1: Categories *505*
35. Triadism 2: The Twelve Consuming Energies *507*
36. Energy-Qualified Nondualism 1: Categories *509*
37. Energy-Qualified Nondualism 2: Evolution of the Universe *511*
38. Energicism: Categories *513*

INTRODUCTION

Hindu theology is the intellectual climax of the world's most ancient and varied corpus of religious speculation—that of the Indic faiths, which today enjoy a great vogue in the West. It can be compared only to Christian theology for architectonic organization and depth of insight, but excels it in antiquity and in manifoldness of religious archetype. Coming into existence around the second millennium B.C., it began to grow articulate around the seventh century of that era, and to crystallize in the age between the seventh and the seventeenth centuries A.D., which may be called the *Millennium of Hindu Theology*. What the West, through translations, knows of Hindu religious writing, belongs to the time preceding this millennium—partly because the earlier texts are much easier to translate than the later ones, written as they are in a far simpler Sanskrit, and partly because of the pioneer translators' bias for "origins." Especially neglected have been the works of the second half of this millennium—precisely the age of Hindu theology's consummate performance.

It is on this period that I shall concentrate in this book. One reason for this neglect, as I suggested, is the difficulty of the language in which those works are expressed. The root of this difficulty is, no doubt—in the words of William Jones, one of Orientalism's modern pioneers—its "wonderful structure; more perfect than the Greek, more copious than the Latin, and more exquisitely refined than either."[1] To begin with, the syntax of Sanskrit—with its inordinate love of nouns and adjectival compounds, and its near aversion to verbs—is wholly dissimilar to that of any language known in the modern West. This intimidates translators, as do some of the language's other peculiarities. Among them is an inflectional intricacy that permits the creation of composite words —words succinctly encapsuling ideas of a richness of nuance that tongues of a lighter digestion (such as English) can assimilate only with difficulty, or not at all. Another peculiarity is its phenomenal capacity for abbreviation, combined with a contrary penchant for diffuseness and ornamentation—the latter propensity being further stimulated by the language's luxuriance of synonyms.

A main purpose of this book is to render the selected texts into readable English. As some eminent and successful modern translators have shown, such a task can be achieved, not by a literal rendering of the text, but by endeavoring to say in English, and in a manner consonant with its genius, what the writer in Sanskrit said (again) in accordance with the genius of his chosen medium. The translation will therefore strive not to be a mechanical copy of the outer (Sanskritic) expression of the writer's thought, but to embody faithfully the thought itself in English: in other words, to be an English avatar of the idea that had earlier assumed an avatar in Sanskrit. One hopes that this effort will encourage more intensive translation, thus making the thought of the great Hindu theologians familiar to Western readers.

The intelligibility of that thought is based on characteristic assumptions, generally unfamiliar to our readers. I have therefore sought to explain some of them in Part One of this work, "An Overview of Hindu Theology."

It was given to this theology to contemplate the first epiphanies of religion's speculative archetypes, and to perceive with unsurpassed clarity how its own cardinal problem, the relationship between the transcendent and the phenomenal, may be described—as one of Difference, Identity, or Difference-in-Identity. This is the scheme I have followed in Part Two, to classify the "Selected Writings" of the systematic theologians of Hinduism.

Works of systematic theologians presuppose systematic theologies. Hindu thought has been marvelously fecund in the creation of speculative systems. A work such as this requires that they be outlined comprehensively, but in the briefest manner possible—that is, in schematic form. I have done this in Part Three, "Schemes," and have also in course of the work indicated where they can be most fruitfully consulted. Schemes 1–12 are pictorial: I have tried in them to integrate conceptual exactness with appropriate pictorial symbols. The drawings are my own, as is the calligraphy; that of Devanagari is based on Western Indian inscriptions of around the thirteenth century. As for the names of the Hindu theologians, most Western readers find them unconscionably long; so I have broken them up wherever possible—as for instance Abhinava Gupta, instead of Abhinavagupta.

Part One

AN OVERVIEW OF HINDU THEOLOGY

THE SIGNIFICANCE OF THE INDIC RELIGIONS FOR THE WEST

What interest can Hindu theology have for Western readers? Can it only be that of the heirs of one great tradition of thought for the works of another, in some ways more ancient than their own?

In attempting to answer this question one must remember that the West has a special relationship to the world's other cultures, in that it has concerned itself with their ideas more than they have with its own. It is the analytical and historical techniques developed by its scholars that have made an exact and profound study of non-Western cultures possible. Also, these cultures, when not secluded from one another, were only partially linked, until they were drawn together into one world scheme by the West, which is thus more ecumenical than they.

However, like other more parochial civilizations—whose complacency about their own achievement was fostered by their ignorance of that of the others—this most universal of civilizations has also tended to exalt its own achievements excessively (as students of comparative culture have observed), though less so now than before. Its historians of thought give one the feeling that the writings of its thinkers are the only fit expression of human ideas. If (they seem to imply) these ideas, as they grant is possible, take birth in a non-Western brain, it is only through their Western interpretation that their integral nature comes to be revealed: so to their first outstanding Western interpreter rightly falls the honor of being their real discoverer. In other words, the archetypes of human thought are *in their plenitude* Western: their Western interpretation is thus to be taken as the "model" by which all the others are to be judged.

But we cannot permit the most ecumenical of civilizations both to enjoy the benefits of an informed and extensive curiosity in other cultures, and to indulge in a flattering but parochial complacency about its own uniqueness. One main reason for this contradiction—at least in theology—is that the informed curiosity is mainly confined to the specialists in the other cultures, and the parochial complacency to (shall we say?) mere theologians, few of whom have the time and the patience to study Chinese or Sanskrit. Few great non-Western works have been readably translated, and most not at all. This is the kind of situation that books like this one can help remedy.

To come back to our question, and to frame a possible answer. The interest that Hindu theology can have for Western readers is chiefly an interest in religious insights which today, as never before, confront, and even challenge, those long traditional in the West. It is arguable that these insights first arose in the Indic world. It is, moreover, possible that the expression they received at the hands of Indic theologians, after centuries of brilliant and unflagging speculation, and in a linguistic medium unequaled for its philosophical finesse, is the model by which all their other expressions are to be judged.

If these assertions are valid, the originality of some of Western thought is diminished to the merely parochial level. Western thinkers may indeed have acquired some of these insights independently of Indic or other influence, but what they gained was previously unknown only to themselves, not to the human race as a whole—much as America was discovered for Europeans only, not for its inhabitants, hence not for mankind.

A knowledge of Hindu theology is particularly relevant to the theology of our times, for the Indic works contain so many of the ideas that modern Western theologians seem to believe are their discoveries: one is led to assume that a closer inspection of the same works will bring to light the other "discoveries" as well. Indeed, they are sure to contain the insights that future theologians will no doubt claim originality for, and which we can now avail ourselves of by merely learning Sanskrit. We can thus, with some malice, rob our successors of the pleasure of believing that the world would have wanted much invaluable wisdom, had it not been revealed to them for the first time in human history.

One of the several ways of envisaging the evolution of Western thought is that of a progressive *Indicization*. From a knowledge of the Western and Indic traditions a different picture of religious speculation emerges than was projected, say, by the secularist Western historians of the nineteenth century.[1] According to their neat scheme, philosophy shone forth to the world in Greece, and moved from splendor to splendor until it encountered the world of Semitic religion—the source of its obscuration, triumphant in the Dark Ages, when philosophy was supplanted by theology. After a long eclipse Descartes restored its brightness, which from that moment ever increased in strength, attaining to its noonday dazzle in our own times. On the periphery of the focus of light and the mass of darkness was the outer "Oriental" world, a sort of penumbra, of little interest—except perhaps to intellectual adventurers and to lovers of the exotic. Thus there were two main bodies of speculative thought—the "enlightened" (comprising the Greek and modern Western philosophy) and the "obscurantist" (including the "medieval" and the "Oriental," both a jumble of superstition and ingenuous reasoning).

In consequence of research into Scholastic, Indian and Chinese thought, this scheme passed from history into mythology—in other words, acquired a more tenacious life. A great number of Westerners still behave as though they wished the nineteenth-century scheme were true, witness their comparative neglect of the two "obscurantist" traditions. Of course there is a vogue in Oriental religions, but its stimulant is less the erudition of scholars than the unctuousness of gurus. But the great Indic theologians combine knowledge and unction—another reason why their thoughts must be made easily available in translation, if only to correct the distortion present in the minds of the aficionados of Oriental teachings. This can be realized by the simple expedient (which, alas, few have had the ability or desire to employ) of presenting the theologians' thought in a comprehensible English guise.

To revert to the nineteenth-century scheme. From the Indic standpoint, as I said, an altogether different picture emerges. In outlining it we must recall to mind the two great bodies of world religion, the Indic (comprising Hinduism, Jainism and Buddhism) and the Semitic (consisting of Judaism, Christianity and Islam). Indic religion was speculative from its inception. But the Semitic, born among non-intellectual peoples, needed a speculative race like the Greek to teach them philosophical habits. Thus one cultural background supplied the *credere* and another the *intelligere,* a fact also largely true of East Asian religions. In the Indic religions, however, both reason and faith existed in symbiosis, or formed their unique amalgam that is theology. Not for these religions the conflict between the Church and the Academy[2] that was so long in resolving (if it ever fully was) in the world of the Semitic faiths.

There were of course religious beliefs long before there was any Indic civilization, but their very first philosophic epiphanies were undoubtedly radiated by the Indic genius. One of the few archetypes that India, the *terre natale de la plus haute philosophie,*[3] seems definitely to have lacked was the unambiguously transcendent God who creates out of nothing—a Semitic concept that itself had long to await its theological efformation. As to the other archetypes, they were sometimes disseminated through contact, as to East Asia. Sometimes they were born anew, without apparent filiation to their matrix, as, centuries after their first Indic epiphany, in Greece. It is as if, following the law of transmigration, they had passed from one avatar to another without contact between avatars. But they were first assembled into an elaborate architectonic framework by Greek, not Indian, thinkers. Indeed, again apparently without contact, the Indian phase of elaboration began just as the Greek was about to end.

Prominent among the rare Greek archetypes that lack equivalence in India is the analogical metaphysics of Aristotle, later used as the chief basis for the "metaphysics of the Exodus,"[4] that is, of monotheistic creationism. This metaphysics was developed to its full speculative potential by the three Scholasticisms—Muslim, Jewish and Christian—attaining its model expression in the work of Aquinas and Suárez (see Scheme 2). Contemporary with the Scholasticisms was the definitive formulation of the "Indic" archetypes by Indic theologians—like Śāntirakṣita, Abhinava Gupta and Madhva—excelling the Greek achievement (and sometimes even the Christian Scholastic) in subtlety, depth and comprehensiveness. This age, in the West, extends roughly from Origen to Suárez; during its course, the avatars of the Indic archetypes invade the West less frequently than before or after. We may thus call it the *Christian Interlude* to the Indicization of the West, and it is perhaps the climax of the West's speculative creativity.

Scholasticism was superseded in the West by two antithetical trends—rationalism and empiricism—that Aquinas and Suárez had sought to balance, and that had also existed contentiously in India. From Descartes began an age during which the West's speculative power is supposed by many to have been at its highest. But this is just the age when the irruption of Indic ideas into Western thought is resumed, and nearly overwhelms it. It is as though the archetypal energy of religious and philosophic thought had worn out its original container and had been transmitted by an invisible conductor to a newer receptacle. I say "invisible" conductor because there was no significant contact between the two civilizations before the mid-eighteenth century. The only Oriental literature that Westerners of the preceding age knew was the Confucian, and in the translations of the Chinese texts available to them the Indic archetypes then active in the West are not in vivid focus.

At all events, most of these archetypes did not first enter world thought through the creative labors of the West. Now even those long traditional in it became imbued with more distinctively Indic nuances. Furthermore, notwithstanding the brilliance of the new interpretation, the character of model expression eluded the writings of this emerging tradition, so preoccupied with innovation and so convinced of its singularity. This was because it now seethed with the two contrasting groups of archetypes efformed by the Indic and the Scholastic traditions. At least on the surface, they were rife with areas of discord. The archetypes that Scholasticism had so consummately expressed and which had now become somewhat coarsened, tended to obfuscate those which had earlier and perhaps with greater purity been embodied in Indic thought, and so prevented them from shining in full strength. Or to use another, and somewhat contradictory metaphor, it was as though the compact substance of one group of ideas, worn to gravel, had become embedded as so much grit in the crystalline mass of the other, thus marring its transparency.

However, through the impact of Orientalism, developed from the mid-eighteenth century, there was a gradual approximation to the purity of the Indic model. In the nineteenth and twentieth centuries, as never before, prominent Western (especially Germanic) thinkers advanced theories and constructed systems directly inspired by the Indic model: among them were Hegel, Schopenhauer, Nietzsche, Engels and Jung. This process of approximation can logically have no other end but the full possession of the model itself—not only in its earlier and scriptural facets (now generally accessible), but also in its later and theological ones. This cannot be achieved through Sanskrit, but through the modern Western tongues, chiefly the best known of them, English. The inaccessibility of the theological facets, as I said, is due to their difficult language and complex thought patterns, but an attempt must be made to render them comprehensible.

From the viewpoint just described it appears that the creative heights of human thought were reached in the two "obscurantist" traditions, with the most "enlightened" one, the modern Western, attaining (for all its mighty upsurge) to a comparatively lower level of originality. Like all good theories, this one is an oversimplification, but I think that it has at least two merits—of being less parochial than the theory it challenges, comprehending as it does the two great bodies of world speculation, the Indic and the Western; and of being less naïve, though, alas, as liable to be turned into a mythology.

To come to these archetypes. I shall take a random thirteen, leaving the mention of others to their appropriate places in the anthology. All these exist anteriorly in the Indic world, and later elsewhere. Some of them reappear in the Greek world, and a few in the modern West without Greek mediation.

1. The West's "modern" age begins with the Copernican Revolution, that is, the supplanting of the Greek ideas of the universe by the Indic. As imagined by the Greeks, the universe had a fixed center, the earth, over which was a succession of astral spheres, topped by the empyrean. But Copernicus and Galileo, as the latter claimed, "by marvellous discoveries and clear demonstrations . . . enlarged [this universe] a hundred thousand times beyond the belief of the wise men of bygone ages."[5] "The Europeans of the 17th century were quite unaware that 'the wise men of bygone ages' in India had for a long time already done justice to the immensity of time and space, not, however, through *marvellous discoveries and clear demonstrations,* but through the intuitions of their cosmic imagination."[6] Space, constituted of numberless world systems, is what the Buddhists call the "Saha world."

2. Idealism, the belief that physical objects exist only in relation to an experiencing subject—a major philosophical concept without clear Greek precedent—was developed by the Buddhists and consummately formulated in the third or fourth centuries A.D. by Asaṅga and Vasubandhu. It appeared in the West with Berkeley, reached its zenith with Hegel in

Germany in the early nineteenth century, and was later revived in the English-speaking world, there to be supplanted by realist and nominalist philosophies.

3. Materialism. From these nominalist, particularly the neopositivist, philosophies developed the belief that all knowledge of supersensible things is void of meaning, that sensation is the sole norm of knowledge; and that inference is valid only if used for clarifying the data of experience, and not for going beyond them. Some have traced these views to Uddālaka in the ninth century B.C., but they are clearly articulated in the doctrines of some Śramaṇa, or Wanderer sects, three centuries afterwards, as far as the denial of the supersensible is concerned; the epistemology was formulated later. A century afterwards Materialism appeared in Greece with Democritus.

4. Skepticism, perhaps the only direct borrowing of Greek thought from the Indic, was introduced into the West by a soldier from Alexander's Indian campaign, Pyrrho (fourth–third century B.C.). Pyrrho's theories are a Greek version of some early Buddhist and Jain dialectical ideas, ambiguously developed in Greece by the Skeptic Carneades (third–second century B.C.), and unconfusedly in India by the Buddhist Nāgārjuna (mid-second century A.D.). Among its procedures is the undermining of the foundations of theology and metaphysics through the disclosure of their supposed antinomies, formulated with expertise by the great Nāgārjuna and (in the West) proudly attributed to Kant.

5. The "non-soul" doctrine of the self as no more than a bundle of perceptions and void of substance—claimed by the Buddhists as belonging to the very essence of their founder's doctrine, and by modern Western philosophers as one of Hume's chief contributions to world thought.

6. The elimination of the thing-in-itself as a knowable, common in Buddhist doctrine, also (in the West) one of Kant's great discoveries.

7. Reality as flux. The Buddha's conviction (echoed by his Greek contemporary Heraclitus) that becoming is the universal form of reality, was magnificently elaborated by his disciple Kamalaśīla in the seventh century A.D. It almost overwhelmed Rousseau during a reverie in 1765, and with an ecstasy that was more Buddhist than Heraclitean, since it was accompanied by the experience of a state comparable to that of nirvana, or of undifferentiated awareness.[7] Conspicuous

among the innumerable contemporary avatars of this doctrine of flux are the Process Theology of the bourgeois world and the dialectical metaphysics of the Communist.

8. Non-violence. This is a Jain archetype, stemming from its fundamental doctrine of life as constituting the primary essence of all things, in consequence of which the attempt to destroy it is the greatest of sins, and non-violence the greatest of virtues. Gandhi, who grew up in a Jain environment, fashioned this doctrine into a political ideology that soon became popular in the West. And today, in so far as our political world may be said to have an ideal, it is surely non-violence.

The above archetypes are mostly non-Hindu in origin or development. The remaining archetypes are all Hindu.

9. Reality as *bipolar*. This is first stated in the Upaniṣads around the ninth century B.C. "There are two forms of the Brahman, the formed and the unformed, the mortal and the immortal, the static and the moving, the actual and the beyond."[8] This doctrine has two modes, which may be called the substantialist and the evolutionary. In the former—the traditional model of Hindu theology, sponsored in the West chiefly by Spinoza—the changes are but the modal aspects of an immutable substance. In the latter, the changes (or process of becoming) constitute the concrete or moving aspect, while the immutable aspect remains abstract or ineffable. First systematized by Asaṅga and Vasubandhu, this variant has two major contemporary versions, the Process Theology and dialectical metaphysics already referred to. Reality, for the bourgeois system, is "God"; for the Communist, Matter or Nature. Its abstract and immutable aspect, for the former, is the eminently relative One, considered as "the absolute ground of any and all real relationships"[9]; for the latter, it is Law, "the eternal laws of Nature."[10] Its concrete or mutable aspect, for both, is the world of change, or process, described by the theist system as "the sum total of all real relationships," and by the Communist as "the modes of existence of matter." For the latter the process is a necessary one, a view which the former does not seem to share.

10. The "conditioning" of man's being, the inquiry into which led the Buddhists to create the world's first empirical psychology, and led both them and the Hindus to the related quest (of which the West is only now becoming aware) of its "de-conditioning" through yogic discipline.

11. Matter as energy, not inert "stuff," as classical Western physics held it to be: hence more like "mind" (one way of translating the Sankhya *buddhi,* one of Matter's evolutes) and "life" (whose principle, say the Sankhyas, is Egoism, or *ahaṅkāra*). By an inner tension this Matter proliferates into evolutes—a doctrine reincarnate in the thought of Marx and Darwin. Combined with the Taoist dialectic of Yang-Yin-Tao (re-embodied in the Hegelian thesis-antithesis-synthesis) it forms part of the metaphysical foundation of Communist dogma.[11]

12. Energy as pervading the universe, subject to human control through correct knowledge. This conviction, basic to the earliest Vedas, was partially formulated in the Hindu system of Ritualism (*Mīmāṁsā*). But there is an important difference between the ancient and modern views. For the former, the "correct knowledge" is the ritual formulation of the hidden sound structure of physical reality through incantations, or *mantras;* for the latter, the "correct knowledge" is (or was) a scientific formulation of nature's immutable laws.

13. Yogic interiority. This is a new archetype, unknown to the West before our times—a conviction that the self can be experienced immediately, and not just as reflected in the experiences of the external world, and that this intuitive awareness can be arrived at through gradually eliminating our multiple concepts of phenomena by means of a systematic (yogic) control of mind and body. This direct contact confronts us with the unimaginable magnitude of power latent in the self, which we can use to control even the limitations of the body. The transplanting of this archetype into the mentality of the West was to a large degree the work of Jung, who "through the practice of depth psychology . . . has done in the twentieth century A.D. what the Hindus did in perhaps the eighth century B.C.; he has discovered empirically the existence of an immortal soul in man, dwelling outside time and space, which can actually be experienced."[12]

Consonant with the experience of yogic interiority is the Christian belief, vehemently stressed from the eighteenth century, of the supreme value of the human individual and of his free decision. A great force in Western religion today, this belief explains contemporary unwillingness to countenance any religious values not open to personal experience or imposed regardless of individual choice. This conviction draws strength from the Indic archetype of yogic awareness, whereby we are assured immediate and intuitive contact with the source itself of this personal autonomy.

THE CONTEMPORARY VOGUE IN ORIENTAL FAITHS

Oriental philosophies have always intrigued the Western mind, mostly because their archetypes sometimes complement, sometimes challenge, but always enrich, the religious vision of the universe projected by the archetypes of traditional Western faiths. Their popularity today is intensified by yet other reasons, for their archetypes are of particular significance in the religious context of the modern West—as we see in the following four of its many situations: (1) The fact that religious feeling has been corroded by Skepticism, which has itself decayed, unable to provide an alternative for traditional belief or to smother the yearning for faith. (2) That the religious intolerance traditional in the Semitic faiths, and with which the West was once bedeviled, has also abated, being replaced by a desire for mutual tolerance. (3) That the style of the traditional Western religions, perhaps through long familiarity, has lost some of its stimulus, giving rise to a craving for new symbols and imagery. (4) That Christianity is no longer seen as a body of wholly singular doctrines, but as having beliefs reflected in the world's other faiths, even the beliefs that are in a fashion specific to itself. Theologians are thus challenged to re-examine the question of whether Revelation was communicated to one or more peoples.

From the eighteenth century a mode of thought skeptical of the supernatural has grown roots in the West. In latter times its force has somewhat waned, but the habits of thinking it fostered still persist—of explaining phenomena mechanically, wholly within a naturalistic framework, and without reference to supernature or to final causes. So while a yearning for faith has grown with Skepticism's enfeeblement, an ingrained deference to its prejudices prevents an immediate return to Semitic-style religions, with their unambiguous certainties and their total commitment to a wholly transcendent God. Only the faiths of the Orient seem to be accordant with Skepticism's postulates, some of which are the following:

a. That words or propositions are inadequate to describe the Absolute. Religions with clearly defined dogmas are suspect; not so the non-dogmatic faiths, of which Buddhism is believed to be a prototype.

b. That experience is the most important kind of knowledge, and that the intuition of the divine is of primary value, while doctrinal and theological knowledge of it is secondary. There is a search for first-hand experience of the divine without commitment to any conceptual definition of it.

c. That no one body of doctrine can possess all the truth, and that all doctrinal teaching contains valid insights—which brings us to the problem of pluralism.

"The one reality is described variously by the wise."[13] This conviction is stated early in the Vedas, the scriptures of Hinduism. From it the Jain thinkers developed the theory that every religious teaching has its true and proper extent of meaning—which, overextended, becomes erroneous. The true religion is therefore the coalescence of all these doctrines restored to their proper dimensions, thus rendered capable of existing in mutual harmony. This conception was later embodied in Christian thought, chiefly by Nicholas of Cusa, who held that there is only one faith in a variety of customs [*non est nisi religio una in rituum diversitate*].[14] Nicholas also suggested that the method just described be employed to reduce "the great diversity of religions to one concordant peace [*ut in unam concordantem pacem tanta religionum diversitas conducatur*]."

This pluralism permits many religious and cultural modes to coexist, even in one communion. It is the ideal of many contemporary Catholic thinkers, as their Church, in her present state of renewal, and for all her bimillennial experience, has found it hard to come to terms with the contemporary world without jettisoning not a little of her cultural heritage. But in the pluralism traditional in the more sophisticated Indic world, it is possible for Scholasticism to coexist with post-liberal theology, and for plainsong to coexist with the Baluba mass. In such a pluralistic environment, newness and modernity have limited value, since the archetypes of thought are believed to have always coexisted. The acceptance of a mode of thought felt to be new does not mean the supersession of another imagined to be obsolete. Those convinced of the validity of the latter do not have to wait in patience until (as so often happens in today's West) fashion capriciously restores respectability to it.

The aesthetic character or style of religions in presenting their messages has tranquil and dramatic elements, some stressed more than others, and further distinguished by particular symbols and imagery. Hinduism seems to maintain a balance of emphasis on the tranquil and the dramatic; Buddhism, Jainism, Confucianism and Taoism accent the tranquil; and Christianity, decidedly the dramatic. In turbulent times such as ours, the tranquil exerts a greater allure—one more reason for the fascination for Oriental faiths.

Hinduism has two main gods, Śiva and Viṣṇu, and two main cults, Śaivism (of Śiva) and Vaiṣṇavism (of Viṣṇu). For Śaivism, God is a terrifying, almost consuming, vitality, embodied in libidinousness and destructive power, and expressed through images of poison, fire and death. Śiva is Eros and Thanatos in one. Intoxicated, frenzied, obsessed by the dance and by love-making, the god—covered in an elephant hide, surrounded by herds of wild beasts and throngs of fiends, and adorned with serpents and skulls—lives in cemeteries, amid cremation fires, himself smeared with ashes from corpses, and accompanied by his female counterparts, the *Śaktis,* or Energies, as fierce and sanguinary as himself. At the end of each aeon his destructive dance burns the world to ashes. Undoubtedly one of religion's compelling symbols of terrifying divinity, this god has supplied Śaiva theologians with symbols of potency and fire for their theologies of creation and liberation. Vaiṣṇavism, on the other hand, accents the majesty and sweetness of God, who is constantly becoming incarnate to save His creatures from harm. While absorbing into himself the animal hierophanies of primitive religion, Viṣṇu also embodies the Aryan fire sacrifice, through which the energy pervading the universe is controlled. He is also the very incarnation of passion, in the form of Kṛṣṇa—but of passion as delight, not (as in Śiva) an overmastering vitality. This passion furnished Vaiṣṇava theologians with some of their loveliest symbols of mystical ecstasy.

Yet, for all this variety and color, these gods also truly personify yogic contemplation, a state of passionless luminosity. They are then symbols of the divine as reposeful, as manifesting itself in subtle and unobtrusive theophanies. Of course, the supreme expression of this tranquillity is the Buddha himself.

On the other hand, Christianity's style, like that of its Judaic predecessor, is more dramatic than tranquil. The Law is revealed on a mountain amid thunder and lightning, a truly sublime spectacle of *son et lumière*. The Redemption is consummated by Christ's "dense and driven Passion,"[15] displayed, also on an eminence, amid scenes of apocalyptic pomp and cosmic pageantry. The Church, channel of the Redemption, is founded amid the shower of incandescent tongues, and man's final end is either the unconsuming fire of hell or the "supreme Fire, Which, though possessing infinite power to consume and annihilate you, does not, it is certain, consume you, but *consummates* you incommensurably in glory" [*este sumo fuego, en el cual, pues hay infinita fuerza para os consumir y aniquilar, está cierto que no consumiendoos, inmensamente os consuma en gloria!*].[16]

In other words, a style dense with power and glory and terror, though without Śaivism's macabre nuances. Yet Christianity has also a distinctively tranquil dimension, more strongly developed in Greek Christianity than in the Latin, but not perhaps to its full potential. This it will no doubt do as its confrontation with the Indic faiths increases; in particular, through contact with Buddhism. For some of Christianity's supreme symbols are those of gentleness and peace, like the lamb and the dove. And in Christ's passion, notwithstanding its drama, what stands out (as Bossuet tells us) is the profound and inviolable silence of Jesus.[17]

If Christian Revelation consists of truths inaccessible to reason, and if, as Augustine contends, the Christian religion has always existed,[18] there is no better proof of this than the Indic faiths, especially Hinduism, where "supernatural" truths are more clearly adumbrated than in any other religion outside Christianity, including Judaism. Catholic theology tells us that our happiness consists in our participation of the inner life of God, in the vision of that aspect of Him which has no reference at all to the creature. This is God as truly God, *deus sub ratione deitatis*. For Mahāyāna Buddhism the Ultimate is totally irrelative with respect to the phenomenal, so empty of any reference to it that it is best described as *Emptiness*. It is in the realization of this Emptiness that our liberation consists. Mahāyāna Buddhism also believes in the compassionate Savior, the Bodhisattva, who helps mankind attain this liberation.

The Mahāyāna thus adumbrates the two chief Christian

mysteries—of the end and of the means. Of the end, that is, God's inner life (whose highest expression is the Trinity); and of the means to that end, the Incarnate Savior. Hinduism enunciates these mysteries in language approaching the Christian. Constantly, if ambiguously, it maintains that God is both one and three, especially in its teaching on the Triad of Gods, the Trimūrti. It confesses God's incarnation in the person of the Trimūrti's second member, Viṣṇu. Indeed, it gives the doctrine a wider application, not only through multiplying the incarnations, but in varying the hypostases to include (beside the human) the main forms of creaturely life.

Again, Hinduism was the first, if not the only, religion before Christianity to tell us that our happiness lies in the possession of God,[19] chiefly the possession through love (mystery of the Beatific Vision); of the primacy of love in attaining to this possession (the mystery of Charity); but of its unattainability without God's gratuitous help (the mystery of Grace).[20] It also postulates a mediatorship between God and men, especially as embodied in a feminine form (like Lakṣmī or Śakti, the counterparts of the Madonna). Lastly, Hinduism (in its Triadic School) affirms the doctrine of *kenosis,* that the divine has in some fashion to empty itself in order to realize its supreme grandeur.[21] For the most part Hinduism had these and other Christian beliefs before the birth of Christianity, which goes to support the contention of Christian universalists like Clement of Alexandria that Revelation was not given only to the Jews.

THEOLOGY, THE ARCHITECTONICS OF RELIGION

Of the various dimensions of theology, two are of supreme importance, the mystical and the intellectual—which we may call, respectively, its illumination and its architecture. Illumination, of course, has the pre-eminence, as architecture itself does little but glorify light, whether in its radiance or absence, on solid spaces or in empty.

It is understandable then why the claim is made that architecture is the greatest of the arts. Its impact, in great measure, derives from the varied articulation of its parts being simultaneously perceived, the formal qualities of each part enhancing those in the others, and being themselves enhanced by the juxtaposition. The insights of religion, individually inspiring, acquire an intenser impact when related to each other, an impact that is never stronger than when one perceives a harmony among them. In some senses, these insights have inevitable connections, but in most are combinable manifoldly, the harmony of one set of combinations differing from the harmony of another.

Thus arises a plurality of theological systems—a fact for which we cannot be sufficiently grateful. Reality has a richness far in excess of the power of the imbecile human mind to grasp it, and the order that this mind can impose on the complexity of things can never be absolute or complete, especially if the dimensions of the reality it seeks to understand exceed its understanding. Our insight into reality can thus be said to grow with the number of viewpoints from which it can be apprehended. The harmony perceptible from one viewpoint is what we may loosely call a system. The other systems may be erroneous in the view of any one of them, but error, if nothing else, serves to focus attention on a certain aspect of reality, through, shall we say, overemphasis—an aspect which might have otherwise eluded the human mind, a faculty notoriously incapable of giving equal attention even to the few aspects of reality known to itself.

Emphasis is thus an essential factor in the mind's understanding of reality. And, transcendent as they are, the insights of religion would be especially bewildering if the mind were not to emphasize some over others, thus considering some basic and others secondary but all precious; and to strive to understand the secondary in relation to the basic, and so to perceive the unison between them all. But according as the insights judged primary are different, so will be the kinds of unison perceived, and this, as I suggested, is what makes for the difference of the theological systems.

Still, as I said, there is a certain inevitability of connection among the insights of religion, or among the concepts which aid in discovering the harmonies among them. This is particularly true of the concepts employed to systematize theology. I have not been able to discover more than two basic schemes, which I shall call the *bipartite* and the *tripartite*—the former general in Hindu theology, and the latter in Christian theology.

The *bipartite*—or, as we may also call it, the *critical*—scheme (see Scheme 1 and Selections 12 and 13), divides theology into knowledge and the knowable: more precisely, the norms or means of knowledge, and the things that these means disclose to us—in other words, the rules and the objects of faith. The logic of this division is that if one first makes sure of the soundness of the means of knowing transcendent (or any other) reality, the knowledge which the means provide us will inevitably be assured.

The *tripartite*, or dogmatic, scheme (see Scheme 2), defines theology in terms of the supreme Reality, God. It is basically a bipartite division—God in Himself and God in relation to His creatures. But the latter member is itself found to have two very clear divisions—God as Creator, from Whom the creatures proceed; and as Goal, to Whom all creatures return. In Scholastic language, God as God, as efficient cause and as final cause.

The logic of this division is that a science's very existence depends on its object, and so must be determined according to the latter alone—particularly if it is the Object of objects, God Himself.

The schemes are complementary, and each is valid in its own way. The bipartite scheme is more logical from the viewpoint of a human science. Theology is a human way of knowing God, and so must start with human knowing. The tripartite scheme is more logical as a theology, since, in the framework of transcendent values, God is more important than human knowledge. All in all, perhaps the bipartite scheme is the more logical, as it displays both norm and object prominently, while the tripartite scheme, magnificent as it otherwise is, relegates the study of norms to a very minor position, as part of the treatise on faith, itself a subdivision of a subdivision of its vast structure (see Scheme 2). Both schemes are Hindu in origin, and Hindu theology might itself have chosen the tripartite scheme if the views of its chief systematic thinker, Bādarāyaṇa, had prevailed. His *Aphorisms on the Brahman,* the foundation of Vedanta systematics, are concerned with God alone, without any special treatment of norms (see Selections 38, 39, and Scheme 9).

It is sometimes customary to treat the architectural and illuminative aspects of theology as antithetical, but this is no doubt due, again, to the weakness of the human intelligence and personality, where the integration of powers is such an extraordinary event. The integration of architecture and illumination is found in the great theologians, with the illumination usually veiled, being translucent through the passion for the concordance and profundity of thought; but occasionally unveiled, as in the divine Juan de la Cruz (in Christianity), and in the no less divine Abhinava Gupta (in Hinduism). There architecture *is* illumination, and illumination, architecture.

THE TRICHOTOMY, OR THE THREE BASIC TYPES OF THEOLOGY

How do these basically simple classifications connect with the bewildering number of theologies? One reason is the numerical problem of reality (if we may so call it), a problem that may be stated in metaphysical and theological terms.

Metaphysically, it may be stated thus: Is reality one or many? We perceive a multitude of things, but, at the same time, our minds are incorrigibly given to conceiving them in unitary fashion, as, say, "being," "reality" or "existence." Which of these are real and which unreal—our plural perception, our unitary conception, or both? In other words, which is real and which unreal—Difference or Identity, or both?

To this question three basic answers have traditionally been given, and from them our three basic types of theology have arisen:

1. Difference is real, Identity unreal: the theologies of Difference.
2. Identity is real, Difference unreal: the theologies of Identity.
3. Both are real: the theologies of Difference-in-Identity.

The theologies of Difference claim, with Madhva, that "Difference is of the nature of things"[22]; that through the very fact of something being known, its distinctiveness and individuality are discerned; that, moreover, it is impossible to impugn Difference or to prove the ultimacy of Identity, without first positing the truth of that very Difference (Selections 14 and 18).

The theologies of Identity argue in similar fashion, that Identity is of the nature of things; that Difference is basically unintelligible; that to conceive Difference (or multiplicity) one has first to conceive Identity (or singularity), and, when one has done so, the conception of Difference, the contrary of Identity, becomes inconsistent or superfluous; that, moreover, the very appraisal of the nature of Difference leads to its dissolution into Identity (Selections 33 and 35).

The theologies of Difference-in-Identity assert, with Bhāskara (Selection 65), that "Difference is an attribute of Identity," no more, and that "everything is . . . innately one and manifold, neither wholly indivisible nor wholly divisible"[23]; or, with Pico della Mirandola, that "contradictories coincide in a unitary nature"[24]; or, with Engels, that "most natural scientists imagine that identity and difference are irreconcilable opposites, instead of one-sided poles the truth of which lies only in their reciprocal action, in the inclusion of difference *within* identity."[25]

Theologically, the problem may be stated thus. Reality has a transcendental and a phenomenal dimension: are these dimensions different or identical, or both? The answers are our three types of theology, which we may call the Trichotomy.

Christian theologies are traditionally theologies of Difference; the Islamic, of Difference and Difference-in-Identity; the Buddhist and the Hindu, especially the latter, are trichotomous. Theologies of unqualified Identity are hard to find outside the Indic traditions, what is known as Monism being usually a Difference-in-Identity theology. Identity theologies of the pure type are the Buddhist Vacuism (or *Mādhyamika*) and its Hindu derivative, Nondualism.

In this way Hindu theology, representing as it does the Trichotomy more clearly than any other theological tradition, is aware of it as no other tradition is. Hence Hindu theologians set themselves a twofold basic task of expounding the logic of their own branch of the Trichotomy, and of demonstrating the illogicality of the other two branches.

In Indic theologies, the emphasis seems to be on the Trichotomy's metaphysical side; in the Semitic, it appears to be on the theological. One of the most forceful statements of the logic of Difference, theologically conceived, is in the words of Lateran IV:

> *inter creatorem et creaturam non potest tanta similitudo notari, quin inter eos maior sit dissimilitudo notanda.*
> one cannot discover so much similarity between the Creator and the creature, without being able to discover an even greater dissimilarity among them.[26]

Or, in the words of Suárez:

> *haec duo, Deus et creatum ens, involvunt in suis conceptibus primariam diversitatem.*
> these two, God and the creature, involve a primary difference in their concepts.[27]

Concepts cannot imply a greater contrariety than that of God and creature, and if what such concepts signify can be identified in one reality, then things might well never be different.

Which brings us to the theology of non-Difference, or Identity, whose logic I have nowhere found more decisively stated than by that great theologian of Difference Juan de la Cruz:

> the creature's lowliness is much less capable of the exaltedness of God than darkness of light. Because all the things of the earth and of heaven, compared to God, are nothing . . . the entire being of the creatures, compared with the infinite being of God, is nothing.[28]

Unlike the logics of Difference and of Identity, the logic of Difference-in-Identity is not one of apartness or of union, but of wholeness and integration. The multiplicity of things is *inclusive;* or, to put it differently, God is perfection, and perfection can exclude nothing that is real. In the words of Spinoza:

> nothing can be known, or be conceived, without God . . . All things, I declare, are in God.[29]

But these three logics are interconnected. To push the reasoning of any of them to its limits seems to transform it into one or both of the others. The following are some examples.

Islamic theology is the starkest theology of Difference. God so utterly transcends the creature that the latter can in no way be "associated" with Him. Yet to say that the creature participates in being, which belongs exclusively to God, is, to that extent, to make the creature God's associate. This can be avoided only by denying existence to anything but God.[30] The dualism of the Quran is thus transformed into Al-Ghazzali's Monism, with the logic of Difference leading to that of Identity.

Similarly, the logic of Identity, pushed to its extreme limits, precipitates into the logic of Difference. Reality is absolutely one; it is the principle of unqualified oneness; all Difference is wholly illusory. But what is the principle of the illusory Difference: is it the one Reality itself or something other? The first alternative compromises the Reality's absolute oneness; the second accepts *two* principles—the unique Reality and the principle of Difference. A duality of principles is thus needed to preserve the unqualified oneness of the one Reality.

And so, almost imperceptibly, the logic of Identity is transformed into that of Difference-in-Identity. The postulation of two principles to safeguard one reality, reasons Abhinava Gupta (Selection 100) is to deny reality's ultimate oneness. The same reality, then must explain both Identity and Difference, though in different aspects.

Finally, the logic of Difference-in-Identity leads either to that of Identity or of Difference, its main difficulty being the principle of contradiction. The poles of Identity and Difference, it is felt, compromise, if they do not cancel, each other. So great is the contrariety between them, that it is difficult to perceive where they identify. The Identity pole, for instance, is said to be immutable, and the Difference pole to undergo transformation. What is the relationship between these poles, asks Dualist Vedantin Jaya Tīrtha (see also Selection 17): "is it that of Identity or of Difference-in-Identity? Not Identity, because both would undergo transformation [since one of them does], so the postulation of *two* poles would be futile. Not Difference-in-Identity either, for there would be ambiguity as regards the Identity pole. 'Can it be said that the Difference pole is for checking the undifferentiatedness of the Identity pole?' Why conceive the unnecessary Identity pole then [since it cannot remain undifferentiated]? We must therefore postulate the total Difference between the poles."[31] Or, as the Nondualist Vedantin Prakāśātman (Selection 32) reasoned, one must affirm a total Identity between them, with Difference being no more than an illusion.

HINDUISM'S DUAL NORM AND DUAL ASPECT

The Trichotomy is a principle for differentiating theology

anywhere, but there is a special principle of differentiation within Hinduism—what we may call its Dual Aspect—the polarity between the Vedic and Tantric traditions.

Both traditions—indeed all the Indic faiths—accept the Dual Norm, of *transmigration* and *liberation*. In contrast, the Semitic religions postulate only one norm for all rational creatures, though admitting of degrees. Life in the transmigratory world has three aims—social life, work (or wealth) and pleasure (see Selection 75). The actions that these aims inspire lead one from rebirth to rebirth without end. To free oneself from this condition of unending misery one has to renounce those three aims and strive for liberation, the nature of which is variously explained in the different Indic systems. The Dual Norm thus comprises the four Aims of Life—social life, work, pleasure and liberation.

Vedic Hinduism has three features that distinguish it from the other faiths maintaining the Dual Norm. For its revelation it accepts the four Vedas—*Ṛg, Sāma, Yajur* and *Atharva* —generally held to be authorless or impersonally originant. For its social structure it accepts the four castes—priest, warrior, laborer and servant—believed to be of divine origin. For its division of the human life-span it accepts the four states—studentship, marriage, mendicancy and renunciation —held to apply only to the three higher castes.

These features persist to our day. But in its beginnings the Vedic religion was centered on the fire sacrifice, its performance giving one access to magic powers capable of realizing all ends, these powers being later concentrated in the Power of powers, the impersonal Brahman, attainable pre-eminently through knowledge.

Tantrism, in contrast, postulates personal deities, who save through grace and with whom one is in communion through love. Tantrism admits neither castes nor Vedas, at least in its earlier periods. It has its own personally originant scriptures, the Āgamas, or Tantras. And it is predominantly mystical, having three kinds of mysticisms. Following the language of Sankhya theology (School I) we may call these the bright (mysticism of Yoga), the passionate (mysticism of sex) and the dark (mysticism of violence). As opposed to Vedism's emphasis on the masculine and the neuter, Tantrism stresses the masculine-feminine polarity of the universe (Selection 25), and, in one of its facets, proclaims the supremacy of the feminine (Selection 109).

Both traditions are dominant, but in different senses—the Vedic chiefly in form, and the Tantric mainly in substance. The Vedas are the norm of all transcendental knowledge, and the Tantric scriptures are justified only if shown to be accordant (see Selections 69–71). At the same time, the Hinduism of the theologies is overwhelmingly Tantric in content. This anomaly is resolved by the distinction between the Vedas and the texts of Tradition, including the Tantras. The message of the Vedas is held to exceed the understanding of our degenerate age, so its truths were restated by sages or divine incarnations in the texts of Tradition and the Tantras in a manner comprehensible to the age. Of Hinduism's two principal denominations, the Vaiṣṇavas fully conformed to the Vedic standard—and so triumphed over the Śaivas, who did not submit till late, and never fully. The chief recusant school was Triadism, which nonetheless (to my mind) produced Hinduism's greatest theologian, Abhinava Gupta, the emperor of Indic speculation.

THE EVOLUTION OF HINDU THEOLOGY

Hindu, Buddhist and Jain thought is a theology, concerned with clarifying, with maximum critical rigor, insights supersensibly guaranteed—either by a Revelation (personally or impersonally originant) or by the vision and authority of an enlightened sage. These insights originate in the Vedas—in the minds of those seers whom we may call the Fathers of Hindu Theology (Scheme 11), indeed, the Fathers of Theology—and in the Tantras. Combinable indefinitely, these insights disclose new meanings with every new combination, and thus constantly generate new systems. And Indic thought is remarkably fertile in theologies (Schemes 3 and 4). Comparable in fecundity are the systems of Catholic theology (Scheme 5), but Catholicism, with its greater dogmatic unity, cohibits a more luxuriant proliferation. Hinduism, lacking a visible authority in which such unity may be embodied, is tolerant of a richer manifoldness, but its theologies have nonetheless an impressive consensus of basic assumptions within which their complex thought is articulated (Scheme 1).

The evolution of this thought extends over three millennia, and may be viewed from three angles. The first concerns the systematics of theology, the logical consistency of structure, and the character of the expression—whether it is inspirational and poetic, or metaphysical and rigorous. The second and third angles bear on theology's two main preoccupations —man's final end, and the means to attain it.

1. From the first angle, systematics, Hindu theology has three *epochs*—of Fecundation, Germination and Flowering. In the *Epoch of Fecundation* (extending from about 1300 to 600 B.C.), the ideas are poetic and inspirational, not systematic and logically formulated. Most of the archetypes of Indic religion appear during its course, but their architectonic juxtaposition is still to be achieved.

In the *Epoch of Germination* (from about 600 B.C. to A.D. 1000), these archetypes acquire more articulate structure through the development of logical and exegetical techniques. The theologizing impulse is notably intense in the Buddhists. It also possesses the Jains and the Hindus—inspiring the latter to create their basic Six Systems, all with a comparative looseness of systematic structure in the beginning, but gaining greater compactness around the middle of the period.

In the *Epoch of Flowering,* a perfection of form and structure is attained, as well as a refinement of detail, assisted by the elaboration of logic and exegesis, and (in the thirteenth century) by the discovery of symbolic logic by Gaṅgeśa. There is an effort to synthesize the various systems into a comprehensive one; at the same time, there is a proliferation of the Vedantic schools. This period lasts from the eleventh to after the eighteenth century: it has not wholly ended today.

Our second and third angles relate to man's supreme end, and the means to it. The end is always supreme state, and often a supreme reality, both being usually identified. One of the names for the state is nirvana, and for the reality, Brahman. The means to this ultimate end are Works, Knowledge, or Devotion.

2. As an inquiry into the ultimate end of man, Hindu theology has three *ages*—of the Gods, the Impersonal Absolute and the Personal God. In the *Age of the Gods* the ultimate state is a kind of glorified creaturely existence in heaven; the ultimate reality, or realities, are the Aryan gods. This age corresponds to the Epoch of Fecundation. In the *Age of the Impersonal Absolute* the ultimate state is liberation from endless rebirths—conceived as painless inertia, undifferentiated consciousness or ineffable joy. The ultimate Reality ranges

from the Absolute Irrelativity, or Emptiness, of the Buddhists to the undifferentiated Brahman of the Hindu Nondualists. This age corresponds to the Epoch of Germination. Finally, in the *Age of the Personal God,* the ultimate state is the loving possession of God, or a Beatific Vision, and the Ultimate Reality is the Supreme Person. This age corresponds to the Epoch of Flowering.

3. As an inquiry into the means of salvation, Hindu theology has three *eras*—of Works, of Knowledge and of Devotion. In the *Era of Works* one attains to heaven (perhaps even to nirvana) by observing the ritual prescriptions of the scriptures, especially those on the fire sacrifice. This era corresponds to the Epoch of Fecundation and to the Age of the Gods. In the *Era of Knowledge,* discriminative gnosis puts an end to ignorance, the cause of misery and transmigration, and leads to a liberation which is identity with an Impersonal Absolute. This era corresponds to the Epoch of Germination and the Age of the Impersonal Absolute. In the *Era of Devotion,* the loving service of God is or leads to supreme joy. This era corresponds to the Epoch of Flowering and to the Age of the Personal God.

The task of compiling this anthology was made easy—indeed, possible—by Karl Potter's excellent *Bibliography of Indian Philosophies,*[32] which lists both Sanskrit texts and secondary literature. But it was not easy to find many of the books listed there, and, when some had luckily been found, the task of translating passages from them was even less easy. So I used as many commentaries and translations as I could find (mentioned in the footnotes), though I have unfortunately not been able to consult those oracles of erudition, the traditional pandits, as often as I would have liked.

Translation from the Sanskrit, "the language of the gods," into English is at once onerous and challenging, for several reasons. One is the difficulty presented by the widely differing genius of the two languages, exemplified in the following sentence, the translation of an aphorism of Bādarāyaṇa's by a prominent guru of our times:

> Besides, in this the union of this with that [scripture] teaches.[33]

What depths of meaning that statement may contain is not for me to guess, for I have not understood the sentence. Consequently, I cannot pronounce on its faithfulness to the original, but I am persuaded that my own rendering is at least more intelligible:

> Revelation also teaches the union of the soul with the Brahman.

While I crave the indulgence of scholars for my errors in translation, I remain convinced that intelligibility, with occasional (and unintended) aberrance, is preferable to a scrupulously faithful imperspicuity.

Another reason is obscurity of allusion. Hindu theology is the work of extraordinarily erudite men, familiar with the literature and lore of an integrated civilization (see Scheme 10). The knowledge of this civilization, as is possessed by an Indology employing Western methods of scholarship, is, alas, as yet too fragmentary. The traditional pandits, mnemonically trained, have access to that civilization's secrets, and not everyone has the good fortune of being able to consult them constantly.

A third reason is the passion for concision in Indic thought, which leads its thinkers to skip several stages in their argument, for in their traditionally oriented ambience, these stages were known to other thinkers, and only needed to be recalled by a few words. More than most traditions, the Indic is based on memory—a fact which explains the concision of thinking, the numerosity of the classifications and the compendiousness of literary forms in which its scientific achievement is embodied. I have sought to supply the lacunae in the very text of the Selections, through the use of parentheses, so that everything within parentheses is not a translation of the original, but comments derived from glosses and other sources. The vocabulary and categories of each system can only be understood through using the Schemes at the end of the book.

A fourth difficulty, connected with the first, is that of expressing the concepts of a supremely speculative language in one which is by no means the ideal vehicle for metaphysics—especially as (or perhaps because of which fact) the philosophers of the latter language have come to be chiefly, and at times somewhat pugnaciously, empiricist. One feels much like the shepherd Philetas (of Longus's novel *Daphnis and Chloë*) asked to play the music requiring a great instrument (*μέγα ὄργανον καὶ αὐλῶν μεγάλων*)—listening to which one seems to hear many instruments at once (αὐλῶν τις ἄν ᾠήθη συναυλούντων ἀκούειν)—on the reed flute of Daphnis, too small for great art, being just right for the mouth of a boy (ἡ δέ ἦν μικρὰ προς μεγάλην τέχνην, οἷα ἐν στόματι παιδὸς ἐμπνεομένη).[34] But we must be thankful for the lightness of English, and its ability to convey at least some metaphysical tone; for not everyone can be expected to master "the language of the gods," or to be capable of the heavy concentration it demands, to appreciate some of the noblest thoughts that have ever coursed through the human mind, and seemingly for the first time in that faculty's speculative history.

In my choice of topics I have always kept in mind the fact that this anthology is only an introductory one, and so have sought to include as many of Hindu thought's summary compendia of theology as I could. I have also tried to represent as many thought archetypes as possible, but I have often been unlucky in not being able to find texts to represent important archetypes, or of requisite length. Still, the fact that I have chosen some texts over others of equal value is due to my own Catholic convictions, and my preoccupation with the problems of Catholic theology. It is also to the immanent architectural genius of Catholicism, with its impatience of fragments, that I owe what ability I possess of seeing Hindu theology as a connected whole. The catholicity, richness and immemorial duration of Hindu theology itself is for me an archetype, in Bossuet's words, of

> *cette immortelle beauté de l'Église catholique, où se ramasse ce que tous les lieux, ce que tous les siècles présents, passés et futurs ont de beau et de glorieux.*
>
> this immortal beauty of the Catholic Church, wherein everything is amassed that is lovely and glorious in all places, and at all times, present, past and future.[35]

Part Two
SELECTED WRITINGS

Theologies of Difference

PRELIMINARY NOTE

See Schemes 3, 4, 6, 7 and 8

The theologies of Difference may be divided into the earlier and later schools. The *earlier schools* include five of the traditional orthodox Six Systems, comprising the following binaries:

Sankhya (School I) and *Yoga* (School II)
Logicism (School V) and *Atomism* (School IV)
Ritualism (School III) and *Vedanta* (Schools VI, VIII–XIII, XV–XXI, XXIV and XXV)

The Vedanta is the only trichotomous school (see Scheme 6), and it unequivocally proclaims one absolute cause of the universe. The other schools began as atheist or as ambiguously theist, and, except for Yoga, are mostly unmystical. Only Logicism became unmistakably theist, while Ritualism remained atheist. The last of these earlier schools, from which Logicism and Atomism apparently originate, is *Dualist Pastoralism*. None of its works survives.

These six theologies of Difference have at least three characteristics in common:

1. They are the *first* systems of Hindu thought, that is, they precede the Vedantic and most Tantric systems.

2. They are Hindu theology's *basic* systems, furnishing concepts and intellectual techniques to the later schools. For instance, logic and the bipartite scheme are supplied by the Logicists, exegesis by the Ritualists, Yoga disciplines by Yoga, cosmology by the Sankhya, and physicist notions by Atomism.

3. They tended, in consequence, to become *tributaries* of the later systems, chiefly the Vedanta, especially in both its Monist forms of Identity and Difference-in-Identity. It was as though their strength had been sapped in the arduous battle they had to wage against Buddhism, as they were coming of age, for they were unable to prevail against later full-fledged Hindu systems. Only Logicism successfully resisted absorption

into Monism, but, in its later history, shed its metaphysics and became almost exclusively a system of logic.

The *later schools* are three—Śaiva Orthodoxy (School VII), Madhva's Dualist Vedanta (School VI) and its derivation, Śuka's Differentism. The last is also a Vedanta school, but seemingly of little importance. Śaiva Orthodoxy is not always successful in resisting Monism's solvent power—unlike the Vedanta of Madhva. Endowed with perhaps the finest structure of any Vedantic system and with some of Indic thought's sharpest dialecticians, Madhva's school not only repels the Monist onslaught, but, through its own superb intellectualism, intensifies the anti-intellectualism of the Monisms both anterior and subsequent to itself, and indelibly stamps its own character on succeeding theological systems.

I. SANKHYA, or DISCRIMINATIONISM

See Schemes 13 and 14

The Sankhya is perhaps the first system created by Indic thought. Its basic archetype is the polarity between an inactive consciousness, or Spirit, and a dynamic "thinking" Matter—as opposed to the Greek concept of an indeterminate Matter and a determining Form. Experience, deriving from the Sankhya Matter, is dynamic and fettering, and liberation, quiescent. However, "Spirit" is only a category comprehending individual Spirits of unlimited number.

This polarity suddenly springs up in the Greek world with Plotinus in the third century of our era, with the important exception that for the manifold Spirits there is a solitary One. But the Sankhya and the Plotinian categories appear to correspond almost exactly:

	1	2	3	4	5
SANKHYA	Spirit (The Transcendental Soul)	Matter	Instinct "Mind"	Egoism (The Phenomenal Soul)	(Evolution)
	puruṣa	*prakṛti*	*buddhi*	*ahaṅkāra*	(*sarga*)
PLOTINUS	The One	Matter	Mind	Soul	Sensible World
	Τὸ ἓν	ὕλη	Νοῦς Λόγος	Ψυχή	Κόσμος αἰσθητός

The difference is only that Plotinus' fifth category is absorbed by the Sankhya into its fourth.

No less significant is the idea of the evolutes of Matter; indeed the very idea of *evolution* in an unconscious principle, of Matter as the primal source of things—ideas later developed in different senses by Darwin and Marx, and which occur in the hymns of the *Ṛgveda.* Or the idea of emanation, a principle first clearly stated by Uddālaka in the *Chāndogya Upaniṣad* (6:2) in the ninth century B.C. The Sankhya doctrine of the two selves, one in its pure state and the other as invested with the "I"ness or Egoism, has a curious modern avatar in the thought of Thomas Merton:

> There is an irreducible opposition between the deep transcendent self that awakens only in contemplation, and the superficial, external self which we commonly identify with the first person singular . . . this superficial 'I' is not our real self. It is our 'individuality' and our 'empirical self,' but it is not truly the hidden and mysterious person in whom we subsist before the eyes of God.[1]

Another curious fact is that the Sankhya proves the existence of Spirit by means of the *cogito* (see p. 70).

Indic thought, as I said, antedates the Greek in the creation of the thought archetypes, but is posterior to it in their elaborate systematic interrelation. The Sankhya can be said to originate around the tenth century B.C. in the hymn to the Cosmic Man in the *Ṛgveda* (10:90), but, from that moment, had a long period of development, pullulating into a multitude of concepts, not all of them consonant among themselves, until Īśvara Kṛṣṇa (c. A.D. 460)—who had been preceded in the task of systematization by Pañca Śikha in the fifth century B.C. and Varṣagaṇya in the second—selected some of these concepts and organized them into the classical Sankhya system (Selection 1). Some of the concepts he had left out—like necessity and time—were absorbed into the theology of the Pāñcarātra (see Scheme 28) and of the *Bhāgavata Purāṇa,* source book of the later Vaiṣṇava theologies. The Sankhya, like Buddhism, is a very numerative doctrine, the numbers (as for instance "the Eleven," "the Sixteen") being obviously aids to the memory.

The classical Sankhya did not long survive as an independent system. Its cosmology was taken over by most of the Hindu theologies; and its basic polarity was transformed into the Brahman–Ignorance polarity of the Nondualist Vedanta (see Scheme 22). An aphorismer who called himself after Kapila, the Sankhya's reputed founder, sought to revive it around the fourteenth century (Selection 4). But the Vedanta remained dominant, again absorbing the Sankhya—together with the Yoga—in the synthesis of Vijñāna Bhikṣu (Selections 67 and 68; excerpt in Selection 4).

We have three other Sankhya theologians in this section. Gauḍa Pāda the Sankhya (seventh century? Selection 2) seems to have belonged to the still unabsorbed Sankhya: he explains his school's teaching on the dynamic, unconscious and evolutive cause of things.

The versatile Vācaspati Miśra (tenth century, Selection 3), was a convinced Nondualist, but was one of the many Hindu theologians who wrote treatises on systems other than (sometimes contrary to) their own, in order to understand them fully. So completely did they identify themselves with the doctrines of those systems, that the latter's followers used their treatises as authoritative statements of their systems' doctrines, as equal in value with the works of the systems' own teachers. And the Hindu theologians achieved this abstraction from their own doctrinal postulates without the benefit of the phenomenologically epocheic bombast.

In our selection Vācaspati seems to be challenging the tenets of—shall we say—Francis Bacon in an earlier birth, for whom philosophy was not

> to lose itself in fumes of subtle and sublime speculations, but to work efficiently to remove the discomforts of human existence,[2]

without, presumably, soliciting the aid of religion—a philosophy, with some misgivings of recent occurrence, dominant in our world today.

Our third thinker, Aniruddha (excerpts in Selection 4) is a theologian of the restored Sankhya, concerned mainly with the elucidation of "Kapila's" thought. I have mostly followed Aniruddha's interpretation of the latter's aphorisms.

1

ĪŚVARA KṚṢṆA

The Sum of Sankhya Teaching

I. LIBERATION

1. Assailed as we are by the triple sorrow [internal, external and superhuman], we desire to know if the means exist to counteract it.

'Is this desire not futile, since we see that such means do exist?'

No. Those means are neither guaranteed nor absolute.

2. *The Sankhya teaching the sole means.* The means set forth in Revelation are like the obvious ones—impure, perishable and open to improvement. Another and more excellent means is the knowledge of the Evolved, the Unevolved and the Knower (or Spirit).

II. MEANS TO LIBERATION

3. *Objects investigated by the Sankhya.* Prime Matter (the Unevolved) is not a transformation. The Seven [evolutes], of which the Prodigious is the first [the others being Egoism and the Five Subtle Elements], are both transformed and transforming. The Sixteen [the Five Gross Elements and the Eleven faculties] are transformations only. Spirit is neither Matter nor a transformation.

4. *Norms of knowledge.* As we see, there are three norms of knowledge—experience, inference and Word. Valid norms of knowledge invariably ensure valid objects of knowledge.

5. *Objects of knowledge.* Experience is decidedly knowledge of particular objects. Inference is declared to be threefold [through effect, cause and analogy], comprising the inferent sign and the inferendum. Trustworthy Word is trustworthy Revelation.

6. The knowledge of the supersensual is arrived at through inference from analogy. Therefore, too, whatever is unproved and not directly experienced is known through trustworthy Revelation.

7. *Encumbrances to experience.* Experience is hampered by excessive distance or nearness, damage to organs, wandering attention, subtility of object, interposition between object and organ, obliteration of one object by another, and confusion with like objects.

8. It is owing to subtility, and not to non-existence, that the principles [like Matter] are not perceived. Matter's effects—like the Prodigious [or Instinct]—are dissimilar to it in some aspects and similar in others.

III. THE EFFECT

9. *Reasons for the existence of the effect.* Nothing can be produced if non-existent; an effect is related to its cause; not everything conceivable is possible; a cause only produces something it is capable of producing; a cause is in essence the effect. For these reasons, an effect is existent [in its cause].

10. *Contrast between the Evolved and the Unevolved.* The Evolved has a cause; it is neither eternal nor all-pervasive; it is active, multiple, supported, dissoluble, composite and dependent. The Unevolved is the opposite.

11. *Contrast between the Evolved and Spirit.* The Evolved, like Matter, is endowed with three Attributes, lacks discrimination, is an object, is general, unconscious and endowed with productive capacity. Spirit is the opposite, though also alike.

12. *Description of the Attributes.* The three Attributes have the nature of pleasure, pain and insensibility, and serve to illumine, activate and deaden. They overpower, support, generate and accompany one another.

13. The Attribute of Brightness is held to be light and luminous, that of Passion to be impulsive and mobile, that of Darkness, heavy and obfuscating. They function together for one purpose as [do oil, wick and flame] in a lamp.

14. Lack of discrimination and such other qualities in Matter is proved by the existence of the three Attributes, and from the fact that the Attributes are absent where the qualities are [as in Spirit].

IV. MATTER

Reasons for the existence of Matter. The existence of the

Unevolved is also proved, because the attributes of the effect are essentially those of the cause;

15. Distinct objects are limited; things are homogeneous; things exist through causal capacity; cause and effect are distinct; and the world of effects is inextricable:

16. For these reasons, the Unevolved cause exists.

Operations of Matter. This cause functions through a coalescence of the three Attributes, and also through modifications brought on by the qualitative diversity in the Attributes' various recipients—like water [a coalescent and tasteless liquid, acquiring various savors according as it is received into receptacles sweet, sour or bitter].

V. SPIRIT

17. *Reasons for the existence of Spirit.* The aggregate of objects exists for something other than itself; a something that needs to be of a distinct nature from the Attributes [inherent in objects]; something capable of taking control [over the aggregate]; and endowed with the ability to experience. Also, there is the urge to Isolation. For these reasons, Spirit exists.

18. *Reasons for the plurality of Spirits.* Birth, death and the faculties are allocated severally; activity is not the same in all; besides, the three Attributes are severally apportioned. These reasons prove that a multiplicity of Spirits exists.

19. *Properties of Spirit.* The contrariety in the Attributes also proves Spirit's character as Witness, his Isolation and neutrality, his nature as uninvolved observer and his inactive essence.

20. *Results of the union of Matter and Spirit.* Thus, from the connection of Matter and Spirit, the evolutes appear as though conscious; and Spirit, innately indifferent, appears as an agent through the Attributes' activity.

21. *Purpose of the union.* In order that Spirit see Matter, and Matter be isolated from Spirit, both are linked like a lame and a blind person. From this union is evolution.

VI. THE INSTRUMENT

22. *Conspectus of evolution.* From Matter evolves the Prodigious [or Instinct], then Egoism, and from it the Six-

teen, and from the Sixteen proceed the Five Gross Elements.

23. *Instinct.* Instinct [or the Prodigious] is the determining force. Virtue, knowledge, detachment and power comprise its Bright Form. Opposed to it is the Dark Form.

24. *Egoism.* Egoism is self-conceit. From it is a twofold evolution—the group of Eleven [the Faculties: Mind, the five perceptual and the five motor faculties] and the Five Subtle Elements.

25. *The Eleven Faculties.* The Bright Eleven issue from Egoism's Modified Form [the basis of the evolutes]. From its Dark Elemental Form issue the Five Subtle Elements. Both issue from Egoism's Fiery Form.

26. *The Five Perceptual Faculties.* The perceptual faculties are eye, ear, nose, tongue and skin. The motor faculties are speech, hands, feet, anus and privities.

27. *The Mind.* The Mind is both perceptual and motor. While it is reflective, its resemblances with the other faculties make it one among them. Its manifoldness and its external diversities are due to modification in the Attributes.

VII. FUNCTION OF THE INSTRUMENT

28. *The Ten Faculties.* Perception is the sole function of the five perceptual faculties with regard to its objects, such as sound. The functions of the five motor faculties are speaking, holding, motion, excretion and delight.

29. *The Three Internal Faculties.* The function of the three internal faculties [Instinct, Egoism and Mind] comprises their specific characteristics, and is not shared in common. But common to them is the function of the Five Vital Breaths, such as the Ascending Breath [and the Descending, the Even, the Pervading and the Vertical Breaths].

30. *The Four Faculties.* Simultaneous and gradual are the functions of the four faculties [the three internal and any one external], with regard to visible things. With regard to the invisible also, the functions of the three inner faculties presuppose a knowledge of the visible.

31. *Purpose of the Faculties.* The faculties, through mutual fostering, each accomplish their own functions. Spirit's aim is their sole motive; none other moves Instinct to act.

32. *Classification of the Instrument, or the Thirteen Faculties or Organs.* The Instrument is thirteenfold [In-

stinct, Egoism, Mind and the ten faculties, perceptual and motor]: it holds, sustains and reveals. It has a tenfold effect [comprising the objects of the ten faculties], which is held, sustained and revealed.

33. The Inner Faculty is triple. The external tenfold faculty makes the objects known to the Inner. The external faculties function in the present; the Inner, at all times.

34. *Objects of the perceptual faculties.* Of these the five perceptual faculties have specific or non-specific objects. Of the motor faculties, speech has only sound as its object; the others have all the five.

VIII. OBJECTS OF THE INSTRUMENT

35. *Gradation of the faculties.* Since Instinct and the other internal faculties penetrate every object, this triple instrument is the doorman, and the others the doors.

36. *Superiority of Instinct to the other faculties.* The faculties being different one from the other, and being particular modes of the Attributes, they clarify the whole purpose of Spirit and place it at Instinct's disposal.

37. Since Instinct accounts for all Spirit's experience, it alone explicates the inapprehensible difference between Matter and Spirit.

38. *Specific and non-specific objects.* The Five Subtle Elements are not specific objects of experience. From these five the Five Gross Elements emerge. Tranquil, turbulent and stupefying, it is they that are known to be the specific objects of experience.

39. Specific objects of experience are of three kinds—imperceptible entities, procreated bodies and the gross elements. Of these the imperceptible entities endure; procreated bodies perish.

40. *The Subtle Body.* Primordially formed, uncircumscribed, enduring, comprising the evolutes from the Prodigious to the Subtle Elements, devoid of experience and endowed with dispositions—the Subtle Body transmigrates.

41. There is no painting without a support, no shadow without solid objects like pillars. So also, the Subtle Body never exists without a support, without the Subtle Elements that are not objects of experience.

42. Existing only to serve Spirit, and aided by Matter's power, this Subtle Body performs like an actor [connected

with numberless roles], by means of the connection between causes and effects.

43. *The Causes and Effects.* Dependent on the Instrument [Instinct] are the Dispositions; they are connatural—like virtue, knowledge, dispassion and power—natural, and acquired. Dependent on the effect [the body] are the embryo and such other things.

44. Through virtue one rises to the heavens; through vice one plunges into the hells. Through knowledge is deliverance, and through its contrary, thralldom.

45. Detachment leads to absorption into Matter; passionate attachment, to transmigration; power, to freedom from encumbrance; and its lack, to encumbrances everywhere.

IX. EVOLUTION

46. *Subjective Evolution.* [Evolution is of two kinds, subjective and objective.] Subjective evolution comprises what is known as Error, Incapacity, Contentment and Success. Precipitated by the strife between Attributes of uneven strength, its variant forms [or divisions] are fifty.

47. *The "Fifty Divisions."* The varieties of Error are five; of Incapacity—through injury to the faculties—twenty-eight; of Contentment, nine; and of Success, eight.

48. *The Varieties of Error.* [The five varieties of Error are known as Darkness, Delusion, Extreme Delusion, Thick Darkness and Total Darkness.] Darkness has eight [sub] varieties; so has Delusion. Extreme Delusion has twenty-eight, Thick Darkness eighteen and Total Darkness two.

49. *The twenty-eight varieties of Incapacity.* Incapacity is specified by injury to the Eleven Faculties and to Instinct. With Contentment and Success frustrated, seventeen injuries result.

50. *The nine varieties of Contentment.* [Contentment is of two kinds, internal and external.] Internal Contentment is quadruple—related to nature, means, time and luck. External Contentment is quintuple, owing to detachment from the objects of the five senses.

51. *The eight varieties of Success.* Investigation, teaching, study, the suppression of the triple sorrow [internal, external, superhuman], the acquisition of friends, and generosity—these are the eight varieties of Success. The three factors

mentioned earlier [Error, Incapacity and Contentment] are as goads that inhibit Success.

X. THE BODY AND MATTER

52. *Need for the twofold evolution.* There is no Instrument without the Dispositions; the Dispositions cannot function without the Instrument. Thus evolution proceeds in dual fashion, known respectively as subjective [from the Dispositions] and objective [from the Instrument].

53. *Objective Evolution.* The divine order is eightfold, the subhuman fivefold, the human unique. Such, in brief, is Objective Evolution.

54. *Threefold nature of Objective Evolution.* Brightness predominates in the evolution of the world above, Darkness in the worlds beneath, Passion in the middle world—from the god Brahmā down to the blade of grass.

55. *Evolution, the cause of sorrow.* In that world the conscious Spirit, undiscriminated as he is from the Subtle Body [or the Instrument], experiences sorrow deriving from decay and death. Thus sorrow is of the essence of things.

56. *Matter, sole cause of evolution.* Matter precipitates this evolution, from the Prodigious down to the specific elements, seemingly for her own benefit, but really to promote the liberation of each Spirit.

57. *Purposive actions in unconscious things.* Milk, though lacking awareness, acts to nourish the calf. So Matter [though unconscious] acts to liberate Spirit.

58. *Matter's sole objective, the liberation of Spirit.* As people act to satisfy desires, so too Matter acts to liberate Spirit.

59. *Why Matter's operations cease.* An actress, her parts played before an audience, desists from the dance. Likewise Matter, having shown herself to Spirit, refrains from action.

60. *Matter's generosity.* In a variety of ways Matter, generous and endowed with qualities [Attributes], does things profitless to herself only for the sake of her Master [Spirit], who is ungrateful [indifferent] and lacking in all qualities [the Attributes].

61. *Matter's Isolation from Spirit final.* There is nothing more bashful than Matter: I am convinced of this. "He has seen me," she thinks—and never again shows herself to Spirit.

62. *Only Matter is bound or freed.* Hence no one is bound,

or freed, or even transmigrant. It is Matter alone that transmigrates, is bound or is freed.

63. *Matter, cause of her own bondage and freedom.* By seven forms [virtue, detachment, power, vice, ignorance, attachment and weakness] does Matter bind herself. But she unlooses herself by one form only [knowledge].

XI. ESSENCE OF LIBERATION

64. *Nature of discriminative wisdom.* Thus, through constant study of the Principles, one obtains the knowledge "I do not exist, I am not I, nothing is mine"—a knowledge leaving nothing to be known, unstained by error, absolute.

65. Composed, like a spectator, Spirit watches Matter, who has ceased production—his purpose having been served—and is now divested of her seven forms.

66. *Finality of liberation.* He thinks, "I have seen her," and loses interest. She thinks, "I have been seen," and refrains from action. Even though they are still together, there is no need for further evolution.

67. *Brief persistence of body after attainment of liberation.* Perfect knowledge has been attained, and factors like virtue no longer function as causes: yet the embodied Spirit, impelled by previous impressions, continues as embodied, like a spinning potter's wheel [which spins awhile, from the potter's previous impulse, though the pot is now formed].

68. *Final Isolation.* On separation from the body—Matter, her purpose realized, having stopped functioning—Spirit attains to an Isolation that is both guaranteed and absolute.

XII. EPILOGUE

69. *Greatness of the Sankhya's founder, Kapila.* This secret knowledge that fulfills Spirit's goals, and which reflects on the existence, origin and dissolution of things, is fully explained by Kapila, the supreme sage.

70. *Authenticity of the Sankhya tradition.* In his compassion, Kapila imparted this highest of sacred sciences to Asuri. In turn, Asuri taught it to Pañca Śikha, who elaborated it fully.

71. This orthodox teaching, come down through a line of pupils, and thoroughly understood by that Aryan ["noble"]

intellect, Īśvara Kṛṣṇa, has been concisely formulated by him in noble verses [in the *Āryā,* or "noble," meter].

72. Leaving aside illustrative instances and omitting the discussion of other views, the subjects treated in this seventy-verse compendium comprise the entire science of the Sixty Topics.

73. Concisely presented though it is, this science is not deficient in content. It is, as it were, an image of the massive Sixty Topic science in a mirror.

—*Explicative Verses on Sankhya*[3]

2

GAUḌA PĀDA THE SANKHYA

Matter, Sole Cause, Selfless Servant, of Spirit

Effort in another's interest, though seemingly in one's own. Like someone who, neglecting his own interests, looks after those of a friend. This is what Matter does, and Spirit does nothing to repay her kindness. Though seemingly in self-interest, all she does is for another. This interest is awareness of sense objects, like sound, and of the difference between the Attributes and Spirit. Matter's purpose is to provide the Spirits who live in the three worlds with objects of sense, like sound, and finally with liberation. So it has been said that "Matter, fulfilling Spirit's purpose, is discarded, like a pot."

One might observe here that Matter is unconscious, while Spirit is conscious, and ask how Matter, as though conscious, imagines to herself, "I have to furnish Spirit with objects like sound in the three worlds, and finally ensure his liberation." There is truth in this statement. However, activity and its termination have been found to exist even in unconscious beings, which is why Īśvara Kṛṣṇa goes on to say:

> *verse 57.* Milk, though lacking awareness, acts to nourish the calf. So Matter [though unconscious] acts to liberate Spirit.

As grass and other foods eaten by the cow are converted into milk and go to nourish the calf, but when the calf has grown stop their action, even so Matter acts "to liberate Spirit." In other words, the unconscious "acts." Also:

> *verse 58.* As people act to satisfy desires, so too Matter acts to liberate Spirit.

As people, moved by some desire "act to satisfy" it, through acts like coming and going, and when they have attained their ends, rest, so too does Matter, "to liberate Spirit," by achieving his two aims—the experience of sense objects, like sound, and the realization of the difference between the Attributes and himself. Besides:

> *verse 59.* An actress, her parts played before an audience, desists from the dance. Likewise Matter, having shown herself to Spirit, refrains from action.

"As an actress, her parts" embodying emotions like love, and events like those recorded in history, supported by vocal and instrumental music, "played before an audience," that is to say, with her work done, "desists from the dance. Likewise Matter" also "shows herself to Spirit" in the role of Instinct, Egoism, the Subtle Elements, the Faculties and the Gross Elements "and refrains from action."

How and what is the cause of this cessation of activity? In answer Īśvara Kṛṣṇa says:

> *verse 60.* In a variety of ways Matter, generous and endowed with qualities [Attributes], does things profitless to herself only for the sake of her Master [Spirit], who is ungrateful [indifferent] and lacking in all qualities [the Attributes].

"Matter" is "generous" to the "ungrateful" Spirit "in various ways." How is she generous? Because she takes on the guise of gods, men and animals, and the forms of happiness, sorrow and delusion, and of the objects of sense, like sound. Thus Matter shows herself to Spirit in various guises, as though saying, "I am of one sort, you of another," and then stops acting. This she achieves in the interest of the eternal Spirit, by "doing things profitless to herself." Like a selfless person who is helpful to all, and who does not want his kindness repaid, even so Matter realizes Spirit's aims by "doing things profitless to herself."

It was said above [in verse 59] that "Matter, having shown herself to Spirit, refrains from action." The next verse explains what she does when she has so refrained.

> *verse 61.* There is nothing more bashful than Matter: I am convinced of this. "He has seen me," she thinks—and never again shows herself to Spirit.

"There is nothing" in the world "more bashful than Matter. I am convinced of this," convinced because she works entirely in another's interest. If you ask why, it is because she thinks "he," Spirit, "has seen me" and "never again shows herself to Spirit." In other words, she disappears from Spirit's gaze.

Īśvara Kṛṣṇa goes on to describe why "nothing" is "more bashful than Matter." It is [not Matter, but] God who is the cause, some say:

> This ignorant creature [man] has no control over his happiness or suffering. Impelled by God, he goes to heaven or to hell.[4]

Others speak of Spontaneity as the cause

> Who has painted the ducks white and the peacocks with gorgeous hues?[5]

—meaning none but Spontaneity.

And here is what the Sankhya masters say. How can God, lacking as He does the Attributes, be the origin of the creatures who possess them? Or how can Spirit, equally devoid of Attributes? Causality, then, logically belongs to Matter. From white threads only white cloth can be woven, and from black threads, black cloth. One therefore deduces that the three worlds, fabricated from the three Attributes, derive from Matter, whose fabric is the Attributes themselves. God lacks those Attributes, and hence the origin of the Attribute-possessing worlds cannot logically be from Him. That means Spirit too. And this is why some have affirmed that Time is the cause. It has been said:

> Time ferments things, Time destroys the world. Time is awake when all sleep. One cannot overtake Time.[6]

However, as the Evolved, the Unevolved and Spirit are the only three categories, Time is included in them, and is Evolved. Matter, the cause of everything, is also the cause of Time. Spontaneity too comes under Matter. Therefore neither Time nor Spontaneity is the cause; only Matter is; besides Matter, no other cause exists.

Matter "never shows herself again to Spirit." Hence "there is nothing"—no other cause, like God—"more bashful," more delightful "than Matter. I am convinced of this."

In ordinary language it is customary to say that Spirit [or a man] is freed, and that Spirit [or a man] transmigrates. To counter this Īśvara Kṛṣṇa says:

> *verse 62.* Hence no one is bound, or freed, or even transmigrant. It is Matter alone that transmigrates, is bound or is freed.

"Hence no one," no [man or] Spirit "is bound, or freed, or even transmigrant." Since only Matter, inherent in so many forms—of gods, men and animals—"is bound, freed or transmigrant" in its roles as Instinct, Egoism, the Subtle Elements, the Faculties and the Gross Elements.

For how can Spirit—innately free and all-pervading as he is—really transmigrate? Transmigration is for acquiring the unacquired. So when people say that Spirit is bound, is freed, and that he is transmigrant, it is because they do not know why transmigration happens. When the distinction between Matter and Spirit is known, the truth about Spirit becomes clear, and it then becomes evident that Spirit is Isolated, pure, free and secure in his own nature.

'Now, if Spirit is not bound, it cannot be liberated either.'

The answer to this is that Matter alone binds and frees herself. For everywhere the Subtle Body—formed of the Subtle Elements and furnished with the triad of inner faculties—is bound by the triple bond referred to in the following verse:

> Nothing else [besides knowledge] frees a man bound by the bonds of Matter, of its Modified Form [Matter's evolutes] and of its third or Ritual Form [works].

And that Subtle Body is linked with Virtue and Vice.

—*Commentary on the "Explicative Verses on Sankhya"*[7]

3

VĀCASPATI MIŚRA

The Need for Theological Inquiry

In this world a teacher who imparts ideas on subjects that people wish to be informed about always has an audience. If he imparts ideas on subjects they have no wish to know, they say things like "this man has no knowledge of life, and he is no scholar either," and spurn him as though he were insane. And the kind of teaching people want is the one which, when understood, leads to the fulfillment of man's highest aims. Now, as the science I will now proceed to clarify has the means of attaining those aims, Īśvara Kṛṣṇa broaches the inquiry into it in the following words:

> Assailed as we are by the triple sorrow, we desire to know if the means exist to counteract it.
>
> 'Is this desire not futile, since we see that such means do exist?'
>
> No. Those means are neither guaranteed nor absolute.

No one would examine the import of this science (a) if sorrow were not to exist in the world; (b) if, though existent, no one were to abhor it; (c) if, though abhorred, it were incapable of being rooted out. This incapacity to uproot it would be owed to two reasons—the eternity [or irreversibility] of sorrow, or the ignorance of the means of extirpating it. (d) If, though capable of being rooted out, the knowledge afforded by the science were not to include the means for doing so, and (e) if another and more easy means were to be found.

But to begin with, it is not true that there is no sorrow, or that the desire to terminate it is lacking, which is why Īśvara Kṛṣṇa says, "Assailed as we are by the triple sorrow." By "triple sorrow" he means the three kinds of sorrow—the internal, the external and the superhuman. The *internal* is again of two kinds, physical and mental. The physical is caused by disorders of wind, phlegm and bile; and the mental, induced by lust, anger, greed, infatuation, fear, envy, dejection, and by particular objects not being perceived. All these sorrows are internal, because they are amenable to internal remedies. Sorrows amenable to exterior remedies are of two kinds, the external and the superhuman. The *external* are caused by men, cattle, wild beasts, birds, reptiles and inanimate things. The *superhuman* are induced by spirits, fiends, demons, planets and such other malevolent godlings. One cannot therefore question the existence of sorrow, which every individual experiences, and which is a differentiated mode of the Attribute of Passion.

When the Mental Energy inherent in the Inner Faculty is in close connection with the triple sorrow—a connection marked with a feeling of distaste—then we have the assailment that Īśvara Kṛṣṇa speaks of. This feeling of distaste is what excites the desire to put an end to sorrow. And even though pain cannot be wholly suppressed, it can be checked, as will be explained later. Therefore his words "means . . . to counteract it" are apposite . . . The sense of his words is that these, and none other, are the counteractive means that the sacred sciences teach.

Here a doubt arises: 'Is this desire not futile, since we see that such means do exist?' What the objector means is this: 'Let us admit that the triple sorrow exists, that its extirpation is desirable, that it can indeed be extirpated, and that the sacred sciences possess the means of extirpating it. Even so, inquiry into them is useless, since there are other obvious and easy means of putting an end to sorrow. On the other hand, the knowledge of truth [the means that the sacred sciences prescribe], is most difficult, needing constant study over many lives to acquire. Hence there is that proverb:

> If one can find honey in town, why go look for it on
> a hill?
> When a wise man has got what he looked for, should
> he bother to look for it still?

There are hundreds of remedies that counteract *bodily* ills; they are very easy to apply, and have been prescribed by outstanding doctors. And we can counteract *mental* afflictions through acquiring things like delightful women, drinks, foods, ointments, clothes and jewelry—all very easy remedies. In the same way, easy remedies for counteracting *external* sorrows are to be found: like expertise in morals and politics and residence in safe areas. As for counteracting *superhuman* ills, we have easy remedies for them too—as talismans, incantations and magic broths.'

Īśvara Kṛṣṇa answers with a "No." And why? Because "those means are neither guaranteed nor absolute." "Guaranteed" implies that the termination of sorrow will be assured; "absolute," that the terminated sorrow will not occur again. These means, then, lack guarantee and absoluteness . . .

This is what it all means: even if we apply, as prescribed, remedies like medicines, girls, moral and political expertise, incantations and so on, we do not find that the three kinds of sorrow are removed; hence the means lack guarantee. And even when the sorrows are removed, they are seen to return; hence they lack absoluteness. Consequently, no easy means that is also guaranteed and absolute has been found. So the desire to know if the means to terminate sorrow exist is not a futile one at all.

—*The Moonlight of the Sankhya Principles*[8]

4
"KAPILA"

Final Sum of Sankhya Doctrine

I. LIBERATION

1. The Self exists, as there is no proof that he does not.

> [Vijñāna Bhikṣu's *Cogito*:] The experience "I know" is a general proof of the existence of Spirit, as no means of knowledge contradicts it.[9]

2. He is distinct from the body, because (a) he supports so much diversity, and
3. (b) He speaks of himself in the possessive case ["my body"].
4. His use of the possessive case does not however have the same sense as when used with regard to a statue ["the statue's

body"], because our norms of knowledge inform us that the possessive case there does not imply a possessor.

5. With sorrow totally removed, his final end is attained.

6. Spirit's delight from happiness is not as great as his annoyance from sorrow.

7. Possibly someone, somewhere, is happy.

8. Happiness is mixed with sorrow; so the discerning include it under sorrow.

9. 'Can it be that the termination of sorrow is not life's aim, because happiness is not thereby attained?'

No. Life's aim is twofold [happiness and avoidance of sorrow].

10. '[Suffering is an attribute, and] the Self lacks Attributes, since, as Revelation informs us, "the Self is unattached to anything." '[10]

11. Though not an attribute of the Self, suffering exists in it through non-discrimination.

12. Non-discrimination is without beginning. Else we should be faced with two difficulties.

> *Aniruddha on the two difficulties.* If non-discrimination has a beginning, liberation would have preceded it, and with the former's rising, bondage would have resulted; hence too, the bondage of those already free. This is one difficulty [for the free can never relapse into bondage]. With non-discrimination having been null previous to its arising, liberation would have been realized, and the religious practices for its destruction [subsequently indulged in] would be futilely undertaken. This is the other difficulty.[11]

13. But non-discrimination is not eternal in the sense that the Self is, else it would be indestructible.

14. Bondage is destroyed by its particular cause, as darkness by light.

15. In the case of discrimination too, its specific causal character is determined by presential and absential induction [where liberation is present, there is discrimination; where liberation is absent, there is no discrimination].

16. No other explanation being possible, non-discrimination alone is bondage.

17. The liberated are not linked with bondage again, since Revelation declares that bondage is not renewed.

18. Otherwise liberation would not be the aim of Spirit.

19. And both liberation and bondage would be indistinguishable.

20. Liberation [does not intrinsically affect the Self, it] does nothing but destroy an impediment [to the recognition of a freedom already there. It is no more than an illusion].

21. [Revelation, it is true, speaks of liberation as being more than mere illusion.] Even so, there is no contradiction [for it is illusory on the absolute level, and real on the pragmatic].

22. As candidates for liberation are of three sorts, it is not a requirement [that they follow only one of the three liberative practices, hearing—the other two being reflection and meditation].

> *Aniruddha's comment.* The postulants to liberation are of three kinds, the weak, the middling and the advanced. The advanced are liberated through hearing; the middling through hearing and reflection; the weak, through hearing, reflection and meditation. Not all the means are for all.

23. The three means are to fortify the others [the weak].

24. No yogic posture is necessary for stability and mental ease.

25. The mind devoid of an object is in meditation.

26. 'Can it be that there is no difference between both states [meditation and dreamless slumber]?'

No. The difference lies in the removal [in meditation] of the tinge [of conceptual latencies found in dreamless slumber].

27. Though the Self is unattached, its tinge derives from non-discrimination.

28. As with a China rose and a crystal. There is really no color [in the crystal], only the fancy that it is there [caused by the reflection of the flower].

29. [Likewise Matter "colors" Spirit.] This color is removed by practices like meditation, restraint, discipline and detachment.

30. It is also removed by eliminating the states of unconsciousness [dreamless slumber] and distraction [the waking state], say the ancient masters.

31. Meditation rises from tranquillity of mind only. There is thus no rule about the locality it is to be engaged in.

II. CAUSALITY OF THE WORLD

32. Primordial causality belongs to Matter, since Revelation tells us that all its evolutes are effects.

33. Eternal though the Self is, this causality does not belong to it, as it lacks the suitability.

34. As he is in conflict with Revelation, that wretched man, the quibbling logician [or Logicist, who believes the Self to be the cause of the world], does not attain to the Self.

35. If only through its effects, we do deduce Matter's existence, as the Atomists do the existence of their atoms.

36. Its products being everywhere, Matter is all-pervasive.

37. Matter's linkage with motion does not destroy its character as ultimate cause, as in the case of the atoms [likewise related to motion, while remaining the ultimate cause, according to Atomist belief].

38. Matter transcends the categories [of the Logicist and Atomist schools]. The categories themselves are not invariable.

39. Brightness and the other Attributes are not Matter's qualities, as they belong to its very essence.

40. Matter evolves for the sake of Spirit, though itself unable to enjoy the experience, like a camel carrying turmeric [for its master, being itself unable to enjoy the rich flavor of the condiment].

41. The variety of evolution derives from variety of karma.

42. The two effects, dissolution and evolution, result, respectively, from a balance and an imbalance in the Attributes.

> *Aniruddha's comment.* When Matter is balanced in its Attributes, the equalizing modification that results precipitates dissolution [where all diversity coalesces, and is equalized]. When it is imbalanced, the differentiating modification that results gives rise to evolution in the form of effects like the Prodigious.

43. When liberation is realized, Matter does not again start to evolve, as happens also in everyday life.

> *Aniruddha's comment.* Just as people strive for liberation from bondage, and when bondage has been loosed, desist, so does Matter [which, after all, acts only for the liberation of Spirit].

44. Even when Matter associates with the other selves [in a fresh round of evolution], the liberated selves do not experience again, as the cause for such experience [non-discrimination] is lacking.

45. The fact that the selves are multiple follows from the fact that the states [such as those of bondage and release] are multiply allocated.

46. ['Can it be that a unique Self is rendered multiple through association with an incidental limiter?'] If you accept limiters, you accept duality.

> *Aniruddha's comment.* Positing a limiter, you explain Difference. If the limiter is unreal, where does Difference come from? If it is real, you have accepted duality [as you have the real limiter in addition to the real Self].

47. Whatever alternative you accept, you clash with logic.

48. In the texts that teach nonduality, Revelation disaccords with neither alternative [here the oneness or multiplicity of the selves]. It does not reject the first tenet, the oneness of the Self [in the sense of its being an indivisible universal concept]; or the second, the multiplicity of the selves [in the sense of many beings participating in that concept]. If Nondualism implies that its own justifying authority is unreal, its own teaching will obviously be devoid of justification.

49. [If you assert that no justifying authority is needed, that] the Self's uniqueness is established by its self-evident luminousness, you imply a duality of action [the illumination] and agent [the illuminator]—and so contradict yourself.

50. Consciousness in essence, the Self illuminates [not itself, but] something other than itself, the unconscious.

51. There is no conflict with the "Nonduality" Scripture ["there is no manifoldness here at all"][12] as it is only for promoting detachment in those still swayed by desires [as desires, derived as they are from Matter, are best overcome by assuming that Matter does not exist].

52. [Nonetheless] the world is real, (a) because it is produced by an unexceptionable cause, and (b) because no evidence to the contrary exists.

53. As no other explanation is possible, only the real can be said to evolve from the real.

54. Egoism, not Spirit, is the agent.

55. Gained as it is by [what, as long as non-discrimination

lasts, is taken to be] the karma of the Self, experience terminates at the Self [discriminately realized].

56. One returns to mundane existence even from worlds such as that of the moon, because there really is a cause for such a return [non-discrimination and karma].

57. In the other worlds, as in this one, liberation is not attained merely through people's counsel [the liberative practices—or salvific means—are needed].

58. Liberation is more easily attained in the Brahmā world [of course not merely by going there], but with the aid of the liberative practices. This is the import of the "Liberation" Scripture.

> He who has learnt the Vedas from a family of teachers . . . and concentrated all his senses on the Self, inflicting pain on no living creature, except at sacred places—he who behaves in this way as long as he lives reaches the world of Brahmā. And he does not return, no, he does not return.[13]

59. Though the self is all-pervasive, as we gather from the "Departure" Scripture[14] it only finds the place and time of its experience through association with an incidental limiter.

60. A body is not formed unless supervised by a Self, for a body, unsupervised, putrefies.

61. 'Cannot a body be formed merely through the agency of karma?'

Karma lacks immediate connection with the factors that cause a body [like semen], and so cannot produce it. Like water: not connected with seeds, it cannot produce sprouts.

62. The Self, through karma, cannot be the cause of the body, since qualities like karma belong to Egoism [not to the Self].

63. The marks of the soul belong to the Self conditioned by Matter's evolutes [not to the unconditioned Self], as is seen from presential and absential induction [in conscious beings, where Matter's evolutes, like Egoism, are present, there the soul is; where Egoism is absent, there is no soul].

64. The realization of works depends on Egoism; it is not dependent on God, and there is no proof that it is.

65. Exactly as in origination from karma [which has no beginning].

66. All the rest evolve from Instinct.

67. The relation between possessor and possessed is also

beginningless, as is the relation between seed and shoot. It is [as some believe] produced by karma.

68. Or, as Pañca Śikha holds, produced by non-discrimination.

69. Or, in the teacher Sanandana's view, by the Subtle Body.

70. No matter how it is produced, the severance of the relation is Spirit's objective, the severance of the relation is Spirit's objective.

The Sankhya Aphorisms[15]

II. YOGA, or SELF-INTUITIONISM

See Scheme 15

Metaphysically, Yoga is Sankhya. From the latter's doctrines it evolves what we may call the "yogic principle," distinctive of Indic speculation. Consciousness is believed to be of itself luminous, but polluted by an external world invading it in the form of a multiplicity of concepts and feelings. The tendency of the mind toward the outer polluting world can be controlled, according to this principle, by the elimination of all concepts but the one on which concentration is focused, and finally (as an ideal state), by the elimination of all concepts absolutely, with the consciousness reverting to the unclouded luminosity of its original nature.

In short, a faculty like the mind, when deprived of its dependence on the object, realizes the force latent within itself and increases its powers of concentration—thus acquiring a greater command over the object, should reversal to the latter become necessary.

This principle was carried to East Asia by Buddhism, and in its long history its characteristic discipline was sought to be applied to those human forces whose great power can lead to disturbing excesses—the powers of thought, sex and violence, objects of the three Tantric mysticisms, bright, passionate and dark. India's Rāja Yoga and Japan's Zen are among the yogas of thought; Tibet's Tantra, among those of sex; and Karate, Kempo and Tae Kwon Do are among the yogas of violence.

As I said, Yoga is metaphysically Sankhya—with one exception. Among the plurality of Spirits is one Spirit (the Supreme Lord) who is never bound by Matter, and so never needs to be liberated. Here too, we have an unusual archetype, of a supreme Spirit who is not a cause, but only an exemplar—of liberation.

But, as I suggested, Yoga differs from Sankhya in its being a mystical discipline, where the contemplator endeavors to experience, not the supreme Spirit, but his own Spirit (or Mental Energy). Hence Yoga is the intuition of oneself by oneself through discipline, meditation and ecstasy. Sankhya, it will be noted, has the same goal—but a goal realized through intellectual discrimination alone.

Frustrating this realization are several conditionings, compelled on Spirit by the evolutes of Matter. Some of these are on the surface, such as our psychological and social ones; others are deeper, and belong to our subconscious—our "conceptual latencies." These conditionings are brought about by Matter, through one of its evolutes, Time. Yoga thus seeks to liberate man from his temporality; indeed, to annihilate time.

Like the Sankhya, Yoga had an all too brief existence as an independent system. Patañjali (third–fourth century A.D.?) created the Yoga system, a brilliant combination of Sankhya metaphysics with the immemorial mystic disciplines of self-intuition, formulas for concentration, meditation and ecstasy. The only theologian of the autonomous Yoga seems to have been the great Vyāsa (fifth–sixth century A.D.?).

Yoga was absorbed into almost every system of Indic thought. It is the one system common to the three Indic faiths, and was given its final systematic form by the Vedantin Vijñāna Bhikṣu, who believed it to be the greatest of the systems and himself to be a Yoga theologian (see Scheme 15).

5

PATAÑJALI

Principles of Yoga

1. Now, to explain Yoga.
2. Yoga is the suppression of mental states.
3. The Witness then abides in his own nature.
4. Elsewhere he identifies with the mental states.
5. These states, antipathetic and not, are fivefold.
6. They are valid knowledge, error, verbal fiction, sleep and memory.
7. Experience, inference and Sacred Tradition are modes of valid knowledge.
8. Error is a knowledge of the false, based on forms not those of things.

9. Verbal fiction follows from verbal knowledge and lacks objectivity.

10. Sleep is a mental state sustained by the awareness of an absence [of being awake and of dreams].

11. Memory is a mental state that does not transgress the limits of already acquired experience.

12. All these states are restrained by practice and passionlessness.

13. Practice is the effort to realize undisturbed calm.

14. Long cultivated, without interruption, and with constant attention, practice becomes firmly grounded.

15. Passionlessness is the feeling of being in control—in one who lacks the craving for things seen, or known about from Revelation.

16. When a lack of yearning for the qualities of objects results from a knowledge of Spirit, that is the highest passionlessness.

17. Unifocal Awareness rises from percipience [of gross objects], introspection [of the Subtle Elements], rapturousness [in the use of the faculties] and apperception [of Egoism].

18. The other [undifferentiated] Awareness comprises conceptual latencies and follows from the practice that terminates mental states.

19. Natally induced concentration is attained by the disembodied and by those whose bodies dissolve into Matter.

20. Others [the yogis] attain to a concentration following from faith, strength, mindfulness, meditation and wisdom.

21. For yogis of severe intensity, concentration is soon attained.

> *Vyāsa's comment.* Now, these yogis are of nine sorts, according as their method is soft, middling or severe—in other words, the followers of the soft, middling and severe methods. The soft method followers are of three kinds—those with soft, middling and severe intensities. The same divisions apply to the followers of the middling and severe methods. The followers of the severe method, who have severe intensity, soon attain concentration and its results.[16]

22. There is also the division of soft, middling and severe.

23. Concentration is also attained by devotion to the Supreme Lord.

24. Untouched by obstacles, by karmas and their conse-

quences, and by conceptual latencies, the Supreme Lord is a unique kind of Spirit.

25. In him the seed of omniscience is unexcelled.

26. He is the teacher of the ancients, as he is not limited by time.

27. The sacred word OM is his symbol.

28. It must be repeated and its meaning meditated upon.

29. Also following from it are the understanding of the individual soul as well as the annulment of obstacles.

30. The obstacles, which discompose the mind, are illness, languor, doubt, heedlessness, lack of energy and dispassion, confusion, and the incapacity to attain or to persist in any state of concentration.

31. Accompanying these obstacles are pain, frustration, bodily trembling, and inhaling and exhaling without control.

32. These are restrained by fixing the mind on a single truth.

33. Mental calm is attained by cultivating friendliness, compassion, gladness and indifference toward those who are affected by happiness, sorrow, goodness and evil respectively.

34. It is also attained by the expulsion or retention of breath.

35. The rise of the activity that immediately experiences objects [above the senses] reinforces mental calm.

36. So does the State of Painless Radiance.

37. So does the mind intent on passionlessness.

38. So does an object which supports the knowledge gained in dreams or in sleep.

> *Vācaspati Miśra's comment.* When the yogi, as he adores in his dream the entrancing image of the Great God, the Blessed, as it stands in a remote forest, being as though carved out of the moon's orb, soft in every limb like pieces of lotus stalk, fashioned of the purest moonstone, covered with fragrant garlands of Spanish jessamine and Arabian jasmine—when, as he adores this image, he wakes up with mind filled with calm, he reflects that it alone is the support of his dream-knowledge, and his mind, one in form with it, attains at that very moment a condition of equilibrium.[17]

39. So does meditation on any chosen object.

40. His control extends from the infinitesimal to the infinite.

41. The mind, with its states dwindled, is like a transparent gem. It acquires the forms of the knower [Spirit], the knowing faculties [organs] and the known [objects], through coloring. This is the Balanced State. [It is of four kinds: the Notional and Non-notional, and the composite and incomposite.]

42. The Notional State is one in which the distinct factors of word, object and idea are confused.

43. The Non-notional State is one in which the memory is purified; the mind seems devoid of its own essence [as knowing faculty] and appears solely as the known.

44. The Balanced State also describes its composite and incomposite varieties, whose objects are subtle things.

45. The subtle object terminates into irresoluble Prime Matter.

46. These Balanced States belong to Seeded Concentration only.

47. With the Non-notional State acquiring clearness, the yogi becomes unshakably calm within.

48. In that calm, insight is only truth-sustaining.

49. The object of this insight being a particular [and transcendent] one, it is not that of the insights derived from Word or inference [which are only general].

50. The conceptual latencies born of that insight are inimical to the other conceptual latencies.

51. When even these are suppressed, all is suppressed, and there is Seedless Concentration.

—*The Yoga Aphorisms*[18]

6

VYĀSA

The Glorious Yogic State

PATAÑJALI'S APHORISM 1

Now, to explain Yoga.

The word "now" opens the topic. We are now to assume that the science of Yoga has been initiated.

Yoga is concentration. It is a quality possessed by the mind on all its levels. These levels are the fitful, the obtuse, the distracted, the unifocal and the suppressed. [The first two have little to do with Yoga.] The concentration in the *distracted* mind, swamped by the flux of distractions, cannot really be included under Yoga. But the concentration on the level of the *unifocally concentrated* mind radiates the object as it really is, wears away the obstacles to liberation, loosens karma's bonds, and makes for the total suppression of mental states. This is called the Yoga of Unifocal Awareness. It is classed into the percipient, the introspective, the rapturous and the apperceptive, as we shall see later on. Finally, when the states of mind have all been *suppressed,* a concentration which is Undifferentiated Awareness is attained.

The aphorism that follows is concerned with the definition of Yoga:

PATAÑJALI'S APHORISM 2

Yoga is the suppression of mental states.

As the word "all" has not been used [before "mental states"], Unifocal Awareness is included under Yoga too. The mind is stamped with the three Attributes, disposed as it is to clearness, activity and inertia. Clearness in essence, the mind's Brightness, when commingled with Passion and Darkness, becomes enamored with power and the objects of sense. But when this Brightness is interfused with Darkness, it inclines to vice, ignorance, lack of detachment, and the loss of its rightful power. That same Brightness, its screen of delusion fallen away, fully radiant yet permeated with a trace of Passion, inclines to virtue, knowledge, detachment and rightful power. Then, with that slight trace of Passion eliminated, the Brightness abides in its essence, becoming no more than the awareness of its difference from Spirit, and intent on the contemplation of the Cloud of Knowable Things. As thinkers call it, this state is the Highest Reflection.

Mental Energy [or Spirit] is unmodifiable; though objects are displayed to its gaze, it does not impinge on them; it is immaculate and everlasting. [On the other hand] the awareness of difference [between Spirit and Matter] is Brightness in essence, and is therefore alien to Mental Energy. Becoming disillusioned with it, the mind suppresses this awareness too. When that state is reached, the mind inclines to conceptual latencies and is Seedless Meditation. It then knows no object, and is hence called a "Not-Knowing" [or Undifferentiated] Awareness. Thus we see how it is that Yoga, the suppression of mental states, is twofold.

'In that state of Undifferentiated Awareness, with the objects removed, what is the condition of Spirit, whose very essence it is to know through the mind?'

PATAÑJALI'S APHORISM 3

The Witness then abides in his nature.

Then, as in Isolation, Mental Energy [or Spirit] abides in its own nature. In its extroverted state, that Energy, though the same, appears not to be so.

'How does this happen?'

Because, as objects are displayed before it [or him, the Witness]:

PATAÑJALI'S APHORISM 4

Elsewhere he identifies with mental states.

When extroverted [that is, "elsewhere"], the Self is in fact indistinguishable from the states of mind. Hence we have the aphorism [of Pañca Śikha's]:

> There is only one knowledge, and awareness [of difference] is that knowledge.

The mind, like a magnet, functions merely by being near. Its knowability renders it the possessor Spirit's possession. Hence the cause of Spirit's experience of the mental states is its beginningless association with the mind.

Commentary on "The Yoga Aphorisms"[19]

III. RITUALISM, or *MĪMĀṀSĀ*

See Scheme 16

This system is in some ways the most original in Indic thought. It began as an inquiry into the meaning of Vedic revelation, traditionally held to have a twofold object, ritual and the Brahman. The first integrated and systematic Vedicism or Vedic "Inquiry" (*Mīmāṁsā*) was achieved, probably in the fifth century B.C., in a work of twenty chapters, sixteen on ritual and four on the Brahman. Of the sixteen ritual chapters at least twelve are the work of Jaimini; the four Brahman chapters, of Bādarāyaṇa. These chapters also summarized the thought of theologians that appear to have been the contemporaries of Bādarāyaṇa and Jaimini; most of those mentioned in Bādarāyaṇa's part (see Scheme 9) are found in that of Jaimini. These two parts were respectively called the Precedent Inquiry (*Pūrva Mīmāṁsā*) and the Subsequent Inquiry (*Uttara Mīmāṁsā*).

The first Vedicists to follow these two founders commented on all the twenty chapters, but some of their successors began to confine their comments to Jaimini's *Ritualist Aphorisms* alone, thus preparing the way for a scission between the two Inquiries. Vedic theology developed slowly; in contrast, the Buddhist, from around the first century B.C. blazed all of a sudden in a pleiad of geniuses, like Nāgārjuna, Vasubandhu and Dinnāga, a powerful menace to Vedic thought. But its challenge was met, among others, by the brilliant Śabara (first century B.C.?), creator of the independent Ritualist system, its object no longer the total meaning of the Vedas, but only Observance (Selection 7). Nonetheless he developed the theology of sacrifice, giving structure to the thought of the Vedic religion before its acceptation of the Dual Norm, when its final goal had been, not liberation, but a heaven of delights. He also seems to have first stated the problem of the determination of meaning (Selections 9 and 10), and originated theories like that of the Occult Virtue in sacrifices (Selection 8). As a result, his system became uncompromisingly realist, and thus came to be opposed to Buddhist Idealism, with its doctrine of "consciousness-only" as Reality, as it was not believed that sacrifices existent only in consciousness could assure concrete ends. He also elaborated, if he did not first conceive, the idea of an authorless or impersonally originant Revelation, an archetype without parallel in religious thought.

These theories helped the Ritualist theologians to work out a rationale for the belief, also professed by some Christian and Muslim thinkers, that the scriptures' truth is self-evident. But can one ask why is it self-evident? "This is as though someone were to inquire," replies the founder of a Christian sect, "how it is that we learn to distinguish light from darkness, white from black, or sweet from bitter."[20] But the Hindu theologians, not content to beg the question rhetorically, worked out the following theory. Knowledge—among whose modes are experience and Word—is intrinsically valid (Selection 10), all doubtfulness in it deriving from accidental circumstances. The innate validity of Word is occluded when it is dependent on human wills for its expression, the wills of creatures capable of deceiving and being deceived. If Word can be dissociated from personal factors, said the Ritualists, its innate validity will shine unobstructedly. This happens in the case of the Vedas. Of these most carefully preserved and studied of all texts, no memory of author survives in any tradition. They are therefore impersonally originant, meaningful sound, expressive of transcendent things, existent from eternity.

Śabara's innovations were spurned by Bhartṛ Mitra, but enthusiastically embraced by Kumārila Bhaṭṭa (seventh century A.D.), one of Buddhism's most penetrating, informed and determined foes. Bhartṛ Mitra seems to be the opponent in Selection 7, against whom Kumārila defends Śabara's theory of the Occult Virtue. Prabhākara (seventh–eighth century) again rejected those innovations, and strove in vain to re-establish the original undivided Vedic Inquiry. Ritualism was now permanently split into Prabhākara's and Kumārila's schools, their differences deepened by other disagreements, chief among them the problem of error. The school of Prabhākara, which may be called the Vericist, held that all knowledge is veracious, and error practically non-existent. That of Kumārila, the Contrarist, held that error is existent, as a knowledge contrary to reality.

Among the most important later theologians of these

schools are the Vericist Śālika Nātha Miśra (tenth century), who develops his school's arguments for the veracity and objective character of the Vedic message (Selection 9); and the Contrarist Pārtha Sārathi Miśra (eleventh century), who elaborates his own school's reasoning concerning the assumptions on which this veracity is based, the veracity or innate validity of all knowledge, strongly attacking the related Vericist theories (Selection 10).

The Ritualists seem to have finally developed an anti-metaphysical pragmatism—challenged by Madhva (Selection 16)—holding that the Vedas are not concerned with informing us of the nature of transcendental things, but with "achievability," the realization of the practical ends in the manner enjoined. If by pragmatism we mean the doctrine that the truth of an idea is established by its practical effectiveness or "success," then the "father of pragmatism," whoever he was, was born well before 1839, and his name was not Charles S. Peirce.

7

ŚABARA

The Nature of Religious Observance

JAIMINI'S APHORISM

Injunction-signed good is Observance [Observance is injunction signifying the good].

"Injunction," as they say, is the word that motivates activity: it is seen to function in statements like "I do this because enjoined by the master." A "sign" is what signifies; as they declare, smoke is the sign of fire. The object signified, that is the "good." The good, we maintain, is what relates man to his paramount goal. An injunction can make known things past, present, future, subtle, hidden, remote and such other intangibles—something that no sense can do.

'Can Vedic injunction also speak of an inexistent good, as

do statements in common life, as "there are fruits by the river"? Such statements can be true; they can also be untrue.'

I reply: to say that the Veda both "speaks" and "untruly" is a contradiction in terms. When we say, "the Veda speaks," we mean that it makes known, that it becomes the cause why something is known. When, through A becoming the cause, B comes to be known, then A is the cause which makes B known. For instance, when with the injunction enunciated, one *understands* that heaven results from performing the Fire Sacrifice, how can one say that it does not result? And if indeed it does not, how can one say that it comes to be *known?* "An inexistent object comes to be known"—such a statement is self-contradictory.

Statements like "one who wants heaven must offer sacrifice" convey no ambiguity as to whether heaven exists or not. What is positively known cannot be untrue. A false notion is one which, when it has appeared, is annulled by the notion "It is not so." But the notion of heaven is never annulled—at any time, by any person, in any circumstance or in any place. So it is never untrue.

As for statements in common life, they are either made by reliable people, or have to do with things experienced by the senses: in which cases they are never untrue. Else they are made by unreliable people, or concern things beyond the senses: in which cases they are unfounded, as their only source is the human mind. Man cannot know such supersensory things without Word [derived from a superhuman, impersonal, source].

'Can it be that human statements about supersensory things are derived from earlier human statements?'

The earlier statements will be as valid as the later ones, as in such intangible matters human statements can never be the norm of knowledge, like statements on color by persons born blind.

'The unknowing are not the right persons to give instruction. But sages like Manu do instruct. Therefore there are men both good and knowing. To draw a parallel, it is only through sight that we know the eye to perceive color.'

I answer that instructions can also be given when delusion prevails; when it is absent, they can proceed from the Veda as well. When we hear a human statement, our thoughts are "this is how the man understands the sense," not "this is the sense," for all too often the sense goes adrift from statements that some men make. On the other hand, there is no proof at all for the falsehood of the Vedic Word.

'Human statements being commonly perceived to be untrue, and Vedic statements being like the human in so far as they are *statements,* can we not conceive them to be also untrue?'

No, because the cases are different. The fact that one statement is untrue does not imply that a different one is so too, precisely because it is different. Devadatta's being dark does not mean that Yajñadatta has to be dark also. When you say that from their similarity to human statements, Vedic statements are conceivably false, your knowledge is derived from reasoning. But the notions got from the Vedic Word are directly experienced, and the norm of reasoning is not one that contradicts experience. Therefore, the injunction-signed good is conducive to happiness.

'If we are to inquire into what is conducive to happiness, what becomes of our inquiry into Observance?'

I answer: What conduces to happiness is what the word "Observance" signifies.

'How do you know that?'

A man who offers sacrifice is commonly said to be "observant." It is by the things that he does that a man is described as for example, a cook and a reaper. Similarly, what relates a man to the paramount good—that is described by the word Observance, not only in common life, but in the Veda as well:

> The gods sacrificed with sacrifices. These were the first observances.[21]

Thus Sacred Tradition denotes Observance through the word "sacrifice." The injunction here signifies both the good and the evil.

'What is the good?'

What conduces to the paramount goal, sacrifices like the Fire Chant sacrifice.

'What is evil?'

What conduces to the contrary; sacrifices such as those of the Hawk, the Thunderbolt and the Arrow. In order that Observance may not be taken as evil, the word "good" has been inserted in the aphorism.

'But how is it evil?'

It is injury, and injury is forbidden.

'Why then is the practice of evil recommended?'

I answer: acts like the Hawk sacrifice are nowhere spoken of as acts to be done, but only that they are the means to adopt should someone wish to inflict injury. That is the form the Vedic instruction takes, as in the line:

> If one wishes to inflict injury, one should offer the Hawk sacrifice,

and not

> One should inflict injury.

'The aphorism cannot express both these meanings at once—that Observance is injunction-signed, not signified by the senses; and that Observance is good, not evil. The aphorism is but one sentence: were it to have those meanings, it should have to be divided.'

I answer: the meaning one derives from the sentence is the sole meaning—this is true only as concerns the Vedic words, not aphorisms. An aphorism only indicates what has been gathered from other sources. Only parts of propositions are threaded together in aphorisms ["threads"]; hence their name. We must therefore understand our present aphorism to comprise parts of two different propositions.

Else we can interpret our aphorism thus: "Observance is a particular good action signified by the injunction," where we have only one proposition.

Commentary on the "Ritualist Aphorisms" of Jaimini[22]

8

KUMĀRILA BHAṬṬA

The Occult Virtue in Sacrifices

To all this I reply: you imagine the Occult Virtue to have a visible form and then proceed to disprove it, but you do not thereby contradict our position in any way. We accept nothing of what you ascribe to us. What we do accept is a certain capacity in the principal action, or the in the agent, even before the sacrificial actions are performed. We know it from

Revelation; it is invisible and named the Occult Virtue. Before the actions, principal or secondary, are performed, men have an incapacity to reach heaven, and sacrifices have an incapacity to produce results. With these incapacities dispelled by the performance of the principal and secondary actions a capacity is generated—this is a conclusion that none can fail to admit. With this capacity lacking, it is as though no actions had been performed. This capacity, in the agent or in the sacrifice, is what our science terms the Occult Virtue.

If you say that experience and other norms do not prove it, you are right. It is proved by nothing but circumstantial inference founded on Revelation; so the fallacy you impute to us does not apply. [I repeat:] Our sole norm for ascertaining the existence of the Occult Virtue is circumstantial inference based on Revelation. As this norm is part of the sacred Word, we can know of Occult Virtue through Revelation alone. Which means to say that Revelation declares heaven to result from sacrifices, and sacrifices to be supplemented by sacrificial preliminaries. From this we cannot but conclude that these actions, destroyed or not, have a certain capacity to produce their effects, for causes devoid of capacity cannot produce effects. We must concede that a capacity emanates from the action itself, even of sacrifices past.

And why? Because—all actions being transitory—if a single action is unable to affect the Ritual Fruit at once, how much less will many actions together? In other words: an action taken in hand, formed as it is of transient and subtle parts, is unable simultaneously to affect the Ritual Fruit. How much less will complex rituals like the New-Moon-Full-Moon Sacrifices? When the Full Moon Sacrifice is being performed there is no New Moon Sacrifice; when the New Moon Sacrifice is taking place, the Full Moon Sacrifice has long ceased to be performed. Thus too, in singly constituted sacrifices, when the Fire Sacrifice is being offered, then the Fire-and-Soma and the Secret Sacrifices are not. If one of them is, the other two are not.

Simultaneous action is therefore impossible. Consequently, if the New-Moon-Full-Moon Sacrifice—or any part of it—were to be destroyed without any capacity accruing to the agent, things would be just as they were before the sacrifice took place. The actions that followed would lack coefficiency with those that preceded, either directly or through some surviving capacity. A principal action, performed by itself, would in no way be different from the same action supplemented by subsidiaries. Hence the Ritual Fruit that Revelation speaks of would not result through the coefficiency of principal and subsidiary, as the coefficiency itself would be non-existent. For it is nowhere declared that the New Moon Sacrifice, or any other, can produce the Ritual Fruit by itself.

Even those who postulate that the Ritual Fruit, derived from the sacrificial action, follows that action, will have to admit that this can only happen after *all* the sacrificial actions have been completed. Hence only the very last of these actions will realize its end, the others having long ceased to exist. However, the capacities of all these actions endure, and they are known as Occult Virtues. The actions themselves need not exist factually; so even when they do cease to exist, the simultaneity referred to, the basis of all mundane activity, will function all the same.

I say therefore that the functioning of all things is consequent on their capacities. Even if the actions themselves arise at another place or time, it is the capacities that account for the functioning. Even in mundane actions, where the fruits follow on at a later time, a capacity exists beyond doubt; only we do not call it the Occult Virtue. Mundane actions like farming, drinking ghee and study, which are known to bear fruit at a later time [in the form of harvest, health and knowledge], cannot themselves factually endure, but survive in the capacities they generate, and so fulfill all functions. As they are not ordained to Vedic ends, these capacities are not conventionally known by the term Occult Virtue.

Consequently, before sacrificial action is performed, when we listen to the Vedic injunctions, we learn that the Ritual Fruit follows upon the performance of many transient actions, principal and subsidiary. Then our faith in Revelation produces in us the conviction that all actions, principal and subsidiary, must even now persist in some form—until the Ritual Fruit obtains. As we see actions factually perish before our eyes, we infer that they can nowise exist but as capacities.

This, you demur, amounts to a rejection of what the Vedas actually say and an acceptance of what they do not say. You are wrong. The Ritual Fruit is either realized from the sacrifice, by means of the capacity, or is itself realized as the capacity in a subtle form. The flaw you point out would apply if the Ritual Fruit had been realized by something wholly unconnected with the sacrifice. What a capacity left over by the sacrifice realizes, is as though realized by the sacrifice itself, for all causes need intermediary dispositions in order to realize their desired results. To put it in another way. No effect that evolves—as curd does from milk—attains its gross form all at once. Rather, it goes through several subtle intermediary conditions. In the same way, results like heaven attain what may be termed the "condition of a sprout," so that when the condition germinates, the results blossom too. In this connection [what we may call] the "present time" extends from the moment the decision to offer sacrifice is made, up to the savoring of the last particle of the Ritual Fruit. As has been remarked:

> When one hears it said that food must be cooked with firewood, one realizes that it involves combustion. When a shoot sprouts, one assumes that [practically speaking] the tree has grown.

If you say that we have yet to grant the possibility of an Occult Virtue able to realize the Ritual Fruit, your doubt lacks any basis. Whether mundane or Vedic, means are known to be transient. If an enduring capacity is not granted to be possible, why are those means enjoined? In other words, unless it is recognized that the capacity of an action now perished is able to survive until the realization of the Ritual Fruit, it will be futile to enjoin an action sure to perish. Hence both the possibility of the Occult Virtue and its recognition have been assured in advance.

You cannot say that the Ritual Fruit arises through men who have performed sacrifices. According to your assumptions, there can be nothing to distinguish a performer from a non-performer. If sacrifices were to disappear, leaving no capacity behind, things would be as they were before the sacrifices had been performed [or it would be as though no sacrifices had been performed], so there would be no difference between performers and non-performers. The character of *soul* belongs indifferently to both; the character of *sacrifice* is the same in a sacrifice that has perished and one that has not been performed; and the character of *performer* cannot survive in a man either devoid of sacrificial action, or who has turned to an action of a different sort.

'Can it not be said that the performer's capacity persists?'

No. That capacity has existed previous to the performance,

and has no innate ritual causality. And if the performer [in his person or soul] were to be the means to the Ritual Fruit, all his actions, good or evil, would have a cause indifferentiably one; in consequence [no matter what the action] the Ritual Fruit would be indifferentiably one [or always invariably the same]. In the fact of having performed sacrifices, there would be nothing to distinguish the performer of one sacrifice from the performer of many, which would be a rebuff to the performers of many sacrifices. When the perception does not specify the performer, can such a meaning be discerned [whether a person has performed one sacrifice or more]? But one who believes that Occult Virtues are produced, perceives a correlation between a single action and a single Occult Virtue, and through this differentiation discovers how the multiplicity and variousness of the Ritual Fruits is justified.

With regard to the subsidiaries too, if the performer himself is conceived to be the means, the aid afforded by those subsidiaries would inhere in him, and they would not need to be performed again in secondary sacrifices.

In your theory ritual acts, like sacrificial preliminaries, can perish, and sacrificial acts are not contiguously connected with Ritual Fruits. Hence it is the sacrificer, not the subsidiary acts, that will have to aid the principal action. And as there is no Occult Virtue, the principal action will need to be aided by the performer's person [or soul]. Hence one who has performed the sacrificial preliminaries in relation to the main sacrifice, will always be furnished with the aid that these subsidiaries afford. And without following the ritual's rules in their regard when performing another sacrifice, he would still obtain its fruits. Thus the subsidiaries would not need to be performed again, and there would be no justification for injunctions such as "he should offer black berries during the preliminaries of the sacrifice."

'Can it be that the times between the primary and secondary sacrifices are wholly different, so the contingency of not repeating their performance does not arise?'

No, it cannot. The reply to this objection will be given by Jaimini in the aphorism "Because the object remains the same."[23] If the aid of the performer's own person is assumed for primary sacrifices that are proximate, it will not make any difference if the secondary sacrifices are distant.

These criticisms also apply to the destruction-of-actions theory. One who holds that Ritual Fruit results only from the destruction of actions, must believe that actions, good or evil, one or many, or even the negations that annul their use, like antecedent or subsequent non-existence [the one preceding origination, and the other following destruction]—one must hold all these actions to be non-entities, and as such indifferentiable. Consequently, the difference and variety between Ritual Fruits will not be possible.

To take an example, one man may be cured of one disease, and another of ten diseases. But in so far as they are cured of disease, there is no difference between them. That being so, if we assume that variety derives from the destruction of each action, then the destruction will have become something positive. As no other entity fulfilling this function exists, it will only be Occult Virtue that we are describing as "destruction."

It has not been revealed that heaven is the fruit of actions destroyed. Such a condition is contrary to sacrifice: and nothing following on destruction can be said to be a thing that follows from sacrifice.

What is revealed is that "a man who desires heaven should sacrifice" and not "a man should effect a negation of sacrifices." The relationship of inferendum and inferent sign that those sentences establish is one between *existents;* but if we imagine it to be a relationship between *non-existents,* we will be invalidating the Vedas as a norm. Nothing that proceeds from a destroyed action can be said to be causally connected with action, as they are both wholly contradictory. The heat emanating from fire can never be said to be connected with coolness. Else let us say that when something is revealed to follow from sacrifice, we may assume it to follow from its non-existence, so also when the fruit is revealed to be heaven, we can assume it to be the nullity of heaven.

'Might not these objections apply to the Occult Virtue theory too?'

The Occult Virtue, in essence, is the capacity resulting from action, and so is not wholly different from it [let alone being its negation]. I said above that whatever the Occult Virtue produces is produced by sacrifice itself, and when the Occult Virtue is realized, the Ritual Fruit is realized too. In common life we never see that negation has causal power. Even if something is shown to exemplify it, we can always attribute the causality to some positive entity. In this case no entity of the kind exists besides the Occult Virtue. If you urge that the causal power of Occult Virtue has also never been seen, you are mistaken, because capacity of a general sort is everywhere seen, and Occult Virtue is only capacity of a particular kind.

—*Commentary on the Sacred Science*[24]

9

ŚĀLIKA NĀTHA MIŚRA

Self-evidence of Revelation

1. The disciples of Master Prabhākara engage in the task of dispelling the doubt that Word lacks contact with objective truth.

DISSENTIENT VIEW

2. On the assumption that mundane language is inconsistent, some argue that Word [which comprehends all language, mundane or revealed] lacks contact with objective truth.

3. Contact with objective truth is ascertainment, determined by norms, like experience, that do not deviate from the truth. But [the dissenters maintain] Word does so deviate. [In their view, explained in the following thirteen paragraphs, the knowledge generated by Word is faultless, but devoid of objective correlation.]

4. Word produces concepts even in the absence of that truth. For instance, in sentences like "There is a herd of elephants in front of your finger."

5. This knowledge cannot be compared with that of silver falsely perceived in nacre. One does not really apprehend silverness in nacre, so that knowledge is delusion [abrogated when one becomes aware of the nacre]. But Word is the cause of knowledge, irrespective of abrogation.

6. Deficient causes are unable to produce an effect that is entire. So it is understandable why the difference between silver and nacre-appearing-as-silver is not [at first] perceived.

7. In our case the cause of knowledge is Word, unaffected

by the qualifications of deficiency. Affected by them is the speaker, but he is not the cause of knowledge.

8. If the speaker, too, were to be the cause of knowledge, like the faculties of sense, then his deficiencies [like theirs] would lead to lack of apprehension. [But Word is eternal and not produced, though manifestable through contingent causes in time.]

9. The speaker serves only to make [the pre-existent] Word manifest. Knowledge is generated by Word alone, irrespective of the speaker's character.

10. No deficiencies of any sort can be found in Word. Such deficiencies are the cause of non-apprehension: when they are removed, apprehension is unobscured.

11. Such then is the knowledge generated by Word. It pays no regard to objects: how then can it serve to ascertain objective truth?

12. Something whose significance obtains when the object is absent, but is the factor in the object's ascertainment—such is a felicitous description of Word.

13. 'If this is so, how can one conduct daily life on the basis of the words of reliable people? How can life be lived without assured knowledge?'

14. I answer: Life is generally seen to go on even when there is doubt, so your argument does not disprove our position.

15. However, objective truth can be ascertained to some degree by investigating the speaker's reliability, and with the aid of other norms as well.

16. But the Veda has a transmundane significance, and lacks a speaker [and so cannot be valid norm]. Alas to what an unfortunate pass have these pundits brought us!

ORTHODOX VERDICT

17. The intelligent strive to proceed carefully in this matter. As to the theory of inconsistency in knowledge, I have disposed of that in my fourth chapter, "The Way of Reason," below.

18. Listen attentively to what the condition of human words is. The learned are unwilling to allow that their meaning is other than what can be derived by inference.

19. Mundane language depends for its production on men.

Suspectable of deviation from the truth, it does not ascertain the truth of itself.

20. We have seen men produce words that are inconsequential in meaning. So human words by themselves cannot ensure meaning.

21. Some men talk inconsequentially through delusion, others through flaws in their thinking, others through pride and still others through weakness.

22. Words spoken by reliable people are apt to be consequential in meaning. But they also are sometimes seen to be inconsequential. Therefore there is no intrinsic ascertainment of their meaning.

23. The word "ascertainment" signifies nothing but knowledge. If a meaning is not ascertained, knowledge is null in it.

24. Human words therefore produce sense suspectable of deviation from the truth. So the mere listening to them does not bring ascertainment of their meaning.

25. As long as one has not become aware—through a norm different from the preceding one [the reliability of witness]—of the content of the meaning in the speaker's mind, especially if connected with the objects of sense,

26. Then knowledge of what is in his mind is gained through sentences that have become inferent signs. When we have assured ourselves with the thought "He must know what he is talking about,"

27. Determined by that thought, the speaker's sentences become the index to the knowledge in his mind.

28. With the object ascertained, the speaker's sentences apprise us of it. In this condition, the sentences are only an explicative restatement of his meaning.

29. Earlier employed as inferent signs to determine the speaker's knowledge, his sentences, proceeding as they do from his knowledge, must be postulated to be his effects.

30. According to the reasoning accepted by all, effect establishes cause. Human sentences [affected by human qualities] cannot embody sacred authoritative knowledge.

31. If inconsistency [between sense of words and objective correlation] appertains to the inferent sign and not to sacred knowledge, how can the latter be said to lack contact with objective truth?

32. However, inconsistency does not appertain to the inferent sign either [as when it relates to a reliable person's state-

ments]—except that dull minds cannot tell what is an inferent sign and what is not.

33. It is perverse to use as an inferent sign what is not one [the words of the unreliable], because similarity connects it with the veritable sign [the words of the reliable].

34. I have disposed of this fallacy at length in the section on the "Marks of Revelation" [in my fifth chapter, "The Objectives of the Norms," below]. There is therefore no inconsistency between inferent sign and sacred doctrine.

35. 'Surely what one first understands from a man's sentences is their meaning—else how can the speaker's specific intent be inferred?

36. Since the mind is of itself undetermined [or formless], this intent can only be gathered from the meaning. It cannot be considered possible when the meaning is not perceived.'

37. To this I say: the speaker's words are suspectable of deviation from the truth, so their meaning is not *ascertained*, and if not ascertained, it is not *known:* this much is certain.

38. But even if the meaning of the sentence is not known, when the intelligent listener hears the assemblage of the speaker's words, he deliberates to himself in this fashion:

39. "The assemblage of words used by the man I am listening to is consequentially connected. So he must be a reliable person." And so their integral significance becomes apparent.

40. The listener also deliberates thus: "This person will not say things that are incoherent, or whose coherence he has not perceived." Our theory, therefore, presents no difficulty.

41. 'You must have forgotten about the horse who rode a horse. Your missing person has turned up here to prove the Veda's validity.

42. Word, which discloses the Veda's sense, derives its capacity [or its significance] from everyday usage. And you say that it is apprehended in daily life through inference. [So inference must be needed to understand the Veda too.]'

43. The solution to this problem is given in this context by the teacher Jaimini himself [in his *Ritualist Aphorisms* 1:1:5], where he treats of the relation between Word and sense. [In that aphorism he declares that "The natural connection between Word and sense is the means of knowing Observance. And Revelation's teaching is inerrant, though its object be imperceptible."]

44. Hence it is only when the consequential connection be-

tween the words has been ensured that the specific intent of the speaker's mind can be understood, not otherwise.

45. When the listener has understood the meaning of the words he has heard, he can relate to the speaker. Consequentiality of meaning between words is not possible otherwise, as I have proved.

46. A natural capacity for this exists in the meaning of words, but it is occluded by the suspectability of falsehood in sentences produced by men.

47. But the Vedas, by nature, preclude the recollection of any author; they enlighten us on truths which are free from contact with any other norm:

48. It is therefore not possible to apply to them the Logicist syllogism [of which the *proposition* is:] "The Veda is personally originant [or has an author]"; and the *inferent sign:* "Because it is composed of sentences"[25] [all sentences needing authors to fashion them]. No author can fashion sentences that relate to supranormal things.

49. I conclude that no suspicion of falsehood can exist with regard to the [impersonally originant] Vedas. As they ascertain objective truth, their connection with that truth is demonstrated.

50. Cleaning it of verbal filth, clearing it of the manifold thorns of the reasonings of other thinkers, Śālika Nātha has restored this most straight "Road of Wisdom."

The Pentad of Chapters, chapter 2, titled "The Road of Wisdom"[26]

10

PĀRTHA SĀRATHI MIŚRA

A Critical Inquiry into the Validity of Knowledge

I. THE FOUR THEORIES OF KNOWLEDGE

'The mere fact that the mind conceives knowledge does not make it valid, as the mind equally conceives in the case of sentences expressive of falsehood.'

True. In such cases invalidity is justified by the recognition of flaws in the knowing faculty, or of invalidating factors in the knowledge itself. Such being absent in the Veda, validity is there perceived to be self-evident and is never abrogated.

And how does one perceive this validity to be self-evident? To resolve this I shall focus on all modes of knowledge and propose the following questions:

1. Are both valid and invalid knowledges perceived to be self-evident?
2. Are both indeterminate in essence, and ascertained through the recognition of a faculty's flawlessness or flaws?
3. Or is invalid knowledge self-evident—but valid knowledge ascertained through the recognition of the faculty's flawlessness, the consistency of the knowledge with other experience, or its practical efficiency?
4. Else, is valid knowledge self-evident—but canceled by the invalidity perceived through the knowledges of deviation from the truth, or of flaws in the knowing faculty?

Some [the Sankhyas, or Discriminationists, support the first theory, and] hold that all causes have an innate capacity to produce their effects. In virtue of this capacity, they believe, both kinds of knowledge are self-evidently perceived. This view is untenable. Knowledge cannot disclose the truth as well as the falsehood of its object at once, because that is a contradiction.

Others [also supporting the first theory] maintain that one knowledge discloses its own validity, and another knowledge its own invalidity. But this also is unacceptable. For in the matter of ascertaining knowledge, it is impossible, without reference to its faculty, to decide which kind of knowledge it is.

Still others [the Naiyāyikas, or Logicists, adopting the second theory] affirm that both are indeterminate in essence, ascertained through recognition of the knowing faculty's flawlessness or flaws. But such a view [as the Buddhists remark] is not clever. Before the recognition of the faculty's flawlessness or flaws, knowledge does not disclose itself in either form, valid or invalid, and so will remain devoid of character. Therefore [as the Buddhists, followers of the third theory, believe], it is invalidity that is self-evident, while validity is discernible through factors like consistency of experience.

This view is also fallacious. To explain. [According to this view] the mere fact that knowledge has arisen does not qualify it for ascertaining the truth of things, because of its averred deviating and dubious character. The invalidity of knowledge is perceived at the time of its arising, but is afterwards overruled by the recognition of its consistency with other experience, or of its practical efficiency. Utterance by a reliable person is a positive quality in Word, but is not found in the Veda, since [as the orthodox believe] the latter happens to have no personal cause. It is also full of madmen's ravings like "The forest trees offered the Soma sacrifice," and "Listen, you stones!" Uttered as it is by persons wholly unreliable, the Veda [conclude the Buddhists] is unquestionably invalid.

II. THE TRUTH OF THE FOURTH THEORY

To all this the reply is as follows:

> A validity dependent on another will never discover itself. Whoever will consider a theory that cuts at validity's very root?

If all knowledge were incapable of ascertaining the truth of its object, and were to depend on another knowledge—then the knowledges of the faculty's flawlessness, of consistency of experience, and of practical efficiency, would depend on still another knowledge to ascertain the significance of their content, and that knowledge on still another. In this way, no one would know anything with certitude even in a thousand births, and the validity of the norm itself would be null.

'Well then, can we say that the knowledge of *practical efficiency* is self-evident?'

What is special about it?

'Its consistency [as of knowledge with object], wouldn't you say?'

No. In dreams there is knowledge of practical efficiency [but no consistency between knowledge and object. There is the knowledge, for instance, that water is being fetched], though actually no water is brought.

'Let us say then that the knowledge of *happiness* has practical efficiency. Here is a fact unquestionably consistent, for there is never any knowledge of happiness when that happiness itself is non-existent.'

You are right. But the happiness itself does not determine

the validity of the knowledge referred to. The knowledge of intercourse with a loved woman in a dream is invalid, but happiness is still experienced. Consequently, we cannot escape the conclusion that *validity* is self-evidently perceived, but canceled by the knowledges of deviation from the truth and of flaws in the knowing faculty [precisely what the fourth theory maintains].

In the same way, contact with unreliable people produces flaws in Word. But such contact is null in the impersonally originant Veda, and there is no evident knowledge of its being deviant from the truth; its validity is therefore undispelled. But human sentences, born as they are in human minds imbued with delusion and deceitfulness, and infected at their very root, deviate from the truth, and so differ from the Veda.

III. CRITIQUE OF VERICISM

Some [the Vericists, according to their peculiar theory, believe that error is non-existent. So they cannot explain the inconsistency in human speech between words and intent—as it can neither originate in the innately veracious Word nor in flawless human speech. In consequence, they] hold that even in everyday life Word is not deviant from the truth, because, in that life, Word is simply not a norm. [For the Vericists, Word is norm in the Veda only.]

Word is not norm in everyday life [they say] because human words are taken as inferent signs of their speakers' intent. [Where then does the inconsistency come from, inference or Word?] Inconsistency [they claim] is to be attributed to inference, not to word; [on second thoughts] it cannot be attributed to inference either, because the listener, unable to discriminate [between words and intent], employs as inferent signs what really are not such signs. On the other hand, if the inconsistency is attributed to Word, invalidity will be innate to it, for defects in Word do not derive from human defects, the human speech function consisting only in giving expression to a pre-existent Word. [And so the Vericists, wishing to avoid the conclusion that Word is anything but innately veracious, argue that it is not normative in everyday life, but only in the Veda.]

This is nonsense. If Word cannot be a norm in common life, how can it be a norm in the Veda? As I have said in my

Necklace of the Jewels of Logic, "No norm can justify the significative power of Word that has ceased to function as an inferent sign."[27] As for your argument that inconsistency in Word would make it innately invalid, because its defects cannot derive from those of men, it might be so if all that a man did was to make manifest pre-existent sentences taken to be his. However, those sentences are his own creation. It is true that sounds are eternal, as are words. But the *sentences* themselves are the work of men, because of their very human character. If the words of men were to be merely declarative of pre-existent sentences, they would, like the Vedic Word, be impersonally originant, and thus would no more be indications of their speakers' intent. Vedic sentences declared by reciters do not indicate what is in their reciters' minds: similarly, human sentences would not disclose their speakers' thoughts.

You say that the suspicion of inconsistency is the reason why Word is not accepted as a norm in the everyday world. But such a suspicion applies equally to your theory of words being inferent signs of their speaker's intent. We have all seen how a man feels in one way, and fashions sentences of quite another meaning.

Besides, Word, like sight, has the power to generate knowledge, and even when there is inconsistency this power is not annulled. As for the inferent sign, it has the power to produce knowledge only when it is free from inconsistency; when inconsistent, it is unfit to be such a sign. If you say that inference must be accepted only when the suspicion of inconsistency in the speaker has been removed, then you must also accept Word as a norm, as all invalidating doubt has been expelled from it [especially as you, Vericist, believe that even humanly originated language is free of flaws]. One who wishes to understand what is in the speaker's mind, must first consider the meaning of his words, and their capacity to convey that meaning. Thus considered, they convey the meaning of the speaker's sentences at once, without awaiting the aid of inference.

The doctrine of your school is also that when the speaker's mind has been made known through inference, the sentence, which is no more than an explicative repetition of what is in that mind, makes its own contents known. One must therefore grant that knowledge derived from the sentences of an unreliable person—who had been taken to be reliable—is a knowledge which deviates from the truth. If it is deficiencies that determine invalidity, and if the defects of the speaker are unable to infiltrate Word, defectiveness will be innate to Word *as such;* and the invalidity of the Veda [which participates in the essential nature of Word] will follow as a necessary consequence. This is a kind of discussion we [orthodox believers] can well do without.

Given therefore that invalidity, dependent as it is on the speaker's faults, derives from the words of unreliable people [as we Contrarists maintain], and since defects of this kind are absent in the Vedas, it follows that the latter are valid absolutely.

We must therefore [to return to our discussion of Jaimini's aphorism] conclude that only injunction-signed Observance conduces to happiness. By Observance, people generally understand the means that help realize happiness, like sacrifices and burnt offerings. Things like the Occult Virtue and [yogic] states of mind are not accepted as such means in the everyday world.

'Cannot Occult Virtue be such a means?'

No; because it serves to realize happiness only mediately [its power to do so originating from sacrifices]. Therefore only sacrifices and such things, as means to happiness, constitute Observance: when they are absent, as in the case of the lowest castes, observancy also is.

—*Light of the Sacred Science*[28]

IV. ATOMISM, or *VAIŚEṢIKA*

See Scheme 17

Atomism conceives reality as made up of unchanging particles rearranged but never altered. The oldest proponent of this doctrine may have been Uddālaka in the ninth century B.C.; but the Determinists, or Ājīvikas, in the following century, clearly held the later Atomist theory of the four kinds of elements—aerial, watery, fiery and earthy. This doctrine appeared in Greece with Democritus in the next century, and, in India, was systematized by Kaṇāda, probably in the first century B.C. The Atomist vision of the world was also that of Newton, which exploded with the explosion of the atom itself.

According to the Indic Atomists, especially the later ones, atoms exist only singly, and need to be combined by a *mind* to give rise to the complex structure of the visible world. This is the Methodizing Mind, of the same character as ours; only a mind which methodizes the constituents of the cosmos needs to be cosmic; hence God (Selection 15). Atomism's conception of the dissolution and creation was accepted by many systems of Hindu theology (Selection 11).

Atomism was originally one system with Logicism. It later became autonomous, in which form it was standardized by Praśasta Pāda (fifth century A.D.?), who worked into it many of the concepts of the great Buddhist logician Dinnāga (fifth century A.D.); it was Dinnāga's brilliant efforts which permanently sealed the critical conviction of the Indic theologies that "the norm of knowledge is in truth the principal object of this science [theology]" (Selection 76). Atomism was again reunited with Logicism by Udayana in the eleventh century.

11

PRAŚASTA PĀDA

The Creation and Dissolution of the Universe

I shall now describe the creation and destruction of the four Great Elements. After a hundred years, by Brahmā reckoning, the moment draws near for the present Brahmā's liberation. It is then that the Supreme Lord, Master of the worlds, wills to destroy, so that living beings, weary of transmigration, might find repose. All the unseen forces of karma, which manifest the bodies and organs of beings and the Great Elements, and which inhere in souls, are suppressed. Impelled by the Supreme Lord's will, the actions deriving from the union of soul and atoms, and the differences in the atoms that underlie bodies and organs, together destroy that union, so that the bodies and organs are reduced to the atomic state. Then the four Great Elements, earth, water, fire and air, in that order, are dissolved—each previous element being destroyed before the others. After that the separated elements remain, and to that moment also survive the souls, permeated with merit and demerit.

Afterwards the Supreme Lord wills to create, so as to make experience possible for living creatures. Atoms combine with all the souls, through the karmas—whose powers have been restored—implanted in those souls. Activity begins to stir in the *aerial* atoms, and, through a sequence of dyads and other atomic combinations, a mighty wind is generated, filling the sky with its gusts.

Later in the same wind the *watery* atoms combine in the same sequence and generate a vast sea that floods space with its billows. In the same sea the *earthy* atoms then draw close together to form the great mass of earth. In that very sea the *fiery* atoms next combine in dyad and other sequences, erupting in a mighty blaze, which, unquenched, stands there flaming.

And now that the four Great Elements have arisen, the atoms of fire, solely through the Supreme Lord's will, combine with those of earth, and a great egg starts to form. The Supreme Lord then creates in it the four-faced Brahmā, the Grandfather of the worlds, his every face as lovely as a lotus. Together with Brahmā he creates the worlds too, enjoining Brahmā with the creation of living things.

Commanded by the Supreme Lord, Brahmā, endowed with surpassing knowledge, dispassion and sovereignty, creates, as his sons, the Lords of Creatures, and mind beings, and multitudes of progenitors, gods, sages and ancestors—furnishing them with faces, arms, thighs and feet—and the four castes and other beings, high and low. He then associates them according to their karmas, with the qualities of merit, knowledge, dispassion and power.

Commentary on the "Atomist Aphorisms"[29]

V. LOGICISM, or *NYĀYA*

See Schemes 12 and 18

Atomism theologizes on physics, and Logicism on logic, proclaiming a liberation through clear reasoning (Selection 12)—an idea surely without parallel in religious thought. Unlike most Hindu theologies Logicism postulates a personally originant Revelation, with God as its author. To prove His existence—indeed, to clarify and develop all its concepts—it employs a complex instrument of reasoning. This is the Nyāya syllogism (Scheme 12) comprising three basic members, the *proposition* ("The mountain has fire"), the *reason* ("because it has smoke"), and the *example* ("as in a kitchen"). It will be noticed that most theologians in our Selections employ this syllogism *in forma;* they also generally adopt the other terms of Nyāya logic.

Organized by Gautama, whom some scholars place in the fifth century B.C. and others in the third century A.D., Logicism was elaborated by Vātsyāyana, probably in the third century A.D. (Selection 12). It then faced the severe challenge of Buddhist dialectics, which Uddyotakara (A.D. 550–625) tried to meet, with less effectiveness than zeal, for logic, in Uddyotakara's fervent belief, is the prime salvific means and the light of the sciences, that is, of all knowledge (Selection 13). Logicism's greatest theologian was Udayana (975–1050), whom we may well call the dialectical mind of Hinduism. Against the Buddhists, the major foes of his school, he ably defended the doctine of Difference (Selection 14) and the existence of God (Selection 15).

The devotion to God that Udayana's writing breathes—and Udayana was a sensitive poet—seems incongruous in a system whose ultimate goal is not the loving possession of God but a state of painless inertia. For by Udayana's time the Age of the Impersonal Absolute was ending and that of the Personal God, worshiped with absorbing devotion, beginning. For such intense feeling the ontology of Logicism appeared somewhat colorless, which is probably why its thinkers, from the thirteenth century, turned their attention to what had always been the special contribution of their school, logic—a specialization which bore a noble fruit in Gaṅgeśa's (thirteenth–fourteenth century) discovery of symbolic logic.

12
VĀTSYĀYANA
Liberation through Logic

The norm of knowledge is efficacious, because only when things are known by it is efficient activity possible. If there is no norm, things cannot be known; if things cannot be known, efficient activity cannot take place. When a knower ascertains a thing through a norm, he either chooses or rejects it.

The will attended by this choice or rejection is called activity. And its efficiency is connection with results. When one wills in relation to a thing [or end], either in choosing or rejecting it, one gains or loses it in consequence.

The end is either happiness and its causes, or unhappiness and its causes. Ends knowable through norms are without number, because the varieties of living beings are without number. When the norm of knowledge is efficacious, the knower, the known and the knowledge become efficacious too.

Why so? Because the end cannot be gained by any other means. The person who engages in the activity attended by choice or rejection is the knower [the "normator"]; that by which he knows the thing is the *norm;* the thing itself is the *known* [the "normated"], and the understanding of the thing is the *knowledge* [the "normation"]. In these four categories is comprehended the truth of things.

And what is this truth? The existence of being and the non-existence of non-being. When being is understood as being, as it is, without distortion, that is truth. When non-being also is understood as non-being, as it is, and without distortion, that is the truth.

'How can the latter be apprehended through a norm?'

Because when being is apprehended, non-being is not. As happens with a lamp. Through its revealing light the revealed object is apprehended: then one believes that what is not apprehended is not existent; that if it were existent, it would be known; that as there is no knowledge of it, it must be non-existent. Similarly, when an existent thing is apprehended through a norm, one believes that what is not apprehended is not existent; that if it were existent, it would be known; that as there is no knowledge of it, it must be non-existent. This is how a norm, when it discloses being, discloses non-being as well.

This being is to be described as differentiated into sixteen categories. The following is the exact way of classifying them:

GAUTAMA'S APHORISM

(1) The norm (2) the knowable (3) doubt (4) relevance (5) example (6) tenet (7) syllogism (8) conjecture (9) demonstrated conclusion (10) discussion (11) sophistical disputation (12) polemic (13) paralogism (14) quibbling (15) specious reasoning (16) fallacies—it is through the true knowledge of these that the supreme good is attained.

. . . These are the true categories, and the instruction here given is to ensure that they are understood without distortion. It must be remarked that the contents of the whole treatise are incomplexly discussed in this aphorism. The true knowledge of knowables like the soul results in the attainment of the supreme goals, as will be said in the aphorism that follows.

The undesirable, its causes, its total cessation, and the means to achieve the latter—when these four topics are properly known, the supreme goal is realized.

—*Commentary on Gautama's "Aphorisms of Logic"*[30]

13
UDDYOTAKARA

Logic, the Light of the Sciences

VĀTSYĀYANA

This dialectics, articulated as norms and other categories, is the light of all the sciences, the means of all ends, the basis of all actions: it is enunciated at the very start of all inquiry.

Theory and goal are to be determined in each particular science. In this science of the soul the theory is the knowledge of the truth; the goal is the attainment of liberation.

UDDYOTAKARA

"This dialectics," or science of logic, "articulated as norms and other categories, is the light of all the sciences," because of its power of irradiation, like that of a lamp. The meaning expressed by its norm is then expressed by the other sciences.

'Have the other sciences no norms then?'

Vātsyāyana says they have not.

'How not?'

Having norms is not their specific function. They have not been formulated in order to ascertain norms: but once the meaning of the norms has been clarified, these sciences begin to have a function. Vātsyāyana goes on to say that logic is "the means to all ends." The means is by reason of their being illumined; because of it the other sciences make the illuminated meaning their object. Vātsyāyana, further, calls logic "the basis of all actions": it is their basis because it is beneficial to all the sciences. It benefits all the sciences, and is their support by virtue of its beneficialness, as a king is of his servant.

"Theory and goal are to be determined in each particular science." All sciences have their theoretical knowledge and their practical objective. What is the theory and goal of the

Triad of the Vedas? The theory is the knowledge of how to procure ritually clean materials for the Fire Sacrifice and other oblations, and the knowledge of what makes these materials free from defilement. The goal is the attainment of heaven—which is why the Vedas, in this context, declare that heaven is the fruit [of ritual activity].

What is the theory and the goal in agriculture? The theory is the knowledge of soils and similar things; the knowledge also of what makes the soil free of parasites like thorns; the goal is the realizing of a good harvest as the fruit of cultivation.

What is the theory and goal of politics? Its theory is knowing when to make equal use of gifts and punishments, according to time, place and ability; conquest of territory is the goal.

"In this science of the soul the theory is the knowledge of the truth; the goal is the attainment of liberation."

—*Gloss on Vātsyāyana's "Commentary on Gautama's 'Aphorisms of Logic'"*[31]

14
UDAYANA

Vindication of Difference

BUDDHIST (*JÑĀNAŚRĪ MITRA?*)

'Is Difference (a) an object's *essence,* (b) the *reciprocal negation* that exists between objects, or (c) a *distinct attribute* inherent in the object itself?

It cannot be the object's *essence.* [For then we shall be unable to conceive any object, say a pot, without explicitly conceiving it as different, and describing it as such. We shall have to say things like] "A pot is different." Such concomitant use [of "different" with "pot"] is not meaningful.

It cannot be *reciprocal negation* either. [Such negation involves the two concepts of "different correlative" and of "negation." An object, say a pot, must have a correlative, say a cloth, different from itself. The essence of an object must be the negation of all that is not itself: the essence of a pot must be the negation of all that is not pot. And the correlative must be comprehended in the negation: the cloth must be something that is not pot. Attempts to characterize these two concepts will be fallacious.] The apprehension of reciprocal negation will be circular. For only when we have characterized the different correlative shall we have characterized the negation, and only when we have characterized the negation shall we have characterized the difference. [In other words, when I ask, "What is cloth?" you say, "Something that is not pot." And when I inquire, "What is not pot?" you reply, "Things like cloth."]

Neither can it be a *distinct attribute,* as that involves an infinite regress. [For that attribute too is different from other attributes, and its own difference will need another attribute to explain it, and so on, without end.]

How then can it be described meaningfully?'

LOGICIST (*UDAYANA*)

Are you meaning to imply that (1) the knowledge of Difference is non-existent; (2) if existent, is eternal; (3) if transient, is causeless; (4) if caused, is object-less; (5) if with object, then with an object capable of invalidation?

The first alternative hardly deserves a reply, evidently contradictory as it is [to the facts of the present controversy; the fact of the *difference* between the views of the Buddhist and Logicist disputants on Difference can hardly have escaped the objector's notice].

The second alternative can be disregarded, considering the state of dreamless slumber [where knowledge of Difference is absent].

The third alternative must be rejected, as implying contradiction. [According to your Buddhist doctrine, you maintain that all existents are transitory and caused: here you postulate that the existent and transitory knowledge of Difference is causeless.]

The fourth alternative must be dismissed, since we do have an object—the characterization of Difference.

The fifth alternative needs to be examined. What is this object capable of invalidation: is it one of the three meanings [proposed at the beginning of this inquiry and which, as you imply, cover all the possible illogicalities of the doctrine of Difference], or is it some other?

If it is some other, how can it be invalidated by the illogicalities, deriving from those three meanings, devoid of any connection with itself? This was how the ascetic Māṇḍavya came to be arrested for a crime committed by the thief [as we all know from the popular tale].[32]

It must therefore be one of the three meanings: let us take it to be the third of them, the *distinct attribute*. Through fear of an infinite regress we are to abandon the superfluous series of attributes [superadded to the first]. But where is the need to abandon the knowledge of Difference? It is not the infinite regress that annuls the evident distinct attribute: it is the attribute that interrupts the regress, as the first smell does every succeeding one. [The Atomist thinkers say that smell is the distinctive attribute of the earth. To the remark that the earth has a fragrant smell, one asks what makes that smell fragrant, and in answer postulates another smell, and then another, in an infinite regress. The fear of the regress can only cause the abandonment of the series of smells, but not the fragrance of the earth.]

Let us therefore say that the knowledge of Difference depends on [the second meaning] *reciprocal negation*. There circularity exists: but does that mean that the knowledge of Difference does not? It does, incontestably. So let it override all other reasonings. Let it not invalidate itself as though it lacked all justification.

'Can it be that the knowledge of Difference is due to ignorance?'

Well, what of it? Ignorance cannot rid us of the fallacy of circularity. [If ignorance could do away with fallacies, it could relieve us of causes too.] Pots would then be able to form by themselves, without potters and other causes.

'The knowledge of Difference, tainted as it is by the fallacy of circularity, is not its own cause. Therefore, whatever its origin, it is difficult to explain, which is why it is called ignorance.' This is the fruit of the inquiry [on the part of the opponent, into the objects of the knowledge of Difference that are capable of invalidation].

What are we arguing about then? Is it not equally difficult to explain what it is that makes the understanding of reciprocal negation possible, when we describe it as the perception of the subject without the correlative being perceived, and the recollection of the correlative, without the subject being perceived? [This explanation, difficult but not implausible, frees our position from the fallacy of circularity.]

Let us say [finally] that the object of the knowledge of Difference is the object's *essence* itself. There we may renounce the concomitant use of words, but now that we have accepted Difference [however we choose to explain it], what can be amiss in their use?

'But we do notice such a use.'

Yes, but it is only accidental, not essential. When saying things like "Fetch a pot" or "Look at the pot," a sensible man does not use the word "Difference" [as "Fetch a pot which is different from other things"]. But to make his meaning clear and to adapt it to the understanding of the dull, he may say, "Jar, I mean to say, pot." In such cases the concomitant use of words is not a fault.

What then is the truth about Difference? Its three meanings [essence, reciprocal negation and distinct attribute], but in different aspects. One does not in fact perceive the cloth through the pot-nature; one does perceive it through the negation of the pot-nature. Experience is also familiar with perceptions of things qualified by distinct attributes.

[If we now go on to correlate the three kinds of Difference with the seven categories of Atomist theology, we will find that] the only kind possible to *non-being* is that of the difference of essence, because a separate non-being or a distinct attribute can have no existence in it. The categories of *generality, particularity* and *inherence,* cannot have the difference of distinct attribute. The remaining three categories, *substance, quality,* and *activity,* can have all three kinds of Difference. Some examples: "This is a cloth, not a pot; it is made of threads. This is a smell, not a color; it is fragrant. This is motion, not upward propulsion; it is oblique."

The characteristics of the *difference of essence* are the perception of an essence without explicit perception of its differential nature; of the *difference of reciprocal negation,* the apprehension of denial, but with its correlative base unrevoked; and of the *difference of distinct attribute,* contradiction, with the inhesion of only one attribute permitted. So much for the response to the critique of Difference.

—*Investigation on the Reality of the Soul: A Discourse with the Buddhists*[33]

15
UDAYANA
Proofs of the Existence of God

I. THE SEVEN WAYS

From (1) effects, (2) atomic combinations, (3) the suspension and other states of the world, (4) the existence of human skills, (5) the existence of authoritative knowledge, (6) the existence of Revelation and (7) the numerical combination of atoms—from all these we can prove the existence of the all-knowing, imperishable God.

1. *Argument from effects*

Things like the earth must have a cause.
Because they are effects.
Like a pot.

By having a cause I mean active production by someone possessed of the intent to produce, and a direct knowledge concerning the matter from which the production is to be.

2. *Argument from atomic combinations*

[The world, it must be remembered, is a combination of atoms, in different degrees of complexity.] Combination is an action, and hence an action occurring at the beginning of creation that brings about the bonding of two atoms, thus originating a dyad. Such a combination is always consequent on the activity of a conscious agent.

Because it is action.
As, for instance, the action of our bodies.

3. *Argument from the suspension of the world*

The world is supported by an active being which impedes it from falling.
Because it has the character of something suspended.
Like a twig held in the air by a bird.

By "*suspension*" I mean the absence of falling in things that possess weight. When I say "the suspension and *other states* of the world," I mean destruction. For the world is destructible by an active being; because its nature is destructible; like that of a torn cloth.

4. *Argument from the existence of human skills . . .* or the arts of life.

Traditional arts, like weaving, need to be launched by an independent person.

Because of their character as human usages.

Like modern writing and such other usages.

5. *Argument from the existence of authoritative knowledge.* Authoritative knowledge, that is, knowledge through authoritative norms.

The knowledge produced by the Veda is due to positive qualities in the cause of that knowledge.

Because of its character as normative knowledge.

As in a norm such as experience.

6. *Arguments from the existence of Revelation.* Revelation, that is to say, the Veda.

a. The Veda is personally originant.

Because of its capacity to instruct [instruction being conveyed through one person dialoguing with another].

Like the Veda of medicine [which all accept to have been humanly, or personally, produced].

b. Again, the Veda is personally originant.

Because it is composed of sentences.

Like the *Mahābhārata* [epic of the Great Indian War].

c. And the Veda's sentences are personally originant.

Because they are sentences.

Like our own sentences.

7. *Argument from numerical augmentation*

[Physical objects, which have measure, are produced from combinations of atoms, beginning with the dyads. But atoms themselves have no measure. How then do dyads? For the following reasons:]

a. A dyad's measure is produced by *number*.

Because, though not produced through the aggregation of measures, it still remains a *produced* measure.

As, for instance [of pot sections of equal size], the measure of a pot composed of three sections is greater than that of a pot composed of two such sections [the former's greater size thus being due to number alone].

b. An atomic measure does not produce measure.

Because its measure is eternal [and hence incapable of the temporal change that all production entails]; or because its measure is infinitesimal.

In this way, at the beginning of creation, the dual number

—the reason for the dyad's measure—needs to be implanted in atoms. [According to the tenets of our combined Logicist-Atomist system, things exist singly, or monadically, and can be combined only by a faculty that reduces these monads to unity and order—the Methodizing Mind]. The combination cannot have been produced at that [primordial] time by the Methodizing Mind of beings like ourselves [then non-existent]. Hence there exists such a Mind coeval with that time, that is to say, God's.

Finally, by the words "the all-knowing, imperishable God," I mean that the quality of imperishableness belongs to Him essentially [and is inconceivable apart]. It is certain then that an everlasting knowledge embracing all things exists.

II. FIVE OBJECTIONS TO THE ARGUMENT FROM EFFECTS

'There are five fallacies in your inferent sign, "effectness."

a. Causality is qualified by corporeity. [A cause always has a body; the body is thus the qualifier and the cause the qualified.] To negate the qualifier is to negate the qualified. [You deny that God is corporeal: so you must deny that He is a cause.]

b. And there is the counter-syllogism [that serves to neutralize your argument]:

There is no production by a cause [in the case of things like the earth].

Because the invariable concomitance between "production by a cause" and "production by a body" is there lacking.

c. "The cause is always corporeal"—here is a concomitance that counters yours [that "effects always have causes"].

d. From a concomitance unfolded by the perception of things as they are, we infer that a cause is corporeal [for experience shows us that causes always have bodies]. In your argument, however, the inherence of the inferent sign "effectness" in the subject "the earth," does not serve to prove the inferendum ["God"] as qualified by incorporeity. There is, besides, a contradiction between qualifier [incorporeity] and qualified [the cause, always perceived as corporeal].

e. We can also introduce into your argument a vitiating contingency [a contingency which invalidates the concomitance, basic to your whole argument, between your inferent sign "effectness" and your inferendum "cause." It is as if you were to assume the concomitance between fire and smoke, and argue that "The mountain is smoky, because it has fire." But the concomitance is vitiated by the contingency of wet fuel, and I could contend that "The mountain is smoky, because it has wet fuel"]. Here this vitiating contingency is "being produced by a body" [and the argument could be presented thus: Things like the earth must have a cause, because they are produced by a body"]. But then your concomitance between effect and causality [the causality of an incorporeal being] would be inconclusive.'

III. REPLY TO OBJECTIONS

Our argument is not invalidated, because of the efficacity of its inferent sign; and it is not contraposed, because of the feebleness of the disproofs. But whether demonstrative or not, our reasoning is free of contradiction, and its inconclusiveness is baselessly alleged.

a. The negation of corporeity, the qualifier, in God, the subject qualified, does not imply negation of causality. Without knowledge about the subject, there cannot be knowledge about what the subject lacks. [God, the subject, is as you say not known: so it cannot be known whether He has a body.] Greater cogency has that effectness which both demonstrates the existence of the qualified subject and generates a knowledge of it, since it is a reason we are all constrained to recognize. Our argument is also not overridden by your syllogism "God is not a cause, because He has no body."

b. "Things like the earth have no cause, because they are not produced by a body." This is not a valid contraposition to our argument because, for the purposes of a counter-syllogism, the qualification "body" has no probative relevance. [It is as if you argued: "The mountain is fiery, because it has golden-colored smoke." Smoke and fire are concomitant; the color qualifying the smoke is immaterial.] So qualified, your concomitant [between no production by cause and no production by body] is inconclusive; so your disproof is feeble.

c. As for your third objection, the effect-cause concomitance has the greater cogency, because of the inherence of the inferent sign "effectness" in the subject "earth," and because of the presence of reasons precluding all instances to the contrary [as there are no effects ever devoid of causes]. To this your own postulated concomitance "the cause is always corporeal" is too feeble to be a contrapositive.

d. As for your fourth objection [contradiction], the inherence of the inferent sign "effectness" in the subject "earth" either entails the incorporeity of the cause, in which case there cannot be contradiction, as the correlation between causality and incorporeity has been recognized; or it does not, in which case there can be no contradiction either, as there is no subject to which the contradiction can be predicated.

e. As for your fifth objection, since our argument has reasons preclusive of contrary instances, there cannot be any inconclusiveness in the shape of ignorance occasioned by their absence. Neither is there the inconclusiveness of concomitance [between cause and effect]. The vitiating contingency "being produced by a body," unable as it is to preclude contrary instances [such as God] can be disregarded.

IV. HARMONY BETWEEN FAITH AND REASON

'If God is a cause, He must be corporeal. Thus we are confronted with adversative reasoning and the absence of supportive proof.'

To this I say: the flawed reasoning of some thinkers has only the semblance of logic, and so is no refutation at all. But the supportive reasoning from the absence of effects [resulting from absence of causes] is our own position's enhancement.

The adversative arguments, supposing God as unproved, are devoid of a subject [to which they can predicate corporeity, in which the main force of their reasoning lies]. Hence they have only the semblance of logic. On the other hand "There is no effect without a cause"—such a reasoning is an enhancement: in other words, efficacious.

Our view is supported by Sacred Tradition too:

> I am the source of all: all things evolve from Me.
> The wise know this, and filled with emotion worship Me.[34]

[And as the sage Manu says:]

> A man who determines the sages' teachings on the Law through a logic not discordant with Revelation

> and the sacred sciences, only he, no other, knows that Law.[35]

These words evince the greater cogency of Sacred Tradition when reinforced by logic.

—*Flower-Offering of Logic,* bouquet 5[36]

VI. DUALIST VEDANTA, or *DVAITA VEDĀNTA*

See Scheme 19

The multiple insights of the Hindu sacred tradition first coalesced into a unity in the system of Bādarāyaṇa, probably in the fifth century B.C. Over a millennium of patient thought on its implications elapsed, when Madhva (1238–1317), furnished with the insights of this accumulated wisdom, again surveyed the entire tradition, discovering, within Bādarāyaṇa's scheme, an architectonic model differing from the patterns perceived by the old theologies of Difference-in-Identity, and seemingly more compact and logical. He grounded his system on Difference, the metaphysical postulate underlying the oldest Vedic speculation, the Jain and the older Buddhist thought, Dualist Pastoralism, and five of the traditional Six Systems. To justify Difference, of whose existence experience informs us, he postulated the inner Apperceiver, or Witness. Our knowledge has to be tested to be verified, and so has the test itself. But we cannot apply test to test indefinitely; we terminate in a final guarantor of all knowledge—the intuitive Witness.

It is the Witness, then, who discloses to us the validity of the three norms—experience, inference and Word—and guarantees our understanding of Revelation's salvific import (see Selection 16).

With these principles Madhva then endeavored to absorb the basic insights of the other theologies of the Trichotomy, leaving out what, in his view, were their inconsistencies. Thus the insight of the theology of Identity, of a reality wholly unique, can be freed from contradiction if we interpret it to mean a unique reality that is plenary and independent, with the other reals being imperfect and dependent on itself. This reality, God, does not need assistance from other causes, though He chooses to employ them (Selection 19). Still, He is not a creationist God; the creature is not innately nothing, dependent for its *entire* being on His causality. In fact, the souls are uncaused, and intrinsically good or evil (Selection 20).

The insight of the theology of Difference-in-Identity can be preserved integrally in the doctrine of the Specific (Selection 18), whereby we have a difference that is real but does not divide. This is an original explanation to the problem that bedeviled so many theologies, that of God's essence and attributes (almost the basic problem of Islamic theology). The problem is that if the essence and attributes are identical, the attributes must be tautologous; and if they are not tautologous, they must mean more than the essence, and so be different from it, thus imperiling the unity of God. Madhva replies that they are identical with the essence in reality, but differ in a real sense as its Specific nuances, signifying aspects of God's reality that the essence as such does not.

This distinction was used by the Christian Scholastics to resolve the same problem—a problem which caused the Muslim Scholastics much perplexity, apparently because they were unfamiliar with the distinction. The Christian Scholastics called it "the conceptual distinction with a basis in reality [*distinctio rationis cum fundamento in re*]." This distinction, says Suárez,

> is realized through *inadequate concepts* of the same reality. For though the identical reality is conceived by either concept, by neither is all that exists in the reality conceived exactly, nor is its entire essence and objective significance exhausted . . . which is why the distinction always has a *basis* in reality, though *formally* it is said to be realized by inadequate concepts of the same thing.[37]

Concerned to show how his scheme could apply to the whole corpus of Hindu sacred tradition, Madhva wrote commentaries on its principal texts, and the enormity of his task compelled him to adopt a style of more than usual concision. The import of his thinking might have ever remained obscure, but for his brilliant disciple Jaya Tīrtha (c. 1335–85), who illuminated its perfect structure with a limpid radiance (Selections 17, 18, 19). His monumental *Nectar of Logic* is one of the pinnacles of Indic theological achievement.

Now in full possession of its powers, Dualist Vedanta could proceed to attack its main foes—Logicism, the principle school of Difference before Madhva's arrival, and Nondualism, the deadly opponent of both. This it did through that very embodiment of dialectical power, Vyāsa Rāya (1460–1539; Selections 20 and 22). The latter school defended itself with brilliance and spiritedness, in the person of Madhusūdana Sarasvatī (Selections 22 and 35)—worthy heir of Nāgārjuna—but was pursued with relentless logic by Vyāsa Rāmācārya (fl. 1566–1616; Selection 22), whose critical penetration seems to exceed that of the great Vyāsa Rāya himself. For if Nāgārjuna may be said to have invented the dialectic, the criticism dissolvent of metaphysics, Madhva may be said to have perfected the dialectic of the dialectic—the criticism dissolvent of the criticism, and reconstitutive of metaphysical thought.

At last, unchallenged as a legitimate system of the Vedanta, the Dualist school could turn to the contemplation of its own powers, so to speak, which it did through Vādi Rāja (1480–1600), one of Hindu theology's most literary minds. His *Jasmine of Logic* is a sustained poetic meditation on the harmony and depth of Madhva's thought—though also luxuriating in polemics—which for him is the definitive system of theology (Selection 21). Last of the great Dualist masters is Vanamāli Miśra (c. 1590–1655; Selection 23), who restates his school's main doctrines with incisiveness and elegance.

16
MADHVA

The Foundations of Dualist Vedanta Theology

PROLOGUE: OPENING PAEANS

1. Moved by devotion for that Being Whose only body is the plenitude of perfections, for the immaculate God supremely attainable through the totality of the sacred words, for the Cause from Whom all this has originated, Whose excellences render Him worthy of adoration, for the Being most dear to me, Viṣṇu Nārāyaṇa—I prostrate myself before Him!

2. I worship in sincerity the Source of the sacred sciences, the Teacher of universal teachers, and particularly my own, and proceed, myself, to explain the science called the supreme, in sequence.

3. Entreated by the gods headed by Brahmā and Śiva, Viṣṇu manifested Himself as the sage Vyāsa, and produced the unsurpassed science known as the supreme Wisdom.

4. Bādarāyaṇa, the teacher of teachers, the origin of the sacred sciences—from him arose the norm of sacred knowledge, for the sake of such beings as the gods.

5. The harmony between the speaker, the listener, and the conditions of their dialogue make for reliability. Hence—because of its reliable pronouncements, its basis in Revelation

6. And its foundation in reasoning—we see, concentrated in one, the great triple authority of Bādarāyaṇa's *Aphorisms on the Brahman,* an authority that is elsewhere dispersed.

7. Hence nothing is known which is so consummately the norm of knowledge. I have written a commentary on the *Aphorisms* before, but I write this one for greater clarity.

I. THE BEDROCK TERMS OF THE SACRED SCIENCES: *OM,* "NOW" AND "THEN"

8. All the sacred sciences are known to have the mystical monosyllable OM and "Now" as their basis. As OM accompanies every one of Bādarāyaṇa's aphorisms, it is intoned separately with each.

BĀDARĀYAṆA'S FIRST APHORISM

OM! Now then is our inquiry into the Brahman. *OM!*

9. OM signifies "interlaced," and so enunciates a contexture of perfections [in God, Whose name is Viṣṇu]. It also signifies the word "Brahman" expressed in the name Nārāyaṇa [or Viṣṇu]. [*OM,* as Madhva sees it, is derived from the verb *av* "to weave," through its passive participle *ota.*]

10. OM is also the meaning of the word "Splendorous," and of the three ritual exclamations of the Sacred Incantation —because of God's plenitude [import of the first exclamation], His causality of existence [import of the second], and His possession of joy [import of the third]. OM also signifies that "He is that Person" [as Revelation describes Him].[38]

[The Sacred Incantation is the *Gāyatrī.* It refers to the "Splendorous" One (*bharga,* made up of the syllables *bhar* and *ga*), taken to mean the one who "supports" (*bhar=bharaṇa* "supporting") and who "moves" (*ga=gamana* "moving") beings. The three ritual exclamations of the Gāyatrī are *bhuḥ, bhuvaḥ, svaḥ. Bhūḥ* is interpreted as "plenitude" (*bhūmataḥ*), *bhuvaḥ* as "causality of existence" (*bhāvanāt*), and *svaḥ* as "possession of joy" (*sutvāt*).]

II. GOD, UNIQUE OBJECT OF THEOLOGY

11. He alone is the import of the Vedas, the Being into Whom Bādarāyaṇa enjoins inquiry. "The man of knowledge is most dear to Me."[39] "A man who knows Him becomes immortal."[40]

12. "He can be attained by the one He chooses, none other"[41]—these words and others proclaim that liberation is attained only through the knowledge born of theological inquiry, [itself originating] through His grace.

13. "Substances, actions, time, essences and souls—all these exist through His favor, not in His despite."[42]

14. "Without You nothing is done."[43] Words such as these reveal that without God there is no liberation for anyone anywhere, even through the essence of knowledge.

15. "To the ignorant Viṣṇu gives knowledge; to those who have knowledge, He gives liberation; to those liberated, Viṣṇu, 'Upsetter of Men,' gives joy."[44]

III. CRITIQUE OF NONDUALISM

16. These pronouncements disclose that liberation has no reference to an unreal bondage. And neither is bondage unreal, as experience is to the contrary.

17. If misery and such things are unreal, we should know of them chiefly through Word. [But all else besides the Brahman is unreal, so Word is unreal too.] And the opponent has not shown that the unreal can validly establish anything [or has any probative power].

18. How do you prove the unreality of things—through a real norm or an unreal one? A real norm will establish Dualism [since there will be a real norm in addition to a real Brahman]. Any other kind of norm is not proved.

19. [The Inner Witness, you say, testifies to the unreality of things.] To wish to prove anything through the Inner Witness is to assert the probative power of the real. If you say that the Witness is indifferentiated, we shall have to determine the probative power of the indifferentiated.

20. That will require another indifferentiated norm [or

Witness]—and so on, into an infinite regress. Also, if the reality of the world is not accepted, no debate is possible.

21. That is why the conventions of debate are all ascertained to be real; it is then that the "pragmatic" is perceived to be "real" indeed.

22. The same arguments apply to the probative power of your "pragmatic" reality [as opposed to your "absolute" and "illusory" realities]. As for this triple level of reality—by what norm, may I ask, do you prove it [absolute, pragmatic or illusory]?

23. So, according to the reasoning indicated, the triple level will remain undemonstrated.

[Now, to take some of your definitions of unreality.] The arguments given above invalidate your concept of unreality as "difference from being and non-being."

24. Besides, difference *from being* is itself real for the theologian of Difference. And as for the world's difference *from non-being,* how can that be unacceptable to him?

25. If you say that difference is from *all* being, the difference *within* all being will persist. If you say that the Brahman is pure being, that too we can accept.

26. [The other definition of unreality,] "something which knowledge can abrogate" [as, for instance, when a subsequent and true knowledge invalidates a previous and untrue one] has not been proved by the opponent. But then he accepts the existence of a correct knowledge of something disparately known [earlier or elsewhere, thus postulating two kinds of knowledge: that of *abrogation,* proper to the Nondualists, and of *disparate perception,* proper to the Dualists].

27. To assert difference from non-being, one must *know* non-being. How then do you contest our doctrine that non-being is apprehended?

28. "Non-being" means "being otherwise than"—which is why we perceive non-being in illusion. We must therefore agree that we have an awareness of the realness of non-being [as an object of thought].

29. If you affirm that awareness to be indefinable, we shall have an infinite regress. [For to define it we shall need another indefinable awareness, and so on. And here is another argument:] If the indifferentiated Brahman is self-illuminant, how can ignorance *conceal* it?

30. [It is not the indifferentiated Brahman that is concealed, you say, but the Brahman relativized by unreal differentia-

tions.] But these differentiations assume that Ignorance is given [and that it gives rise to them. However, they *are* unreal]. And Ignorance cannot conceal what does not exist.

31. Ignorance cannot be ascribed to the non-self-illuminant unconscious [which you say your unreality is]. And if this Ignorance is non-existent, the sacred sciences will be in vain.

32. If the unreality of Ignorance is said to derive from Ignorance we shall have an infinite regress or circularity.

33. Our own doctrine, that ignorance has a real nature, offers no difficulties; so no such fallacies will rise. Are you saying that Ignorance is unintelligible? [If its unintelligibility is absolute and unqualified, how can we have any intelligence of it? If it is qualified by partial intelligibility, how can we be sure that any of our intelligences are not tainted by it? Our intelligence of] the Self might be similarly unintelligible.

34. So all right-minded people must shun this doctrine of Illusion, lacking as it does the four conditions of all salvific action—an eligible subject, an object, a result, and the connection between them [as all are unreal]—besides being vitiated with innumerable other defects.

35. Therefore misery is real, as experience, in guaranteeing it, discords with your doctrine. So the Veda can never ascribe the nature of the [impassible] Brahman to the [passible] soul.

36. When Revelation says "the sacrificer is a handful of grass," it does not mean that literally. So also when it affirms the soul's Brahman nature. Experience is equally contrary in both cases [to literal identity].

37. Revelation [in some places] proclaims the Lord endowed with perfections like omniscience to be different from the soul. Subordinate to this is Revelation [in other places] in so far as it proclaims identity [hence "Identity" Scripture is subordinate to "Transcendence" or "Difference" Scripture].

38. The "Identity" Scripture can have no authority in so far as it discords with its suzerain "Difference" Scripture. In scriptural texts declaring independence, excellence, the identity of place and thought

39. And similarity [between God and soul]—in such texts, affirmations of identity are literally true. Such texts, according to occasion, allow for a breadth of interpretation. But the "Difference" Scripture is tolerant of no such breadth. How then can it fail to have the greater force?

40. The doctrine of illusory Difference implies [as I have shown] the impossibility of Ignorance, and is hence un-

founded. Hence too, without Viṣṇu's grace, bondage, which is real,

41. Cannot be terminated. Which is why inquiry into the Brahman is enjoined. As a king who, pleased at the sight of a prisoner, has him freed from his chains,

42. So also, God the blessed, when seen, will bring bondage to an end.

IV. CRITIQUE OF RITUALISM

[You say that the central teaching of the Vedas is "achievability" for its own sake, injunctively declared. You are wrong.] Nothing is achievable [or worthy of being achieved], except as a means of realizing a desired end.

43. [And what is "the achievable?"] The achievable is not (a) something that is connected with activity. Prohibited actions [like the murder of a Brahmin] are equally connected with activity [as are injunctive actions; but a Brahmin's murder is hardly something "achievable"]. It is not (b) any future action either. When we say, "God will create" [we are not implying that a future creation]

44. Is an achievable action [that the Veda enjoins on God. The Veda cannot counsel God or remind Him of His "duties"]. Neither is it (c) something that one is not at liberty to avoid doing [an action we were necessitated by command to do]. For the same definition would also apply to a prohibited action [which, when compelled by desire, we believe we lack the ability to avoid doing]. Hence, the desired end and the means to realize it—

45. That is what "the achievable" means. The Blessed One, God the beloved, is the means to the end. And He is Himself the supremely desired end of the just. As Revelation testifies, "That which is dearer than son, than friend, than everything else, that being most intimate of all—this Self!"[45]

46. "Breath, instinct, mind, the faculties of sense, the soul, the body, children, wealth—all such things are dear through contact with the Self alone, and also whatever else is dear."[46]

47. These and other words show that—as the three conditions, of *expectation*, of *contiguity* and of *coherence* are fulfilled in Him—all are able to perceive His significance as the supreme desirable end.

[The three conditions are needed to turn words into a sentence, and so constitute its significance. *Expectation* is the incomplete sense of a word that leads one to expect more sense to complete it; *contiguity* is the juxtaposition of words in phrase or sentence; *coherence* is their conformability in meaning. These conditions are fulfilled in God in a different sense. Expectation in Him as supreme end and means to the end; contiguity, through His omnipresence; and coherence through the absence of any norm capable of abrogating His being.]

48. [You say that the significance of the Vedas lies principally in their injunctions to action, and only secondarily in its indicative affirmations. You prove this by alleging that the meaning of words is learnt principally through injunctions like "Bring the cow." You are wrong again.] It is through *indicative* statements like "Your brother is eating cakes," through the presence of some elements and the absence of others, through the object denoted being on the spot, and through the force of the three conditions of sentence construction—

49. It is through such indicative sentences that a child begins to apprehend meaning, and not through injunctive statements like "Bring the cow." The apprehension of injunctive statements becomes possible only through the child's actually perceiving the cow being brought.

50. How can the child perceive the action of bringing that is still in the future? But he will have apprehended the meaning of an action occurring in the present.

51. When he has seen the object again, and heard the word which denotes it, then will he apprehend its meaning—as occurring in the present, the past and the future: in that order.

52. How can the apprehension of meaning, linked as it is with the three conditions of sentence construction—the first of which is expectation—rise in the case of an injunction? But when the meaning of a word has been learnt through perception [in the present], then expectation will be possible [in the case of an injunction, which counsels action in the future].

53. The apprehension therefore relates to an object first in the present and afterwards in the future. All have expectation for desired ends, independent of activity.

54. It is through knowledge, direct or indirect, that ends are realized. There can also be activity for the sake of knowledge, as when one eats to find out the taste.

55. Besides, things sometimes become desirable through the mere knowledge of a statement's meaning.

[Furthermore, believing as you do that the Veda's sense is

mainly pragmatic, you deny that its indicative statements have much real significance, and that they ever describe the nature of things. Your views are inconsequential.] For then scriptural statements that refer to the characteristics of such ritual objects as the little and big butter ladles, and of the sacrificial fire, will be lacking in descriptive significance.

56. And [its essential characteristics being irrelevant] any implement whatsoever will be fit for use in sacrifice. It is clear, then, that besides their cultic significance, things must have an essential significance too.

57. [You say that when we come across scriptural statements like "let him revere the Self,"[47] we must put things like the "Self" in quotation marks, so that they will have a purely symbolic sense, and be taken as symbols that the sacrificer can mentally evoke during the ritual. Your belief is unwarranted.] If you can use quotation marks [for theological realities like the Self], you can use them also for [your ritually useful realities like] fire, by reason of which they too will become mentally evocable symbols.

Besides, scripture has ever so many words lacking such quotation marks.

58. If you choose to relate those marks to ["metaphysical"] realities like the Self, you might do so with ["pragmatic"] realities like fire too. But if you relate all the Vedic texts to a unitary enunciative significance,

59. The breaking up of the Vedic texts [into two groups, one interpreted pragmatically, and the other metaphysically] will be unfounded. All the Vedic texts [interpreted in both ways] are to be related to the one ultimate Fruit [of all activity and knowledge].

[If you insist on keeping the groups apart, on the plea that words in quotation marks never occur in the pragmatic portion of scripture, you are wrong again.] There is a scriptural passage in which the words "let him say thus" [which clearly implies quotation marks] are juxtaposed with "he pours a libation into the fire." [All your conceptually redundant hypotheses, which enable you to move capriciously from literal to symbolic sense, serve you nothing.]

60. You allege that our postulation of multiple meanings in Vedic statements entails conceptual redundancy. It is rather *your* conceptual redundancy that entails a total loss of meaning in those statements.

61. If you say that this can be decided through a norm,

then the norm will determine meanings too, and in this way, there will be meanings both for words and sentences.

62. [You accuse us of breaking up sentences referring to the Ultimate, like "The Brahman is truth, knowledge, infinity,"[48] and of relating each word separately to It as "The Brahman is truth," "The Brahman is knowledge," "The Brahman is infinity." But we do this in harmony with a unitary norm of interpretation, whereby all Vedic words and sentences are referrible to the Brahman: the *words* to His metaphysical essence, the *sentences* to actions that lead to Him. This brings us to our second reason.]

The division of phrases is not a fault when it is based on a distinction of relationships to the *object*, with the phrases [and words] being interlinked. [Attributes like truth and knowledge are all distinctly related to the Brahman, in so far as each signifies in Him what the others do not; yet none of these relationships contradicts the others.]

63. The division of phrases is a fault when they [the Ritualists] postulate that each word, taken by itself, is separately related to the term expressing the *action*.

[*Comment of Padmanābha Tīrtha.* To say that "he buys soma for the price of a red, brown-eyed, yearling cow" one says: "he buys a cow," "he buys a red," "he buys a brown-eyed," "he buys a yearling."[49]]

64. [You accuse us further of capricious interpretation of the Vedic texts. Some passages, you allege, we interpret literally, like the passage referred to; others, metaphorically, like the statement "You are It,"[50] which for the Nondualists clearly signifies that the soul is identical with God. Our interpretation is not capricious.] One is permitted to find a metaphorical sense in revealed statements when the literal one is contradicted by norms like experience. [These other norms clearly tell us that the soul is unidentical with God.] But we are not to imagine such a non-literal sense if no other norms contradict.

65. To conclude: actions have knowledge as their fruit, and knowledge dispenses eminent grace, which subserves the inquiry into the knowledge of Viṣṇu.

V. THE TRANSCENDENCE OF REVELATION

66. The inquiry must therefore be conducted in accordance

with the authority of Revelation. Like that of experience, the validity of the Sacred Tradition is intrinsic.

67. Else there will be an infinite regress. If Revelation derives its validity from another source, it will be innately void of it. Only things like false knowledge and deceitfulness go counter to the Veda,

68. And therefore have no authority. We have also to accept the eternity of the Vedas, for without any eternal Word, it will not be possible to guarantee Observance [or the Moral Law].

69. ['Why must we postulate a Revelation that is impersonally originant? Why can it not have a personal author?' Because that would give rise to difficulties.] One would have to suppose the author to be free of intent to deceive, to have knowledge of the things he was revealing, to be in fact the author of the revelation imputed to him, and such other things. The consequent redundance of explanations would be fallacious; so a personal author's word cannot be truly authoritative.

70. If you object that some person [like, shall we say, the Buddha, whom you, Buddhist, hold to be omniscient] must have perceived the Moral Law, because it is real, your argument can be disproved in this way: "The Buddha is not percipient of the Moral Law, because he *is* a person [or a man]."

71. The word of one who rejects the Moral Law [that is, of the Materialist] is of no value at all. Granting the non-existence of the Moral Law, *non-existence* cannot be perceived by experience [the only norm that the Materialist accepts].

72. Therefore, with so many doubts arising, we affirm that Word is a norm, as experience is.

[Here you say that the Veda cannot be a norm, as it does not tell us how to determine the meaning of its own words and phrases. I reply that it need not do that, as we know how to do so through other norms. We have to distinguish between *words,* their *meanings* and the *connection* between the words. The Ritualists say that there is a power in words which expresses their meaning clearly, before any connection takes place, and that the connection, or relation, is brought about through the conditions of expectancy, contiguity and coherence. This is the Expressed Relation theory. But I maintain that the meaning of words is not clear before the connection takes place.]

The power of words is indeed experienced in the meaning of each, but only in connection with other words. [When we know "cow" firstly in connection with "bringing," secondly with "tying," thirdly with "seeing," we perceive a varied connection between a word and its several significations. Only thus can the power of the word be apprehended, as referring to an invariable object capable of innumerable applications.]

73. Hence the Connectional Meaning theory [is the only valid one]. In the other theory there is explicative redundancy. [There is need of *two* powers there: one to express the meaning of the words, and another to make their connection known. The Ritualists reply that there is only one power, inherent in the words, not in their meaning—which, *through* the meaning, brings about the connection between words. The meaning then, has an intermediary, connective function. But a distinct function means a distinct power.] There can be no function lacking in power to signify [so it is clear, why], in the other theory the power to signify is twofold.

VI. THE THEOLOGICAL SYNTHESIS OF BĀDARĀYAṆA

74. All this, diffusely treated with differentiation of discipline in the science of logic and in *The Science of the Brahman,*[51] is here briefly indicated.

75. The science of logic develops the true teaching on the rules of normative knowledge. With these rules fixed, we can engage in inquiry—the ascertainment of objects normatively knowable.

76. As for *The Science of the Brahman,* it was produced by the Master [Bādarāyaṇa] himself, from a work, five hundred million verses long, that Viṣṇu, as Nārāyaṇa, had composed.

77. Bādarāyaṇa reduced it to five thousand verses. For that reason, then, he refers to *The Science of the Brahman* with the word "then," as being that work's epitome. [He does this in his next work, the *Aphorisms on the Brahman,* in his very first aphorism "Now, *then,* is our inquiry into the Brahman".]

78. All that exists is guaranteed by experience [so Bādarāyaṇa does not expressly affirm the reality of this world.] Besides, he was engaged by the gods on difficult questions, and so refrained [in his *Aphorisms*] from treating all topics elaborately.

79. [These apparent lacunae in the *Aphorisms* were exploited by the Nondualist opponent to insinuate his own ideas into the Vedanta, on the pretext of commenting on that great work.] But the opponent's philosophisms merit nothing but scorn. Unable as he is to perceive what *experience* shows him, what *doctrine* will he be capable of scrutinizing?

80. His doctrine is incompetent: so the treatise on liberation [the *Aphorisms on the Brahman,* or the Veda] ignores him.

VII. VIṢṆU, THE ABSOLUTE

The blessed Vyāsa [Bādarāyaṇa] himself tells us that the Brahman is Viṣṇu.

81. At the end of his work *The Science of the Gods,*[52] he declares, "Because Viṣṇu Himself said it." Vyāsa himself wrote the beginning and end of the book,

82. But the intervening portion was composed at his direct orders by his pupils Śeṣa and Paila. As in that work the Brahman's Viṣṇu nature has been proved, he refers in the *Aphorisms* to the Brahman alone.

83. [Viṣṇu is the God who moves on the waters, whose abode is the deep. One of His chief names is Nārāyaṇa, which may be divided into *nāra+ayana. Nāra* itself may be broken up into *na+ara.*] *Ara* is synonymous with "flaw" and "blemish," So we are to understand that *nāra* means "perfections" [*na* "no" *ara* "blemishes"], and their possessor *Nārāyaṇa* ["the refuge of perfections"; *nāra+ayana* "refuge"].

84. The word "Brahman" itself denotes this plenitude of perfections. Hence what the first aphorism enjoins is the inquiry into Nārāyaṇa Himself.

85. As Revelation evidently designates Viṣṇu by the word "Brahman," when it speaks of Him who is "on the shoreless ocean,"[53] it is referring to the same God as Nārāyaṇa.

86. Bādarāyaṇa says [in the *Mahābhārata*] that "the waters are said to be *nārā,*[54] and He is declared to be "in the midst of the waters."[55] Lady Glory [His consort], who at her pleasure gives Brahmā and Śiva their roles [of creator and destroyer], herself

87. Says that Viṣṇu is the matrix from which she arose, Viṣṇu, in Whom, as Revelation affirms, the worlds "dwell,"[56] "in Whom the gods dwell"[57]—that is, in Him Whose own abode is the deep.

88. He is the One Whom "the verses"[58] refer as to "Him named the Imperishable"[59]: He is the One Who, when declared to be "that whence she arose,"[60] is proclaimed to be "He Who is the Brahman Itself."[61]

—*Explanation of the "Aphorisms on the Brahman"*[62]

17
JAYA TĪRTHA
Critique of Difference-in-Identity

MADHVA

All imperfection is absent in the all-powerful God.
He is said to be "endowed with all power." Then
how can He identify with the imperfection-laden
soul?
If endowed with all power, how can He be imperfect, independent that He is? Void of identifying experientiality identity is no identity.
The norm that determines identity of consciousness
is identifying experientiality, and no other. Identity is
merely agglomerative if that experientiality is lacking.
Such an identity is nominal only, and is possible in
conscious beings. As it is not *total* identity, one may
impute it to conscious beings even when that experientiality is absent.

I. IDENTITY OF GOD AND SOUL REPUGNANT TO OMNIPOTENCE AND PRUDENCE

JAYA TĪRTHA

Proposition: The soul and the Brahman are not identical. *Reason:* because they are the subjects of contradictory attributes. *Example:* as, for instance, shadow and sunlight. This proof is not without basis. Bādarāyaṇa himself declares

> And, as we see from Revelation, the Brahman is endowed with all power.[63]

Thus it is on the basis of His all-powerfulness that His freedom from all imperfection is confirmed. Also because the soul's misery and other imperfections are attested by experience. If subjects supporting contradictory attributes can identify, posts and pots might well be identical.

'Let us admit that the Supreme Self is all-powerful and free of all imperfections. Even so, differentiated through conditioning, His particle, the soul, becomes laden with imperfections of His own creation. How is this contradictory? The fact that the differentiation is a modal one resolves the contradiction.'

To this Madhva replies, "If endowed with all power, how can He be imperfect, independent that He is?" If you accept that the Supreme Self is endowed with all power, then, His independence being the cause of the conditioning itself, how can something that He Himself has caused be laden with imperfection?

What Madhva means to say is this. Modal differentiation may or may not resolve the contradiction. It is the modal differentiation itself that is unfounded. To explain. Conditionings like the Inner Faculty, the products of Ignorance and such factors, sunder the Supreme Self and invest His particle, the soul, with misery and other imperfections. This is unacceptable, as it nullifies the Supreme Self's all-powerful independence.

So we must postulate that the Supreme Self personally sunders His own being by means of those conditionings dependent upon Himself, and furnishes His particle, the soul, with misery and other imperfections. This is even less acceptable. For then He will be lacking in prudence. No prudent person is ever seen to make himself experience acts at variance with personal happiness, through means—such as snakes and thorns—that are dependent upon himself. Because of His plenitude, the Supreme Self, unlike an ascetic, gains nothing by inflicting pain upon Himself. The beginningless character of this self-inflicted pain, caused by such factors as Ignorance, is no justification, because such a beginningless succession of painful events is dependent on the same Supreme Self. Neither can it be ascribed to cosmic play. Those who act according to prudence do not indulge in play to thwart their own personal happiness. It is a fallacy, then, to commingle imperfection with the Supreme Self in any mode whatsoever, so He cannot logically "identify with the imperfection-laden soul."

II. IDENTIFYING EXPERIENTIALITY, SOLE CRITERION OF IDENTITY BETWEEN CONSCIOUS BEINGS

'And even if the soul and the Brahman are in fact identical, the Brahman does not have the experientiality which identifies with the misery existent in the soul. So the fallacy alluded to does not apply, because the contradiction may possibly be resolved through the modal differentiation described above.'

Madhva calls this into question with the words: "Void of identifying experientiality, identity is no identity." Identifying experientiality is the apperception of states like misery, comprehended under experience, recognized as belonging to oneself. Madhva retorts with the words just quoted. For the soul, in fact, does not experientially identify with the impassible Brahman nature: this is indisputable. Neither does the Brahman identify experientially with the misery inherent in the soul. Hence, as I said before, there is no identity between them. Madhva now explains why, in the words "The norm that determines identity of consciousness is identifying experientiality, *and* no other." The word "and" carries the force of the reasoning.

'Let us agree that identifying experientiality is the norm to determine identity. What of it? If we are deprived of one norm we need not be deprived of the identity itself. Absence of smoke does not always mean absence of fire.'

It is to this objection that Madhva's words "and no other" apply.

'A pot is identical with itself, but there is no identifying experientiality involved. How do you explain that?'

This objection is anticipated by Madhva's words "The norm that determines identity of *consciousness*." Let me put it this way. Identity determined by consciousness, with identifying experientiality as its sole norm, becomes the basis of discussion only when that experientiality is posited. The sentence "my soul, Bhadrasena"[64] is one in which such experientiality is affirmed. You cannot demur that the soul, in this life, does not experientially identify with the miseries of its previous lives, though it is the identical soul which experienced those miseries. I am not alluding to an identifying experientiality which is incessant [aware at all times of all that befell it]. What I do mean to say is that when a conscious being identifies with some *nature* experientially, it is identical with that *nature,* and if it does not so identify, then it is not identical with it. If this norm is negated, then the identity is. When the perception of color is negated, sight is negated too. [If we have to choose between identity and consciousness] we cannot negate consciousness, since both sides in the dispute accept it. So it is identity that we shall have to negate.

Consequently, in the syllogism that presumes to establish the identity of the soul and the Brahman from the fact that they are both conscious beings, the hypothetical character of the concomitance between consciousness and identity becomes manifest. Invariable [or non-hypothetical] concomitance exists only between consciousness determined by identity and identifying experientiality, as is seen in living men like Devadatta. It does not exist between identity and consciousness pure and simple. Such a consciousness is lacking in the syllogism referred to, hence it is easy to formulate the following argument:

> *Proposition:* The soul and the Brahman, though conscious, do not mutually identify. *Reason:* because they lack identifying experientiality. *Example:* as in the instance agreed on.

In the proposition, the predicate ["do not mutually identify"] is not devoid of significance. As in the argument "Sound is not a specific quality, like touch" it serves to counteract any objections that may be brought against the reason.

III. ACCIDENTAL IDENTITY BETWEEN GOD AND THE SOUL UNOBJECTIONABLE

Madhva now raises a fresh doubt with the words "Identity is merely agglomerative, if that experientiality is lacking." The agglomerative identity I speak of is not identity in an absolute sense. Therefore, even when identifying experientiality is lacking, it can be imputed to conscious beings. What Madhva means is this. The believer in agglomerative identity accepts the difference-in-identity of the soul and the Brahman. There the absence of identifying experientiality, produced by difference, and confirmed when the difference becomes known, does not negate identity. In agglomeratively identical things, as, for instance, threads-and-cloth, the attribution of contradictory characteristics [difference between threads, identity of cloth], confirmed when the difference comes to be known, does not negate the identity. Else it would be difficult to posit identity even in such cases, so identity is not unacceptable there, as we may agree without much trouble.

Madhva comes to another point of agreement in the words "As it is not total identity, one may assign it to conscious beings even when that experientiality is absent." Let us by all means accept an identity between the soul and the Brahman free from mutually identifying experientiality. To accept anything else would be to go counter to the adduced instances and would be fallacious. Hence Madhva says, "Such an identity is nominal only, and is possible in conscious beings." But if your identity is only nominal and not real, its postulation is not fallacious.

Madhva's meaning is as follows. The absence of the attribution of contradictory characteristics is not the sole norm for determining the identity between a cloth and its threads. Experience [quite independently of that norm] attests that identity. Hence the connection of contrary characteristics [difference between the threads, identity of the cloth] is freed by identity's abrogative power [the fact that cloth and threads are unmistakably one] from the fear represented by the time sequence [for it seems that contraries can be true only successively, not simultaneously. But simultaneity between cloth and threads does not wholly identify them or annul their contrariety, which is] confirmed when their difference is certified. If the identity of the consciousness is arrived at by means of another and improper norm, then the absence of the identifying experientiality will not go counter to identity, and will be confirmed only with the declaration of difference. But this is not what happens, because, as I said, the identity of the consciousness is invariably concomitant with identifying experientiality and with nothing else. If the concomitance is negated, so will the object it determines be. Identity will of necessity be null, and all talk about it will again be to no avail.

—*The Nectar of Logic*[65]

18

JAYA TĪRTHA

Specifics, the Nuances Innate to Identity

MADHVA

Hence, to speak of something as attributeless [or "void of Specifics," lacking in a distinctiveness whereby it may be identified and named, is a contradiction in terms, since "attributelessness" is distinctive of itself in relation to other things. It] is like saying, "I am dumb." The Specific is therefore inevitable, even in an undifferenced reality [like the Brahman]. It is also self-determining. However, when real difference is absent, the Specific's presence is indicated by the use of non-tautologous words. What we call the Specific exists universally in things.

I. THE SPECIFIC AS DIFFERENTIAL EQUIVALENCE

JAYA TĪRTHA

"The Specific is therefore inevitable, even in an undifferenced reality." As, in the manner discussed, there is otherwise discord between the Great Pronouncements [of Revelation on the Brahman] and the Supplementary Pronouncements, we are constrained to postulate the Specific even in the Brahman that is devoid of difference. To explain: The oneness proclaimed in the Great Pronouncements, and [multiple] attributes like truth, knowledge and infinity,[66] declared in the Supplementary Pronouncements, are mutually identical in the Brahman, according to the Scripture that affirms the Brahman's uniform essence:

> Only in one way can It be perceived—that immeasurable, changeless being, immaculate, beyond ether, the increate Self, the great Immovable.[67]

Your imputed fallacy does not apply, as, even in a thing devoid of real difference, there is a specific potency whereby difference flashes yet does not flash, and is thus plausible for this reason and others. It is speculations like these that make us aware of the Specific, as you yourself cannot fail to admit.

'Even if we were to take the Specific for granted, the discord between the scriptural texts would not be stilled. If that Specific is different from the thing it specifies [its own specificity will require explaining, and we shall need a different Specific, and so] we shall be involved in the fallacy of an infinite regress in differences. If the Specific is non-different from the thing, it will thereby have shed its differentiating character and so have lost its capacity to specify.'

To this Madhva replies: "It is also self-determining." To complete the sense of these words, it must be premised that non-difference is the sole relation possible between the Specific and the specified reality, and that the capacity to specify is to be explained in virtue of the Specific alone.

'Still, the sequence of Specifics [each explaining its predecessor] will lead to an infinite regress.'

Madhva's words "self-determining" pointedly refer to this objection. It is that very Specific which *intrinsically* constitutes any other Specific as well as its own capacity to specify. We must assume that the determinability and determinateness of each Specific exists in virtue of its own essence.

'By what norm do you prove the Specific's capacity to determine difference in a reality that is undifferenced?'

Madhva replies with the sentence beginning with the words "However, when real difference is absent"—the word "however" being used for emphasis. He continues: "the Specific's presence is indicated by the use of non-tautologous words"—such words being the secondary characteristics determining all the vestiges of difference,

To explain: The scriptural text, quoted above, which speaks of the uniform way in which the Brahman can be perceived, only gives us a conception of His essence as consciousness [and not of the attributes or quasi-attributes which are identical with that essence]. Thus, though the self-luminance of the consciousness is certain [because the latter is demonstrably identical with the former], it is still not certain [because "consciousness" and "self-luminance" are by no means tautological]. Hence the informative power of non-tautologous words. The fact that the Consciousness-Luminance [in your Nondualist system] cannot be dispelled by Ignorance, and that the latter can be dispelled by the knowledge of nonduality—such are specific differences of function. Also, the fact that Consciousness is one, and that the terms like truth, knowledge and infinity used to describe it are many, implies numerical incongruity [since all these multiples apply to a thing that is not thereby multiplied].

These are some of the vestiges of difference that we become aware of. Both oneness and multiplicity being otherwise incompatible, we must conceive a *differential equivalence*—some eminent quality accountable for those vestiges—to exist even in an undifferenced consciousness, as no other explanation is possible.

In consequence, through this hypothesis, which fathoms the essence itself, the Specific is established as the determinant of the vestiges of difference. What need, then, to search for any other norm? All this also enables us to formulate its definition: *the Specific is the cause of the functioning of a non-metaphorical difference even where difference is absent.* In this way the Nondualist, obliged to admit the Specific, will be constrained to accept other ideas as well.

II. PROOF OF THE SPECIFIC FROM THE VESTIGES OF DIFFERENCE

Madhva then says: "What we call the Specific exists universally in things." The Illusionist is not the only one obliged to accept the Specific in the Brahman: in fact all believers in the world's reality also need to posit it in every object. To take an example, a cloth and its whiteness are really not different, as they are not perceived differentially as are two fingers, for instance.

[Logicist objector:] 'Can this be due to *steadfast unconnectedness* [which we Logicists define as the inhesion of something destructible, say the whole, in something indestructible, say the parts]?'

What, pray, is this steadfast unconnectedness?

'The necessary existence through the relationship of inherent and inhered, shall we say?'

Does such a relationship preclude a perception of difference [as happens with a cloth and its whiteness]? A cloth is not like a pot [though both may have the same color and be similarly used, as receptacles, for instance]. The cloth, made into a receptacle, shows its berries [as a pot can do], and in its surface character, its whiteness [a pot too can have a white surface]. Does that make cloth pot? And such a conception [as that produced by the Specifics] is not error, because [error is an abrogable conception, and here] no abrogator can be found. The abrogator, in our case, would be the conception, derived from experience, which had fathomed the difference between a cloth and its whiteness. But as there is direct perception of their non-difference, other abrogating norms, such as inference, have no occasion to appear.

As I said, there is no conception that fathoms the difference between a cloth and its whiteness: their identity is thus certified by experience. However, vestiges of difference are also perceived, such as the following:

a. The fact that neither of the concepts "cloth" and "whiteness" has a significance that is adequate or redundant [in relation to their object as a whole].

b. The fact that the words [signified by those concepts] are not synonyms.

c. The rememorative capacity of such non-synonymous words.

d. The distinction between object and function in actions like fetching water.

e. The fact that when one is told, "Bring a cloth," one does not bring any white thing; or when one is told, "Bring something white," one does not necessarily bring a cloth.

f. The fact that to say, "A cloth is not white," is not to make a contradictory statement like "A cloth is not a cloth."

g. The inability of a blind man to form the conception "this is white," in contrast to his ability to form the conception "this is cloth." As he is unable to know white, he is not unable to know cloth.

h. Contact with saffron does not conceal cloth as it does its whiteness; conversely, the non-concealment is absent in whiteness through the contact, as it is not absent in the cloth.

Many other examples could be given. The conception of Specifics [as I said] is not an error, both because the possibility of abrogation is absent, and because the Specific conforms to usage. Consequently—those conceptions of non-difference and of the vestiges of difference being otherwise incompatible

—we are obliged to postulate a certain eminent quality even in the undifferenced cloth, differential equivalence, by reason of which all will be rendered consistent. This eminent quality, possessing as it does the capacity of specifying even the undifferenced, is celebrated as the Specific. We must therefore posit its existence in other substances too.

'If we accept the notion of Difference-in-Identity, the inconsistencies will be removed, and there will be no need for your Specific.'

You are wrong. To make it possible for the mutually contradictory Difference and Identity to coexist you will have need of the Specific.

'But we do experience such Difference-in-Identity. How then can they be contradictory?'

You are right. But when we inquire how this is possible, we find it consequent to admit that eminent quality [I spoke of] in the thing's essence. We are also obliged to postulate the Specific's existence to avoid the abeyance between Difference and Identity, as I said.

MADHVA

> The Specifics are themselves infinite, and are mutually specifying. Endowed with self-determinateness, they are found in things universally. Hence, infinite as He is in perfections, the Brahman is also called undifferenced. That non-difference is proclaimed by Revelation in these words:
>
> "As rain water splashing on a high mountain rock flows down the mountains, so one who sees the attributes as different, flows alongside them."[68]

III. INFINITY OF SPECIFICS

JAYA TĪRTHA

'If the Specific is found in all things, it is not differentiated from them, so we arrive at the oneness of all things!'

Madhva replies. "The Specifics are themselves infinite." Intrinsic to nature, these Specifics are found in things universally; there are, in fact, infinite Specifics in infinite substances, and not just one Specific everywhere. Hence the fallacy you speak of does not apply. When Madhva earlier said, "What we call the Specific exists universally in things," he was using the singular number to signify a collective unity.

'Now, if each substance has a single Specific only, then manifold situations [or contexts]—expressed in sentences like "The cloth is large, white and flutters"—would not be possible. Manifold and mutiple effects are never seen to proceed from a single unmanifold thing. If such were to happen, things would be lacking in explanation, and the postulation of the Specific would be futile.'

Madhva counters this with the same words, "The Specifics are themselves infinite." The Specifics, described above, existing universally in things, are also infinite in each thing, so there is no occasion for the fallacy you allude to. "Infinite" is a secondary definition of the Specific. It must be known that there are as many Specifics as there are functions [or situations]. While each substance remains one, its Specifics must be conceived through mutual difference, because multiplicity cannot exist without difference. Thus the differences being identified in the substance, the substance will also be differentiated.

Which is why Madhva says that the Specifics are "mutually specifying." Multiplicity is possible through mutual specification only, because, as I said, the Specific has the capacity to produce the vestiges of difference.

'But these Specifics will need other Specifics, so there will be an infinite regress.'

Madhva answers: "Endowed with self-determinateness, they are found in things universally." We earlier inquired into the Specific's non-difference from the standpoint of the substance; we now inquire into the Specifics' non-difference among themselves. The meaning in the two cases is thus clearly different. However, all that is proved through the hypothesis which establishes the Specific's nature; hence no separate proof is given. Nothing which is itself implausible can serve to counteract another implausibility, but is conceived through the essence-insightful hypothesis according as it arises. If a Specific is open to experience, it can, as we shall see, be known through experiential proof. But if it is a Specific of another sort, it cannot be known by experiential proof alone. That is why our hypothesis has been proposed, and also why all thinkers [in an open or tacit manner] acknowledge the Specific's existence.

IV. THE THEORY OF THE SPECIFIC AND THE INFINITY OF DIVINE PERFECTIONS

Madhva observes at this point: "Hence, infinite as He is in perfections, the Brahman is also called undifferenced." The Brahman, though undifferenced, is declared to possess infinite perfections. If someone remarks that there is always a difference between the attribution and the attributed, he can be answered in Madhva's words "the Brahman is also called undifferenced." And if someone were here to say—

'An undifferenced reality, qualified by multiple attributions, must itself be multiple. Else it will follow that the attributions themselves are not multiple, and that the words denoting them are synonymous. The [difference-involving] relationship of qualities and the qualitied will also not be possible'—

He could be applied to in those very words of Madhva's, "the Brahman is also called the undifferenced." In virtue of the Specific, there is at the same time an infinity of perfections and the Brahman's oneness. As His perfections are infinite, He is endowed with the qualities-and-qualitied relationship; and the unconfused assertion "The Brahman and the perfections" is perfectly plausible.

In this connection, when [following Bādarāyaṇa's second aphorism] we say that the Brahman is the cause of the world's creation and other states, we are saying that He is infinite in perfections. This aphorism gives us to understand that infinity of perfections is indeed the definition of God. The aphorism then makes it clear that, as proof of this, it is proceeding to lay down the definition of the causality of the world's states like creation [as the "manifestative" definition of God]. Consequently, there is nothing to disprove the claim that world causality pertains to the essential definition of God; so it is not proper to conceive it as His accidental definition [as some Nondualist theologians have thought fit to proclaim].

—*The Nectar of Logic*[69]

19

JAYA TĪRTHA

The Limitlessness of God's Causality

MADHVA

Though able to act otherwise, God, by the determination of His own will, always creates the world with determinate causes.

JAYA TĪRTHA

By "otherwise" Madhva means that though God can create without causes, He always creates the world through causes that His own will determines, with the thought "I shall create only with the help of other causes [besides My own omnipotence]."

"Otherwise" can mean that He can create Egoism through Matter, and the Prodigious [or Instinct] through Egoism [thus reversing the usual order of evolution: Matter-Instinct-Egoism]. Similarly, though He can make Matter the efficient cause and Time the material cause, still, He has the thought "I shall make the former the material cause by means of the latter, and only then create the world." Thus, by the determination of His own will, He always creates the world with determinate causes—meaning by "determinate," fully equipped and endowed with existence and powers defined by Himself. That is how Madhva's words are to be construed.

To elaborate. If the question is raised whether God does or does not follow a determined order of efficient and material causes, I answer that He does. It is thus proper to ascribe causality to Matter. But that order does not, as in the case of a potter, involve a failure of power when those causes are missing or change during causation—so implying a loss of His independence and of their dependence: it is an order unreservedly subject to His will. Thus it is also proper to ascribe independence to God.

And neither are those causes self-dependent for their existence and powers—so implying a lapse in His unrestrained sovereignty. On the contrary, their existence and all else they possess is subject to God alone. His association with them thus emblazes His sovereignty eminently. It has been said:

> When the instruments' instrumental nature owes its being to the Self, then the instruments' coming into being becomes an emblazonment for sovereignty.
>
> —*The Nectar of Logic*[70]

20
VYĀSA RĀYA
The Problem of Evil

BĀDARĀYAṆA'S APHORISMS

OM! There is no partiality and harshness in God's treatment of souls, because He acts in compliance with their karma. Revelation discloses this [in lines like, He "leads us to the good through our good, and to evil through our evil"].[71] OM!

OM! 'Can it be maintained that there is no karma, as it lacks an independent existence?'

No, because it is eternally existent. OM!

OM! [Though God complies with karma] independence is still proper to Him [because karma is dependent on Himself]. Partiality and harshness in compliance with karma are justifiable. OM!

VYĀSA RĀYA

The previous section was concerned with the good altruistically produced [that is, with creation brought about for the creature's benefit, not the Creator's]. This section intends to show that the reasoning behind that doctrine is incontrovertible.

THE PROBLEM

The question here is whether the causality of all things is proper to Viṣṇu or not. To resolve that we shall have to decide whether or not His causality of happiness and misery leads to His being unfair and cruel. This question can be decided only if we determine whether He acts without conforming with the karma of souls, or in conformity with it. And that problem can be determined only if we ascertain whether karma's capacity is independent of God, or whether, because of His supremacy, it is dependent on Him. To solve this difficulty we must make make certain whether, granting karma's dependence on God, the partiality and harshness that lies in causing happiness and grief, which befalls the soul in conformity with the eternally existent capacity of the karma dependent on God—whether this partiality or harshness is blamable precisely because it is that, or because it contravenes the authority of the Veda [the impersonally originant Law of morality, which strongly condemns such behavior, and which declares that virtue leads to happiness and vice to pain].

DISSENTIENT VIEW

. . . It is not logical to postulate an altruistic creation, such as was described in the previous section. In such a creation all would be happy at all times. God would not gladden some and vex others, and so be unfair and cruel. You cannot say that He is not to blame, because He is only acting in compliance with the soul's karma, because karma itself, as Revelation declares, is caused by God:

> He alone makes a man do a good deed, and brings him up from these worlds. He alone makes a man do a bad deed, and leads him down from the worlds.[72]

'Is it not reasonable to postulate that He makes men do their later deeds in conformity with their earlier karmas? You cannot argue that if a fault terminates, then it must originate also; because the flux of karmas has no beginning.'

Such reasoning cannot be sustained. The essence of the reality of karma's beginningless flux is dependent on God, as we have seen from the arguments presented in the earlier section [of the *Aphorisms on the Brahman*] entitled "The Beginning" [or "Material Causality"].[73] Hence there will still be inequity and callousness on His part [for He will have been the cause of that which causes Him to act unfairly]. And if karma is independent of God, then independence will not be properly attributable to Him [as His exclusive attribute, since karma will share it too]. So on both counts the Brahman is not free from defects. Such is the opposite view.

ORTHODOX JUDGEMENT

. . . Are inequity and callousness defects

(1) Because God causes happiness and pain without regard to the soul's good and evil actions, and so contravenes the authority of the Veda in its teaching of the causality of happiness and pain [since it declares that they are due, respectively, to good and evil deeds]? Or (2) because, though God acts with regard to the soul's deeds, and so does not contravene Revelation, yet the karma itself [which accounts for the deeds that lead Him to act callously] depends on God for its existence?

It cannot be (1), because God does regard the soul's deeds. If it is (2), would inequity and callousness be defects (a) because, as in souls, they would have been caused by unlawful behavior [on the part of God] or (b) because they would contravene the teachings of the sacred science [as declared by Kṛṣṇa Himself in the *Gītā*, in these words]:

> I am the same to all beings: I detest none and am partial to none. But those who worship Me are in Me, and I am also in them.[74]

Or (c) because the noble attribute of impartiality would be frustrated and so conduce to God's own degradation?

It cannot be (a), because God is above the prohibitions of the Law. As for (b), He who conforms with the aptitude [for good and evil] eternally inherent in souls, is one to whom the word "impartial" can be truly applied. It has been said:

> He will not give to His own in excess of what is due to their service, nor to others in excess of their misdeeds: so is Viṣṇu impartial.

And also that:

> The ordaining of life or even knowledge in accordance with the character of place or persons—that is impartiality: partiality is otherwise.[75]

Hence it is that the impartiality of Yama, the god of death, is universally accepted.

> The mind that looks impartially on persons like mother, wife, teacher and pupil, on the sage Vasiṣṭha as on the despised Pulkasa tribesman—such a mind is not said to be impartial.

And a king who is harsh with criminals and gracious to the law-abiding cannot be called partial. Furthermore:

> The wise have an even appreciation for a Brahmin learned and modest, for a cow, an elephant, a dog, and a dog-eating outcaste.[76]

These words [from the *Gītā*] reveal that an unevenness in the subjects does not imply an unevenness in the God on Whom those subjects depend.

If it is (c), the frustration of impartiality that conduces to degradation,

i. Is it that He is unfair and cruel because He creates a variety of natures in souls [some innately good, and others evil];

ii. Or because He contravenes their natures that are beginningless and everlasting;

iii. Or because, though able to transform their eternally established natures into others, refrains from doing so;

iv. Or because He controls them with regard to their beginningless and innate proclivities?

It cannot be (i), because the nature of conscious beings is eternal [or increate].

It cannot be (ii), because God gives the fruit only in accordance with the nature of each conscious being.

It cannot be (iii), because to refrain from transforming natures is not what makes for partiality and callousness:

> A person who, though able to change one nature into another, refrains, is not called unjust even by the world. The sage who can turn geese into crows, but does not do so—do people call him unfair? And

> the sage who can turn crows into geese, but does not do so—do people call him cruel?

It cannot be (iv), because the control that respects innate proclivities is accordant with the great perfection of independence, and does not conduce to degradation. In God, the compassion consequent on His nature does not correlate with the absence of merit. Else God, through His compassionateness, could turn pain into happiness and evil into good, and, like a tender-hearted human being, be distressed at the sight of pain in living things. It has been said:

> A partiality which contravenes good and evil is a fault, and such has been repudiated in the *Aphorisms on the Brahman.* But control of good and evil is not a fault, but rather a virtue. Hence this is what Kṛṣṇa [not the god but a sage also named Vyāsa, later incarnate as Bādarāyaṇa], the author of the *Aphorisms,* accepts. There is never any partiality in Viṣṇu which does not regard the soul's innate aptitude [for good and evil]. With that aptitude determined there might be partiality of some kind.

And as Madhva says in his *Explanation of the "Aphorisms on the Brahman":*

> We cannot accept the partiality and callousness that void the Veda of authority. Anything else is not partiality and callousness.

In Bādarāyaṇa's aphorisms on this topic [referred to at the start of this discussion], the first two aphorisms repudiate the first [of the two views] referred to in the *Explanation.* But the next aphorism resolves the doubt that independence might not be proper to God, with

> Independence is proper to Him.

[These words constitute the first part of the aphorism. And in its second part] with the words

> Partiality and harshness in compliance with karma are justifiable,

it adopts the second view referred to in the *Explanation.*

CRITIQUE OF OTHER SOLUTIONS TO THE PROBLEM

. . . [The Nondualist argues as follows:] God is the general cause [of good and evil], like rain to crops. The karmas are the particular causes, like seeds. The seeds differ in potentialities, so there is a divergence in crops, like rice and barley. So God is not unfair and cruel: such [the Nondualist claims] is the sense of the aphorism.

But he is mistaken. Revelation and Tradition assure us that even the particular causes have God as their author. Revelation says:

> He alone makes a man do a good deed.

And Tradition:

> Viṣṇu will cause virtue and vice.

Hence God cannot be acquitted of unfairness and cruelty. It cannot be argued that to avoid contradiction with a large number of scriptural declarations, it is right to interpret them in an implicative sense, because, as has been said, "such meaning is scripture's intent." Vācaspati Miśra himself, in his *The Irradiant* [commentary on the *Aphorisms*] asserts that "there are scriptural texts like

> He alone makes a man do a good deed.

which speak of the creatures' dependence of God in all things. We are not to understand them in that strict sense, but are properly to interpret them as only signifying the praise of God."[77]

. . . [The Qualified Nondualist reasons thus:] "The soul, entirely through the general and independent power given it by God, performs good and evil deeds. But God disregards the evil and approves the good, so He is not unfair and cruel. As was said before, man—through the independent power given him by God—engages in efforts to realize knowledge and cherished activities. Then God disapproves or approves them, and in apportioning punishment or reward, gives every man's every action the fruit it deserves."[78]

This view is also untenable. It is impossible to acquit of cruelty One Who, through the endowment of freedom [or independence] provides the cause for the performance of good and evil deeds [which lead Him to react to them harshly]. Also this view discords with Revelation:

> He Who controls the soul within . . . He alone makes a man do a good deed.
> Without You nothing is done, nothing![79]

and with Tradition:

> As a man, standing steadfast, whirls a wooden doll [so, O Arjuna, the Lord of all beings, ensconced in the heart] whirls all beings—puppets on a machine—by means of His Mirific Power.[80]

And if God incites the soul to *independent* activity, how can the soul be God's body [which the Qualified Nondualists say it is and define as something wholly subordinate to, and never independent of, the embodier]? And how can the soul direct its activity to its own harm? You cannot say that it believes—deludedly—that this harm is a good, because the delusion itself will have been caused by God. Hence the charges of unfairness and cruelty will remain unchallenged.

Besides, if God disregards the evil, even when He has the power to prevent it, the accusations of unfairness and cruelty will hold. If He lacks the power, then there will be conflict with the following aphorisms of Bādarāyaṇa, among others:

> Such mirific powers [or energies] indeed exist in the Self, and so scripture declares [in texts like "the ancient Person is endowed with mirific power, such powers as are not to be found in another"].[81]

> And the Brahman is endowed with all powers, as is revealed [in passages like "The deity furnished with all powers is the highest, and so they say that it possesses irrestrainable power"].[82]

And with Revelation itself:

> No effect or cause is known of Him, no one is seen to be like or greater than Him. His supreme Energy is revealed to be inborn, and to be the activity of knowledge and power.[83]

In this way too the position of the Logicists [or Naiyāyikas] —according to whom God's will has a general character, expressible as "Let it be so," and not a specific one—is also refuted. For anything at all would accrue to any person whatever from that [undetermined, permissive] "Let it be so" character of will—sometimes pain for God Himself, sometimes hell for the man who does good. I myself find that "Let it be so" character hard to accept, because what this character might consist in has not been described to this day. Supposing that—given the "Let it be so" character—happiness befalls any man as a result of a particular karma of his, if that karma is independent of God, there would be disaccord with Revelation; if it is dependent, the charges of unfairness and cruelty will be hard to rebut. Therefore, unless we accept an innate aptitude [for good and evil] that is beginningless [and is not caused by God], the charges of partiality and callousness will be difficult to controvert . . .

—*The Moonlight of Meaning*[84]

21

VĀDI RĀJA

Finality of Madhva's Doctrine

The heterodox Buddhist and Jain teachings are tentative [or heterodox] systems with regard to the whole body of Sacred Tradition. After them, other schools unfolded in succession, one tentative system following another, until Madhva's system arose.

This system, no other, is the definitive doctrine; that is to say, the doctrine definitively [or finally] established. Those who can judge between valid and invalid positions can decide this for themselves. That is why there is no system after Madhva's, up to this day. It is therefore the definitive theology.

Having made up my mind about this, I have submitted to its teaching, sublime above all, and exalted by Revelation. Enjoying logical discussion as I do, I have fashioned [this book] *The Jasmine of Logic.*

—*Jasmine of Logic,* perfume (chapter) 1[85]

22
VYĀSA RĀMĀCĀRYA
The Inevitability of Dualism

VYĀSA RĀYA

Your second definition of falsehood is unsound. [Reality, you claim, has three levels: the *absolute,* which no knowledge can abrogate; the *pragmatic,* abrogable by the knowledge of the absolute; and the *illusory,* abrogable by the knowledge of the pragmatic. These levels, you maintain, are the result of the superposition of the veil of Ignorance on the luminous and undifferentiated Brahman-substrate. The latter, flashing in its true essence, is absolute reality; but as flashing through the veil it gives rise to the other two levels—which together constitute the false world, its falsehood consisting in its liability to total abrogation. Let us see what your theory entails.]

If this total abrogation is real absolutely, Nondualism collapses [for we shall have two absolute reals, the Brahman and the abrogation]. If it is real illusorily, the point is obvious, and in no need of demonstration [for that is precisely what we Dualists say—the real world is abrogable illusorily, but not truly]. If it is real pragmatically, a pragmatic abrogation does not contravene a thing's absolute reality, so you are inconsequent with your own definition of falsehood. [In other words, a thing may be absolutely real, but pragmatically abrogable, like your Brahman, appearing as the world, abrogable only in its superposed and pragmatically real world-appearance, not in its basic substrate reality. In our Dualist view, the world is similarly real.] Moreover, the "Nonduality" Scripture ["there is no manifoldness here at all"][86] would be teaching a falsehood, and the non-illusory world, the correlative of the pragmatically abrogable, would acquire the status of absolute reality.

VYĀSA RĀMĀCĀRYA

With the words "your second definition is unsound," Vyāsa Rāya proceeds to demolish the second definition of falsehood —taken to mean "what, in a cognized subject, correlates with its own total abrogation." [When I say that I see silver, when in fact I see nacre, I am positing silverness in nacre, nacre being in this case the cognized subject. But a closer inspection shows the subject to be nacre, not silver, and that subsequent knowledge abrogates the previous one. In other words, silverness is totally abrogated in the cognized subject, nacre; hence the silver in nacre is false.]

When Vyāsa Rāya says "Nondualism collapses" and so on, what he also means to imply is this:

If, according to your way of thinking, you assume the falsehood of silver to be pragmatic, your definition of the subject will be faulty, as correlativity with total abrogation, in the absolute sense, is lacking in the silver itself. [The "pragmatically" real world and the "absolutely" real Brahman, have the same substratum or subject, the Brahman. But the "pragmatically" real silver and the "absolutely" real silver do not have the same subject, but *two* subjects—nacre for the former and silver metal for the latter.] And if you assume this silver's falsehood in an absolute sense, the experience that manifests this silver will be disclosing what is untrue [and hence nonexistent].

MADHUSŪDANA SARASVATĪ

'[Your objections against our Nondualist teaching cannot be sustained, whether we imagine this abrogation to be real or unreal. Let us take the first alternative.] The world-abrogation is no other than the Brahman-substrate, so its reality in the absolute sense does not lead to Nondualism's collapse.'

VYĀSA RĀMĀCĀRYA

You are mistaken. Necessary as it is for the Brahman-substrate to flash in order to project the world illusion—with the world-abrogation, indifferentiable from the Brahman, also flashing, the world illusion itself will be rendered impossible. You cannot argue that the [world-revealing] substrate-flash is not the same as the world-abrogating substrate-flash, because according to your doctrine the world-abrogation is the Brahman unqualifiedly—else your other doctrine of Its undifferentiated nature will also collapse.

Vyāsa Rāya's words "the point is obvious and in no need of demonstration" also imply that the object to be demonstrated is itself defectively defined. And in the sentence which begins with the words "If it is real pragmatically, a pragmatic abrogation does not contravene a thing's absolute reality," we are also to understand that, as in case of objects like pots, the abrogation of the world is itself abrogated, else sensory experiences like the sight of pots will not be possible.

Here the opponent says:

MADHUSŪDANA SARASVATĪ

'In fact the abrogation is false [our second alternative], and its falsehood is not of the illusory order, but of the pragmatic. You cannot now argue that if the abrogation of the world is itself annulled, then the world becomes not inaccordant [in fact, identical] with ultimate reality, and that the abrogation is therefore inconsequential. [Absolute reality will remain inaccordant with the annulment of world-abrogation, just as] the content of a dream—as we all perceive—is inaccordant with its abrogation's own annulment. [The annulment of a dream in which one event, say, an elephant, is abrogated by another, say, a lion, does not make the elephant real.] There is no necessary connection between the annulment of the world-abrogation and the world's equivalence with absolute reality. What is necessary is that the abrogated thing belong to a lower order of being than the abrogator. In our case both abrogated and abrogator belong to the same order of being [as do the abrogation and the reality of the world], so how can the inaccordance between them be denied?

You cannot therefore reason that the annulment of the abrogation confers reality on the abrogated. It does that only in cases where the reality of the abrogated is established *by virtue of* the annulment, and not through the mere *fact* of the annulment being abrogated. In the case of silver, for instance, the knowledge expressed in the sentence "this is not silver" is countered by the knowledge "this is *not* not-silver" which establishes the silver's reality. However, where abrogator and abrogated are both annulled, then the abrogated does not become real. When a pot is being destroyed, its antecedent non-existence [the fact that there was no pot before it was produced] and the subsequent abrogation of that non-existence [by the making of the pot] are both annulled [when the pot is broken; but that annulment does not make the pot whole again]. The annulment of both the world and its abrogation does not therefore confer reality on the world, because both are equally conditioned by the abrogable character of phenomenal perception.'

VYĀSA RĀMĀCĀRYA

To this I say: that we perceive some things *not* to exist in dreams, and we do not find this perception abrogated on waking, so it is not abrogated in fact. [It is not true, then, that waking knowledge is always a *total* abrogation of dream knowledge.] Also mere perception in a dream does not abrogate a thing, for then even the Self [so perceived] could be abrogated.

'In our case,' you remark, 'both abrogated and abrogator belong to the same order of being.' You are wrong. With the abrogation annulled, the very hypothesis that they do belong to the same order becomes open to doubt.

You also deny 'that the annulment of the abrogation confers reality on the abrogated.' Here again you are mistaken. Since what is annulled is a *total* abrogation [an event inalterably final, unlike experiences in dreams], reality is inexorably assigned to the abrogated correlative, as your own example of silver shows. Impossible as it is to annul an abrogation unless there is an abrogable correlative reality, the very fact of the annulment of the abrogation implies that the correlative is real, as a third alternative is not possible. The same is not the case with a thing's antecedent non-existence, so when that is negated the thing does not necessarily become existent. There is a third possibility there—the thing's non-existence subsequent to its destruction. It is therefore logical to conclude that the annulment of a total abrogation inevitably entails its correlative's absolute reality.

When Vyāsa Rāya speaks of the total abrogation, when considered on a pragmatic level, as "inconsequent with the definition" of falsehood, he also means to imply that there is a contradiction—the contradiction in the attempt to establish both the pragmatic level of reality and its abrogation in [absolute reality,] that level's correlative. [In other words, the Brahman is the substrate as well as the negation of pragmatic reality.] To your way of thinking there must be a contradiction in the reasoning that seeks to establish the heat of fire being common to water. [Water is cool by nature, according to Atomist physics. When heated, it becomes the substrate of the abrogation of coolness, heat. Similarly, the Brahman, absolute reality, is the negation as well as the substrate of the pragmatic level of being.] Else that reasoning can be taken to be another description of Nondualism itself. Such is also the sense of Vyāsa Rāya's words.

He then goes on to speak of "the 'Nonduality' Scripture."

To which the opponent answers:

MADHUSŪDANA SARASVATĪ

'The Revelation that teaches us that the world is identical with the Brahman, and also abrogates the world's reality—both through the same falsehood—cannot be lacking in authority [as the world and its abrogation belong to the same level of being and are equally false].'

VYĀSA RĀMĀCĀRYA

Not true. To proclaim both a correlative and its abrogation through the *identical* falsehood is a contradiction. A norm, in fact, ascertains the truth of its own meaning, and the norm by which we apprehend the negation of the world is precisely of this nature. If, at the same time, we hold the negation to be abrogated, the fact that Revelation is proclaiming a falsehood will be impossible to dispute.

—*The River of the Ambrosia of Logic,*
Commentary on Vyāsa Rāya's *Ambrosia of Logic*[87]

23

VANAMĀLI MIŚRA

The Expressibility of God

Adoration to Kṛṣṇa the august!

BĀDARĀYAṆA'S APHORISM

> The Brahman is not inexpressible, as It is an object of knowledge.

I. TOPICAL CITATION FROM SCRIPTURE

'The Brahman is decidedly inexpressible: how then can your view concord with Sacred Doctrine? Revelation declares:

> The joy of the Brahman, from which words and mind, unable to reach it, turn away: the man who knows it never has any fear!'[88]

Rejoinder: "The Brahman is not inexpressible," that is to say, not indescribable by words, "as," from the following words of Revelation,

> Thus, freed from sin, he is led up by the Sacred Paeans to the world of Brahmā [the Golden Embryo]; from that god, who is intense with life, he apprehends ["as . . . an object of knowledge"] the Person who "reposes in the fortress,"[89]

we hear that "It is an object of knowledge." The intent of these words is to proclaim the Brahman of the Upaniṣads.

II. DISSENTIENT VIEW

'Is it not true that the Brahman is inexpressible from your own point of view? Let me show you how. You yourself hold that, as the Brahman is distinct from the joy of the soul, so also is It distinct from the Brahman-idea conceived at the time of worship. The following words of Revelation,

> That which does not think with the mind, but by which, as they say, the mind is thought—know that alone to be the Brahman, and not this thing which is adored,[90]

deny worshipfulness to the Brahman. Also because the exiguousness of the soul's joy is real, through the Brahman-idea being apprehensible at the time of worship. You yourself have denied apprehensibility to the Brahman when explaining the section which comprises the following aphorism of Bādarāyaṇa's:

> Similarly, the Brahman is different from the Brahman-idea, because Revelation denies their identity.[91]

Therefore it is only the distinctive reflection of the Brahman in the hearts of the worshipers that is the object of worship. We can logically suppose that it is only through the worship of that *idea*—as through worship offered to an image—that the Brahman immanent in it is propitiated. And though really inapprehensible, He comes to be immediately apprehended through the power of His inconceivable and limitless energy. As the *Logic of the Brahman* has it:

> They see the Supreme Brahman reflected in their own minds. The Brahman, immanent in the reflection, is the Brahman that gives them their fruit. Its worship is as that offered to an image, and the Supreme is as though apprehended through immediate knowledge.

In this way, if you maintain the Brahman's non-worshipfulness, then you must agree that He will be lacking in expressibility in the declaratory words of Revelation occurring in those portions injunctive of worship. And if you affirm His expressibility, how can you maintain His non-worshipful nature?'

III. ORTHODOX JUDGEMENT

To this I say: the apperception of the mental object through the conceptual latency produced by listening to the scriptures—that is the contemplation on it. Such is the tenet of our school. As Jaya Tīrtha says in his *The Nectar of Logic:* "The apperception by the mind of the mental object produced by the salvific means like listening and seeing—that is contemplation." This contemplation is realized through listening, which grasps the sense of the words as the teacher utters them. Listening that has to do with the Brahman is not possible without expressibility [that is, unless the words on the Brahman listened to have an expressible sense]. The expressibility of the Brahman is thereby proved. As when the act of of worship, focused on an image, is directed to the deity one concentrates on, and not on the image itself, so too the contemplation is directed to the original, and not to the [reflected] object conceived by the mind. Hence the three salvific means—listening, reflection and meditation—do not have a distinct object, and there is no fear that there will be discord with the Sacred Doctrine on the matter of the reflection itself.

The words of Revelation

> Let him worship the Self,[92]

indicate that a man should apperceive the mental object produced by listening to what scripture says about the Self. This mental object produced by listening and apperceived is not the Brahman, but is a mental image conceived in conformity to what has been listened to. "Know that alone to be the Brahman"—such is the import of Revelation. What is reflected in the mind—in other words, the image conceived in the mind, of an Original—that is the Supreme Brahman that the contemplators perceive, and render immediately known through grace. Since what is apprehended in the reflection is the Brahman itself, and it is what gives the contemplators their fruit, it is to that Brahman that worship is offered, as worship to the image. They see it through an immediate vision conferred by grace—such is the meaning of the *Logic of the Brahman*'s words. Contemplation is the stream of similar conceptions with the exclusion of dissimilar ones, and is synonymous with meditation, the third salvific means. In so far as it relates to the reflected image, it is immediate mental knowledge; and, as related to the original, it is a remembrance.

The words of Revelation,

> That which does not think with the mind, but by which, as they say, the mind is thought—know that

> alone to be the Brahman, and not this thing which is adored,[93]

disclose that the mental concept formed at the time of contemplation is vacuous of object. But other words of the same Revelation,

> Only the mind can perceive that there is no diversity in it whatever. He who sees any diversity in it experiences the deadly essence of death,[94]

give us to understand that the mental concept realizes the object at the time when, by God's grace, contemplation matures.

—*Adornment of Madhva's Countenance*[95]

VII. ŚAIVA ORTHODOXY, or *ŚAIVA SIDDHĀNTA*

See Schemes 20 and 21

Śaiva Orthodoxy derives from the old Dualist Pastoralism (*Pāśupata Darśana*), whose literature has been lost. Pastoralism had five categories—Cause, Effect, Union, Ritual Behavior and Cessation of pain. This scheme was taken over and elaborated by the Monist Pastoralism of Lakulīśa (School XXII, Scheme 33). Cause and Effect, previously different, were now both different and identical.

This was undoubtedly because Monist Pastoralism adopted the emanationist and evolutive concepts of Sankhya (Selection 92). Śaiva Orthodoxy reduced the five categories to three —Master (God or Śiva), Beast (the soul) and Bond (Matter), thus accentuating Hindu theology's triad of categories (Brahman, conscious beings, unconscious beings) more than any other Indic system. These it sought to combine with emanationist concepts, sometimes losing its character as a Difference theology in the process. For emanations are both identical with and different from their source, and when the emanationist concept is applied to some of the basic categories, or to all separately, there is the temptation to apply it to all of them unifiedly, as actually happens in the other Śaiva system, Triadism (School XXIII, Scheme 34). Śaiva Orthodoxy thus seems to have prepared the way for the latter, a system wholly of Difference-in-Identity.

Of the three categories Beast has no emanations. Śaiva Orthodoxy postulates three levels of emanation, one higher in Master, and two lower in Bond. The lowest level comprises the evolutes of the Classical Sankhya, known as the Five Impure Principles. Above them, anterior in time, are the other evolutes, like necessity and time, left out of Īśvara Kṛṣṇa's synthesis, but absorbed into Tantric systems like the Pāñcarātra (Scheme 28), and the Śaiva Tantras—which Śaiva Orthodoxy and Triadism systematize. These are the Five Mixed Principles. Above these are the intemporal Five Pure Principles, one of them Śiva Himself, and the remaining four, single or combined expressions of Śiva's three basic Energies of Will, Knowledge and Action.

Emanationism, as I said, makes it difficult for Śaiva theology to preserve its character of Difference. Śrī Kumāra, represented in Selection 25, believes that the three categories are substantially one, differentiated only by incidental limiters—a doctrine that the orthodox Aghora Śiva condemns. One assumes the categories to be quite distinct, but Śaiva Orthodox texts give the impression that the two conscious categories, God and the soul, are identical and different among themselves; and that taken together they are wholly different from the third, the unconscious. The latter point is specially emphasized by Aghora Śiva in his denial of material causality to God (Selection 26), a doctrine basic to most Vedantic and Tantric schools. Śaiva Orthodoxy is thus a theology of Difference with Monist leanings—which is why I have placed it immediately before the theologies of Identity.

The system seems to have become articulate around the eighth century A.D., and was later divided into two schools, superseding the other. The earlier one used Sanskrit, and proclaimed liberation through knowledge, and may be called Gnostic Śaiva Orthodoxy. The later one chiefly used Tamil, and taught liberation through devotion. It survives to our day.

The tenets of Gnostic Śaiva Orthodoxy seem to have been assembled a little before those of Triadism were, chiefly through the efforts of Sadyojyoti (eighth century?). However, Triadism was systematized first—by Somānanda in the ninth century. Śaiva Orthodoxy's own systematizer appears to have been none other than that most versatile of ancient Hindus, themselves one of the most versatile of races, Bhoja Deva (c. 1018–60), yogi, theologian, architect, aesthetic philosopher, physician, king, poet, legendary patron of poets and other things besides (Selection 24). His concepts were elaborated by several theologians, chief among them the Monist Śrī Kumāra and the Dualist Aghora Śiva (fl. 1130–58). The latter seems to have been the last great theologian of the Gnostic school, and to have prepared the way for its merging into the Devotional.

In the meantime Triadism had produced a parallel, Monist, theology, excelling that of Śaiva Orthodoxy in mystical profundity and architectural magnificence, for it was the school of the Sun King of Hindu theology, Abhinava Gupta. Chief of Triadism's representatives in the Tamil country was the twelfth-century theologian Maheśvarānanda (Selection 104), the contemporary of Aghora Śiva. In the following century arose the Tamilian or Devotional Śaiva Orthodoxy, with Meykanta Tevar (fl. 1221). It endeavored to assimilate the concepts of Triadism with Gnostic Śaiva Orthodoxy (a process already apparent in Aghora Śiva) to my mind somewhat redundantly and unimaginatively (Scheme 21). Some of its theologians also wrote in Sanskrit, like Umāpati Śivācārya (fourteenth century) and Śivāgrayogi (eighteenth century).

24
BHOJA DEVA

The Sum of Śaiva Orthodox Theology

OPENING PAEANS

1. Victorious is Śiva, mass of consciousness, the One, the omnipresent, the eternal, the ever dawning, the Lord, the tranquil, the one cause of the universe, the favorer of all!

2. Victorious is Śiva's glory, knowledge and action by nature. It neither rises nor sets, is never extinguished, and it gives us release!

3. With all my soul do I adore Her, from Whom Śiva receives the power to make the world of the living experience life and to attain release. She is the unique, consciousness in essence, the Primordial Goddess!

4. To be of service to mankind—our mind brimful with the sentiment of compassion—we have in concise fashion produced this work, the *Light on the Principles*.

I. THE TRIAD: MASTER, BEAST, BOND

5. In the Śaiva scriptures the principal triad is Master, Beast and Bond—in that order. Master is known as Śiva, Beasts as the infinitesimal conscious beings, and Bond as the Five Things [Pollution, Karma, the Mirific Power, the world produced by that Power, and the Obscuring Power.]

6. *Free and liberated beings.* Liberated souls are them-

selves Śivas, but attain freedom through His favor. We must know that He Himself is the one eternally free being, His body the Five Mystic Incantations [the four Vedas, and their quintessence, the mystic monosyllable OM].

7. *God's fivefold activity*. Creation, preservation, destruction, obscuration and the work of grace—such is the fivefold activity attributed to the ever dawning God.

8. *Beasts*. Beasts, we must know, are of three kinds—Intelligence-Deconditioned, Dissolution-Deconditioned and Conditioned. Of these, the first are conjoined with Pollution, the second with Pollution and Karma.

9. The [third, the] Conditioned are conjoined with Pollution, the Mirific Power and Karma. The Intelligence-Deconditioned are of two sorts—one with contamination liquidated, and the other with contamination unliquidated.

10. Favoring those of the first sort, Śiva endows eight with the lordship of wisdom [making them the Wisdom Lords]. He makes the others Incantations, and they are said to be seventy million.

11. Among the Dissolution-Deconditioned are those whose Pollution and Karma have matured; they enter liberation. [There are] others [whose Pollution and Karma have not matured, and are] furnished with eight-constituent bodies [or Subtle Bodies]; they enter all wombs through Karma's impulsion.

12. Favoring some [the latter], Śiva confers the lordship of the Spheres on them [making them the Sphere Lords]. Their eight-constituent bodies comprise the [threefold] Inner Faculty [Instinct, Egoism and Mind] and the [fivefold] faculties of perception and action.

13. The rest [of the Beasts] are the Conditioned, linked as they are with Principles like Aptitude at the dawn of creation. He Himself makes a hundred and eighteen of them the Incantation Lords.

14. Eight of these are called the Circle Lords. Equal in number are gods like Krodha. There are also Vīreśa, Śrī Kaṇṭha and the hundred Rudras—one hundred and eighteen in all.

15. Through fulminating a Pollution-dissolvent energy, He links the ones whose Pollution has matured to the Highest Principle. This He does through Initiation, embodying Himself in a teacher's form.

16. All the remaining bound souls He applies to the experi-

ence of the world, in accord with their karma. This is why they are called Beasts.

17. *Bonds.* The soul's Bonds are of four kinds—the first two marked by Pollution and Karma, and the other two originating from Śiva's Mirific and Obscuring Powers.

18. One, but manifold in potency, is Pollution in souls, obscuring, as we must know, their knowledge and action as the husk, the rice, and rust, copper.

19. Karma is said to be eternal; it is virtue, vice and manifoldness in essence. The Mirific Power is a substance; it is the root of the universe and is eternal.

20. The Infinite's soul-obscuring power, promoting as it does bondage, is denoted by the word Bond. This is how Bonds are of four kinds.

II. THE PURE PRINCIPLES

1. *The Five Pure Principles.* There are Five Pure Principles. The first of them is remembered as the Śiva Principle. [The others are] the Energy Principle and the Ever Beneficent Principle, the Supreme Lord Principle and the [Pure] Knowledge Principle.

2. *The Five Mixed Principles.* To enable the soul to know and act a pentad of principles emanates from the Mirific Power—Time, Necessity, Aptitude, Knowledge and Attachment.

3. *The three Impure Principles and their twenty evolutes.* From the Mirific Power also emerges the Unevolved [or Matter], which is the Principle of the three Attributes; and after it Instinct and Egoism, the Mind, the [ten] faculties of perception and action, and the [ten] Elements, subtle and gross.

4. For the soul's experience twenty principles [just mentioned] originate from Matter, and three others besides. Between these and Matter's Attributes there is really no absolute difference.

5. *Śiva.* Pervasive, unique, eternal, the cause of all the Principles, knowledge and action in essence—this is the Śiva Principle that the masters celebrate.

6. Subsisting in it all the Energies—as Will [Knowledge and Action]—accomplish their activities. That is why Śiva is known as the all-favoring.

7. *Energy*. The first expansive movement of Śiva eager to create—so as to be gracious to the conscious and unconscious beings—is called the Energy Principle, and is indivisibly inherent in Him.

8. *The Ever Beneficent*. The emergence of the Energies of Knowledge and Action, with neither being excessive or deficient, is what the wise call the Ever Beneficent Principle.

9. *The Supreme Lord*. When the Energy of Knowledge is in abeyance and that of Action is preponderant, it is called the Supreme Lord Principle, and is the cause whereby all ends are ever accomplished.

10. [*Pure*] *Knowledge*. When the Energy of Action is in abeyance and that of Knowledge is preponderant, it is called the Knowledge Principle. It illuminates, as knowledge is its essence.

11. *The Pure Principles, the abodes of the Conditioned Souls*. The Conditioned Souls of Sound and Nucleus are said to abide always in the Ever Beneficent Principle, the Wisdom Lords in the Supreme Lord Principle, and the Incantations and Knowledges in the Knowledge Principle.

12. *Timelessness of the Pure Principles*. These five Principles have no sequence, since they are untouched by time. The sequence postulated in this teaching is by sole reason of [Energy's varied] function.

13. *Unity of the Pure Principles*. This Principle is in reality one, known as Śiva, though arrayed with a myriad wondrous energies. It is through their different functions that we conceive its differences.

14. *Reason for the pluralization of the Principles*. To favor the conscious and unconscious, the Lord, in assuming those forms, does a kindness to intelligent beings, whose powers are inhibited by the Pollution without beginning.

15. Śiva, the all-favoring, gives experience and liberation to the infinitesimal conscious beings, and to the unconscious the power to accomplish their activities.

16. That liberation, equality with Śiva, is certainly a favor to the conscious being—which cannot, in default of experience, reach fulfillment, since Karma has no beginning.

17. Hence to enable this being to get this experience the omnipresent Lord creates the body, the faculties and the worlds. For there is no effect without an agent, nor yet without a material cause and instrument.

III. THE MIXED PRINCIPLES

1. *Instrument and material cause.* Here His instrument are the Energies. His material cause is postulated to be the subtle Mirific Power. It is said to be one, eternal, pervasive, beginningless, everlasting and beneficent.

2. *The Mirific Power.* The Mirific Power is common to all souls, and is also the cause of all the worlds. Inwrought in the activities of all persons, it breeds infatuation by its very nature.

3. Having past actions in view, Śiva, through His Energies, agitates the Mirific Power and provides each soul with a body and with faculties to make it capable of experience.

4. *Time.* At the very outset the Mirific Power, charged with manifold energies, produces the Time Principle [the "Impeller"], constituted of future, present and past. It impels the world, and is hence called the "Impeller."

5. *Necessity.* Necessity is a constraining force, which next emerges from the Mirific Power. As it necessarily orders everything, it is called Necessity.

6. *Aptitude.* After that, Aptitude originates from the Mirific Power. Concentrating the Pollution in men in one place it elicits the power to action, which is why it is called Aptitude.

7. *Connection of these three Principles.* With Time and with Necessity becoming ever subservient to it, Aptitude exercises its function from its first expansion up to [the last Principle] the earth.

8. *[Impure] Knowledge.* To enable the soul, whose active powers have been roused, to perceive objects, this same Aptitude brings to light the Knowledge Principle, luminous in its essence.

9. Then Aptitude, by its own action, breaking through the obstruction of the Energy of [Impure] Knowledge, reveals the assemblage of objects. It is here the highest instrument possessed by the Self.

10. When Instinct, endowed with pleasure and such like states, becomes capable of being experienced, then [Impure] Knowledge becomes its instrument. In the perception of objects, however, the instrument is Instinct.

11. *Attachment.* Attachment is essentially a clinging, and indeed without a sense of distinction between objects. It is the

general cause of activity in the soul, and distinct from the attributes of Instinct.

12. *The Soul.* When, conditioned by these Principles, Beast is made capable of experience and of the state of being called a soul, it then becomes qualified for listing among the Principles.

IV. THE IMPURE PRINCIPLES

1. *The Unevolved.* From the Mirific Power emerges the Unevolved, and expressly for making experience possible for the soul. This Unevolved is undefined, as its Attributes have as yet been unrealized.

2. *The Three Attributes.* From the Unevolved emanates the Principle of the Attributes, comprising perceptibility, activity and constraint—also respectively known as Brightness, Passion, Darkness, and as joy, pain and delusion.

3. *Instinct.* From the triad of Attributes proceeds Instinct, apt by nature to apprehend objects. Instinct is also triple in its Attributes, in accordance with actions from previous births.

4. *Egoism.* Egoism may be conceived as triple—formed of vitality, impetuosity and pride. Through the partitioning of its being do objects come to be experienced [by the Self, which is unhearing, unseeing, unspeaking and inactive of itself].

5. *Three Forms of Egoism.* Egoism emerges in still another triple form—bright, passionate and dark—and is expressed through the names of Modifying, Fiery and Elemental.

6. From the Fiery springs Mind, from the Modified the faculties, from the Elemental the Subtle Elements. This is the order of their emergence from Egoism.

7. *The Faculties of knowledge and action and their objects.* Mind is in essence desire, and its activity is thought. The faculties of knowledge are the ear, the skin, the eye, the tongue and the nose.

8. Their percepts are sound, touch, color, taste and smell. These in order, are their objects, five of the five.

9. The perception of phenomena like sound is said to be their function. The faculties of action are the voice, the hands, feet, anus and genitals.

10. Speaking, holding, walking, excretion and delight are their actions. The Inner Faculty is threefold—Instinct, Egoism and Mind.

11. The Outer Faculty, divided as it is into the faculties of knowledge and action, is again tenfold.

The Elements, Gross and Subtle. The Five Gross Elements, connected with the Subtle, are ether, wind, fire, water and earth.

12. The Subtle Elements, sound and so on, are known to be five. From them come the Five Gross Elements, through one Attribute being added to another.

13. Giving space, blowing, cooking, gathering and bearing—these in order are described as the activities of the Gross Elements, among which ether is one.

V. INTERRELATIONSHIP OF THE PRINCIPLES

1. The effect produced through instruments operating on a support is tenfold [the five Gross and the five Subtle Elements]. Powerless otherwise, the instruments [then] operate through the effects as their support.

2. The relationship among the first five Principles is through their conscious essence. As for the remaining seven, starting with the Mirific Power, the Śaiva scripture says that the relationship is of two kinds:

3. That between the Principles, starting with the Unevolved, which is through the three Attributes, since their essence is joyful, sorrowful or delusive. This particular characteristic persists up to the last ten Principles [the Elements, Gross and Subtle].

4. As for the group of Principles beginning with sound, we must understand them to have the same relationship, as they share the same Attributes. In some [Principles, as from Time down to the earth], there is a particular relation as exists between a body and its embodier [or between effect and cause].

5. The disposition of the Principles has thus been reported in their order of creation. Through reversive transmutation they dissolve again into the Mirific Power.

6. The Way [of the Pure Principles] that transcends the Mirific Power dissolves into pure Energy [the second Principle]. And She Herself abides indivisibly in Śiva [the first of the Principles], the All-Soul.

7. The Mirific Power [Bond], the Soul [Beast] and Śiva [Master]—this triad survives the dissolution of the Great Principles. It then rekindles as before in creation.

8. Moved by grace, the Lord precipitates the dissolution of the Great Principles for the repose of all things whom transmigration has exhausted.

VI. LIBERATION

1. Prompted by compassion for Beasts, the Supreme Master, avid to promote their karma's maturing, initiates creation and brings that karma to maturity.
2. Sole repository of mercy, the ever beneficent Śiva brings to maturity the karma of Beasts, by means of experience, imparts Initiation to them and liberates them all through His power.
3. Whatever provides all beings with experience and persists up to dissolution is what is termed a Principle [or Truth]. Things like bodies and pots are therefore not Principles.
4. *Epilogue.* He who described the origin [of each of the Principles], their fulfilling Cause and the distinction between them,
5. He who took such pains to tell all the truth about the Truths [or Principles]—it was he who organized this work on the *Light on the Principles.*

—*Light on the Principles*[96]

25

ŚRĪ KUMĀRA

The Masculine–Feminine Polarity of the Universe

BHOJA

With all my soul do I adore Her, from Whom Śiva receives the power to make the world of the living experience life and to attain release. She is the unique, consciousness in essence, the Primordial Goddess!

ŚRĪ KUMĀRA

As the omnipresent, the Isolated, the inactive and the indifferent Being, Śiva is unable to provide experience and liberation for the assemblage of Beasts; so only as endowed with Energy is He able to provide them. Hence the graciousness [that motivates this] is only possible to God charged with Energy. When Bhoja uses the term "the unique" he means that the Goddess has no second.

'But it has been shown that *Śiva* is the One without a second, in the words "only Śiva is all." How then can talk of non-secondness be plausible here?'

I reply that since all reality is essentially the God and the Goddess, the language of non-secondness is applicable to both. To explain. Liberation, defined as subsistence in the Isolated self, is in essence conscious and blissful; these are the characteristics through which we understand its God-Goddess nature. For if liberation were to be voided of its essential happiness, the aim of life would be null, since happiness alone is life's primary goal. You cannot reason that the absence of sorrow is also life's aim, and hence that even if the joyfulness of our ultimate goal were to be naught, the aim of life would still be possible through the elimination of contact with sorrow. One cannot, I say, reason thus because human beings desire the absence of sorrow only because it goes along with happiness; of itself it can never be life's primary aim. Hence, as only happiness can be such an aim, we must seek the joyfulness of our ultimate goal. And unless we can experience that joy it cannot become life's aim; we must therefore seek to experience it too. Liberation is thus joy and consciousness in essence, and so possesses the God-Goddess nature. The Goddess, then, is the consciousness of supreme joy, while the God is the joy of consciousness. This is what one gathers from the words of the puranas and the Āgamas, such as:

> She is the knowledge, He the knower.

And, as the *Rituals on the Incantations of the Goddess* says:

> The Primordial Master is the sage, the divine verse is the Gāyatrī. We are taught here that the Goddess is the consciousness of supreme joy.

Or in the words of the *Rituals on the Mistress of the Worlds:*

> The teachers say that the deity is consciousness described as understanding in its essence.

We gather the same idea from the following words of Revelation:

> The Brahman is knowledge and joy,[97]

and from others as well. Also from an apposite verse such as follows:

> I adore the Mirific Power of the universe, the painted wall formed of the Prodigious and the other evolutes, its visual appearance charged with Passion [or composed of colored space], and outlined with forms of the soul's eternal happiness.

You cannot object that consciousness and joy, being mutually distinct, are two attributes of the Self, because you will conflict with Revelation:

> Śiva is by nature consciousness and joy.

Hence if they were to be distinct, they could never be His attributes.

'But if consciousness and joy are not different, on one side [that of joy] no joyous experience will be possible [there being none in the state of transmigration; and on the other] that of self-luminance, release and transmigration will be indistinguishable [as self-luminance pervades both states].'

You are wrong. There is no contradiction in postulating that in the state of transmigration the Self, through false imagining, is unable to experience joy, like the self-luminous crystal placed next to the rose. [Its luminosity is occluded through reflecting the rose's color. Likewise, while remaining innately luminous, the Self is tinged with the reflection of the world's suffering.] Joy, then, is the Brahman's essence, disclosed in liberation, as Revelation assures us.

'Well, let us say that the God-Goddess nature is found in the Pure Principles. But how can it ever belong to the Causal Principle, variegated as it is by the Mirific Power?'

I reply that it is through being invested with efficient [masculine] and material [feminine] causality. As the *Liṅga Purāṇa* says:

> The eight-formed Śiva, the spouse, has the divine Matter for wife, and for children the Prodigious and the other evolutes.

In the same way the Effectual Principle also has the Goddess nature reflected in its dual form of conscious-unconscious. In the fourteen types of beings too their dual essence as body-embodied manifests the God-Goddess nature as well.

'But how can these beings possess the God-Goddess nature?'

Because of Their illimitable power, I say. Revelation tells us in the *Bṛhadāraṇyaka Upaniṣad:*

> He finds no joy in being alone. He yearns for a partner. He then grows to a certain size, and falls apart into male and female portions. From this "falling apart" is husband and wife. She became a cow, he a bull. From them came cattle. She became a mare and he a horse. From them came horses.[98]

Words such as these declare that the actuality of the two causes of the universe, the God and the Goddess, is in the shape of all living things. The whole universe, then, evinces the illimitability of Their power. As Manu says:

> Dividing his body into two, he became a man in one part and a woman in the other. From them he created the first Male Power.[99]

Or, as in the *Liṅga Purāṇa,* which certifies this doctrine:

> All that is masculine is the God, and all that is feminine is the Supreme Lady.

As the Supreme Lord and the Supreme Lady have nothing to divide Them, nondual language can be applied to both. Consequently there is but one Śiva Principle, differentiated as masculine, feminine and neuter.

—*The Lamp of Meaning*[100]

26

AGHORA ŚIVA

God Not the World's Material Cause

BHOJA

> Pervasive, unique, eternal, the cause of all the Principles, knowledge and action in essence—this is the Śiva Principle that the masters celebrate.

AGHORA ŚIVA

The Śiva Principle, earlier established as Nuclear in essence, in virtue of its being the material cause of the Pure Way—that same Principle is [in Bhoja's words] "pervasive." Which means to say that it pervades the totality of the world, by nature both pure and impure, through its metamorphic forms—comprising its States like Cessation, Stability, Knowledge, Tranquillity and the Elevated-Above-Tranquillity. As they say:

> In the States the Principles abide, and in the Principles the Lord who roams the universe.

And so on. Furthermore, that Principle is "unique," because it is the supreme cause. Since, as has been said, manifoldness is inconscient, manifoldness [in Śiva] would entail his being an effect, like a pot. Consequently, also, he is "eternal," for were he not, there would be no supreme causality, and he himself would need another material cause [and that would need another]—which would constitute an infinite regress. He is therefore himself the material "cause of all the Principles," that is, of the pure Principles, not of the impure ones. The latter, as I said, arise from the [impure] Mirific Power. As he himself is pure, he is not the proper substance for impure causality.

Besides, the "knowledge and action," existent in his *self*, he causes to come into *being* in the souls, which is also why he is called "knowledge and action in *essence*" [or *self-being*]. What Bhoja means to say is that—through propitiation of one or other Sphere Lord, or by Initiation—Śiva reveals knowledge and action to those who have attained the sphere of the Pure Way, his own effect. As the noble *Elephant Tantra* says:

> The Supreme Principle is beyond tranquillity, indestructible and undecaying in essence. The Beasts, their strength made to bloom by his power, arrive at the state of selfhood.

Hence also his power to illumine the mind.

'[There seems to be a contradiction here, as knowledge and essence do not belong to Śiva alone.] It has been said, has it not, that the Mirific Power also reveals knowledge and action, by means of such Principles as Aptitude?'

It has indeed. But the knowledge that derives from the Mirific Power has only *limited* objects, and is the cause of the self being experienced in the not-self, and is hence delusive. On the other hand, this Śiva-knowledge reveals *all* objects, and has illuminative power, as it makes one aware of the pure reality that comprehends Śiva and the other pure Principles, by means of the teaching founded on the sacred science. There is thus no contradiction.

Or else [we may interpret Bhoja's words "knowledge and action in essence" differently, to me in that] he *communicates* or manifests his *own* wealth known as knowledge and action to the souls, and so is called "knowledge and action in *essence*" [or *own-communication*]. Further, Bhoja's words ["knowledge and action in essence" form a Sanskrit compound where the word for "action," ending in an *a*, is joined to the word for "essence." This *a* can also be taken as a prefix to "essence," having the sense of *un-* or *non-*, and so the compound] can also mean that "knowledge and action are *not* his essence." But then we must interpret "not" as referring to an inconscient essentiality, and not to a cognitive one. Material causality is inconscient, like clay, and hence a cognitive essentiality can never be a material cause. It has therefore been said in the *Supreme Tantra:*

> Their efficient cause is the Supreme Lord, their material cause the august Nucleus [also known as the Great Mirific Power].

It has also been said elsewhere:

> She [the Mirific Power] is the pure Serpentine Energy of Śiva, inconscient by essence.

It is this "Śiva Principle," the material cause [of the pure Principles], known as the *Great* Mirific Power [as opposed to the lesser Mirific Power, material cause of the impure Principles], "that the masters celebrate."

The words of Bhoja [quoted in the beginning] must not be understood to apply to the Supreme Śiva or to His Energy, because, as the reference is to the Principles that comprise the emanations from Śiva down to the earth, the words cannot allude to anything that transcends these Principles [as do the Supreme Śiva and His Energy]. Were we to postulate Them as the material cause of the Pure Way in the form of the Śiva Principle, Their [consequent] liability to transformation would entail their being inconscient, which would be fallacious.

It is also not logical to postulate a *transmogrification* [or a merely illusory transformation of this transcendence], because the world, established as existent by all norms, is not unreal, but would be if it were [consciousness] transmogrified. Hence our explanation of Bhoja's words is the right one, as it has been revealed that the Nucleus-Soul's Serpentine Energy, marked as a Principle, does not inhere in the consciousness, and possesses a capacity to be assumed [by Śiva Himself]. It has therefore been said that

> here the energy is not the material cause, because it is conscious in essence, like Śiva. The talk, referred to above, of the transformation of the consciousness, is not proper. Transmogrification [on the other hand] is spoken of with regard to consciousness, but in that case the effect is null. How indeed can the world, established by all norms, be a transmogrification of the consciousness? The Mirific Power is also not the material cause here because it is delusive by its own power. It is the essentially unconscious and pure Serpentine Energy of Śiva; it does not exist in Śiva, the cause, through identity. For this reason it is the material cause [in relation to Śiva], just as clay is to the potter.

Even in Sonic Absolutism the Self, through the sequence of Sound and the other evolutes, cannot exist multiply. As Rājānaka Rāmakaṇṭha says in his *Explicative Verses on Sound:*

> The Self is here said to be untransformable; so is its energy. They are thus not suited to multiple existence. Or else [we may say that] transformation is existent only outside the consciousness.

And so on. Hence even if Sound is conceived [in the manner of the Sonic Absolutists] to be the material cause, the existence of the Great Mirific Power [or Nucleus] is proved. I have shown this at great length in my *Lamp* on Nārāyaṇa Kaṇṭha's *Gloss on the Lion Tantra,* where it may be ascertained.

Gloss on Bhoja's "Light on the Principles"[101]

Theologies of Identity or Non-Difference

PRELIMINARY NOTE

See Schemes 22 and 23

The theology of Identity seems to be archetypally Buddhist, since there is no Monist pronouncement in the Vedic tradition that cannot be interpreted in a Difference-in-Identity sense—and was indeed so interpreted before the time of Gauḍa Pāda (c. 640–90), the founder of the Nondualist schools (Selections 27–29). The main, perhaps the only, problem that Nondualism has to confront is that of Difference, so obviously given in experience, and which has, so to speak, to be dialectically annihilated, and to be dissolved in the perceiver's mind. This is attempted with great skill by that extraordinary philosophical and poetic genius Śrí Harṣa (second half of the thirteenth century), author of one of the most sophisticated of the Sanskrit epics, and the noble successor of the Buddhist dialecticians (Selection 33, where he attempts to answer Udayana's arguments for Difference given in Selection 14).

The theology of Identity has more difficulty in justifying its own assumptions than in destroying those of other systems, which is why it seems to prefer mysticism and epistemology to metaphysics. It is dominated by its grand insight of the ultimacy of the Self (Selection 34). To make the realization of this insight possible, it employs, as I just said, a complex dialectic to dispel all notion of multiplicity—the product, in its belief, of Illusion (Selections 28 and 31), and obstructive of the vision of the Self. But it is willing, on occasion, to abandon logic and to assert that the matter is ultimately inexplicable—except through the mystical experience we can ultimately gain if we unquestioningly accept Nondualism's tenets and follow its injunctions.

To resolve the problem of Difference, Nondualism makes use of Buddhist epistemological distinctions, as between the *two levels of truth,* the absolute and the relative, proposed by the Vacuists (*Mādhyamikas*); or between the *three levels,* absolute, pragmatic and illusory, advanced by the Idealist (*Vijñānavādins*). Difference is said to belong to the lower level or levels, and Identity to the higher.

An then came Gauḍa Pāda, who boldly professed to see this doctrine in one of the Hindu texts of Revelation, the *Māṇḍukya Upaniṣad.* His follower Śaṅkara (first half of the eighth century) made the equally bold attempt at professing to elicit the same doctrine from that comprehensive and concise synthesis of Hindu theology (Scheme 9), the *Aphorisms on the Brahman* by Bādarāyaṇa, whom Madhva calls the "teacher of teachers." Up to that moment (for about thirteen centuries) the *Aphorisms* seem, without exception, to have been interpreted in a Difference-in-Identity sense. This eccentric Nondualist interpretation of the *Aphorisms* was challenging, because it gave the other schools of theology an important basis of agreement—their rejection of the theology of Identity and of its Illusionism. It also encouraged new interpretations of the *Aphorisms,* thus leading to a blossoming of Vedantic systems (Scheme 6). One of the many prominent theologians of the Hindu revival, Śaṅkara seems to have had a keen sense of what constitutes that religion's basic unity (Selection 30).

The new doctrine still lacked a metaphysics—which seems to have been supplied it by the great Maṇḍana Miśra (fl. 690), by taking the Spirit-Matter polarity of the Sankhya, reducing Spirit to a unique being, the Brahman; and of transforming the very real Sankhya Matter into a ghost, so to speak, for it was affirmed to be neither being nor non-being. This seems to have been a wholly novel archetype, even in Indic thought. I have been unsuccessful in finding a copy of Maṇḍana Miśra's *The Proof of the Brahman* except in translation,[1] but I have included instead a penetrating analysis of the concept of the Inexplicable by Madhusūdana Sarasvatī (1540–1647), perhaps Nondualism's last great theologian. Madhusūdana is guarding the doctrine from the remorseless scrutiny of the Dualist Vedantin Vyāsa Rāya (see School VI) and is also developing its ideas to their maximum logical consistency (Selection 35).

It is difficult to decide whether Nondualism is one or many schools. On the one hand, its followers profess adherence to Śaṅkara's commentary on Bādarāyaṇa's *Aphorisms;* on the other, they disagree on most issues. What they do agree on is that the basic categories of their theology are the Self and the non-Self; that the latter is superposed on the former (Selection 31), giving rise to an illusory multiplicity, caused, as it seems, by the transformation of the Self. But this transformation—contrary to what the non-idealist Difference-in-Identity theologians unanimously affirm—is not real in the opinion of most Nondualists, but only illusory; hence what we may with more propriety call a *transmogrification* (Selection 32). In fact, causality itself is not more than an appearance (Selection 29).

But they disagree, among other things, in explaining how this Ignorance functions, and whether it gives rise to one soul or to many. Bondage they all affirm, is the effect of Ignorance. But whose is this Ignorance? Gauḍa Pāda believes that it is that of the Brahman himself (Selection 28)—a Difference-in-Identity solution, positing as it does the principle of Difference *within* the principle of Identity (See Selection 100). Indeed, one way of looking at Nondualism is to consider it an eccentric Difference-in-Identity school. The concept of the Absolute's self-obscuration was developed in Triadism (School XXIII, Schemes 34 and 35), especially by Abhinava Gupta, with a consummate architectonic sense unapproached by any Nondualist; but then structure does not seem to be one of Nondualism's strong points.

Disagreeing with Gauḍa Pāda, Maṇḍana Miśra argued that the Brahman, who is knowledge in essence, cannot be affected by Ignorance. Knowledge and Ignorance are contradictories, as the former is the apprehension and the latter the non-apprehension of reality. Besides, everything inherent in the Brahman is eternal, so if Ignorance were to affect Him, He would be eternally knowing and ignorant at once. So Ignorance must be external to the Brahman, wholly other than Himself.

Wholly other, yes, but not another thing. For if Ignorance were existent, Nondualism would collapse, as there would be two realities; if it were non-existent, it would be unable to make anybody ignorant. Hence it would have to be both existent and non-existent; it would, in other words, be the Inexplicable, or Illusion. Thus was evolved what seems to be the methodological principle of Nondualism, which, stated simply, is: explain logically what you can, and attribute the rest to Illusion (see Selection 32). The question "Whose is the Ignorance?" was not answered to the satisfaction of all the Nondualist schools. Some still said it was the Brahman's, and had to face the above difficulties; others that it was the soul's, which seemed to the others to imply cyclical dependence.

VIII–XIII. THE SIX NONDUALIST or *ADVAITA* SCHOOLS

Whomever it affected, Ignorance did give rise to multiplicity and Difference. But how is this multiplicity to be explained? There were differences here too—so that we have, in all, at least six schools of Nondualism.

1. *Undivided Nondualism,* represented by Gauḍa Pāda and Śaṇkara. This school assimilates the concept of the multiple levels of truth, and suggests the solution to the problem of multiplicity through metaphors, most of them found in Gauḍa Pāda.

2. *Limitationism,* envolved through the ether-and-pot metaphor. The pot only appears to limit the limitless ether (or space), and when it is destroyed even the appearance of limitation vanishes. The apparent limitation depends on the capacity of the pots; some are larger than others and seem to contain more ether. This concept had the strangest of avatars, for it reappears in the Thomism of the early twentieth century, a system that some of its adherents believed was the only orthodox Catholic theology possible. This is the Thomism of the 24 Theses, of which Thesis 2 is:

> Perfection that it is, actuality is not limited except by potentiality—which is the capacity for perfection. Hence, in so far as actuality is pure, it exists only as unlimited and unique; wherever it is finite and multiple, it enters into real composition with potentiality.[2]

This principle is proclaimed to be the very foundation of Thomist metaphysics, and is believed to have been formulated by Aquinas himself, though not in those very words. Of the two systems, the Hindu is probably the more consequential, for it may be asked whether the actuality is intrinsically *capable* of limitation or not. If it is, it is already limited, because it lacks the not inconsiderable perfection of illimitability, found only in God. If it is not, then its limitation can be no more than apparent, and we may find the ether-and-pot metaphor apposite. It is interesting to note that the Thomist potentiality is also neither being (in the sense of actuality) nor non-being (in the sense of total nonentity). If this is Thomism then Maṇḍana Miśra, who seems to have proposed Limitationism, is the first Thomist.

3. *Reflectionism,* expressed through the face-in-the-mirror and moon-in-water metaphor, on the assumption that the reflected image or images are not distinct from the object they reflect, though appearing to be. The Brahman, reflected in Illusion, thus appears multiple. This school, founded by Padma Pāda (mid-eighth century) and represented, among others, by his illustrious disciple Prakāśātman (fl. 975, Selection 32), seems to be the major Nondualist school.

4. *Apparitionalism,* the school of Sureśvara (c. 720–70), founded on the belief that Ignorance, through its diversifying power, elicits diverse appearances or "apparitions" from the substrate reality of the Brahman.

5. *Idealist Nondualism,* proposed by Prakāśānanda (beginning of sixteenth century, Selection 34), seems to revert to Gauḍa Pāda's theory, and indeed to Buddhist Idealism, according to which the universe is only consciousness and perception. From having become a theology of Identity, Nondualism reverts to being once again a theology of Difference-in-Identity.

6. *Syncretic Nondualism,* of which the most prominent representative is Madhusūdana Sarasvatī. Nondualism was unable to resolve its inner conflicts to the satisfaction of all or most of its adherents, but it was unified by the concerted opposition against it by all the other schools of Hindu theology, and also by the dialectical basis it had inherited from Buddhist Vacuism. In its last phase Nondualism is very tolerant of its own diversity. Madhusūdana, with a logic reminding one of Nāgārjuna's, argues with much skill that the opponent's arguments do not touch any of the Nondualist theories, however inaccordant among themselves. For these theories serve to dispel dualism—which is all that matters. Madhusūdana himself effected a minor revolution within the system, which had always believed in the ultimacy of knowledge as a salvific means. But in Madhusūdana's time theology was preeminently devotional, absorbed in Kṛṣṇa and his joys; as was Madhusūdana, who came very close to transforming the venerable gnostic system into a theology of devotion. All other theologies believing in personal deities were committed to Difference-in-Identity—except the theology of Gaṇapati, or

the Gāṇapatya system, centered on the elephant-headed son of Śiva, who destroys all obstacles. This system was given a theology of Identity by Nīlakaṇṭha in the seventeenth century.[3]

27

GAUḌA PĀDA

The Proclamation of Nondualism

1. To know reality differently from what it is, is to dream; not to know it at all is to be asleep. When the error of both conditions is dispelled, the undifferenced state is realized.

2. When the soul put to sleep by the beginningless Illusion awakens, it becomes aware of nonduality—the unborn, the unsleeping and the undreaming.

3. If the world were really to exist, it would undoubtedly disappear. For the duality we perceive is mere illusion, and nonduality is the one supreme truth.

4. If anyone were to imagine a dualizing knowledge [as of a distinct teacher, student and scripture], it would be dispelled. Such a knowledge only serves to teach the truth. Once the truth is known the duality disappears.

—Explicative Verses on the "Māṇḍukya Upaniṣad"[4]

28

GAUḌA PĀDA

The Epistemology of Illusion

I. IDENTITY OF DREAM AND WAKING STATES

1. All objects in a dream are truthless, say the wise, by reason of their being concealed and confined within the body.

2. The time that dreams last is not long, so the dreamer

does not actually go to the locale of his dreams. And when every dreamer awakes, he does not find himself in that locale.

3. Revelation tells us that the chariots seen in dreams are unreal. Hence the wise declare this truthlessness, confirmed by logic, to be proved, and indeed self-illuminated [or self-evident].

[*Revelation says:* And when he sleeps soundly, he takes material from the whole world with himself, himself takes it apart, himself puts it together. He sleeps soundly in his own radiance, in his own light. The man is then self-illuminated.

There are no chariots there, no horses, no roads—but he himself creates those chariots, horses and roads.][5]

4. Confined as they are within the body, the truthlessness of these objects is called to mind on waking. As in the waking state, so in the dream—dream differing from waking state in that the former's objects are confined.

5. The wise, with solid reasons, speak of dream and waking states as one, on the grounds that their objects have a common characteristic [the invariable relationship, existing among them, of knower and known].

6. Whatever a thing is not at beginning or end, it is not in the middle. Entities are like delusions, but taken as undelusive.

7. The usefulness we perceive in objects while awake is annulled in dreams. So they are held to be unreal, since they have a beginning and an end.

8. The extraordinary character of dreams arises from the extraordinary character of the dreamer, as with the dwellers of heaven. [It is the extraordinariness of the latter's condition that causes the wonders they experience.] Someone conversant with a milieu sees the things it possesses, so someone in the milieu of dreams sees the things it evokes.

9. Even during dreams, what the mind imagines as being within oneself is unreal, and what is outside as real. But the truthlessness of both contexts is perceived.

10. And even when one is awake, what the mind imagines as being within oneself is unreal, and what is outside is real. But the truthlessness of both contexts is consequentially conceived.

II. THE IMAGINER OF THE DELUSIONS, THE SELF

11. If the objects are unreal in both states, who knows the objects, who again is their imaginer?

12. The shining Self knows himself by himself through his Mirific Power. It is he who knows the objects. This is the Vedanta's conclusion.

13. The self, his mind turned outwards, imagines the subsistent and contained forms within, and others besides. This is how the Lord imagines.

14. These forms are known within one as long as the thought of them endures [that is, for a moment]; those without endure for two moments [the present, and past or future]. They are all imagined; there is nothing else to distinguish them.

15. Those which are undisclosed within and those which are disclosed without—they are all imagined, distinguished by reference to diverse faculties only.

16. The Lord first imagines the soul, then the different outer realities, and then the inner ones. As one knows, so one remembers.

17. A rope undiscerned in the dark is imagined to be things like a snake or a trickle of water. The Self is imagined in the same way.

18. When the rope itself is discerned all imaginations are dispelled, and nonduality rises into awareness with the words "this is only a rope." Such is the discernment of the Self.

19. This is that shining being's Mirific Power, by which he himself is deluded.

> [From Vv. 20–28. Gauḍa Pāda speaks of thirty-five names, among others, given to Self by its several votaries: (1) Breath; (2) The Elements; (3) The three Attributes of Matter; (4) The Śaiva Principles; (5) The Quarters; (6) sense objects; (7) the worlds; (8) the gods; (9) the Vedas; (10) sacrifices; (11) the experiencer; (12) the experienced; (13) the Subtle; (14) the Gross; (15) the Formed; (16) the Formless; (17) Time; (18) Space; (19) Disputation; (20) the Abodes; (21) Mind; (22) Instinct; (23) Consciousness; (24) Virtue and Vice; (25) the twenty-five Sankhya Principles; (26) the twenty-six Yoga Principles; (27) the thirty-one Pastoralist Principles; (28) the Infinite; (29) People; (30) the Four States of Life; (31) the genders; (32) the Higher and the Lower; (33) creation; (34) dissolution; (35) maintenance.]

29. Whatever form the Self manifests is the form one per-

ceives. Actually becoming that form, the Self protects the perceiver—who, possessed of it, realizes it himself.

30. It is through these beings, inseparate from himself, that the Self is apprehended as separate. One who knows this truth can indulge in imagining unhesitatingly.

III. ULTIMACY OF NONDUALITY

31. As we view dreams, illusions and fairy cities [in the skies], so do the insightful Vedanta masters view the world.

32. There is no destruction and no origin; none bound and no aspirant; no seeker and no one saved. This is the highest truth.

33. The Self is imagined in non-existent forms through nonduality. He is imagined in existent forms, also through nonduality. Nonduality therefore is blessed.

34. This manifoldness is not owing to the nature of the Self, or indeed to its own nature. Nothing is separate or inseparate—as the knowers of reality are aware.

35. Sages free from passion, fear and anger, profoundly versed in the Vedas, apperceive this concept-less nondual cessation of the world.

36. Therefore, when one has known the Self, one should fix one's thoughts on nonduality, and when one has realized it, continue to live his life in the world like one deprived of sense.

37. Eschewing praise, greetings, the performance of rites to ancestors, living in things moving and stationary, the ascetic should live on what chance brings him.

38. When he has perceived the truth within and when he has perceived it without—when he has identified with that truth and found joy in it, he will never lapse from that truth.

—*Explicative Verses on the "Māṇḍukya Upaniṣad"*[6]

29

GAUḌA PĀDA

The Causelessness of All Reality

1. I honor that noblest of men [the Buddha, or Viṣṇu, the "Supreme Man"], who with an ethereal knowledge, indivisible from the known, realized the existences that are also ethereal.

2. I bow to him who taught this touch intangible [to duality], the joy of all things; conducive to well-being, beyond controversy and negation.

3. Arguing among themselves, some thinkers [the Sankhyas, or Discriminationists] postulate that the existent originates. Other clever men [the Logicists and the Atomists], that the non-existent does.

4. No existent ever originates: no non-existent does either. In so arguing among themselves, both sides proclaim non-origination.

5. We applaud their proclaiming non-origination. We do not dispute with them. Know now how this doctrine is free from dispute.

6. These thinkers contend that the non-originant is originated. How can an immortal existent pass over to mortality?

7. The immortal does not become the mortal, nor the mortal the immortal. The alteration of nature is impossible.

8. One who believes that the innately immortal becomes mortal—how can he assume that his own fictitious immortal remains changeless?

9. What is consummate, natural, innate, unproduced and unrelinquent of its nature—that is what we must understand nature to be.

10. All existents are by nature free from old age and death. Wishful of old age and death they deviate from their nature in thought.

11. *Atomist attack on Sankhya.* One who believes that cause is effect—for him, cause is itself produced. [Material cause, clay, is identical with effect, pot. Matter is unproduced,

and is the cause from which its evolutes are produced. But it is at the same time identical with its evolutes—and hence, to that extent, produced.] If a thing is produced, how can it be unproduced? If altered, how can it be eternal?

12. If [unproduced] cause is not other than effect, it must follow that the effect is also unproduced. How then, with the effect being [nevertheless, in your view] produced, can the cause be unchanging?

13. There is no example of anything produced from the unproduced, and to be produced from the produced leads to an infinite regress.

14. The thinkers [the Ritualists] who hold that the effect is the cause's producer, and that the cause is the effect's producer [the cause, the body, produces merit and demerit, the effect—which in turn becomes the cause of the body]—how can they describe cause and effect as having no beginning [or being unproduced]?

15. The thinkers who hold that the effect is the cause's producer, and that the cause is the effect's producer—their kind of production will be like that of father from son.

16. Admitting the cause-effect relationship, what is the sequence between them? If they are simultaneous, they cannot be connected—like an animal's horns.

17. Your cause, which emanates from its effect, is not proved. And how can an unproved cause give rise to an effect?

18. If cause derives its existence from effect, and effect its own existence from cause—then which of these mutual dependents is produced first?

19. Inability to reply, ignorance about the sequence, or even its derangement—for these reasons the enlightened emblazon their doctrine of improduction.

20. The so-called example of seed and shoot is one that has yet to be proved. [It is claimed that seed-and-shoot exemplify a beginningless causal sequence or series. But every individual seed and shoot has a beginning, and there is no such thing as "series" apart from the individual seeds and shoots.] And what is not proved is not an apt inferent sign for proving the inferendum.

21. The ignorance of prior and posterior in the causal sequence is what emblazes improduction. How is it that the origin whence an entity arises is not perceived?

22. Nothing is produced—either from itself or another.

Nothing whatever is produced—be it existent, non-existent or both.

23. From something which by nature has no beginning, no cause is produced, no effect. What has no beginning [commencement] has no beginning [origin or cause].

24. Because knowledge must have a cause [objective reality] —for else both knowledge and reality will be annulled [reality, as supposed; and knowledge, as lacking object]—and because there is the experience of suffering, other systems postulate external reality.

25. Through the insight of *logic* we postulate a cause for knowledge; through the insight of *things* [as they ultimately are] we postulate the causelessness of the caused.

26. The mind touches neither the object nor its appearance. And as the object is non-existent, the appearance is not different from it [the object or the mind].

27. In none of time's three paths—past, present and future —does the mind touch the cause. So how can its error, lacking a cause, exist?

28. In consequence, the mind is not produced, and what the mind perceives is also not produced. Those who can perceive its production can perceive the footprints of birds in the sky.

29. As it is the *unproduced* that is produced, improduction is its nature. The alteration of nature is impossible.

30. An uncommenced world can have no termination, and a commenced liberation no interminability.

—*Explicative Verses on the "Māṇḍukya Upaniṣad."*[7]

30

ŚAṄKARA

The Vedic Law

When the Lord had created the world, he wished to ensure its stability, so He created Marīci and the other Lords of Creatures, and imposed on them the Law of Action proclaimed in the Vedas. Then he created others, like the passionless Youths Sanaka and Sanandana, imposing on them the passion-negating Law of Inaction.

Thus the Law that the Vedas proclaims is twofold—of Action and of Inaction—and it is the cause of the world's stability. The immediate source of the happiness and liberation of living beings, this Law was for long observed by Brahmins and other castes, by the followers of the four states of life, and by the aspirants to the highest goal of existence. After much time had elapsed, desire was aroused in the Law's observers; Lawlessness [Vice] arose with the failing of discriminant knowledge; the Law was overwhelmed, and lawlessness grew. Then Viṣṇu, the Primal Cause, whose name is also Nārāyaṇa, touched by the desire to preserve the world's stability, and to protect the Brahminhood of the god of this world [the Brahmin], was in one part of his nature truly born as Kṛṣṇa, of Vasudeva and Devakī. For with the protection of Brahminhood the Vedic Law would be protected, as upon it the setting of bounds to the castes and the states depends.

Furnished always with that sextet of glorious attributes—knowledge, sovereignty, energy, power, vigor and refulgence—that Lord subjected to himself his Vaiṣṇava potency, the innately triple-Attributed Mirific Power, Primal Matter itself. And unborn as he is, and imperishable, the Lord of created things, the Essence eternal, pure, wise and liberated, became, through his Mirific Power, as though embodied, and as though taking birth, and he can be seen to dower creatures with his grace. Without any benefit to himself, graciousness to creatures his only motive, he taught the twofold Law to Arjuna, when that warrior was sunk in the ocean of sorrow and delusion—so that the Law, accepted with its abundant excellences, and faithfully observed, would attain increase. And the all-knowing noble Vyāsa, in the seven hundred and seventy-seven verses known as the *Gītā,* compiled that Law exactly as the Lord had taught it.

This sacred science of the *Gītā* is thus the quintessence of all Vedic knowledge, mystifying in its meaning. Many lay folk, as I have found, have understood this meaning in an extremely contradictory fashion, even when the significance of its words and categories, its sentences and their content, was free of confusion. So in order to ascertain the *Gītā*'s significance, I shall prepare an exposition of it in a clear and concise fashion.

In brief: the object of the science of the *Gītā* is the highest goal of existence and the total cessation of the causally conditioned world of transmigration. This is achieved by an assured knowledge of the Self heralded by the abandonment of all activity. This is the doctrine propounded by the Lord himself—after he had set forth the Law in the *Gītā* [in the *Anugītā*]:

> This Law is ample for one to perceive the meaning of the word "Brahman."[8]

In the same work it is also said:

> He is neither observant of the Law, nor Law-less, neither moral nor immoral.[9]
>
> Let him remain fixed to a seat and meditate in silence.[10]
>
> Knowledge is characterized by renunciation.[11]

In the *Gītā* itself, towards the end, the Lord tells Arjuna:

> Give up all things of Law and abandon yourself wholly to Me. I will save you from all your sins. Have no fear.[12]

As for the Law of Action, source of happiness though it is, it is enjoined on the definition of the castes and the states; and though it is the means for attaining the abode of the gods, it is conducive to mental purity also, when observed in a spirit of sacrifice to God and purged of all expectation of results. And when the ability inherent in knowledge is acquired, and through the impulse afforded by the dawning of knowledge itself, mental purity conduces to liberation also. With this idea in mind, Kṛṣṇa later says [in the *Gītā*]

> He offers his work to the Brahman, shuns attachment, and works on. He is unstained by sin, as a lotus by water.[13]
>
> The yogi works with his body, mind, instinct and by his unaided senses too, shunning attachment to assure purity of mind.[14]

In sum: the twofold Law ordained to liberation, the ultimate truth proclaimed by Kṛṣṇa, the Supreme Brahman expressed in meaning, explicitly defined and related to specific motives: such is the science of the *Gītā*. As its knowledge leads to the attainment of all human goals, I shall strive to make its meaning clear.

—*Commentary on the "Gītā"*[15]

31

ŚAṄKARA

Superposition, the Basis of Illusionism

"You" and "I," which encompass the conception of object and subject, are polar in essence, as are darkness and light. Their mutual inexistence is thus evidently impossible: all the more the inexistence of their attributes. In consequence, the "You"–encompassed object and its attributes are superposed on the "I"–encompassed subject, which in essence is consciousness itself. Conversely, the subject and its attributes are superposed on the object—superpositions which it is proper to suppose are erroneous.

Nonetheless, it is a natural practice in the world—the work of false knowledge—to impose the essence and attributes of each of these polarities on the other, by not discriminating between substance and qualities that are totally opposed. As a result, truth and falsehood are coupled in statements like "I am this" and "This is mine."

Queries the opponent: 'What *is* this superposition?' I answer: the appearance, in one place, in the form of a memory, of something seen elsewhere before. Some thinkers [the Logicists and Atomists] say that it is the superposition of one thing's attributes on another; others [Ritualists of the Vericist school] describe it as the confusion caused by the imperception of the difference between the things coincident in the superposition; still others [Ritualists of the Contrarist school], as the fiction of characteristics contrary to the thing upon which the superposition occurs. But these views do not in any way disagree that attributes of one sort appear in a thing that is of another sort. Such, in fact, is common experience, for nacre appears to be silver, and one moon as two.

'But how in fact can the object and its attributes be superposed on the Inner Self, which is a non-object? One superposes an object on another that is before one's eyes; and you did speak, did you not, of the non-objectness of a Self free of the conception of the "You"?'

I answer: the Self is not, absolutely speaking, a non-object, because it is the object of the "I" conception. Immediate knowledge also guarantees an Inner Self. And there is no invariable rule that an object must be superposed only on another that is before one's eyes. Even when they are not actually looking at the sky, the ignorant superpose attributes on it like the possession of a dirty surface. In the same way, the superposition of the non-Self on the Self is not a contradiction. So described, superposition is what the wise conceive as Ignorance: in contradistinction to it, the ascertainment of the nature of things is what they call knowledge.

That being so, the object on which a thing is superposed is not in the least constrained by the defects and qualities produced by that thing. And it is on the basis of this mutual superposition—known as Ignorance—of the Self and non-Self, that all mundane and Vedic activities concerning knowledge and the knowable are begun, as well as all the sacred sciences ordained to injunction, prohibition and release.

. . . In this way, one superposes the Inner Faculty, which conceives the "I," on the Inner Self, the Witness to all its activities; and conversely, the all-witnessing Inner Self on the Inner Faculty. Thus this superposition—beginningless, unending, connatural, erroneous conception by nature, the activator of the functions of agent and experiencer—has come to the knowledge of all. It is to destroy this cause of evil, and to realize the knowledge of the Self's oneness, that all the Vedantic texts commence.

—*Commentary on the "Aphorisms on the Brahman," Preface*[16]

32

PRAKĀŚĀTMAN

The Transmogrification of the Brahman

I. TRANSFORMATION AND TRANSMOGRIFICATION

Some hold that the Brahman Himself is transformed into the shape of the world, as clay into the shape of a pot. The teacher Padma Pāda rejects this theory in the words "The world is [the Brahman] transmogrified." *Transmogrification* is the appearance, in multiple and unreal forms, diverse from the primordial one, of a being that has not lapsed from its nature. *Transformation* is the attainment of a disparate and real form, with the relinquishment of the primordial one. The opponent has now to prove why the Brahman does not transmogrify but rather transforms.

'Can we say that He transforms on the authority of the "Creation" Scriptures? [There His transformation is clearly implied, as for instance:

> Being had a thought, "Let me become many, let me generate!" It emitted fire. That fire thought, "Let me become many, let me generate!" It emitted water . . . Water thought, "Let me become many, let me generate!" It emitted food.]'[17]

Does that "Creation" Scripture speak of the Brahman as relinquishing His primordially existent Brahman nature of knowledge, joy and truth, impartible and unlimited, and of so attaining to His effectual condition of unconsciousness, pain, falsehood, partibility and limitedness? Or does it speak of the Brahman as remaining unrelinquent of His primordially existent nature while attaining to the discrepant effectual condition?

Such is the question we must raise. If the primordial form is relinquished, the Brahman nature will decompose, and so become nothing but an effect.

'Can we say that at the time of world dissolution [when

things revert to their original state] He will again transform into His nature of knowledge and joy?'

[No. Having become an effect, He will be unable to relinquish His connection with the transmigrating universe.] It will [consequently] be impossible for Him to attain release. [Things reverting to their original state in dissolution never lose their effectual condition. Also, change is dependent on an efficient cause—lacking in liberation. You cannot argue that scriptural teaching will free Him from bondage, as it does us all.] You will also be in conflict with Revelation [which denies that He is bound]:

> In one way only can that unknowable being be perceived. It is the immaculate, beyond the ether, the unborn Self, the great, the eternal.[18]

And

> The wise Self is not born and does not die. He came from nothing and becomes nothing. He is the unborn, the eternal, the everlasting, the ancient. He is not killed when the body is.[19]

So what the "Creation" Scripture means to speak of is the attainment of the effectual condition, but only with the non-relinquishment of the primordial Brahman nature—and in this way it proposes transmogrification, the latter process having the characteristic signs of things like nacre silver and tigers of magic.

'The "Creation" Scripture has to do with creation only; it is not concerned with the relinquishment or non-relinquishment of the primordial nature.'

[True.] Even so, the relevant pronouncements on the Brahman have a unitary significance. So where Revelation speaks of the attainment of the effectual condition—but only without the [original] nature being relinquished—it teaches transmogrification, a perfectly unobjectionable position.

II. DISPROOF OF TRANSFORMATIONISM

Someone interjects that even the impartible can be transformed. Let us examine the problem. Let us inquire whether, when the gold substance is transformed into a necklace, its particles are transformed or not. If they are, then each [impartible] particle will be, so the transformation will affect the impartible particle itself. If they are not transformed, then the whole formed of them will not be either, because no change is possible in inherent accidents without change in the inhered substance.

Therefore, just as conjunction inhering in one portion of the whole is consequentially connected with the conjunction inhering in the impartite atoms that form the whole—so also the transformation of the whole is connected with the transformation in the impartible parts.

We must now ask our opponent what this transformation is. [Does it consist (1) in the consolidation of parts; (2) in conjunction with a different object; (3) in movement, connected with the emergence of an object, like the spinning of a potter's wheel with a pot; (4) the rise of further qualities in the object, or (5) the appearance of a different substance closely connected with the previous one?]

1. If transformation is the consolidation of parts—either through the anterior conjunction of those parts, the occurrence of a further conjunction, or through conjunction with other parts—then there is no transformation in the impartible, because the latter simply lacks parts. And we cannot describe the transformation of the whole, its acquisition of a further state, or its alteration, independently of conjunction or consolidation.

And neither is transformation

2. Conjunction with another object,

3. Movement, or

4. The rise of different qualities—because they are all absent in the Brahman. With the potter's wheel spinning [hence in *movement*] in space, which is in contact [or in *conjunction*] with an object other than itself, and with red color arising [hence a *different quality*] in the pot, one does not have the idea that any of these factors are causes of any transformation.

5. If transformation is the appearance of a different substance closely connected with the previous one [say, with the gold of the necklace], are the gold particles transformed (a) into the form of the necklace, or (b) into another substance altogether?

Not into another substance, because we do not find that any substance is produced that is different from the gold substance. Neither are they transformed into the form of the necklace, because the particles of gold acquire their alteration precisely in so far as they are coincident with the particles forming the necklace. Independently of states like the form of the necklace we do not, as I said, see altered states in gold particles which can explain differences in transformation. And, as I also said, difference in conjunction alone is not transformation. It is also not logical to assume that the gold particles are transformed into the necklace shape without the gold substance being also transformed, for that would be admitting the Novel Origination theory.

Here [the doubt arises whether] the transformation of the parts, though not perceived, is to be postulated because the transformation of the whole would be otherwise impossible, on the grounds that the change in the inhering accidents cannot occur independently of change in the inhered substance.

This doubt is invalid. For [if that were true] when wholes originate and perish, so would the parts that constitute them, or when the wholes walk, the parts would too.

'Perhaps there will be transformation also [of the parts, as of the whole]?'

No, there will not. The whole [pot] is coincident with the genus of potness, but its parts are not. [Pots are pots, but potsherds are not.]

'[Now whole and parts are identical.] How then can there be an alteration in the whole without there being an alteration in the parts? A distinct quality, like blue color, or a distinct state, does not supervene on a substance, as though it were a substance over and above a distinct state. And, as was said, no effect forms in the parts without an effect forming in the whole. And even if there is an appearance of a further effect [in the cloth, supposing we twist it to look like a rope], the threads of the cloth never appear as not being threads.'

[But threads in untwisted cloth are not quite the same as those in cloth twisted into a rope; they are not similarly "coincident." Can we say then that the twisted stuff is really rope and not cloth?] The coincidence of threads in the effect, cloth, is fixed in its altered state through the coincidence of the cloth [and not of the rope], as was said before. Furthermore, the transformation of the parts is only seen in conditions where the whole undergoes transformation. Hence transformation is not proved of the unconditioned and impartible Self.

If it is maintained that conjunction with the impartible is

what transformation is, then [it must be observed that] the perceptible conjunction in partible wholes is not found in its atomic particles, because [in the latter case] the nature of such conjunction is beyond experience. Besides, one cannot postulate a conjunction in the impartible as though it were a partial conjunction existent in a partible whole. Conjunction is possible only in partible wholes, just as coincidence with a genus is possible only in such wholes independently of their parts. The coincidence of the conjunction in the parts attains to its alteration in the coincidence of conjunction in the whole.

'Can it be that conjunction is found only in wholes, not in parts?'

It cannot. If partible wholes are unconjoined, the effect cannot come into existence. Therefore the conjunction is entirely in the whole and not in the parts.

'If conjunction is coincident with the whole, then the conjunction will be omnifunctional, will it not?'

Then conjunction with the impartible will also be omnifunctional, and there will be lack of all manifoldness [hence no real transformation of the one into the many.]

III. EXPLANATION OF THE BRAHMAN'S IMPARTIBILITY

'How then do you explain the Brahman's impartibility?'

As follows: if the parts and whole are both self-illuminant, neither can be the object of the other's knowledge [because self-luminance, by definition, is objectless and undifferenced awareness]. So the Brahman cannot experience partibility in His own Self. If either parts or whole are non-self-illuminant, then one will be known by the other [as a distinct object], so they will not be related as whole and part [through Difference-in-Identity, but will be wholly distinct], like a pot and the Self.

Revelation also [declares the nullity of action and partibility in the Brahman with the words]:

> He is partless, inactive, tranquil, faultless, immaculate, the exalted bridge to immortality, and like a fire that has consumed its fuel.[20]

'But activity, such as the control of the universe, is also revealed of the Brahman [as in the following scriptural texts]:

> He Who, standing on the earth, is within it, Whom the earth does not know, Whose body the earth is, He controls the earth from within—He is your self, the controller, the immortal.[21]

Revelation also teaches that He is partible:

> Such is its greatness [the greatness of the Sacred Incantation, the Gāyatrī, as the Brahman]. Even greater is the Person. His feet are all beings. Three of His feet are the immortal in heaven.'[22]

[I answer that] where there are contradictions of this kind we must conceive of such appearance [of activity] and non-appearance [of inactivity] through the power of Illusion. To conclude: (a) because the causality of Illusion is revealed in the words:

> To reveal his own form he was transformed into every form. Through his magical powers ["illusions"] Indra appeared to be many. Hundreds and tens of his horses are yoked[23];

(b) because the conscious being attains its goal [undifferenced awareness, not differenced conceptuality] in dreamless slumber; (c) because the Brahman has innately no motive for activity; and (d) because He attains to His dissimilar effectual condition without relinquishing His dissimilar [primordial] nature—for these reasons it is proved that only transmogrification is true.

—*Exposition of "The Five Chapters" of Padma Pāda*[24]

33

ŚRĪ HARṢA

Critique of Difference

Here is another point which deserves scrutiny. The invalidation of the "Identity" Scripture[25] which you announce —an invalidation that grasps the difference between things, like pots and cloths, through norms, such as experience—in what sort of meaning does it express itself? Does it signify (a) the difference deriving from a thing's *essence,* (b) the *mutual exclusion* of things, (c) *difference in attributes,* or (d) some other factor?

It cannot be (a) the difference deriving from a thing's *essence.* In such a case the essence of the pot and of the cloth will lie in what distinguishes the one from the other—something impossible to conceive unless the one object *implies* the other. For difference is difference *from* something: otherwise to say that "essence is difference" is to make the two terms synonymous. If experience apprehends the essence of a cloth through concepts like "the cloth is different from the pot," then even the pot will be included in the cloth's essence. The difference-grasping experience will really have fathomed the essential identity of pot and cloth, and you will have arrived at a conclusion quite the reverse of what you intended.

'The experience you describe is expressed in terms of non-difference. Perhaps you might consider describing it in terms of difference as well! If pot and cloth were not different, experience would express itself in terms of "pot" and "cloth," and not as "the cloth is different from the pot."'

Such a rejoinder could be countenanced if, while upholding absolute non-difference, we were to repudiate the difference rendered extant through Ignorance. Hence a knowledge imperceptive of non-difference is impercipient of difference too. It is then valid only for non-difference, not for difference [its contradictory], for then it would wreck its own foundation.

'Well then, the essence of cloth is unqualified difference. When we add the qualification "from the pot," the essence becomes explicated by means of the pot, which is different from it.'

This theory is also implausible. A difference devoid of a correlative is beyond the reach of normative knowledge: such a knowledge only operates in instances of correlative-connected difference. What kind of logic is this that the essence of a cloth, intrinsically related to something else, only becomes distinct from it after it has been explicated by it? What is intrinsically blue does not become so only subsequent to its explication by yellow.

If you maintain that difference is the essence of the cloth in so far as it is explicated by its correlative the pot, what, in your opinion, does the correlative character of the pot to this cloth consist in: in its essence, or in some attribute?

If we take the first alternative, then the pot's essence will lie only in its being the cloth's correlative, and the cloth will be included in the pot's essence. To what can all this conclude but to non-difference?

'Well then, supposing unqualified correlativeness to be the pot's essence, the qualification "to the pot" will be something superadded.'

This cannot be maintained either. Normative knowledge has nothing to do with correlatives that correlate with nothing. As for the qualification "to the pot," we shall have to ask ourselves whether it is the pot's essence or attribute, and the same logical flaws will apply.

The second alternative will also not hold. Correlation to the cloth is the pot's attribute, and hence included in its nature; thus pot and cloth will be non-different. And if the cloth becomes the pot's attribute, then, by parity of reasoning, the pot will also become the attribute of the cloth. No other relation is possible to the pot, the correlative of the cloth—and the cloth is itself explicated by its own correlative, the pot: we thus land ourselves in a vicious circle. No norm of knowledge exists which has for its object a pot-intrinsic-to-a-cloth or a cloth-intrinsic-to-a-pot.

Besides, if the attribute and its subject are not connected, the attribute would have unrestricted scope [and anything could have any attribute whatsoever]. If they are connected, each connection will need another, and so on, without limit, and we shall have an infinite regress. If [to avoid this] we postulate an immediate and essential connection, either at the beginning of the regress or later, that essential connection would be present in the very essence of the subject of the connection, and would thus entail non-difference. This argument applies no matter what attributes one postulates. Therefore experience, the norm you employ to establish difference deriving from the essence, really becomes the norm guaranteeing non-difference.

> [Śrī Harṣa then proceeds, in great detail, to reduce the remaining three alternatives to absurdity by showing them to be mostly variations of the fallacies of circularity and infinite regress.]

—*The Confits of Confutation*[26]

34

PRAKĀŚĀNANDA

Self-evidence of the Self

On what grounds is the difference between the perceived and the perception valid? This world of moving and immovable flashes as perception only.

The Brahman is perceived as a dream world, diversified as knowledge and known. The waking world of movable and unmoving is consciousness only.

As with the threads removed the cloth is essentially a void, so with the Self removed this phenomenon-only is a void.

As a rope appears a snake to the deluded vision, so the Self appears as world to the hallucinated mind.

Only in the Self does this entire world, whose reality is mere perception, arise, continue to exist and dissolve.

Only in that Being which is the fullness of joy, the nondual, the immaculate, preclusive of sin and imperfection, does this triple world, perception only, flash.

The revered sage Vasiṣṭha says the same:

> In this wide mirror of Consciousness, all these thing-perceptions are reflected, as the trees on a bank in a pool.[27]

and again:

> The world of moving and immobile is His consciousness-frolic. Inbeing of the universe though He is, His unity is never destroyed.[28]

'Hence—on the assumption that Ignorance, made to inhere in the Self, has originated the world, which in essence is perception only—you have splendidly conceived the Self as an object of that Ignorance. There being no norm, mundane or Vedic, on the basis of which we can justify the Self's existence, we can assume it to be as unreal as the horns of a rabbit. So why should there be any desire for studying the sacred sciences to gain an intuition of it, and how, pray, can there be need of argument?' This is a summing up of the opponent's views.

In reply to this reasoning, I shall now declare, and logically justify, that Reality hidden in the Vedas, the joy supreme and absolute, eternal and irrelative by essence, the truth, the subtler than the subtle, this great immortal Being, attainable by the liberated alone. This entire world, whose stuff is mere delusion, is only a pinpoint of a particle of Its substance. That Reality is the essence of the Light within, It is the blessed.

When you say that there is no norm, do you mean to imply that the Self is lacking in essence or in knowability? The first alternative is untenable. The essence of the Self [the knowable whose existence is to be established on the basis of your norm] is eternal, and wholly irrelative; and it is impossible for the norm to cause the existence of the knowable. In the second alternative, even if the norm is granted to exist, a second norm will be needed to justify it, for if that justification is lacking, the first norm will be as unmeaningful as a man's horn, and will therefore lack the power to demonstrate its knowable object. If this other norm exists [it will need to be supported by still another] and with this succession of norms an infinite regress will result. To say that only a norm of knowledge can authenticate an object's existence is therefore no more than a presumptuous postulate.

'A norm is quite independent of any other: it authenticates both itself and its object. What is by nature self-lighting—in things that concern itself and its objects—is not in need of any other light, like the light of a lamp. It does not make sense to suppose that the all-authenticating norm is itself in need of authentication.'

Really! Then how can the Self, which guarantees the world diversified as norm and knowable—how can the Self be guaranteed by a norm dependent on the Self for its own guarantee? Assuredly the Self's own normativeness must antecede that of all norms, for no norm will realize its own nature as norm if a normative *knower* does not exist. Besides, how can the norm make the Knower of all its object? That would land one in the contradiction of identifying the action [knowing] and the agent [knower]. Also, everything other than the Self, being non-Self, cannot [by definition] be a knower. This is why Revelation asks

> Through what, my dear, can one know the Knower?[29]

It is evident then that the Self, the normative knower, the self-guaranteed, cannot be said not to exist even if a norm is lacking.

To continue the argument. Is the non-existence of the Self that you insist on (a) established by a norm, (b) uncertain of nature, or (c) self-evident? Let us take the first alternative. A norm which apprehends a negation [non-existence] must necessarily apprehend the correlative on which the negation is founded. With the correlative—the Self's existence—thus posited by the norm, its non-existence becomes inconceivable. The second alternative is inconsequent, for nothing whose nature is uncertain can be discussed. Obviously one cannot speak of something which has not entered one's mind. As for the third alternative, self-evidence might rather be affirmed of the [existence of the] Self, it being incongruous to assert a non-existence to be self-evident. Else you will only be accepting the Self under another name.

And how is the Self's non-existence known: by the Self or the non-Self? Not by the latter, because the non-Self is not a knower. Not by the former, because that is a contradiction.

Let me explain why. When does the Self become aware of its non-existence—while (a) existent, or (b) non-existent? If (a) while existent, how can it be affirmed not to exist? Also, how can it know something [its own non-existence] which is not there to be known? If (b) while non-existent, how can it know, since it is itself lacking in existence?

'Can one maintain that the Self, while it is existent, is aware of its non-existence to occur at a later time?'

[What you are really saying, then, is] that the Self exists, but is non-eternal. But such a thesis has been disproved, [above, in Section 2], because it has been shown to imply that actions forfeit, and non-actions appropriate, fruition.

And does the believer in the Self's non-existence deny reality to his own self, or to the self of another? If to his own, then, as the denier is non-existent, the self he was to have denied will continue to exist. If to another's, since the denier's own self exists, how can the Self's non-existence be affirmed? As Revelation says,

> If a man knows the Brahman as non-existent, he is as though non-existent himself; if he knows the Brahman as existent, we know him as being existent himself.[30]

Further, does the norm function with regard to [or make known] (a) an existent object, or (b) a non-existent one? If a non-existent one, then it might even guarantee a rabbit's horns, as there is nothing to distinguish between kinds of non-existences [and a chimera, like a rabbit's horn, is one kind]. Also norms [whose objects, by definition, are valid knowables] are unable to authenticate things that do not exist. If (b) an existent one, then the reality of the object does not depend on the functioning of the norm, since it is already assumed to possess the status of valid object. If it is not assumed to have that status, then to affirm that the norm makes known an [invalid] existent object will be to contradict one's own words.

'Can one maintain that the object depends upon the norm for its *manifestation?*'

Perhaps—in so far as the innately non-manifest non-Self, the unconscious, is concerned. But how can this be said of the innately self-manifesting Self? In Revelation's words:

> The sun does not shine there, nor the moon or the stars. These lightnings do not shine—then how much less this fire? When He shines everything shines after Him; by His light all this is lighted.[31]

And now to one who perseveres in the question "By what norm is the Self known?" the answer must be "By all norms." The object of a norm can only be something that Ignorance conceals, and Ignorance conceals only the Self. The unconscious [or the non-Self], on the other hand, is innately self-concealing, so there is no need to postulate something else, in the form of Ignorance, to conceal it. Hence, as it is not the object of Ignorance, the non-Self is also not the object of a norm. But Ignorance is dependent on a norm for its annulment, and it is only through the consciousness [or the Self] stamped with this annulment, that the unconscious [or the non-Self] is capable of being known. Therefore, to say that the Self, authenticated by all norms, is non-existent, because no norm authenticates it, is rashness, nothing more.

'Then how can one say that the Self is exclusively Upaniṣadic? If *all* the norms of knowledge make it known, how can you claim it to be revealed by the Upaniṣads alone?'

I reply: in His inner essence of plenary being, consciousness and joy, the Brahman cannot be the object of any other norm. It is in this sense that He is Upaniṣadic exclusively.

—*The Pearl Necklace of Vedanta Orthodoxy*[32]

35

MADHUSŪDANA SARASVATĪ

The Category of the Inexplicable

VYĀSA RĀYA

[REPORTED BY MADHUSŪDANA]

'What is this falsehood you seek to prove? It cannot be the Inexplicable that is the non-substrate of being and non-being —an idea you derive from Padma Pāda's *The Five Chapters,* where he says that "the word 'false' signifies the Inexplicable."

Is this Inexplicable

1. The absence of being qualified by non-being;

2. The simultaneous presence of two negations—of being and non-being, or

3. The simultaneous absence of those negations?

It cannot be (1). [The definition is supposed to apply to the world and be a basis for proving its falsehood. But it does not apply.] The world—which [for us Dualist Vedantins] is the substrate of being only—cannot be conceived as being qualified by non-being. But if you make a special point of establishing the qualification "qualified by non-being," you will be committing the fallacy of *proving the proven.* [I for one am prepared to admit that the absence of being qualified by non-being is falsehood, as it certainly does not apply to the world as I conceive it. So why postulate it in a discussion intended to prove that world's falsity?]

Neither can it be (2). [For three reasons. First.] Being and non-being are such that where one is absent the other is necessarily present. To postulate them simultaneously is a *contradiction.* [Second.] The world, like the attributeless

Brahman, lacks the attributes of being and non-being. But, like the Brahman, it is being in essence [even in your view, according to which the world, in so far as it is real, is the Brahman itself], and will consequently not be false. So your definition lands you in the fallacy of *inconsequentiality* [for where it intended to prove the world false, in contradistinction to the true Brahman, it shows that the one is as true as the other. Third, your definition does not apply in its entirety to all false things]. In nacre silver, for instance, your definition is true as concerns nacre's difference from being whose nature is inabrogability. But it is not true in so far as nacre is not proved different from non-being whose nature is abrogability. [In other words, being is the inabrogable and non-being the abrogable. So what is different from being and non-being must be neither inabrogable nor abrogable. But nacre silver, your standard example of a false thing, is not inabrogable, so it is different from being. But it certainly *is* abrogable, so it is *not* different from non-being.] In consequence you commit the fallacy of *defective definition.*

Finally, it cannot be (3), for the same three fallacies apply, contradiction, inconsequentiality and defective definition.'

MADHUSŪDANA SARASVATĪ

You are mistaken. Your second alternative, the simultaneous presence of the two negations, being and non-being, is free of fallacy. In the first place, there is no *contradiction* at all. Contradiction can consist in one of three things:

a. The mutual exclusion of being and non-being;

b. The absence of one as coincident with the presence of the other;

c. The presence of one as coincident with the absence of the other.

In our case, it cannot be (a), as we do not accept that being and non-being are mutually exclusive. To explain. Non-being [as we see it] is not the absence of the being whose essence lies in total inabrogability. It is rather inapprehensibility through the notion of being in any substrate whatever. This is the absence to which our definition relates. It therefore comprehends discrepancy from total inabrogability along with apprehensibility through the notion of being in some kind of substrate.

Consequently, the fallacy of *defective definition* will not apply to nacre silver, because the non-being that is merely discrepancy from the being whose essence is inabrogability does not enter into its definition. Hence too there is no contradiction, because being and non-being so defined are not mutually exclusive.

Accordingly, it cannot also be (b). Nacre silver is not what you understand it to be. It lacks being, yes, but it also lacks non-being [but only in the sense defined, and not in the sense of the abrogable].

Neither is it (c), for there is no need to postulate contradiction. The natures of cow and horse mutually exclude each other [without being contradictories], but the absences of both are found to coexist in a camel. [In other words, being and non-being, as I have defined them, are not strictly speaking contradictories; so the presence or absence of one does not imply the presence or absence of the other.]

[Let us revert to the opponent's argument (2), to his second point.] He urges that the attributeless Brahman lacks the attribute of being, but is at the same time being in essence. So too the world, which is also being in essence, will turn out not to be false after all—which will land us [he says] in the fallacy of *inconsequentiality*.

But he is wrong. The universal apprehension of being is conceivable only through one omnipresent Being, and there is no proof that the world, like the Brahman, has the essential conceptuality of "being" as applicable to every existent thing. And a comprehensive concept of "being" would be impossible [if it were to require the knowledge of its application to each being in the universe].

We may also define falsehood as constituted of two differences at once—one the correlative of being and the other of non-being. Therefore, if the world is assumed to be both being and non-being [as Vācaspati Miśra seems to do][33] or either of them [only being, according to Logicists and Dualist Vedantins, only non-being according to some Buddhists], the differences we have defined will not belong to it, so the fallacy of inconsequentiality will not apply.

You cannot argue that as we agree [with our opponents] about the world in so far as it is discrepant from unreality and different from non-being [though not in so far as it is also different from being] we commit the fallacy of a partial *proving of the proven*. [To see why not, let us take a parallel argument.] The theologian of Difference-in-Identity employs the following syllogism: "Qualities and the qualified are both identical and different, because they both have a common substrate," and the Logicist is in agreement in so far as the difference is concerned. Yet, as the proposition is not proven in its entirety, the fallacy of proving the proven does not arise. So in our case also that fallacy does not occur, because our proposition, in its entirety, has a composite significance [difference from non-being *and* difference from being].

[In the Difference-in-Identity argument] there is no real identity [between qualities and the qualified], as between a pot and a jar [which mean the same thing], because we do not perceive them to coincide; so a composite significance [of both identity and difference] has to be proved in their case. So also, in our own case, when we see that [illusory] perceptibility is not perceived in nothingness, devoid of being, and that a composite significance [of being and non-being] serves to make perceptibility possible, composite significance is what we intend to prove. There is thus a parity in both arguments. We can therefore qualify our proposition with equal propriety thus: [the perceptible, or the false] is wholly devoid of being and wholly devoid of non-being.

One cannot argue that the proposition, composite or qualified, being nowhere proven [for where has one seen something wholly devoid of being and wholly devoid of non-being?], will involve the fallacy of *unproven characteristic*. Or that, since its constituents [being and non-being] are separately proven, the composite and qualified proposition is proven too—for rabbits and horns are separately proven, so rabbit horns will also be. One cannot, I say, argue thus, because such a combined significance is proven in nacre silver [which in some inexplicable way, is both silver and non-silver at once].

[Finally] it cannot be objected that as the Brahman is attributeless, and therefore void of the attributes of being and non-being, our definition of falsehood will apply to the Brahman too [giving rise to the fallacy of *latitude of definition*]. The Brahman is being in *essence*, and so cannot be the substrate of the total absence of being. It is also attributeless, and so cannot be the substrate of the *attribute* of the absence of being.

—*The Proof of Nondualism*[34]

Theologies of Difference-in-Identity

PRELIMINARY NOTE

We now enter the mainstream of Hindu theology, agitated with numberless currents, its waters teeming with the forms of life that have since impregnated the seas of human thought.

Its foundational archetype is the bipolar nature of reality, expressed in the following dichotomies among others: substance–modes, essence–attributes, undifferentiated–differentiated, immortal–mortal, unmanifest–manifest, embodied–body, unconceptualized–conceptualized, universal–particular, unevolved–evolved, whole–part, cause–effect, experiencer–experienced, qualified–quality, and supporter–supported.

Bipolarity forms the basis of Sinic theologies, such as that of Chu Hsi; of Islamic theologies, such as those of Al-Junayd, Ibn-Arabi and Al-Ghazzali; and of Western theologies and metaphysics without number, since the days of Giordano Bruno—chief among them those of Spinoza, Hegel and Engels. In our own days no little effort has been expended in constructing Christian theologies of Difference-in-Identity. Some attempts: those of Teilhard, Hartshorne and Tillich.

The Greeks do not seem to have known bipolarity. The Orthodox theologian Mark of Ephesus (1392–1444) was convinced that the distinction between essence and energies was due to divine providence,[1] a distinction which enabled the Church to explain how God is incomprehensible yet known in the Beatific Vision. The Orthodox avatar of Difference-in-Identity seems to appear with Basil of Caesarea in the fourth century (if not before):

> 'Αλλ' *αἱ μέν ἐνέργειαι ποικίλαι, ἡ δέ οὐσία ἁπλῆ* . . .
>
> While the energies are many, the essence is unique. And while we say that we know our God through the energies, we do not affirm that we attain His essence. His energies do indeed come down to us, but the essence itself remains inaccessible.[2]

In Orthodox theology, however, the Difference-in-Identity scheme has the narrowest of applications—only within God Himself. In the Hindu and other theologies, it is applied to reality as a whole, God being its inaccessible pole, and all the other existents its accessible one.

The Hindu Difference-in-Identity schools may be divided into two main groups, the *non-denominational,* which is mainly Vedic; and the *denominational,* professing adherence to Viṣṇu, Śiva or Śakti ("Energy"), which became overwhelmingly Tantric. These groups have further subdivisions. The non-denominational is again twofold. (a) Non-Vedantic Vedic systems, and (b) Non-denominational Vedanta. The denominational systems, as I suggested, are three: (c) Vaiṣṇava, (d) Śaiva, (e) Śākta, or "Energic." Let us examine the further subdivisions of these groups:

a. NON-VEDANTIC VEDIC SYSTEMS. Only one representative.
   1. *Sonic Absolutism* of Bhartṛ Hari (School XIV), the theology of language.

b. NON-DENOMINATIONAL VEDANTA (see Scheme 6). Has three schools:
   2. *Ancient Vedanta* (School XV), of Bādarāyaṇa.
   3. *Conditioned Difference-in-Identity* (School XVI) of Bhāskara.
   4. *Indivisible Nondualism* (School XVII), of Vijñāna Bhikṣu.

c. VAIṢṆAVA VEDANTA (see Schemes 6 and 7), comprising two major groups, which we may call the theologies of Majesty and Sweetness (see Selection 85), emphasizing those particular aspects of the divine. These groups are represented by at least eight schools.
   5. *Pāñcarātra,* not really a Vedantic school, but the foundation of all Vaiṣṇava theologies (see Scheme 28). A Majesty school, it was evolved more in scriptural writings than in systematic theological works.
   6. *Qualified Nondualism* (School XVIII), also a Majesty school, founded by Yāmuna, but represented principally by Rāmānuja. This school has two affiliates—the systems of Rāmānanda and Svāmi Nārāyaṇa. The Majesty schools (among which is also Madhva's Dualist Vedanta, School VI) worship Viṣṇu as unincarnate, rather than in His avatars.

7. *Consciousness Nondualism* (or *Cidādvaita*) of Yādava Prakāśa (tenth century), for whom all reality was spiritual. Nothing seems to have survived of this school.
8. *Innate Difference-in-Idenity* (School XIX), of Nimbārka, which seems a Sweetness school, and incarnational (adoring Kṛṣṇa). It has one affiliate, the *Sakhi,* or Companionist School, of Hari Dāsa.
9. *Immaculate Nondualism* (or *Viśuddhādvaita*), of Viṣṇu Svāmin. Very little, if anything, survives of this school.
10. *Pure Nondualism* (School XX), of Vallabha, a Sweetness school and incarnational.
11. *Ineffable Difference-in-Identity* (School XXI), founded by Caitanya, but provided with a theology by the two Gosvāmis, Rūpa and Jīva.
12. *Established Nondualism* (or *Siddhādvaita*), of Hita Harivaṁśa (sixteenth century), better known as the Rādhāvallabha School (of Kṛṣṇa the Lover of Rādhā). An incarnational and Sweetness school, not fully evolved.

d. ŚAIVA THEOLOGIES (see Scheme 8). They form two main groups and five schools. The first group comprises three independent schools which refused to conform to the Vedic standard; the second group consists of two Vedantized schools.

13. *Monist Pastoralism* (School XXII) of Lakulīśa.
14. *Nandikeśvara Śaivism,* of Nandikeśvara, of whose work little remains.
15. *Triadism* (School XXIII) also known as Kashmir Śaivism, founded by Vasu Gupta. Unequivocally idealist, Triadism is one of the greatest of all Hindu theologies.
16. *Śaiva Nondualism* (School XXIV), of Nīlakaṇṭha, the first Vedantized Śaivism.
17. *Energy-Qualified Nondualism* (School XXV), of Basava, fully elaborated by Māyi Deva, Vedantized by Śrī Pati. It is a synthesis of all earlier Śaiva theologies.

e. ENERGIC THEOLOGIES (School XXVI). Apparently developed more in scriptural texts than in systematic works, and also seemingly affiliated to Triadism.

Besides the foundational bipolarity, all these schools seem to share another principle—that of *play,* or cosmic frolic. The principle links the two poles of reality, explaining how the unicity pole (or God) becomes the multiplicity pole (or the world). It maintains that an innate self-delighting and motiveless impulse causes the transcendental to overflow into the world of phenomena, and to reabsorb that world into itself.

XIV. SONIC ABSOLUTISM, or *ŚABDABRAHMAVĀDA*

The world's first, and for centuries apparently the only, systematic speculation on language was confined to three schools of thought—Ritualism (School III), Logicism (School V), and Sonic Absolutism. They were concerned, among other things, with clarifying the logical procedures involved in our use of language. Sonic Absolutism differed from the others in being exclusively a theology of language. While its modern successors in linguistic speculation, the Vienna Circle and the Cambridge School, merely treated words as quasi-hypostatical entities almost in complete abstraction from the people who used them, the Hindu system hypostatized Word totally, transforming it into the ultimate reality.

Mere glimmers in the Vedas, the concepts of Sonic Absolutism acquire a greater vividness in the thought of the grammarians, Pāṇini (c. 350 B.C.) and Patañjali the Grammarian (second century A.D.), but are fully emblazed in the monumental work of Bhartṛ Hari (fifth century A.D.). The metaphysics of Sonic Absolutism is "energic"—one might even say evolutionary—rather than substantialist. It has a stability pole, the Word Principle, which prevents the mutability pole, the phenomena of the universe, from becoming a dispersed and chaotic mass, but our attention is focused more on its powers of manifestation than on its essence. This metaphysics is formulated in the first chapter of Bhartṛ Hari's *The Book of Phrases and Words* (Selection 36). Though not a flourishing school, its principles acted as a bond between the Hindu theologies, for they, like it, generally affirmed the intrinsic rightness of Word, as well as the inadequacy of human systems in expressing the Absolute—both ideas embodied in the mystical monosyllable OM (Selection 37).

36
BHARTṚ HARI

The Divinity of Language

PAEAN TO THE SONIC ABSOLUTE

1. The Brahman, without beginning or end, the Word Principle, the Phoneme [or the Changeless], manifested phenomenally as things, the source of the world's creation,

2. The Being which Revelation proclaims to be one; yet distinct, as sustaining distinct energies; not divided, but through its energies seeming to be,

3. Where the six states—origin, continuance, change, growth, decay and destruction[3]—implanted in its impartibly irresistible Energy of Time, become the sources of existential differentiations,

4. The unique Being, repository of the germs of all things; to which all these multiple beings pertain, and which endures as experiencer and experienced, and also as experience itself,

I. THE VEDA AND ITS QUINTESSENCE, *OM*

5. The Veda [or Revelation] is the means of realizing that Being and is also its reflection. It is one: but the great seers have separately revealed it, as though it consisted of many ways.

6. Its different parts have many recensions, but the members are ordained to the same ritual. The meaning of its words is fixed in its various branches.

7. The texts of Tradition are likewise multiple, and are concerned with visible and invisible goals. They were devised by sages imbued with Vedic knowledge, with Revelation as their basis, through the aid of indicative signs.

8. The Monist and Dualist opinions, born of their professors' imaginations, pose as Vedic exegesis, and are multifariously excogitated.

9. The true knowledge, known as Purity, is acquired in one

word. Unopposedly to any belief, it is proclaimed in the word OM.

10. From OM, the creator of the worlds, proceed the various sciences with their principal and secondary divisions. They are the sources of salvific knowledge and of purificatory ritual.

II. THE GREATNESS OF GRAMMAR

11. Nearest to the Brahman, the highest of ascetic disciplines, grammar, as the wise tell us, is the first of the six subsidiaries of Vedic knowledge [grammar, etymology, phonetics, prosody, astronomy and ritual].

12. It is the straight path to that most sacred light, to that supreme essence of speech precipitated in divergent forms.

13. The truth about objects and their activities is founded solely on words: the truth about words cannot be understood without grammar.

14. It is the gate to liberation, the medicine for the disorders of language, the purification of all the sciences, illuminating each.

15. The genera of objects are all based on the genera of words. So also, in our world, all sciences are based on the science of grammar.

16. It is the first rung on the ladder of liberation, the undeviant royal road for the aspirants to release.

17. All chances of error surmounted, the Self of the Sacred Incantations [the Lord of the Creatures] sees the Veda, the embodiment and matrix of its mantras, in its isolated purity.

18. This supreme form of Word, where all difference has subsided, the pure light that shines through even in this grammatical darkness,

19. The light, disclosive of forms and actions, that those who have transcended the mutable plane and have passed beyond light and darkness, adore;

20. Where the causes of words, as though vestiges of the memory of the Phoneme, appear, through association with Word, as the Phoneme's reflections;

21. Where the diverse phonemes of the *Atharva* hymns, and of the *Sāma,* the *Ṛg* and the *Yajur Vedas* are seen in their state of separation—

22. That is the one thing which varieties of transformation

render manifold, that is grammar. Those who acquire it reach the Supreme Brahman.

23. The great seers, authors of the aphorisms, the glosses and commentaries, have transmitted to us the eternal relations between its words and meaning.

24. Etymologically derived or fixed meanings; indicative or descriptive words;

25. Verbal relations of cause and effect, or of suitability, which subserve the knowledge of religious duty or of correct and incorrect terms—

26. These have been described in the science of grammar, either through their characteristic features or their own names. Some have been introduced to recall them to memory in conformity with Sacred Doctrine.

27. Fixed by the proficient on the basis of Sacred Doctrine, the correct words help to realize merit when their sense is undeviatingly transmitted. Words of any other kind are incorrect.

III. PREVALENCE OF TRADITION OVER LOGIC IN THE STUDY OF LANGUAGE

28. Eternal or produced, words have no beginning. As with living beings, the continuity of words is said to be eternal.

29. No one can empty this continuity of its meaning. That is why an eternal Tradition, intent on the correctness of words, has been established.

30. Religious duty cannot be confirmed by logic without Tradition. Tradition antecedes the knowledge of the seers themselves.

31. Known as they are by the generality of people, the paths of religious duty, unintermittingly preserved, cannot be abrogated by anybody through logic.

32. Things have a diversity of powers when diversified by various conditions, places and times: so it is very difficult to prove their existence through inference.

33. A substance of a known power—in relation to activities of a particular kind—changes its power when associated with a substance of another kind.

34. Inferred to exist through great effort by expert logicians, a thing can be inferred not to exist by even more expert ones.

35. The knowledge experts have of jewels, coins and such things is acquired by constant study. It cannot be communicated to others and is not inferential.

36. The miraculous powers of ancestors, demons and fiends, the result of their karma, overreach experience and logic.

37. In those people whose minds have been lit by the dawning light and are uneclipsed, the knowledge of past and future is no different from perception.

38. The words of those who with the eyes of seers perceive the truths beyond sense and consciousness, are not unsettled by logic.

39. One who does not doubt what another has seen, as he does not doubt his own knowledge—how can another man turn him away from what he has actually experienced?

40. The moral teaching conveyed in the two sentences "This is merit, this is demerit" is of little use to men, including even the untouchables.

41. A man devoted to Sacred Doctrine—which endures uninterruptedly like Consciousness—is not deranged by logical argument.

42. It is not difficult to foresee the fall of the man who relies mainly on logic, as of the blind man who runs on an uneven road guided solely by the touch of his hand.

43. Therefore the proficient base themselves on the Teaching that has no author [Revelation] and on Tradition and its dependencies, and then proceed to explain the meaning of words.

IV. DUAL ASPECT OF WORD: SOUND AND MEANING-FLASH

44. The word-proficient scholars discern two important terms from the basic ones—one is the cause of words, and the other conducive to meaning.

45. Some ancients believe that a difference exists between words and sense; others attribute this difference to the difference in the understanding of what is in itself without difference.

46. As the fire in matchwood is the cause of other fires, Word inherent in the mind is the cause of audible words.

47. The mind first grasps a word as fixed to a sense; then the organs aid it through the expression of sound.

48. As it is to sound that successive origin belongs, Meaning-Flash has no before or after. Non-succession, through the appearance of succession, comes to appear as multiple.

49. By means of the activity of water, the reflection, existing outside its original, imitates the water's movements. Such is the relation between Meaning-Flash and sound.

50. In knowledge one sees both the essence of knowing and the essence of the known; so also in Word one perceives the nature of the meaning as well as that of Word itself.

V. SUCCESSIONAL REALIZATION OF WORD AND OF ITS CONNECTION WITH THE OBJECT

51. It is as if the power known as Word has the nature of an egg. Its evolution, inherently active, achieves succession in stages.

52. As a form, the object of a unique idea, reproduces another [successively realized] form on the canvas, so too with Word, where also there is a triple phase [successive ideation, its culmination into one idea, then its successive realization].

53. As the speaker's mind, from the first moment, actualizes his intention only in words, the understanding of his hearers is also not formed except by words.

54. The generality of people do not perceive the meaning latent in those senses of words that are secondary to their usual sense, because that is their "other" meaning.

55. Light has two powers, of being seen and of causing to see. Likewise, in all words, these powers subsist separately.

56. Unless they become objects [of hearing], words do not disclose their essence. Unperceived, merely through their existence, they do not elucidate their meaning.

57. [The nature of words is apprehended only when they illustrate their object; it is only then that their sense becomes clear.] So when a word's meaning is not clear, one asks, "What did he say?" However, one does not similarly apprehend the nature of the sense organs when they illustrate their object.

58. The two distinct qualities in Word are perceived separately, and can therefore produce their different effects without conflicting.

VI. THE GRAMMATICAL PROCESSING OF WORDS

59. Though expressed by their own forms, words like "increase" become related to grammatical concepts that signify the quantitative "increase" of vowels in Sanskrit.

60. Based on the word [for the combustible substance] "$fire_1$" is the [denotative] term "$fire_2$". Connected with this aggregate of sounds "$fire_3$" is the grammatically functioning vocable "$fire_4$".

61. Only because it is pronounced, a word is not necessarily subjected to grammatical operations. [And when it is] its capacity for conveying other meanings [besides the usual ones] is not inhibited.

62. A word expressing quality is not grammatically processed merely because it happens to be pronounced, since its meaning depends [on the substance in which the quality inheres]. It is for this that the connection of grammatical operations with these meanings was devised.

63. In every term that is common to an object compared and an object of comparison, there is a quality in the object of comparison distinct [from that on which the comparison rests].

64. A quality is the cause that endows a substance with degree. When the quality is itself autonomously conceived, it is in turn endowed with degree by other qualities implanted in itself.

65. When a word established as denoting a quality is pronounced, another form [the denoted quality itself] becomes distinguished from it.

66. Its own form its object, the noun becomes the cause of the nominative and the possessive cases before becoming linked with the object it denotes.

67. Now that the word has an object, the nominative case is indicated by the noun. Then that meaning is overpassed to give rise to the possessive case, expressed in the word "his" or "its."

68. For some, Pāṇini's aphorism on "the proper form"[4] implies that the individual is the name of the genus. But it is the genus conjoined with the individual that is grammatically processed.

69. For others, the aphorism indicates that the individual

is the thing named. The grammatical rules refer to the individual designated by the genus.

VII. UNICITY OR MULTIPLICITY OF WORD

70. In the hypotheses of Word's nature being effectual or eternal, some believe Word to be unique, others hold it to be multiple.

71. Though the words be different, the identity of the letters is not changed; though the phrases be different, one perceives the identical word.

72. No word exists apart from its letters, no phrase apart from its letters and words.

73. 'There are no letters in a word, as there are no parts in letters. Apart from the phrase, words have no existence at all.

74. In practice, grammar is based on differing viewpoints. What is primary significance for some is the contrary for others.

75. Undivided in duration, Meaning-Flash invests itself with the duration of sounds. Difference in the conditions of its apprehension explains the difference in its diction.'

76. Different as the vowels—long, short and protracted—are from the eternal Meaning-Flash, the duration of basic sound is imputed to it fictitiously.

77. After Meaning-Flash has appeared, the secondary sounds produce differences in diction. But the nature of Meaning-Flash does not change.

VIII. HOW SOUND MANIFESTS WORD

78. The sounds produce a disposition (a) in the sense faculty, (b) in the words, or (c) in both—these are the Manifestationists' three theses.

79. [In the first thesis, the disposition] exists in the faculty only, as, say, concentration of mind or as lampblack [the former, improving the mental vision, enables the yogi to see more than the normal mind can; the latter, improving the eyesight, enables its user to see more than the normal eye can. In the second thesis, the disposition] exists in the object only, as in the perception of the smell [in oil on hot days, where the oil, not the faculty of smell, is heated].

80. [In the third thesis] if the eye operates through contact,

the light, as one finds, creates a disposition in both object and faculty. The same process works with sound.

81. Some hold that sound is perceived separately from Meaning-Flash; some, that sound is imperceptible; and some, that it is independent.

82. One is able to memorize a chapter in the Vedas, or a verse, through repetition, but the text is not perfectly represented in each repetition separately.

83. Word's innate form is exactly determined when Word is brought to light by sounds, and also by ideas of indescribable form but conducive to the apprehension of distinct form.

IX. PROCESS OF WORD DETERMINATION: SOUNDS AND MEANING-FLASH

84. A word is determined when its germ is produced by sounds and its maturity attained with the last sonance.

85. It is owing to his incapacity that a hearer believes verbal elements to exist in the intervals [between letters, words or phrases]. They are only means for apprehending [those words or phrases].

86. A semblance of distinction affects knowledge; difference constantly assails speech; an order of succession is impressed on words, and knowledge is founded on the known.

87. Just as the apprehension of previous numbers is a means of knowing the later ones, different though they be, so also the hearing of words other [than those one wishes to hear is a means of understanding the words one does wish to hear].

88. The manifestative verbal elements are different in letter, word or phrase. Wholly distinct through they are, they commingle their powers, so to speak.

89. In one's first impressions of an object, when viewed from afar or in darkness, one imagines it to be other than it is before discovering that it is different.

90. Similarly, when the causes of the manifestation of a phrase elicit a phrase [in itself impartible], it becomes, before anything else, an idea divisible into parts.

91. The transformation of milk [into butter] and of grains of paddy [into rice] follows a fixed order. The ideas in the hearers' minds also follow a fixed order.

92. Even if ideas were divisible, their structural division would derive from a succession in sounds. However, since

they are indivisible, the fiction of their divisibility is a device [enabling us to know them].

93. Some imagine Meaning-Flash to be a genus manifested through many individuals, and conceive the individuals themselves as its sounds.

94. Modified by the factors [of diction], the sound of the unmodified Meaning-Flash becomes the condition for its perception, and is comparable to light.

95. Manifestation is necessary not only in transient things, but must also be postulated in the eternal genera's supports.

96. Embodied things, as we see, are linked with a place. Yet, in spite of the conceived difference of place, there is no difference between sound and Word.

97. A relation of suitability is established between perceiving and perceived. Similarly, the relation between manifested and manifestation is fixed between Meaning-Flash and sound.

98. In common life, implanted in each substance, we find a determinate cause that reveals perceptions of the same species, like those of smell.

99. Transmitted objects imitate the difference of the media which transmit them, witness reflections in oil and water.

100. It is impossible that mountains and objects of like dimensions exist on the reflective surface of things so divergent in size as diamonds and mirrors.

101. Hence, since letters, words and phrases are undivided in duration, the duration of their diction, and their own proper duration, are distinguished through differentiations in sound.

102. Other thinkers say that Meaning-Flash is something born of the contact and separation of the organs [with the points of articulation], and that words are sounds born of Meaning-Flash.

103. Whether the duration of the sound is short or long, the duration of Meaning-Flash itself does not change. It is the series of other sounds [produced by a variety of acoustic factors] that waxes and wanes.

104. From a distance we perceive only the sound [not Meaning-Flash], as happens with a lamp [only its light being visible from afar, the lamp itself being too small to be seen]. But in the sounds of bells, for instance, the distinction [between sound and Meaning-Flash] is clearly perceived.

105. It is through collision between the substances [the breaths and the points of articulation] that the distinct long and protracted sounds are further lengthened. When the shock has subsided, the sounds which differentiate diction are born.

106. Even before the tremor of the organs has quieted, other sounds start up from Meaning-Flash, like flames from other flames.

X. THEORIES ON THE GENESIS OF WORD

107. Some postulate air, atoms or knowledge as the source of Word's origin. Divergencies in viewpoint are endless.

108. *Theory 1.* Endowed with activity through effort accordant with the speaker's will, and struck against the points of articulation, air becomes Word.

109. Aided by the causal power of someone able to increase velocity, the impact of this air shatters even strong bodies.

110. *Theory 2.* Possessing as they do all powers, the atoms, through separation and conjunction, transform themselves into shadows, heat, darkness—and Word.

111. As their power starts to become manifest, the ultimate atoms of words, assembled through an effort of articulation, start to amass like clouds.

112. *Theory 3.* To manifest itself, this inner knowledge, abiding in the subtle form of Word, transforms itself into an audible speech sound.

113. Word becomes mind. Ripened by an inner heat, it enters the air known as breath. It is then pronounced.

114. Inherent in the Inner Faculty principle and invested with its attributes, it transforms itself into Word through the virtue of that inner heat.

115. Loosening its knots through a diversity of audible sound, breath brings to light the letters and infuses itself into them.

116. *Theory 4.* Perpetually active, Word is not perceived because of its subtlety. Appropriate causes render it perceptible, as fanning does air.

117. *Theory 5.* The power of Word that exists in breath and the power that exists in the mind are transformed at the points of articulation and attain a differentiated state.

XI. UNIVERSALITY OF WORD, THE MEANS TO LIBERATION

118. The power immanent in words binds this universe together. It is this innately brilliant eye [Word], which flashes forth as manifold.

119. Articulated through words, the distinction between the primary notes of music acquires relief. Hence only by words are objects of all kinds ascertained.

120. As the knowers of Revelation have realized, this universe is a transformation of sound. It was from the Vedic utterances that the universe first evolved.

121. All practical behavior is dependent on Word. Even a baby has knowledge of it, through conceptual latencies acquired in earlier births.

122. Without the impulse of Word, the first movement of the vocal organs, the first upward exhalation of the breath and the first collision with the points of articulation would never have taken place.

123. No idea in this world but is accompanied by Word. All knowledge appears as impregnated with Word.

124. If knowledge were to lose its eternal form as Word, the light would not shine, for it is Word that engenders consciousness.

125. Word is the foundation of all the sciences, arts and skills. It is through dependence on Word that every object evolved is individualized.

126. Word is the outer and inner symbol of all living things. Consciousness in all things does not exceed the limits of Word.

127. Word incites all men to activity. With it gone, a man seems insensible, like a log or stone.

128. As in the state of difference, the agent employs Word to produce an effect, so in the state of indifference, Word itself subsists in the form of effect.

129. Self-produced or produced by another, it is the enunciated Word that brings objects into mutual relation. This is how convention is fixed and meaning established.

130. When an objective basis for a verbal expression is lacking—as in a "circle of fire" [an illusion produced by whirling a lighted torch]—the characteristics of that "thing" are derived from words alone.

131. They say that the inner Word is the speaker's own self. It is the Great Bull through which one desires for union [with the Supreme Self].

[*Revelation says:* It has four horns, three feet, two heads and seven hands. Thrice bound, the Bull bellows. The Great God has entered the mortal world.][5]

132. Perfect speech, then, is the realization of the Supreme Self. One who knows the principle of this activity attains the deathless state of the Brahman.

XII. INTERCONNECTED FORMS OF WORD: REVELATION, TRADITION, LOGIC AND GRAMMAR

133. No one admits any Tradition devoid [like Revelation] of a personal author. Were all forms of Tradition to disappear, their source, the Revealed Triad [the three Vedas] would endure.

134. When all schools of thought perish and no other authors exist [to perpetrate new ones], mankind will not transgress the duties that Revelation and Tradition prescribe.

135. If knowledge were innate, there would be no use for the sacred sciences. If religious duty prompts knowledge, then Revelation is its foundation.

136. When not in conflict with Revelation and the sacred sciences, logic is the sight for those unable to see, as the sense of a Vedic utterance is not obtained from its form alone.

137. Allusion to relevant factors without their being mentioned, the comprehension of a related sense in the obvious sense of the words, and the disclosure of a meaning through inferentially connected sentences—these and other manifold semantic niceties are discriminated through the aid of logic.

138. The logic implanted in man is none other but the power of words. Even those lacking Vedic knowledge find a rule inconsonant with the [nature of] Word unacceptable.

139. The powers of visible phenomena like color are restricted to fixed objects. Words are seen to have such powers too, as Vedic incantations in matters like the removal of poison.

140. As words have power in those matters, know that in the matter of merit, too, correct words have power; so those seeking salvation must speak correctly.

141. From Tradition comes all knowledge of unseen rewards. Tradition could also have told us the contrary.

142. One such tradition is grammar, aiming at a knowledge of correctness and fashioned by an unbroken line of educated men.

143. It is the supreme and wonderful abode of the triple speech—the Displayed, the Interjacent and the Visioning—diversified into innumerable qualities of sound.

144. Its continuing function is the treatment of words in analytical terms or as integral units. Those who know the nature of objects also perceive the power of words.

145. Revelation, as they say, is without beginning, interruption or author. Without interruption, too, is Tradition, the work of educated men.

146. Insight in Revelation is of things unfolded unifiedly. When they had comprehended the truth of its message, the sages, employing logical and didactic methods, composed the works of Tradition.

XIII. DEFORMATION OF WORD: BARBARISMS

147. The impurities found in the body, in speech and in the mind are purified by the teaching of medicine, grammar and theology.

148. A barbarism is an incorrect term used to denote a specific object [*goṇi,* for "cow"], where the correct form *gau* is required to be used.

149. The word *asva* ["dispossessed"] and *goṇi* ["sack"] are correct in other senses [but not in that of "horse" *aśva* or "cow" *gau*]. Correctness is everywhere determined by difference of context.

150. Through the use of inference, incorrect forms give rise to correct ones. Identifying themselves, so to speak, with the correct forms, the incorrect ones bring the sense of the Word to light.

151. The educated do not admit such barbarisms as synonyms for the correct words, since they are not directly expressive in the sciences of Tradition.

152. A child learning to speak lisps "ma-ma ma-ma." Those who know the correct word, however, elicit the certain meaning from the indistinct utterance.

153. Similarly, when the incorrect term is used instead of the correct one, the sense is mediately perceived through the correct form.

154. For rude speakers the barbarisms have become es-

tablished by unbroken usage, so that the correct forms have no meaning for them.

155. The divine Word [was pure in former eras, but in this dark age] has become sullied through the incompetence of its speakers. But those who deny the eternity of Word have opposite ideas on this point.

156. But though we postulate that there is no separation between incorrect and correct forms, to use the former while wishing to utter the latter is to employ a word with no meaning.

—*The Book of Phrases and Words*[6]

37
HARI VṚṢABHA

OM, the Undisputed Center of All Thought

BHARTṚ HARI

> The true knowledge, known as Purity, is acquired in one word. Unopposedly to any belief, it is proclaimed in the word OM.

HARI VṚṢABHA

This conception of the same Brahman, the omniformed, is not different from other conceptions believed to be contradictory. In fact, as the knowers of the Brahman declare:

> In none of its aspects does the Brahman cease to be uniform, or become conceptualized.

Further, all systems conceive Him to be indeficient, unconceptualizable—but as though conceptualized—and as the inner Person. The word OM is permissiveness to all opinions, the form of all Revelation, the constituent of all the Brahman's names, the cause of the rise and fall of all the systems, and the compaction of all conflicting meanings. This Brahman is everywhere permissive, everywhere prohibiting. However, the essence of its activity cannot be comprehended through its permissiveness or prohibition. As they say:

> He is neither one nor not-one; also, neither two nor not-two. Those who live on the plane of action think Him irregular in all things, while those who live on the level of thought perceive Him to be regular.
>
> —*Commentary on "The Book of Phrases and Words"* by Bhartṛ Hari[7]

XV. ANCIENT VEDANTA, or *PURĀTANA VEDĀNTA*

See Schemes 9 and 24

It is perhaps possible to place Bādarāyaṇa, arguably the world's first systematic theologian—assuming that theology is systematic reason attempting to understand the message of Revelation—as early as the fifth century B.C.[8] Indeed his synthesis seems to have been known to the *Gītā* itself:

> It [the body–Self relationship] has often been sung by the sages in hymns, each in its separate way, and in aphorisms on the Brahman, well-reasoned and conclusive.[9]

So well-reasoned and conclusive was Bādarāyaṇa's synthesis of Hindu theology, embodied in the *Aphorisms on the Brahman* (see Scheme 9), that no one attempted to supersede it, and it came to be considered the supreme norm of sacred science. It was at once simple, rigorous, and accommodating of a variety of interpretations. Most of its 564 aphorisms are deliberate allusions to the significant pronouncements of Revelation, and so cannot be understood without the latter. No theological work in history has been so commented on, and no system deferring to the Vedic standard was held to have achieved the status of a system unless it possessed a commentary on the great *Aphorisms on the Brahman* (Selections 38 and 39).

With Bādarāyaṇa started a line of theologians who came to be called the Ancient Masters of the Vedanta. All the work of most of them has perished; of some a few fragments remain. Their thoughts were expressed in at least two ways:

1. As comments on the largest and most quoted Upaniṣads, the *Chāndogya* and the *Bṛhadāraṇyaka.* Such theologians were Ṭaṅka, or Brahma Nandin (Selections 40–42), Dramiḍa (Selections 42–46) and Bhartṛ Prapañca (Selections 50–64). Bhartṛ Prapañca (c. fifth century A.D.) seems to have been

one of the Ancient Vedanta's most fecund and architectonic thinkers (see Scheme 24), and it is tantalizing to think of what the systems of the other Ancient Masters must have been.

2. As comments on Bādarāyaṇa's *Aphorisms* themselves. Prince among the commentators was Bodhāyana (or Upavarṣa), of uncertain date, whose work was said to have been vast. Copies of it began to become rare in the tenth century, when Rāmānuja, one of the few who read them, professed (as did Bhāskara) to renew its teachings in briefer form, and thus to restore the Way of the Ancient Masters (see Selection 74).

38

BĀDARĀYAṆA

The Sum of Vedanta Theology

TOPIC 1: THEOLOGY, THE INQUIRY INTO THE BRAHMAN

1. Now, then, is our inquiry into the Brahman.

> Yes, the Self must be seen, heard of, thought about, and meditated upon.[10]

TOPIC 2: THE BRAHMAN, OBJECT OF THEOLOGY

2. Where the world's states of creation, maintenance and dissolution are from—that is the Brahman.

> Where these beings originate from; in which, once originated, they live; into which, on dying, they dissolve—try to know it, it is the Brahman.[11]

TOPIC 3: REVELATION, THE NORM FOR ASCERTAINING THE OBJECT

3. Revelation is our source for the knowledge of the Brahman.

> I seek Him, that Person proclaimed in the Upaniṣads.[12]

TOPIC 4: EXEGESIS, THE MODE OF INTERPRETING THE NORM

4. That knowledge is from a concordance of the source's concepts.

> This is a triad—concepts, bodies and actions. Of the concepts is Speech. Speech is their Hymn, their origin, as from it all concepts arise. It is their Song, their evenness, as it is even with all concepts. It is their Brahman, their support, as it supports all concepts.[13]

TOPIC 5: INTELLIGIBILITY, OBJECTIVE OF THE EXEGESIS

5. The Brahman is not inexpressible, as it is an object of knowledge.

> The word that all the Vedas reveal, that all penances proclaim, and in yearning for which men live as celibate students—I shall tell you that word briefly: It is OM.[14]

6. 'Can it be that the object of our inquiry is really the soul?'

No. Because, in referring to it, Revelation uses the word "Self."

> That subtle essence is the inbeing of all this existence. It is Reality. It is the Self. You are It, Śvetaketu.[15]

7. Revelation also declares that a man committed to it attains liberation.

> When a man really perceives that Self, that God, the Lord of what was and what will be, he is not revulsed.[16]

8. Neither does Revelation declare it undesirable.

> In Him the heavens, the earth and the sky are woven, and the mind with all the Breaths. Know

> Him alone to be the unique Self, renounce all other words! He is the bridge of immortality.[17]

9. Besides, the soul enters into that Self.

> When a man sleeps, my dear boy, he unites with the Real, he goes to his own.[18]

10. The teaching is uniform in this regard.
11. And so Revelation proclaims the Brahman [the knowable, the supreme].

> That is fullness, this is fullness; fullness proceeds from fullness. When one takes fullness out of fullness, fullness remains.[19]

39

BĀDARĀYAṆA

The Brahman's "Equivalent" Names

1. THE JOYFUL

12. The Brahman is the Joyful, because Revelation, when referring to Him, repeatedly uses the word "joy."

> Now this is an inquiry into joy. [Then, describing the degrees of the intensity of joy, from the human to the divine, using the word "joy" over twenty times, the passage concludes.] A man who knows this, when he departs this world, passes over to the Self who is the fullness of food, the Self who is the fullness of breath, the Self who is the fullness of mind, the Self who is the fullness of knowledge, the Self who is the fullness of joy.[20]

13. 'Is it not true that the suffix *-ful* in "joyful" only signifies "having" joy ["made" of joy], and so cannot refer to the Brahman?'

No, because *-ful* here signifies "fullness" of joy [and so denotes the Brahman].

14. And the Brahman is also proclaimed the cause of joy.

> He is truly Savor itself. One who relishes this Savor is filled with joy. If this pervasive Being were not joy, who could exhale, who inhale? He alone is the cause of joy.[21]

15. [The "Joy" Scripture] the *Taittirīya Upaniṣad* celebrates the Brahman as joyful both in its hymnic and in its ritual portions.

16. The fullness of joy is not the other self, the soul, because he is unfit to be that.

17. And because the soul and the Self are declared to be different.

> When he finds fearlessness and security in that invisible, impersonal, ineffable and independent Being, then he will have attained fearlessness. But if he makes the slightest dent within it, he will have cause to fear. But such fear is only for one who is wise in his own opinion.[22]

18. Creation [which ensues from this fullness of joy] cannot be inferred [as the unconscious Matter of the Sankhya can], since that creation springs from His will.

> He willed "Let me be many, let me generate!" Then He kindled with heat. Being kindled, He emitted everything, whatever exists.[23]

19. Revelation also teaches the union of the soul with the Brahman.

> The Brahman is reality, knowledge, infinity. He who knows it to be hidden in the abyss of the heart, in the highest heaven, he relishes all joys along with the wise Brahman.[24]

2. THE SOLAR INDWELLER

20. The Golden Man standing in the sun is the Brahman [the supreme Self], because he is declared to have the Brahman's attributes.

> Now that Golden Man seen within the sun—he has a golden beard, golden hair, and is all gold, to the tips of his nails. His eyes are like the red lotus. "Up"

is his name, because he is *up* above all sin. One who knows him also rises up above all sin.[25]

21. And, from declarations of difference, we know that there is another self, the soul.

He Who stands in the sun, but is other than the sun; Whom the sun does not know, and Whose body the sun is; Who controls the sun within—He is yourself, the controller of your soul, the immortal.[26]

3. ETHER

22. The Brahman is ether, because it has all His marks.

[Said Śālāvatya] "What is the origin of the world?"
"Ether," replied Jaivali. "All these things emerge from ether and disappear into it. Ether is greater than them all. Ether is the ultimate support."[27]

4. BREATH

23. For the same reason, the Brahman is breath.

[Said Prastrotṛ] "Which is that god?"
"Breath," replied Uṣasti. "All things merge into breath, all things emerge from breath."[28]

5. LIGHT

24. The Brahman is light—mentioned as this light is with reference to the Being Whose feet are all things.

The Sacred Incantation, Gāyatrī, is all this being—whatever exists. It is four-footed . . . As the *Ṛgveda* declares in a verse

"Such is its greatness. Even greater is the Person. His feet are all beings. Three of his feet are the immortal in heaven."[29]

[The passage then goes on to treat of the following identities or associated concepts: Gāyatrī—ether—ether within the heart—five gates of the heart—five doorkeepers of the heart—five doorkeepers of heaven—the light above the heaven—the light within man.]

> Now: the light which shines above this heaven—with the worlds that have none above them, and which themselves are the highest, being everywhere and in every way behind it—that light is absolutely the same as the one within man.[30]

6. THE SACRED INCANTATION, THE *GĀYATRĪ*

25. 'Since the reference is to the Incantation, it is not to the Brahman.'

Wrong. The Incantation is a precept for fixing the mind on the Brahman. Hence the similarity between them [as having four feet, in both physical and metric senses].

26. Brahman being the Incantation, "all beings" having aptly been designated as His "feet."

27. 'But the teaching on the Brahman and the Incantation is at variance [the Brahman light shines "above this heaven" and the Gāyatrī is "in heaven"], and cannot refer to the same thing.'

There is no conflict between the two [the same Brahman, in different aspects, can be in heaven and above it].

7. THE IMMANENT BREATH

28. The Brahman is breath, as we can infer from the passage that speaks of Indra as being breath.

> Pratardana, Divodāsa's son, by his fighting and his valor actually arrived at Indra's favorite residence. There Indra said to him, "Pratardana, let me give you a gift." Pratardana replied, "Choose a gift for me yourself, what you judge most beneficial for man." Indra said, "No one chooses for someone else: make your own choice." Replied Pratardana, "Such a gift is no gift for me."
>
> But Indra did not swerve from the truth: Indra *is* the truth. He said. "Know me alone. I judge that most beneficial for man, that he know me" . . .
>
> . . . Indra said, "I am breath, innate knowledge. Meditate on me as life and immortality. Life is breath, breath life. Breath is also immortality . . . He who meditates on me as life and immortality,

> gets his full life in this world and immortality and imperishableness in the world of heaven . . .
>
> . . . In a chariot, the felly is placed on the spokes, and the spokes on the nave. So also objects are placed on knowers, and knowers on breath. That breath, innately knowledge, is joyful, ageless and immortal. Good actions do not increase him, nor evil actions diminish. He alone makes a man do a good deed and brings him up from these worlds. He alone makes a man do a bad deed and leads him down from the worlds. He is the world's guardian, the ruler, the Lord of all. Let it be known that He is my Self, yes, let all know that He is my Self![31]

29. 'The breath in this passage is not the Brahman, because the speaker, Indra, is referring to himself.'

The passage is full of Indra's intimate connection with the Self!

30. The teaching that breath and the Brahman are identical is based on scriptural insight, as happened with Vāmadeva the sage.

> In the beginning, the Brahman was this. He knew only Himself, as "I am the Brahman." Then from Him all came to be. Then any of the gods who awakened became the Brahman in fact. So also the sages; so also men. The sage Vāmadeva perceived It and exclaimed, "I became the moon, I became the sun!" So now, anyone who has the knowledge "I am the Brahman" becomes all this. Even the gods lack the power to stop this from happening, for He is their Self too.[32]

31. 'The passage has to do with the marks of the soul and the principal breath, and hence not with the Brahman.'

You are mistaken. The passage propounds a triple worship [to the soul, the principal breath and the Brahman]. Brahman is the basis of the other two, in virtue of their connection with it [so the passage ultimately has to do with the Brahman].

—*Aphorisms on the Brahman*[33]

40
ṬAṄKA
(OR BRAHMA NANDIN)

Meditation on the Self

UPANIṢADIC TEXT

All this is the Brahman.[34]

One must realize that all this is the Self, because everything finds fulfillment in It.

41
ṬAṄKA

The Attainment of the Self

UPANIṢADIC TEXT

> One who sees this [the fact that being is the Self], does not see death, illness or pain. One who sees this, sees everything and obtains everything everywhere.[35]

The Self is reached through discrimination, dispassion, discipline, ritual, virtue, non-dejection and joylessness.

Discrimination is bodily purity due to food that is untainted in kind, source and producer. *Dispassion* is detachment from desires. *Discipline* is repeated meditation on the "Verbality" Scripture:

> Through a single lump of clay all that is fashioned from clay is known. The changes are only verbal, a mere matter of name: only clay is the reality.[36]

Ritual is the ability to perform actions like the Five Great

Sacrifices. The *virtues* are truth, honesty, compassion, generosity, non-violence and freedom from desire. Dejection is the mental gloom brought about by misery and by reverses in space and time, and by the memory of painful things. Opposed to it is *non-dejection.* Merriment is contentment that is contrary to dejection. Its opposite is *non-merriment* [or *joylessness*].

—Fragments from the *Sentences on the "Chāndogya Upaniṣad"*

42

ṬAṄKA AND DRAMIḌA

God's Body

UPANISADIC TEXT

> Now that Golden Man seen within the sun—he has a golden beard, golden hair, and is all gold, to the tips of his nails. His eyes are like the red lotus.[37]

ṬAṄKA

'Can it be that His body is simulated in order to favor meditation, since He has power over minds?'

Rather, His is a body that exceeds the grasp of sense, since as has been shown, the Inner Faculty perceives it.

DRAMIḌA

Neither is the body purely magical. The Creator's body cannot be anything but genuine. But no eye can grasp it. Only an unsullied mind, possessed of other means of knowledge, can apprehend it. In the words of Revelation:

> He is not grasped by the eye, by speech, or by the other senses, but through austerities and ritual. A man perceives him when, with mind purified by the clarity of knowledge, he contemplates on him as the partless being.[38]

We have not been taught that formless deity has form, and Revelation speaks of things just as they are. In other places the Witness is described in these words:

> And the appearance of that Person [in the Right Eye, the essence of being] is like a saffron-colored vestment, like white wool, like cochineal, like a flame of fire, like a white lotus, and like sudden lightning.[39]

And:

> I know that great Person beyond the darkness, splendorous as the sun. To know Him is to pass beyond death; there is no other way.[40]

43
DRAMIḌA
God's Power

UPANIṢADIC TEXT

> Through that imperishable Being's command, Gārgī, some rivers flow to the east from the White Mountains, others to the west or to any other quarter.[41]

At His command the wind moves, the rivers flow. He marks their limits, and they leap like lustful rams.

44
DRAMIḌA
God's Power and Compassion

Sustained by His will, these worlds do not fall or explode.

When He knows a man to be obedient to His commands, He, the wise and skilled Lord, will make him prosper.

—Fragments from the *Commentary on the "Bṛhadāraṇyaka Upaniṣad"*

45
DRAMIḌA

God's Exalted Omnipotence

Let us take the example of a worldly king who finds himself in a fearsome place fraught with danger and thick with mosquitoes. Fanned as his body is by flabella, he is not only unaffected by these discomforts, but busies himself with the care of his loyal subjects, and has ready delightful things, like perfumes, that all his people can enjoy.

Likewise, the Lord of the worlds, the flabella of His omnipotence waving, is not touched by deficiencies. He cares for the worlds—the worlds of Brahmā and the other gods—and has at His command delights that all creatures can experience.

46
DRAMIḌA

The Perfection of the Liberated

Through union with the deity, bodiless though a man be, he will, in deific fashion, find all his goals realized.

—Fragments from the *Commentary on the "Chāndogya Upaniṣad"*

47

BODHĀYANA

Connection of the Theologies of Ritual and the Brahman

Following on the acquisition of the knowledge of Works, the desire to know the Brahman arises.

48

BODHĀYANA

Brahman the Light

Freed from worldly concerns, the Brahman is like light.

49

BODHĀYANA

The Mystical Honey Science

UPANIṢADIC PASSAGE

> The sun is the honey of the gods. Heaven is its cross-beam, the sky the hive [that hangs from it], and the rays the bee's eggs.[42]

The gods are capable of the mystical Honey Science, since the Brahman may be sought for in everything.

—Fragments from the *Gloss on the "Aphorisms on the Brahman"*[43]

50

BHARTṚ PRAPAÑCA

Unity in Manifoldness

There exists an unmanifold unity in the manifold, as the sea in its waves.

51

BHARTṚ PRAPAÑCA

Duality and Nonduality

In the world of the dual, everything happens through something else. But here, in the universe of the nondual, all forms of existence are non-different, so everything is instantly realized through the nature of the Self.

52

BHARTṚ PRAPAÑCA

The Highest State

UPANIṢADIC PASSAGE

> Then there is His name "the Truth of the truth."
> The Breaths are the truth, and He is their truth.[44]

It is through connection with Him that the Breaths are the

truth . . . The Breaths are connaturally intelligent, and are not a complex of concepts and bodies. Through contact with extrinsic conditions, they are conceived as being effect and instrument, concepts and bodies—only in order to be specified.

So that truth has been elucidated. We now proceed to speak of the essence of the intelligent Self, explicating it from the truth. In that [highest] state the differentiations of someone being an experiencer and others being connaturally intelligent Breaths is non-existent. This difference, caused by the conceptual and corporeal complex, inheres in a substratum. When all this truth has been clarified, it is through inward penetration that the intelligent Self is described. All that [mutiplicity]—identical as it is with the intelligent Self—is [referred to] for the sake of description only. The essence of that Person who is essentially intelligent is explained . . . In the matter of the embodied and the bodiless all forms are consumed. Here the means whereby the Supreme Self, now in a state of differentiation, is realized—that is the form, transcending the Five Elements, which Revelation desires to indicate.

53
BHARTṚ PRAPAÑCA
Identity of the Brahman and the Soul

The Supreme Brahman is intelligence and the intelligent soul is consubstantial with it.

54
BHARTṚ PRAPAÑCA
Restoration of the Sense of All Being

Understanding is sometimes ephemeral . . . and sometimes obscured by ignorance. This ignorance is the incomprehension of the sentence "I am really all this." The understanding of it is eternal in the Supreme Self . . . but ephemeral in the other transmigrant self of obscured intelligence. This being so, one who has lost the sense of all being through ignorance, realizes it again through the vision of the universal Self.

55

BHARTṚ PRAPAÑCA

Perspicacity

The outward actions of that Person inhere in faculties like the mind . . . Then the mental disposition of action draws near and enters into Him. The discernment between them has been explained. But ignorance inheres in His own knowledge. Distorting that knowledge, ignorance applies it to a contrary apprehension of things. Through the mediation of the mind, this special kind of knowledge inspissates, and functions as an outer light for mundane activity. Its discrimination from the aggregate of factors caused by *attachment* has also been explained. To be explained now is discrimination from the aggregate formed by *ignorance*. Exteriorly based, attachment moves through the doors of the objects and the senses, and so enters the Self.

56

BHARTṚ PRAPAÑCA

Mental Dispositions

Desire is the fruit of action, but is in fact a conceptual latency. According as the mental disposition which produces action is, so is the fruit of the intelligent self. With that fruit concentrated in itself, the mental disposition becomes individualized. Imbued with it the intelligent Self, as happens, craves with desire. And knowledge is what sets the limits to mental disposition, and the transformations of action conform to this knowledge . . . And ignorance is a knowledge that perceives contrarily [or perceives things contrary to what they are]. As has been said, it is exterior to the intelligent Self. The mental disposition controlled by the Self destroys action. Hence desire, action, mental disposition and knowledge, being interrelated, have a unitary meaning. So one desires the objects comprising duality through mental dispositions and perceives them through ignorance.

57

BHARTṚ PRAPAÑCA

Desires

Desires [in the scriptural phrase][45] are inherently saffron-hued. These desires, defined by their saffron-hue, are situated in the external heart. It is there that they take their birth. Inherent in a seed, a shoot germinates when implanted in the earth. Likewise the heart is the seedbed of the things that inhere in the understanding.

58

BHARTṚ PRAPAÑCA

The Form of Light

"He mounts higher, and arrives at a world beyond sorrowlessness."[46] These words refer to a state that subsists at this time in the Self as unmingled light . . . Its innate luminosity is due to Its discrepancy [from all else]. A distinctive lack of knowledge of the Self belongs to ignorance, and ignorance is said to be fear caused by the sight of multiplicity. . . . Opposed to it is knowledge, expressed in words such as "I am really all this." This churned-up vision of oneness is always pure and luminous. It is ever blazing in its nature as distinctive knowledge. When this knowledge does not arise there is absence of discernment.

'But such a knowledge would really be darkness, not light.'

[You cannot be serious.] The form of light can with great effort be made to reveal itself, and the orthodox teaching is settled in this regard. One therefore abides in light through one's own self.

59

BHARTṚ PRAPAÑCA

The Ever Seeing Self

UPANIṢADIC PASSAGE

> And when it is said that [in dreamless slumber] he does not see, yet he is seeing.[47]

At that moment He is constantly seeing. But His distinctive knowledge is not manifest, so long as qualities exist in their subjects. For wherever there is fire, there is heat, and wherever there is a seer, there sight is: so there is no exception.

And the seer is eternal. His destroyer is not seen to flourish anywhere. All being the Self, all being nondual, His destruction by someone else is not possible, and hence never happens. For the destroyer is indivisible from the Self. Hence the Self's destruction never comes about. Indestructible, the Self is eternal—and this eternal seer's eternal attribute, sight, is ever present. So He is continually seeing with His undeviating sight; this is indisputable . . .

'If He is ever seeing, how is it that He sees nothing?'

Listen as to whether He sees or not . . . He does indeed see. But there is no second object in relation to which He can manifest His distinctive knowledge. It would not be distinguished otherwise. If that other distinct thing were to be there he would see it. But there is no second thing. Therefore as the power of seeing exists He is ever seeing. But He finds nothing to see, and so does not perceive it. Like a fire which though blazing does not set anything incombustible ablaze.

60

BHARTṚ PRAPAÑCA

Illuminating Knowledge

In this world of duality the distinctive knowledge, beaming like the sun's rays—shines around as though on a waking world. Even when that knowledge exists, it may grasp the perceptible contrarily to what it really is.

61

BHARTṚ PRAPAÑCA

All Is Fire

Speech is divine, and the earth, because of its hardness and density, is a tenebrous body. Speech abides in dual form, earthy and fiery. There is only one divinity, fire, spiritual and elemental . . . the divine is all fire. Absorbing each deity singly, it absorbs all deities into itself . . . hence . . . of the kind that speech, elemental or spiritual, of such a kind. . . . The deity of the earth subsists in various places in several modes. He is that fire . . . seen universally, in every particular subject, in the form of earth or of speech.

62

BHARTṚ PRAPAÑCA

A Conflux of Deities

While from the heart, as from a ball of turmeric, the arteries branch out all around, this subtle deity is implanted in the heart's inner recesses. Every single deity does likewise, for all are linked as cause and effect. When a deity has the function of seeing, all the other deities depend upon it for that function. If a deity has to do with the arteries, it is present there embodying the power of the other deities. As the whole is contained in each member, that deity is spiritual, as it is elemental and divine. . . . As in the case of the spiritual, the arteries are all over the body, so are the arteries that bear the breath in that spiritual Person, described as innately elemental, replete with air. This Person, issuing out of the body, stands pervading the whole earth. Just as in the spiritual order, fulfillment in each member is through the whole, in the same way, is fulfillment in the Cosmic Soul, member by member, in the realms of the spiritual, the elemental and the divine [or the internal, the external and the superhuman].

63

BHARTṚ PRAPAÑCA

Two Kinds of Liberation

Yājñavalkya attained fearlessness and did not forfeit it.[48] But not directly. There are two kinds of liberation: the kind directly realized in this body, is, as they say, not absolute [or Brahmanic] liberation, not absorption into the Brahman. When, after the death of the body, one is absorbed into the

Brahman—that is the second liberation, the one we all hope for.

64

BHARTṚ PRAPAÑCA

Vision of Nonduality

'By the sight of duality all its effects are extirpated, and are no longer germs for appropriating the Subtle Elements. A man is fulfilled by that sight alone, as he has accomplished scriptural teaching. So there is no purpose in the vision of nonduality.'

What is extirpated by the vision of duality are the effects of attachment. Attachment is the stuff of which beings are made. It is extirpated so far as desire is concerned, and desire is related to actions. The dual self is distinct from the intelligent Self and is immanent in the objects of the transmigratory world. "It has to be absorbed into the Brahman; it has to be dissolved." This command, for realizing the unrealized, will hold up to the moment of dissolution. Hence the declaration of oneness. And with ignorance eradicated, the limiting factor would be removed, and not the destructive functioning or attachment of actions. With attachment and actions uneliminated, knowledge will have to be employed once more, since the two are mutually inseparable. For while impurity persists, the vision of nonduality is impossible.

—Fragments from the *Commentary on the "Bṛhadāraṇyaka Upaniṣad"*[49]

XVI. CONDITIONED DIFFERENCE-IN-IDENTITY, or *AUPĀDHIKABHEDĀBHEDA*

See Scheme 25

After the Nondualists had superposed their novel interpretation on the *Aphorisms on the Brahman,* the old Difference-in-Identity school seems to have been thrown into disarray—when Bhāskara (c. ninth century) came to its rescue, defining its logic with a simplicity and cogency never equaled (Selection 65). He employed this logic to develop the theology of negation (or *apophatic* theology; Selection 66), whose principle, together with that of its complement, the theology of affirmation (*cataphatic* theology) had been formulated probably in the ninth century B.C., by Yājñavalkya, the sage in whose mind Vedic speculation can be said to have consummated:

> Now, then, is the teaching "It is not, no, it is not."
> There is nothing higher that the saying "It is not."
> Then there is His name "the Truth of the truth."
> The Breaths are the truth, and He is their truth.[50]

Apophatic theology was to become the basic theology of the Orthodox Church, developed there in great splendor, especially by the sublime Dionysius, who thus states its principle, along with that of cataphatic theology:

> *δέον ἐπ' αὐτῇ καὶ πάσας τὰς τῶν ὄντων τιθέναι καὶ καταφάσκειν θέσεις, ὡς πάντων αἰτίᾳ καὶ πάσας αὐτὰς κυριώτερον ἀποφάσκειν ὡς ὑπὲρ παντα ὑπερούσῃ . . .*

> While it is right to attribute to and *affirm* in the Cause all the positive characteristics of beings, since It is the Cause of them all, it is even more authentic to *deny* them of It, since It is transcendent above them all. And one must not believe that the denials

are opposed to the affirmations, but rather that the Cause, transcending as It does all removing and positing, is above all privation too.[51]

65
BHĀSKARA
The Logic of Difference-in-Identity

BĀDARĀYAṆA'S APHORISM

From reasoning and from other revealed teaching [it can be shown that the effect pre-exists in its cause].

I. DISSENTIENT VIEW

'What then is the proof of the theory of the existence of the effect in the cause?'

The proof that a pot—not curds or rabbit horns—arises from a lump of earth. If a pot that had not existed were to arise, they also could, since there is no differentiation in [kinds of] non-existence.

'Can it be that the determination to one particular effect is due to the determination of the causal power?'

No, I say. I ask the objector repeatedly, how is it that the causal power comes to have that particular determination? As non-existence is undifferentiated, how is the potency of the lump of earth determined to one particular effect? If anyone, explaining the reason for that determination, speaks of the effect's existence in the cause, such a person will not have frustrated the purpose of my polemic. We must therefore conclude that an already existent effect comes into existence.

'But as you admit that the effect is existent as the cause, the action of producing it will be to no purpose.'

Can it be that the action is only to manifest something previously existent?

'Is this manifestation existent or non-existent? If existent, the potter's activity will be to no avail. On the other alternative, you will be accepting the theory that the effect does not exist in its cause.'

II. ORTHODOX VERDICT

I answer: the effect is decidedly existent. And why? For the reason that the effect is only the cause arriving at one state or another. There is no absolute difference between a state and its possessor: there is no absolute difference, for instance, between a cloth and its whiteness, related as they are as qualified and quality; they are in fact the same thing. And there is no substance without qualities and no qualities without a substance, for such is given in experience. Experience is the criterion for deciding about the condition of Difference and Identity. Those who apply this criterion perceive the difference and identity of cause and effect. And Difference is an attribute of Identity. Identity exists as the mighty sea; the selfsame existing in the form of the waves is called Difference. Waves are not seen in rocks, for they are the powers of the sea. Between powers and their possessors both identity and difference are observed: differentiations in fire, for instance, are its powers of burning and shining; differentiations in the wind are the modes of breathing.

Everything is therefore innately one and manifold, neither wholly indivisible nor wholly divisible.

Our position therefore has a triple justification—from experience, inference and Revelation. Your position has no justification in particular.

'To what texts of Revelation do you allude?'

The following:

> In the beginning, my dear boy, there was only this being, one, with no second.[52]

The word "this" indicates the effect's existence in causal form at the time of the world's dissolution.

If the cause of the manifestation of the effect is the proximity of factors like the potter's wheel, that manifestation, or proximity, or even the effect's concealment—all these causes have other causes, and they, in turn, others, and as the world is without beginning, this regress is without contradiction. And since experience is caused by merit and demerit [in previous births], the manifestation or concealment of the salvific means is dependent on merit and demerit. All this is beyond cavil. Hence each of these states of manifestation and concealment prevails through oversetting the other. . . .

We must also here examine the metaphor alluded to in Revelation. The impartite minuteness of the banyan seed, passing through one state after another, is found to have attained a vast bulk. This is seen in the text:

> From that subtile essence [latent in the seed] which you cannot see, my dear boy—from that very essence this great banyan tree exists.[53]

As such a phenomenon is observed, it is not without basis, just as virility, which is real, becomes manifest in youth; else even a eunuch would be capable of virility.

III. CRITIQUE OF THE DOCTRINE OF THE NON-EXISTENT EFFECT

On the other hand, how is origin from nothing to be described? We never see that the non-existent has power to give birth, or that rabbit horns come into being. As for the production of the pot from the potter's rod and wheel—is its cause's capacity eternal or non-eternal? If eternal, then the origin of the effect, unrelated to any other cause, must be eternal also. If it is non-eternal, then the capacity itself needs to be produced by some other, and that by still another: and so there will be an infinite regress. And if these capacities are infinite, we shall never arrive at an unambiguous material cause at all.

You might here suppose that though the capacities are eternal, they bring about the effect through the aid of auxiliaries. To that I say: if the effect arises through the assistance of the auxiliaries, as it arises other auxiliaries will be needed [to explain the previous ones], and thus there will be an infinite regress. And if the causal capacities are eternal, the effect will be eternal too, and thus the fallacy I alluded to will apply. Is it that those who seek gold never apprehend the bracelet, the two being wholly distinct? [Is it not rather that effect-bracelet is really identical with the cause-gold?] And is it that a piece of cloth five *pālas* in weight must have a very great length? Denying as it does the pre-existence of effect in cause, the Atomist system, alien to Revelation and to inference, is therefore also illogical. Similarly too, the [Buddhist] system which propounds the nullity of the means of knowledge, and teaches that existence proceeds from non-existence, both being null—such a system must be taken to be disproved.

The logic of our theory is further clarified by Revelation:

> In the beginning, my dear boy, there was only this being, one, with no second. But others say that in the beginning there was only non-being, one, with no second—and that from non-being being arose.

The word "non-being" means "another being." Revelation goes on to say:

> How is this possible, dear boy. . . . How can being rise from non-being?

And the query is answered:

> In the beginning, my dear boy, there was *only* this being.[54]

IV. CONFIRMATION OF THE DOCTRINE OF THE EXISTENT EFFECT

BĀDARĀYAṆA'S APHORISM

And like a cloth.

As a cloth sometimes rolled up, sometimes unrolled, is not different, so also the cause is not different in its effectual or in its causal form.

BĀDARĀYAṆA'S APHORISM

Or as with the Vital Breaths.

As the wind, restrained in its modes of Ascendant, Descendent, Equilibrious, Pervasive and Vertical Breaths by breath control in the navel and the nose, abides in the heart in its essential form—but when freed from that restraint becomes fivefold—so is the Brahman.

—*Commentary on the "Aphorisms on the Brahman"*[55]

66
BHĀSKARA
Principles of Apophatic Theology

BĀDARĀYAṆA'S APHORISM

> For Revelation denies the characteristics of the Self defined so far, and has yet more to declare.

And now we must turn our attention to the Brahman, Who is unhampered by the configuration of the universe, and is signified as reality and consciousness.

> The Brahman has indeed two forms, the embodied and the unembodied;

Beginning with these words, and going on to speak of the saffron-colored and other forms [of the supreme Person], Revelation proceeds:

> Now, then, is the teaching "It is not, no, it is not."
> There is nothing higher than the saying "It is not."[56]

These words signify the Being who is innately pure and free. The word "embodied" refers to the triad of embodied realities [mentioned in the passage just quoted: mortal, solid and definite], and "disembodied" to the dyad of beings [air and sky]. And the saffron-colored nature of the soul is formed of conceptual latencies. Hence the denial, emphasized by repetition—excluding the pentad of gross and subtle elements, and everything formed of conceptual latencies which arises from the unconscious, or is virtually devoid of the Self—discloses that Self's essence in its purity. It does not affirm the nonexistence of the world, because its words do not have that intent.

Then Bādarāyaṇa says: "Revelation denies the characteristics defined so far," that is to say, the characteristics—the conditioning by the double limiter—of the Person discussed so far. It "has yet more to declare," in other words, there is even more to be known about the Brahman, which is not something fanciful or of little consequence. Here the words are applied to the Immutable. There is no judgement on the Brahman other than that expressed in the words "It is not," which are a negation of the universe. It is with such intention that the words "It is not, no, it is not" have been used, and such is the meaning of Revelation.

To the words "Revelation has yet more to declare," one must relate the subject of names. Now, the names to which Revelation alludes are:

> Then there is His name "the Truth of the truth." The Breaths are the truth, and He is their truth.[57]

But there are some [the Nondualists, commenting on Bādarāyaṇa's *Aphorisms*] who begin a new section with the present aphorism "For Revelation denies the characteristics of the Self defined so far" [thus contravening the practice of the ancient Vedantic school]. They raise the question: 'Do the words "It is not, no, it is not" abrogate the Brahman, or the complex of the notional and corporeal?' They then establish, as their dogma [the answer]: 'It is an abrogation of the conceptual and corporeal, not of the Brahman.'[58]

But this is untenable, as there is no room for any doubt. The principle [laid down by Revelation]:

> If a man knows the Brahman as non-existent, he is as though non-existent himself; if he knows the Brahman as existent, we know him as being existent himself[59]

affirms Him to exist. And this is how He is to be understood. It is by means of such emphasis that all the Upaniṣads teach the nondual Brahman, through eliminating the multiple configuration of the universe. The Upaniṣads, from beginning to end, affirm the Brahman's existence. This aphorism is therefore to show that the Brahman's nature—defined by reality, knowledge and infinity—is not the nature of the universe. It is rather that He acquires a distinct nature comprising that very reality, knowledge and infinity. There reality is the subject, and consciousness its attribute. A relation of attributes to non-existent subjects is impossible. Indistinct like fire and its heat, the attribute is also distinct [from its subject], without being a distinct thing. The form of consciousness, which has the characteristics of the sky, is devoid of specificity. It has no end, and is hence endless, or eternal, with an eternity that is essential, spatial and temporal; it is also eternal in the sense that it is distinct from objects like pots, the earth and the clouds. Thus it is one unique thing, since difference in qualities and subject does not mean difference in nature. For there is no substance void of attributes, nor attribute devoid of substance.

—*Commentary on the "Aphorisms on the Brahman"*[60]

XVII. INDIVISIBLE NONDUALISM, or *AVIBHĀGĀDVAITA*

See Schemes 26 and 27

Vijñāna Bhikṣu (sixteenth century) bears witness to the vigor of the Vedic tradition at a time when the Tantric had almost wholly triumphed. Alone among the adherents of devotion-struck theologies he proclaimed a liberation through knowledge (without any admixture of devotion) consisting in identity with an impersonal Absolute. To a victorious Vedanta he declared the Yoga to be the first among systems, and the Sankhya to possess a superior means to release. His main achievements are three—the final elaboration of the restored Sankhya (School I); the final systematization of Yoga (School II), and the synthesis between Sankhya, Yoga and Vedanta, the three main theologies of the Six Systems (Selection 67).

The theme of concord among theologies and religions is general in Hindu thought (see Selection 37). We can discern at least three models of proposed solution:

1. The *gradationist,* establishing a hierarchy among systems, the lowest being the farthest away from the truth, and the highest the most near to it, if not identical with it. This model is common in Christian and Islamic theologies.

2. The *equivalential,* affirming a basic identity between religions, with variations of little significance, so that one religion is equivalent to any other.

3. The *complementarist,* maintaining that each religion or theology—consisting of a central message and peripheral teachings—is unfailingly true in the former, while open to error in the latter. The whole truth, therefore, can lie only in the synthesis between those theologies or religions. This model, adopted by Vijñāna Bhikṣu, was elaborated more methodically (and somewhat differently) by the theologians of Jainism, like Hemacandra (1088–1172) and Malliṣeṇa (thirteenth century).

67

VIJÑĀNA BHIKṢU

The Concord Among Orthodox Theologies

"Yes, the Self must be seen, heard of, thought about and meditated upon."[61] It is in words such as these that Revelation prescribes the triad of salvific means—listening, reflection and meditation—for the sake of the vision of the Self, whereby man's supreme goal is realized. As to the desire for the means to liberation, in the matter of this triad, Tradition declares:

> He must be heard of from the words of Revelation, thought about through logical discourse, and, once thought about, must perpetually be meditated upon —these are the causes of the vision of the Self.[62]

By "perpetually meditated upon" understand "through the methods of yogic science." So when Revelation had disclosed man's *goal,* the *knowledge* which realizes it, and the essence of the Self, its *object*—the Lord, incarnate as Kapila, unfolded the logical reasons that are not discordant with Revelation, through the six chapters of his Science of Discrimination [the *Sankhya Aphorisms*].

'But the Logicist-Atomist system has its own explanation of the above topics—the system, from the Sankhya standpoint, being therefore void of sense. These systems seek a contrary kind of Self, claimed by the one system to be attributeful and by the other to be attributeless; besides, the logical reasons of the former are dissonant with those of the latter: consequently authority cannot belong to both.'

You are wrong. On the basis of the distinction between the ultimate and pragmatic levels of truth one can avoid the charges of unmeaningness and contradiction. From statements expressive of the experiences of joy and sorrow and through mere differentiation from the body, the Logicist-Atomists, at the very start of their inquiry, infer the existence of the soul—it being impossible, all at once, to attain to a knowledge of the most subtle kind. This knowledge, which denies that the body is the soul, is decidedly a true, pragmatic knowledge; just as the knowledge of a man's hands and feet is decidedly a true, pragmatic knowledge, serving to dispel the illusion [made possible by dim light] that he is a post. Hence when the *Gītā* says:

> Bewildered by the Attributes of Matter, men become attached to those Attributes. And a man who perceives the whole must not derange those dull wits who see only a part[63]

—it declares the Logicist who imagines the Self to be an agent, to have partial knowledge, partial only in relation to the integral knowledge of the Discriminationist [or Sankhya]; it does not maintain that he is totally ignorant. And even the partial Logicist knowledge, through an inferior kind of renunciation, is positively a means of attaining liberation, though in stages. Compared to it the Sankhya knowledge is ultimate; a knowledge, through a superior kind of renunciation, capable of arriving at liberation instantaneously. The *Gītā*'s just quoted words establish the knowledge of the Self's inactivity as being the only kind of integral knowledge. Revelation's authentic texts, by the hundreds, deny the validity of the Logicist-Atomist kind of knowledge on the ultimate level. Some instances:

> He is not followed by goodness, and he is not followed by evil, for he has passed beyond the heart's tribulations,[64] perceiving that desire and such things are merely thought.[65]

> Equable, he traverses the worlds, appearing to meditate, seeming to move.[66]

> Whatever it is that he sees there, it does not follow him.[67]

So do hundreds of authentic texts from Tradition, such as:

> Actions are always being produced by Matter's Attributes. The Self, deluded by Egoism, imagines himself to be active.[68]

> The unsullied Self is all freedom and all knowledge. Attributes are essentially replete with sorrow and ignorance. They belong to Matter, not to the Self.[69]

We cannot, however, conclude from this that the Logicist doctrine is lacking in validity, for in the matter which here concerns us—of the soul as other than the body—it is inabrogable, according to the principle "What a word refers to, that is its meaning." The experience of joy in the self, no doubt, is also pragmatically certain. But it lacks corroboration from a higher mode of knowledge, and so cannot, in that regard, be the object of authoritative teaching.

'Well, let us say we concede that. Let us agree that the Sankhya does not conflict with the Logicist-Atomist system. But it certainly does conflict with the Vedanta and Yoga, since they maintain an eternal Lord's existence, a Lord which the Sankhya constantly rejects. And you cannot resolve the contradiction between these theist and atheist systems on the basis of the distinction between ultimate and pragmatic, and on the claim that the salvific need for worship renders theism plausible, because it is impossible to decide which member of the distinction applies. As it is difficult to know if God exists, atheism is also justified by common experience, and can further be confirmed by the need for denying all craving for lordship, as for denying attributefulness to the Self. On the other hand, in no text of Revelation [or Tradition] is there a clear exclusion of the Lord that might lead us to perceive theism's validity on a purely pragmatical level.'

I reply that even this issue can be settled on the basis of the ultimate–pragmatic distinction. Sacred Teaching does condemn atheism, in texts like:

> "The world is devoid of reality," they say, "it has no Ground, no ruling Lord."[70]

But the very same teaching asserts the propriety of a denial of the Lord, if on a pragmatic level only, to foster the need for renouncing all desire for lordship. But—even granting that eternal lordship is not denied, as the Materialists do—the Sankhya masters hold that the vision of a plenary, eternal and faultless lordship, taking possession of the mind, could act as an impediment to all effort for acquiring discrimination. In addition, theism is nowhere subject to condemnation, with regard to which the Sacred Teaching on worship might need to be qualified. Accordingly

> There is no knowledge like Sankhya, no power like Yoga.[71]

> Have no doubt over this: the Sankhya is known to be the highest knowledge.[72]

Texts such as these declare the superiority of Sankhya above the other systems only in so far as its teaching on discrimination goes, not in as much as it denies the Lord's existence. Besides, one learns of theism's ultimate validity from the consensus of Parāśara and all wise teachers. The following passage from the *Parāśara Purāṇa* makes plain the fact of the Vedanta's greater force in its teaching about the Lord:

> All who believe in Revelation as the sole norm must relinquish whatever aspects of the systems of Gautama [Logicism], Kaṇāda [Atomism], Sankhya and Yoga as are inconsonant with its doctrine. But the systems of Jaimini [Ritualism] and Vyāsa [Vedanta] have no discordant aspects at all. Through the aid of Revelation, in the investigation of Vedic meaning, they have attained to the fullness of revealed insight.
>
> Many thinkers have formulated many reasoned works of knowledge. Whatever the genuine votaries of logic and scripture assert, hold that in esteem.[73]

From these words of the "*Mokṣadharma*" [chapter of the *Mahābhārata*], from the tradition of Parāśara and other wise teachers, one must adhere to the logic establishing the Lord's existence as enunciated in the Vedanta, Logicism and Atomism, because of its greater validity. Besides, Nārāyaṇa himself tells us of the extent of the Sankhya knowledge of the Lord, in the words of the *Kūrma Purāṇa:*

> Illustrious yogis and the Sankhya masters themselves do not see the Great Lord, the Brahman without beginning or end. Let Him be your sole refuge.

Besides, *the Lord* is the Vedanta's primary object, avowedly established by deliberative reasoning. If one were to question the Vedanta in that aspect of its teaching, its authority would be rendered null, according to the principle "What a word refers to, that is the word's meaning." On the other hand, the primary object of the Sankhya teaching is man's ultimate *goal,* and the *means* to achieve it—discrimination between Matter and Spirit. Hence even if it denies the Lord it does not forfeit its authority, according to the principle just enunciated. Open to qualification as the Sankhya is in respect to its denial of the Lord, its teaching is [to that extent] deficient in validity.

It will not do to argue that the Vedanta's prime object is only the Supreme Lord and not *eternal* lordship. Bādarāyaṇa's aphorism:

> 'Can it be maintained that [in evolving a harmonious exegesis of Revelation, there being conflict among the texts of Tradition] the fault will arise of some Traditional texts [those of the Sankhya] not being applicable?'
>
> No. Because then the fault will arise of other Traditional texts [those in accord with the Vedanta] not being applicable too[74]

represents a dissentient viewpoint and is inadmissible. So it must be emphasized that the Vedanta's object has *eternal* lordship as its essential qualification. Also, the word "Brahman" primarily refers to the "Supreme Brahman," which is why Bādarāyaṇa's [very first] aphorism does not read, "Now, then, the desire to know the *Supreme* Brahman."

However, we must not imagine that their disagreement with the Sankhya system means that Vedanta and Yoga accept the Supreme Lord's effectual [as opposed to his causal] nature, for then Matter would become independent, and Bādarāyaṇa's aphorism "Capacity to create being inconceivable in Matter, it cannot be inferred to be the cause"[75] would be out of place [in the chapter where it belongs]. Furthermore, in Patañjali's aphorism:

> He is the teacher of the ancients, as he is not limited by time[76]

and in Vyāsa's commentary on it, one is clearly apprised of the Lord's eternal nature. Hence, as considerations of concord [between the systems] and of the need for personal perfection indicate, and because the Sankhya denial of the Lord is on the pragmatic level only, there is no conflict with the Vedanta and Yoga systems. The point about concord is found in the sacred teaching, for instance, in the *Viṣṇu Purāṇa* [where Prahlāda says]:

> Demons! I have imparted to you ideas on a variety of doctrines, and have arrived at a concord between them. Listen now to my summary.[77]

We can [finally] conceive of a reason to support the partial conflict of the orthodox systems with the sense of Revelation—the purpose of inhibiting salvific knowledge among the sinful. In those particular aspects [where the conflict occurs] these systems will not be authoritative; but in their other, primary aspects, where they are not at variance with Revelation and Tradition, their authority will indubitably hold. That is why one comes across a condemnation of all systems other than the Vedanta and Yoga in the *Padma Purāṇa,* as in Śiva's conversation with [his wife] Pārvatī:

> Listen, goddess, I will tell you of my dark acts as they occurred. Merely to hear about them is degrading, even for those who know. First of all, I myself disclosed the Śaiva and Pastoralist systems. Thereafter, Brahmins penetrated with my power communicated still others. Kaṇāda imparted the great Atomist doctrine, Gautama the Logicist, and Kapila the Sankhya. Next the Brahmin Jaimini, propounding atheism [or Ritualism], created a mighty corpus of teaching imbued with Vedic import. Then Bṛhaspati proposed that most contemptible Materialist system. For the undoing of the demons, Viṣṇu, in the Buddha's form, taught the false Buddhist doctrine; as well as that of the naked and blue-vestured [Jain] sects. Then I myself, goddess, disguised as a Brahmin in the Kali age, enunciated the Illusionist doctrine, that aberrant teaching, Buddhism in camouflage. It makes nonsense of the words of Revelation, and people detest it. It also teaches the abandonment of the very essence of action, and propounds inaction through escape from all activity. In this doctrine, I myself teach the identity of the soul and God. To hasten the whole world's destruction in the Kali age, I have shown the Brahman's highest form to be attribute-

> less. For the world's destruction it was I, goddess, none other, who communicated the unVedic Illusionist doctrine as though it were a great science of full Vedic significance.[78]

I have elaborated on this point in my *Commentary on the "Aphorisms on the Brahman."*[79] I therefore conclude that no orthodox system is lacking in authority or is contradictory, as all these systems, in their own proper fields, are inabrogable and are free from discord.

'But will there not be controversy at least on the possibility of many Spirits?'

No, there will not, as there is no real conflict on this point. The Vedanta itself decidedly teaches the multiplicity of souls, in aphorisms like:

> The soul is a part, since there are references to manifoldness.[80]

On the other hand, the selfhood [in the ultimate sense] of the Spirits, affirmed by the Sankhya, is denied by the Vedanta in the aphorism:

> The wise acknowledge him to be the Self, and teach him to be such,[81]

where selfhood on the ultimate level is said to belong to the Supreme Lord alone.

For all this, the Sankhya's authority is not annulled, since in the doctrine alluded to, there is no dispute that the discriminative knowledge of the soul—the Self on the pragmatic level—is conducive to liberation. In conclusion, the doctrines of the multiplicity of the selves, and of the uniqueness of the Self, on the basis of the distinction between pragmatic and ultimate, are free from contradiction. I have explained this fully in my book on the Vedanta[82] and need not dwell on the matter further.

—*Expositive Commentary on the Sankhya* [*Aphorisms*][83]

68

VIJÑĀNA BHIKṢU

Joy Not the Essence of the Absolute

I. CRITIQUE OF THE DOCTRINE OF THE JOYFUL NATURE OF LIBERATION

In consequence, the doctrine of the Brahman's innate joyfulness is to be rejected. This is also in accord with the principle stated in *The Sankhya Aphorisms:*

> Joy and consciousness cannot belong to the same being, as they are discrepant.[84]

Like sorrow, joy is essentially non-illuminant, because it is seen to exist even in the absence of an adequate concept. On the other hand, by means of the reason that apprehends the substrate [consciousness, on the basis of its attributes, like thoughts, that postulate its existence] it has been demonstrated that consciousness is essentially illuminant. Therefore both [consciousness and joy] opposed as self-illuminant and non-self-illuminant, are contradictory. The consciousness knows itself as an object only through the idea furnished by Instinct. For if we were to suppose it known through a consciousness other than itself, we should be involved in an infinite regress. If it were to know itself immediately, we should fall into the contradiction of action and agent [that is, of knower and known] being the same. Hence illumination [only, not joy] can be logically affirmed of the consciousness.

If we were to try and avoid contradiction by asserting that joy, like consciousness, manifests itself through the idea [furnished by Instinct], contradiction would still occur, for if the one [joy] were to be known, the other [sorrow] would be unknown [since if there is sorrow there can be no joy, and vice versa]—and simultaneously to know and not know is a contradiction. At the moment of cognizing sorrow, consciousness would be ignorant of joy; at the time of blissful absorption, it would not know [sorrow]. You yourself are unwilling to postulate the divisions of knowability and joy [in your undifferenced Brahman], because then you would be in conflict with the text of Revelation which asserts the homogeneity ["uniflavoredness"] of the Brahman.[85] We might even have to predicate suffering of the Self, on the basis of the principle of logical economy.

'All this reasoning is pointless, since it is rendered inapplicable by the greater force of the following texts of Revelation:

> [Bhṛgu, Varuṇa's son] understood that the Brahman is joy.[86]
>
> The Brahman is knowledge and joy.[87]
>
> The Brahman is joy . . . all these beings are undoubtedly born of joy.'[88]

This is not true, for Revelation also tells us that the Self is other than joy, hence there is still scope for reasoning. The sage Manu deplores the ascertainment of meaning [of Revelation] independently of logic in a situation of doubt, in the words:

> A man who determines the sages' teachings on the Law through a logic not discordant with Revelation and the sacred sciences, only he, no other, knows that Law.[89]

The scriptures which conflict on the Brahman's joyful nature are the following. [First, those that accept the joyful naure:]

> One who knows the joy of the Brahman never has any fear.[90]
>
> All this [the coalescence of several degrees of the intensity of joy] is one degree of the Brahman joy.[91]
>
> There is a Self of joy other than that Self of knowledge.[92]

[Second] there are also texts which expressly deny the Brahman's joyful nature. Some of those from Revelation:

> He is not joy; nor is he joyless.[93]

> Contemplating, through meditation on his inner self, the resplendent and ancient Being—difficult to apprehend, who has entered mystery, who is hidden in a cave, who abides in the abyss—the wise man abandons joy and sorrow.[94]

Some of those from Tradition:

> The Brahman, whose essence is past, present and future, is joylessness without sorrow.

> Let those things be joyful and sorrowful, in my mind or at my death. What are they to me now?

> These modes of the mind have joy and sorrow as their secondary characteristics.

In the passage quoted above, the words "not joy" are a denial of the nature of joy [in the Brahman], "nor . . . joyless," an inference of the conditional character of joy. The annulment of joy that the words "the wise man abandons joy and sorrow" indicate is incompatible with a joy innate to the Self, as it would then imply the denial and the attainment [of joy] at the same time [denial, from scripture's words; attainment, as in attaining the Self, the wise man would attain the joy innate in it]. If from the same phrase one deduces that the annulment of joy occurs in the soul only, then, since part [the soul] and whole [the Brahman] are essentially one, and as we are given to understand that the soul and the Brahman are absolutely homogeneous in the words "You are It" and "It is you," it follows that the denial of joy in the soul is equivalent to the denial of joy in the Brahman.

"Joylessness without sorrow" is an appositional compound. Were it an attributive one [it would refer to a "sorrowless and joyless" being, and] we would need to use implication [to signify that being]. The words "as their secondary characteristics" mean that joy and sorrow are attributes, or the compound simply means joy, sorrow and other things of that nature.

Hence, with the denial of the Brahman's nature as joy, the whole group of texts which affirm joy at the moment of liberation are to be understood in the figurative sense of abandonment of sorrow. In passages like "they do not deserve a sixteenth portion of the joy that lies in the calming of desire," the conventional use of the word "joy" to imply the "termination of sorrow" is established. The same was said by the teacher Kapila:

> Joy is a loose way of describing the end of sorrow.

And

> Revelation acclaims release [as joy only] for the sake of fools [so as to entice them into it].[95]

But if one takes joy to mean the "joy" that is beyond sorrow and joy, then the word does not have a figurative sense. Therefore eternal joy, comprising factors like [unimpeded] desire, is conditioned in the Supreme Lord by the Mirific Power, and in the soul by Instinct. And we are to understand the unconditioned lovableness of the Self through its capacity to motivate love, and through its nature as cessation of sorrow.

The word that communicates the idea of the Brahman's essential joy connotes the identity of substance and attributes, as is suggested by Revelation in the text "desire and such things are merely thought."[96] It may be considered only a metaphorical way of connoting supreme lovableness, or a metaphor like space, signifying the fully blissful nature and supreme lovableness of the Self, and expressible in words such as "May I never cease to be, may I always live."

This is why the teacher Bādarāyaṇa will say, "Joy and its attributes belongs to Matter."[97] And in the *Kūrma Purāṇa* this is what the goddess Matter says to [Śiva's consort] Pārvatī:

> Replete with eternal bliss, I am Śiva's supreme energy.

You cannot argue that another and separate joy must be postulated in Matter. For if that were true, since the experience of joy would occur through Matter alone, it would be pointless to imagine yet another joy in the Self also.

We must further postulate an essential knowledge in the Self distinct from the knowledge produced by Instinct's ideas. Else it would be impossible to witness Instinct's functioning. Because of all this [the doctrine of] the essentially joyful nature of liberation is to be rejected and also because the soul [when liberated] has no connection with joy, and because the qualities of the soul's conditioners have been utterly extirpated. Yet even if we were to grant the soul's essential joyfulness, joy would not be its goal during liberation, since experience [without which there is no joy] is not possible in that state. The soul could not immediately experience itself either, for the contradiction of its being both the deed and the doer would result. Because of the total extirpation of the conditioners, the expression "the experience of joy" applied to liberation, is to be understood to refer to what is loosely termed "liberation" in what is known as "the Brahmā world."

II. CONFIRMATION OF THE DOCTRINE OF THE JOYLESSNESS OF LIBERATION

What then, you may ask, is the kind of goal attained in total liberation? I answer that the only goal is the termination of sorrow, as the following scriptural texts bear witness:

> The knower of the Self overcomes sorrow.[98]

> The Self, freed from the body, is quite untouched by pleasure and pain.[99]

> The wise man abandons joy and sorrow.[100]

For the same reason the phrase "goal of man" is commonly used with reference to things like the destruction of ignorance, because the absence of joy and sorrow are intrinsically desirable things.

'The absence of suffering cannot be the aim of life, because the Self is eternally free from sorrow, and at all events suffering was never a quality of the Self.'

I reply that according to the Sankhya it is only because of experience that joy and sorrow are rendered desirable or repugnant—as is seen from yearnings expressed in statements like "May I experience joy." Experience is the immediate apperception of joy and sorrow which are reflected in the Witness. This is implanted in the Self, and is wholly extirpated through knowledge alone. With the conditioner destroyed, the reflection of an attribute such as sorrow and joy, deriving therefrom, is impossible.

'Can it be maintained that experience belongs to Instinct, and not to the Self, because of authoritative statements such as: "like the experience of Instinct in the Self"?'

The answer is no, as the Sanskrit word for experience has a

double meaning . . . protection and enjoyment. A thing is nourished by elements outside itself, just as the gross body is by food. Likewise, all things being essentially joyful and sorrowful and deluding, Instinct undergoes experience, [that is to say] Instinct is nourished [in its experiences] of joy and sorrow by the states of joy and sorrow latent in the objects of its experience. This nourishment [or enhancement] is like that of the sweetness of milk by the sweetness of sugar. This experience belongs to the conscious Spirit, and since the latter, the subject of the reflection, is unmodifiable, the experience of Spirit is an immediate apperception of joy and sorrow. But it is impossible for Instinct to have such an apperception, or indeed an experience of even a metaphorical sort, because it is unconscious. [If Instinct were open to experience], the postulation of a Spirit would be without foundation. This is why the Sankhya theologians say:

> Spirit exists, because it is endowed with the capacity for experience.[101]

So also the *Gītā:*

> Matter is said to be the explanation of the *activity* in effect and cause, while Spirit is said to be the explanation of the *experience* of joy and sorrow.[102]

'Well, let us grant that the soul experiences sorrow. Even so, as you see it, the aim of life cannot be supposed to be the end of sorrow, because the soul absolutely lacks the sense of "I." '

This objection cannot be sustained, for the cause of activity in Instinct is knowledge serviceable to the experiencer. If not, the conscious Spirit would not be capable of the activity which only the knowledge signifying *thisness* renders possible, such as is conveyed in statements like "*this* is useful." Hence, even if non-soulness is valid on the ultimate level, the state of Spirit being an experiencer remains, and each particular soul needs a particular activity of Instinct [to become capable of experience]. It is therefore certain that the Brahman and the souls, related as whole and parts, are in essence consciousness only. This is the definitive doctrine of the Vedanta.

—*The Nectar of Knowledge Commentary on the "Aphorisms on the Brahman"*[103]

XVIII. QUALIFIED NONDUALISM, or *VIŚIṢṬĀDVAITA*

See Scheme 29

Qualified Nondualism is an event of great moment in Hindu theology. On the one hand were the theologies of knowledge, developed to the highest imaginable point of sophistication; on the other, the ebullient newer trend of devotion, clamoring for theological synthesis. It was Qualified Nondualism that combined the architectonics of the one with the fieriness of the other, thus becoming the first Vedanta theology of devotion.

Though devotion appears in the late Upaniṣads and is prominent in the *Gītā,* its expression was mainly popular; a great deal of it in the spoken languages, and not in the hieratic Sanskrit; chiefly, in the beginning, in the non-Sanskritic ones, like the southern Tamil—blessed with numerous poets and mystics, among them the Vaiṣṇava Alvars. Their ideas and other like ones were co-ordinated in Sanskrit, on the basis of the Difference-in-Identity scheme, in scriptural texts comprising two principal groups—the earlier Pāñcarātra corpus, of uncertain date, and the later *Bhāgavata Purāṇa* (ninth–tenth century); the latter, unlike the former, fully integrated into the Vedic tradition.

The Pāñcarātra corpus is mainly concerned with ritual, but has a most spectacular metaphysics and cosmology, one of its prominent archetypes being the four Theophanies, and an elaborate cosmogony of emanations (see Scheme 28). This astounding world view could not be integrated into Vedanta theology, the pre-eminent Hindu orthodox system, unless the Pāñcarātra corpus were shown to be consonant with the Vedic teaching—a task successfully achieved by Yāmuna (date given as 918–1038; Selections 69–71), who seems to be the founder of the school.

His successor Rāmānuja (dates given as 1017 or 1056–1137) proceeded to turn Qualified Nondualism into an integrally Vedantic system, based almost wholly on the sources accredited within the Vedic tradition, with the minimum use of Pāñcarātra texts. He therefore reverted to the most venerable of the Vedantic systems, the Ancient Vedanta, as elaborated by Bodhāyana (School XV), chief interpreter of Bādarāyaṇa's thought. As the basic polarities or dichotomies of his theology he adopted the concepts of body–embodied (Selection 72). His thought is nonetheless infused with the most ardent mysticism, as we see in his meditation on the glories of God, of His transcendence and accessibility (Selection 73).

Associated with God is His Consort, the Lady Glory (or Śrī or Lakṣmī). The Divine Feminine had been sublimely treated in Triadism (School XXIII), but there it is either delusive, projecting the multiplicity of the universe, or destructive, reverting it to its primordial and undifferenced unity. In Rāmānuja the Divine Feminine becomes the embodiment of divine gentleness and mercy—a concept developed to its fullness only by his successors, notably Lokācārya (thirteenth–fourteenth century). Triadism, like the schools of knowledge, had placed the impersonal above the person. But Rāmānuja returns to the doctrine that the *Gītā* affirms as its greatest secret:

> Listen again to My highest word, most secret of all —you are very dear to Me, so I will tell you your good.[104]

In other words, that God is a Person, and that the highest relationship He has to His creature is that of love and concern. From now on Vaiṣṇava theology will call God by the *Gītā*'s name for Him, the Supreme Person.

Rāmānuja's thoughts, expressed with dialectical rigor and with a somewhat overpowering exuberance, were elaborated with clarity and elegance by Sudarśana Sūri (thirteenth century), who was convinced that his illustrious predecessor was a sage, like Bādarāyaṇa, and the restorer of the Ancient Vedanta (Selection 74). Through the efforts of Rāmānuja and Sudarśana Sūri, the Vedantic orthodoxy of Qualified Nondualism became inexpugnable. However—successful as its synthesis was between the architectonics of the Vedanta and the devotion of the Alvars—it had not sufficiently clarified the nature of devotion, so within four centuries of Yāmuna's death, Qualified Nondualism split into two schools.

The first of them was the Passivist, or the Cat School,

affirming that God alone is the author of salvation; the creature's entire share in that act consists in totally *surrendering* itself to Him—as the kitten does to its mother, remaining quite still while it is being carried around. This branch was initiated by Lokācārya, author of a brief sum of theology of Qualified Nondualism (Selection 75). The other school was the Activist, or the Monkey School, proclaiming the creature's need for *co-operating* with God, as the young monkey does with its mother, by clinging to her as she carries it around. The founder of this branch was Vedānta Deśika (dates given as 1268–1369/71), in many ways the greatest theologian of Qualified Nondualism, his voluminous writings being the most consummate treatment of his school's doctrines. Among his preoccupations was to strengthen the critical foundations of theology, starting of course with the basic problem of whether certainty in knowledge is possible (Selection 76).

A basic doctrine of Vaiṣṇavism is that of incarnation, but the theologies of Majesty emphasize the transcendence of the unincarnate God rather than the accessibility of the incarnational. Now with Viṣṇu's Vedantic character securely established through the theologizing of the Qualified Nondualists, it was possible to explore the theological character of the incarnations, and in doing this thinkers constructed new Vedantic systems. Their attention was centered mainly on Viṣṇu's incarnation as Kṛṣṇa, embodiment of delight. Almost equally popular was Rāma, the incarnation previous to Kṛṣṇa, symbol of virtue and respectability, whose name, in Northern India today, is synonymous with that of God. Rāma devotion was not as theologically fecund as Kṛṣṇa devotion, but it did produce one school of theology, that of Rāmānanda (fifteenth century), which accepted the theological world view of Qualified Nondualism, rather than a wholly new one of its own, or one affiliated to the newer Vaiṣṇava systems. The latter were strongly erotic in character and imagery, and hence not to the liking of more puritanical thinkers, like Svāmī Nārāyaṇa (1781–1803). A worshiper of Kṛṣṇa, he rejected the erotic Kṛṣṇa theology of Vallabha's Pure Nondualism (School X), and reverted to the chaster thought of Yāmuna and Rāmānuja, thus fashioning a Kṛṣṇa theology of Majesty.

69

YĀMUNA

The Vaiṣṇava Scriptures, the Pāñcarātra Corpus, Easy Summary of Revelation

The Lord, to Whose unerring and innate vision the entire corpus of Vedic Revelation is directly displayed, saw that His devotees' minds were too infirm to study and retain the many branches of the Vedic schools embodying scattered and multifarious injunctions, preceptive explications and incantations. Moved to compassion for the devotees, He condensed the meaning of the Vedas in a manner easy to comprehend, and then promulgated it [in the Pāñcarātra corpus].

70

YĀMUNA

Two Faultless Revelations: The Impersonal in the Vedas and the Personal in the Pāñcarātras

In the Pāñcarātra corpus too, no suspicion about its validity appears, since it can be certified to be free of faults, having as it does the omniscient Lord of all for its enunciator. To explain. Both Veda and the Pāñcarātra being self-evident, there is the assuredness that faults are excluded in both—in the one instance, because of an assured absence of a person in whom they can inhere; and in the other, because of the assured presence of an enunciator possessed of qualities preclusive of those faults. As, for instance, in the assured absence of heat—in the sky, because of the assured lack of a substrate for it to inhere; and in water, because of the presence of a coolness preclusive of heat.

71

YĀMUNA

The Truthfulness of God in the Pāñcarātras

If we suspect that God, without cause, simply because He is all-powerful, wishes to damn us, then, alas, He will fling the good into hell, just because He is omnipotent! And the suspicion that He might do so will cause the whole world to desist from activity!

Besides, on the assumption that He deceives us only because He is all-powerful: we doubt whether in the beginning He did or did not create the Vedas containing preternatural and untruthful meaning; whether or not He deprived Brahmā, the Golden Embryo, of the power of remembering that he also is their author [thus leading people to imagine them to have originated impersonally]; and whether or not it was He who in consequence initiated the tradition of their recitation —if we doubt all this, how can we have any trust in Him?

On the other hand, while admitting that He does indeed have omnipotence, we find no proof that He exploits it in all its latitude; that He has no occasion to do so; that He is by nature gratified and so has no need to deceive; that He is untouched by even a suspicion of such faults as injustice and cruelty; that He continues steadfastly in His natural kindness to all living creatures: moreover, that even if He had indeed composed the Pāñcarātras to deceive, that the wise, who up to this day have recited, studied and followed them could hardly have been oblivious to these defects of God's making —if, accepting all this, would our suspicions persist? If the answer is no, it will apply to the Vedas as well.

In other words: what can He Who is fulfilled in all His desires, Who is omnipotent and is the abode of mercy, gain from the deception of insignificant creatures who have not understood the Vedas' meaning? If the Pāñcarātra corpus was composed to deceive, how is it that the great sages, such esteemers of the Vedas, praise it as their equal on every occasion?

—*The Authority of Sacred Tradition*[105]

72
RĀMĀNUJA
Darkness the Body of God

It is my belief that at this point the core of Bādarāyaṇa's teaching on transformation does not consist in assigning imperfection to the Supreme Brahman, but rather in according Him unconstrained power. And this is how the transformation is explained:

The Brahman is concentrated goodness, abhorrent of all imperfection, diverse from all things other than Himself. He is all-knowing, the realizer of all His wishes, fulfilled in His desires, limitless and sovereign joy. Embodied as the mass of all conscious and unconscious beings that subserves His cosmic play, He becomes the soul of that body. Then [at dissolution]—through the successive regression of Matter's evolutes, the Elements, Egoism and Instinct [into Prime Matter itself] —the universe that has become His body survives as an unconscious substance extremely subtile, known as Darkness. With this body of Darkness, now arrived at a state of subtlety so extreme that it can hardly be called different, the Supreme Brahman attains a condition of oneness. [Later, at the time of creation] He conceives the thought "Let me become the world body, composed of conscious and unconscious beings, differentiated, as previously, in conceptual and corporeal fashion"—and then transforms Himself, in His world body, through entering one evolute of Matter after another. This is the doctrine of transformation in all the Upaniṣads.

—*The Glory Commentary on the "Aphorisms on the Brahman"*[106]

73
RĀMĀNUJA
The Transcendence and Accessibility of God

Lady Glory's Lord

Repellent of all evil, concentered goodness

Essence dissimilar to all other than Itself, uniquely unconstrained knowledge and joy,

Great ocean of innumerable perfections amassed—as knowledge, power, sovereignty, vigor, energy and refulgence—perfections innate, unlimited, august

Treasury of qualities without end—as glory, fragrance, beauty, tenderness, harmony and youth—qualities complacent, consonant, undeviating, inconceivable

Form empyreally divine

Body divinely adorned—with adornments becoming, multiform, variegated, infinite, stupendous, unending, unflawed, limitless

Figure divinely panoplied—with arms conformable, numberless, of unimagined power, eternal, incorruptible, exalted, propitious

Lover of Lady Glory—the Beloved, the figure of His substance, the eternal, the immaculate, participant in His essence, adorned with the perfections of His divine form—as majesty, sovereignty and goodness—qualities exalted, numberless, blessed

Worshiped without pause by Eternals without number—beings whose nature, unfailing existence and diverse actions conform to His will; their sole delight total dependence, their endowment a host of qualities innumerable, as knowledge, action and sovereignty, qualities intransient, immaculate and incomparable

Of essence and being incircumscriptible by word or thought

Dwelling in the Highest Empyrean—an abode befitting, manifold and variegated; a place of delight furnished with delightful things and means of delight without count; perfect, replete with endless wonders and of magnific splendors; limitless in extent, immaterial, unalloyed, intransmutable

Indulging in the cosmic frolics of projecting, displaying and dissolving the entire world filled with the ranks of experiencers and objects of experience beyond number

The Highest Brahman

The Supreme Person

Nārāyaṇa!

Creating the whole world on all its levels, from the god Brahmā down to the unmoving objects, He abides in His nature, inaccessible to the contemplation and the worship of gods and men, even of the god Brahmā himself.

Shoreless deep of compassion, benevolence, tenderness and generosity, He did not abandon His nature when He transformed His essence into a nature such as theirs; becoming incarnate among diverse creatures, He became adored among them.

He offered them the fruits of life's four goals—duty, wealth, pleasure and liberation—according as they wished. On the pretext of bearing the world's burdens He became incarnate on earth to calm the pains of transmigration for people of as little consequence as ourselves, to be the refuge of us all, and so became something that the eyes of all could see.

He performed divine deeds that ravished the minds and eyes of all kinds of beings, high and low. He killed the demoness Pūtanā,[107] the cart-fiend Śakaṭa,[108] the two tree demons [Nala-kūbara and Maṇigrīva],[109] the bull demon Ariṣṭa,[110] the cowherd demon Pralamba,[111] the ass demon Dhenuka,[112] the serpent demon Kālīya,[113] the horse demon Keśī,[114] the elephant demon Kuvalayāpīḍa [also the mount of the wicked king Kaṁsa],[115] Cāṇūra and Muṣṭika and Tosala, Kaṁsa's wrestlers, and finally Kaṁsa himself[116]—and then satiated all creatures with the ambrosia of His speech and glances filled with limitless compassion, tenderness and affection. Revealing the multitude of His unexcelled qualities—such as beauty and lovableness—He turned people like Akrūra[117] His uncle and the florist Mālākāra[118] into consummate devotees. And on the pretext of inciting Pāṇḍu's son, Arjuna, to war, He revealed the discipline of devotion—a discipline which has Himself for its object, which the Vedanta proclaims, and which is supported by the diciplines of knowledge and ritual action—as the means of attaining liberation, man's highest end.

Then, as the war between the Pāṇḍavas and the Kauravas was beginning, that Lord—the Supreme Person, the Master of All, the God become mortal for the service of the world and overwhelmed by tenderness for His suppliants—that Lord brought the chariot-warrior Arjuna and Himself the charioteer to the sight of the whole world.

—*Commentary on the "Gītā"*[119]

74

SUDARŚANA SŪRI

Rāmānuja, Restorer of the Ancient Way

There are men who ascertain valid objects of knowledge through valid norms, of the good to be striven for and the evil to be shunned, and of the means to these ends: in so far as all this relates to things that exceed human power, it can be known only through Revelation, that corpus of syllables we call the Vedas. But fouled as this corpus is by the soot discharged from defective and less than human brains, resort to a more perfect norm becomes imperative.

Before all else one has to understand the first half of Revelation, dealing with things favorable to life in this world and in the next, and the means to realizing them—things like cattle, sons, rain, food and heaven. Then the nobler half of Revelation will awaken one to the understanding of life's highest goal and to the way of reaching it. That way is the royal ["bell"] road dear to the Ancient Masters, now wholly beset with the numberless thorns of the impious language of various sorts of insightless theologians. They have disclosed a new and wrong way, in following which the world has chosen to fool itself.

Wishing then to revive that original teaching; to clear of thorns the old and proper road completed by the Ancient Masters, men skilled in discerning the true from the false; to content the seekers of life's highest goal by rendering them service; to ensure the happiness of those tormented by the fear of transmigration, and moved by divine power to become incarnate—Rāmānuja, the most compassionate, noble author of the Commentary on Bādarāyaṇa's *Aphorisms,* undertook to explain the Vedantic science of which those *Aphorisms* are the embodiment.

The supreme sage's [Bādarāyaṇa's] *Aphorisms* need exegesis, and if a great sage's [Rāmānuja's] exegesis can be obtained, it is the one to adopt, for no one who is not a sage can be endowed with a profound insight. A sage's thought can be understood only by another sage, and not by any fool.

—*The Revealed Illumination,* Introduction[120]

75

LOKĀCĀRYA

The Five Principles: Compendium of the Theology of Qualified Nondualism

PROLOGUE: THE FIVE PRINCIPLES

1. As the awareness of the truth dawns, and when the urge to a new life appears, it is necessary that the knowledge of the Five Principles arise in the transmigrant conscious being.

2. The knowledge of the Five Principles lies in the exact perception of the natures of oneself, the Supreme Self, the goal of man, the means to the goal, and the frustrations to its attainment.

3. Each of these truths is in turn fivefold.

4. By the nature of oneself I mean the nature of the individual soul.

5. This, again, is of five kinds—the eternal, free, bound, isolated and aspirant of liberation.

6. The nature of the Supreme Self is fivefold—the Supreme Form, the Theophanies, the Incarnations, the Inner Controller and the Iconic Embodiments.

7. The goal of man, that is, the goal that man must strive

for, is also fivefold—social duty, rewarding work, delight, the experience of the soul and the experience of God.

8. The means to the goal are fivefold—ritual activities, knowledge, devotion, surrender to God and reverence for the teacher.

9. The frustrations are fivefold, frustrating the nature of the soul, the nature of the Supreme Self, the goal of man, the means to the goal and the attainment of the goal.

I. SOULS

10. Of the five types of souls, the Eternals are those who are ever free from the turpitude of the transmigratory world. Their sole delight lies in being conformable to God. They are graced with diadems, and are the ministers of the glorious Vaikuṇṭha's Master. Commanded by the Supreme Lord, they are able to engage in the acts of creation, maintenance and dissolution. They attend the Lord in any of His forms—such as the Supreme Form and the Theophanies—and are prompt in His service. They comprise Viśvaksena, the commander of the divine armies, and other immortals.

11. The Freed are the sages, imbued with ecstasy and joy. God's grace has liberated them from their sorrows and sins, the consequences of their association with Matter. Their home is the Great City of Vaikuṇṭha: there they experience God's essence, the beauty of His form, and His majesty. Overflowing with the love generated by that experience, they insatiably glorify Him to the limits of their power.

12. The Bound are conscious beings who believe that the body is the soul—the body, that mixture of the five elements, that transient entity, that aggregation of the experiences of pleasure and pain, that object unfit to see and touch once it is separated from the soul, that receptacle of impurities, that generator of ignorance and of false and distorted knowledge. On that assumption they hold that the goal of man is nothing but the pampering of the body through the experience of object sensations—sound, color, touch, taste and smell. Once in enjoyment of these sensations, they make use of them to destroy the order of the four castes and states, they serve things not fit to be served, they inflict violence on living things and snatch at other men's wives and goods. They are turned away from God and swell the flux of transmigration.

13. The Isolated is a solitary, tortured by extreme hunger

and thirst, unable to discriminate between what is and what is not fit to be consumed, but happy when he has consumed his own body. The conflagration in the wood of transmigratory existence scorches him. To free himself from the torments of that existence, aided by the knowledge brought on by the sacred sciences, he succeeds in discriminating between Matter and Spirit.

[He is not thereby liberated,] Matter's painful essence predominating, but he becomes attached to the little joy that that discrimination affords, and is unable to discriminate Matter and Spirit from the Supreme Self Who is the fullness of knowledge and joy. He then applies himself to the Yoga of knowledge as a means of realizing the soul—and comes to experience the fruit of yogic endeavor, the experience of the soul, and of nothing else, as though it were man's supreme goal. In consequence he remains without any links with transmigratory existence and also without having attained God, continuing to roam, bodiless, yearning for the Self.

14. The Aspirant of Liberation is one who strives for liberation. Such aspirants are of two kinds, the Devotees and the God-Refugees.

II. THE SUPREME SELF

15. The supremacy which regards the Supreme Lord denotes "The intelligent being, whose body is breath, whose form is light, whose thoughts are true, whose nature is the sky, who is all actions, desires, odors and tastes, who embraces all, never speaks and is never surprised,"[121] Who abides in the highest heaven, Who is by nature the Primordial Light and Whose name is the Supreme Vāsudeva.

16. The Theophanies [or the "clearly comprehended" forms] are Saṅkarṣaṇa, Pradyumna and Aniruddha, the causes, respectively, of creation, maintenance and dissolution.

17. The Incarnations ["manifested" or "majestic" forms] are the avatars, Rāma, Kṛṣṇa and others.

18. The Inner Controller is of a twofold character—both God "abiding within His servant" and the servant acknowledging Him as "my life breath." In this manner, "abiding with Your servant, You know" all his thoughts—thoughts such as "You have entered the inner lotus of the soul," "Lotus-indwelling Goddess [Lakṣmī, Lady Glory] enter You also," and "the soul You have entered is of a beauty that in-

creases reverence." In this way God, attended by the Lady Glory, and assuming an unexampled form, unceasingly watches all activity and quiescence within the lotus of the heart.

19. The Iconic Embodiment [the "avatar for worship"] is God assuming the form His servants like, and the names His servants like. Accordingly, He Who needs no forms and names for Himself, assumes the forms and names desired; Who, although knowing everything, is as though knowing nothing; although all-powerful, is as though powerless; although fulfilled in all His desires, is as though in need; and although the Protector Himself, is as though in want of protection. Reversing the relation of owner and owned, He becomes easily accessible to all as an object of sight, and dwells in shrines and homes.

III. MAN'S GOAL

20. Of man's goals Social Duty is an activity fulfilled by the protection of living things.

21. Rewarding Work is the accumulation of wealth and grains in harmony with the imperatives of caste and state of life; and its expenditure, with a sense of duty, on the things of God, on services to ancestors, and on charities to living creatures, with regard to the merits of place, time and recipient.

22. Delight is of two kinds, the this-worldly and the other-worldly.

23. This-worldly delight is a particular experience of joy, linked with the sensations of objects, like sound, and to things like father, mother, jewelry, wealth, grains, food, drink, wife, son, friend, cattle, home, field, sandal, flowers, betel, clothes and so on.

24. Other-worldly delight is the enjoyment of sensations of objects, like sound, through going to the worlds of luminous substance, like the heavens, where sensations are of a different nature from those of this world. There, free from the afflictions of hunger, thirst, sorrow, delusion, old age and death, in accordance with the merits a man has earned, he drinks ambrosia in the company of heavenly nymphs.

25. Isolation is no more than release from sorrow, and the experience of the soul merely, which some call liberation.

26. Man's supreme goal, liberation, is a state where one abides in one's eternally obeisant nature. In its attainment

those unavoidable experiences, merits and demerits, the result of inchoate karma, are destroyed. The gross body, the abode of the six transformations of being traditionally described in the words "is, is born, changes, grows, decays, is destroyed"[122]; the receptacle of the three sorrows—internal, external and superhuman; which, occluding the essence of God, gives rise to distorted knowledge, and which augments transmigration: this body is contemptuously abandoned. The skull is broken and escape effected through the spinal cord. The soul then enters the region of heat, and the Subtle Body sheds the dust of its conceptual latencies through a bath in the river Dispassion [or Dustless]. One receives a touch from the hand of the god No-man which removes all affliction; one then obtains an immaterial body, of unmixed Brightness, compounded of the five celestial elements,[123] a body which generates knowledge and joy, is intent only on the experience of God and is all-luminous. Then diademed immortals come forward to greet him, and he arrives at the great Jewel Pavilion —and there sees the eternal and glorious Lord of Vaikuṇṭha, Consort of Lady Glory and Lord of Lady Sky and Lady Earth, attended by multitudes of gods, and revealing His form in a torrent of flame.

IV. MEANS TO THE GOAL

27. Among the means to the goal of man is Ritual Observance. It consists in offering sacrifices, giving gifts, performing austerities, contemplation, reciting the morning and evening hymns, offering the Five Great Sacrifices, maintaining the fire for the sacrifice of the fire-god, going on pilgrimage, living on holy sites, doing rigorous penance like the Moon Fast, bathing in sacred rivers, living temperately during the four rainy months, subsisting on fruits and roots, studying the sacred sciences, propitiating God, murmuring prayers, offering libations to ancestors, and performing one's duties. All these sear the body and precipitate the destruction of sin. Qualitative Consciousness, issuing through the senses, does not dwell on sensations like sound, and so lacks object. Nonetheless it has need of one, and as long as yogic discipline—comprising the eight members of Yoga: disciplinary precepts, spiritual precepts, postures, breath regulation, abstraction, consideration, contemplation and concentration—as long as

yogic discipline lasts, that Consciousness treats the soul itself as object.

28. Ritual Observance is the auxiliary of the discipline of knowledge, and is the chief means to the attainment of power.

29. The discipline of Knowledge arises from the discipline of Observance. It makes its object of contemplation the Lord of All, as enthroned in such special places as the circles of the heart and of the sun. Next, it experiences that object, the Lord Himself, armed with conch and discus, apparelled in yellow robes, diadem, anklet and other divine adornments. It then prolongs the duration of this experience through yogic methods, transfiguring it into an unbroken vision.

30. The discipline of Knowledge is the auxiliary of the discipline of Devotion and is the chief means of attaining Isolation.

31. The discipline of Devotion is the experience of sequent memories, flowing unintermittedly like poured oil, transformed into a fulfilled state of love. With God's essence contemplated on, and—through the extirpation of the inchoate karmas—with the means to liberation and the goal itself realized, a state of maturity is produced where the means diminish and the goal expands.

32. The means of Total Surrender is easy and productive of quick results in those who have been unable to follow the discipline of Devotion, linked as it is with Ritual Action and Knowledge. As this means has to be used but once, the moment it is employed, the experiences of God arise and the range of liberation is attained. It is thus an easy means and consonant with the aspirant's nature.

Total Surrender has two varieties, the anguished and the confident.

33. Anguished Surrender is found when the aspirant, prompted by the unprompted grace of God, studies the sacred sciences and follows a good teacher's guidance. Then, as knowledge dawns, he becomes impatient of the [common] experience of God, of the bond with his contrarious body, and of association with his teacher. Growing excessively anxious to acquire an experience of God, as well as a body, a region and a teacher all his own and without parallel, and in order to rid himself of the ills of conception, birth, age, affliction of mind and of death, he abandons himself wholly to God

Viṣṇu, the Lord of the Veṅkaṭa mountain. "Noble Lord Veṅkaṭa," he cries, "You are all I have; I am Your slave. Receive my adoration, dweller on Veṅkaṭa's crest! You have shown me too much of the world, and have broken me. I am weary of standing on its shore striving to reach You. Have mercy! I entreat You solemnly by the Lady Glory! I shall no longer allow myself to endure all this." Importuning God in this fashion, the aspirant surrenders himself totally.

34. Confident Surrender arises when an aspirant becomes disinclined to undergo heaven or hell in another birth. To free himself from that eventuality and also to attain God, he follow's a good teacher's instruction and applies himself to the means to liberation. Wishing to terminate all perverse activity, he fulfills the duties of caste and state of life that the Vedas enjoin, and also submits himself to God's service, to the best of his ability, through acts of word, mind and body. He then reflects on the Supreme Lord's nature as whole, as Governor, Protector, Experiencer, All-knower, All-powerful and as Plenary Perfection—in contrast with his own nature as part, as governed and owned, as body, as pervaded, supported, protected, as object of divine experience, as unknowing, helpless, imperfect and destitute, exclaiming, "You may or may not free me, but I have no Savior but You!" In this way, he makes over to God the whole burden of his salvation and the means to it, and then rests in a state of fearless calm.

35. Reverence for the teacher is the means for one who lacks the power to avail himself of those discussed so far. It arises when a great devotee of Viṣṇu, a teacher supremely compassionate and capable of affording his disciple sure guidance, reflects that helping him attain God would be pleasing to God. [Conceiving his pupil's faults to be the result of his own] the teacher himself has recourse to the salvific disciplines—like a mother with a suckling infant who is ill. The child's illness, she believes, is a result of her own lapses [in the matter of diet] and so she takes medicines herself. The pupil, lost in reverence for his teacher, resolves to look up to him in all contingencies and to follow all his counsels. In consequence, he develops the habit of dependence on his teacher, for all his activity and inactivity.

Though the Lord is Himself immediately accessible, He is even more so through the teacher, since He abides as Inner Controller in all the gods. This reverence for the teacher is thus an independent means, and in the complex of all the means, it is both auxiliary and autonomous.

V. THE FRUSTRATIONS

36. Of the frustrations, that of the nature of the soul is a belief that the body is the soul, that one is subject to a being other than Viṣṇu, or that one is subject to none at all.

37. The frustrations of the Lord's supremacy consist in attributing sovereignty to another god, or even his equality with Viṣṇu; of attributing sovereignly divine powers to godlings, mere humanity to the Incarnations, and impotence to the Iconic Embodiments.

38. The frustrations of the goal of man are the desire for other goals beside liberation, and disinclination for the soul's cherished goal, the service of God.

39. The frustration of the means to liberation is the unjustifiable acceptance of the efficacy of other means, the belief in the inadequacy of the right means, of the excessive arduousness of the goal, or in the numerousness of the frustrations.

40. Lack of repentance, offensiveness to the teacher, persistent insult to God, rudeness to the devotees and other ill-mannered behavior are all said to be frustrations to the attainment of the goal.

41. Defective food frustrates knowledge.

42. Bad company frustrates the enjoyment of the fruits of one's good acts.

EPILOGUE

43. Thus, when the knowledge of the Five Truths has arisen, the aspirant soul, continuing to exist in this world, should until liberation adopt the following mode of life, to free himself from transmigratory existence. He should find food and clothes according to his caste and state of life. He should consider to himself that a man's food is his deity's food, and so offer all that he uses to God. He should do what he can to provide for God's devotees, and take what is left, as a favor from God, only for sustaining his body. He should, as often as he can, be with his teacher, who gave him his knowledge of the truth, serving him in every possible way and earn-

ing his esteem. In God's presence he should evince his own inferiority.

44. In his teacher's presence, a man must always evince his ignorance.

45. In the presence of devotees, one must always evince one's sense of dependence on God.

46. In the presence of the worldly, one must always evince one's difference from them.

47. Alacrity in all that concerns the goal, assiduousness in the practice of the means to the goal, fear of the frustrations, indifference to all else, knowledge of the soul's nature, powerlessness in one's own salvation—when the aspirant pursues all these, he will be endowed with knowledge and fulfillment. Such an aspirant will be preferred to the Eternals and the Divine Consorts themselves.

—*The Five Principles*[124]

76

VEDĀNTA DEŚIKA (AND SRĪ NIVĀSA)

Theology: A Critical Science

The norm of knowledge is in truth the principal object of this science. It inquires into undesirable and desirable goals, and so offers the prudent the true knowledge of the normatively knowable, to help them achieve their cherished salvific ends: this knowledge is the cause of man's ultimate happiness. It further inquires into the norm with its attendant conditions, and consequently discloses the normatively knowable, so as to propose its object clearly. And it treats of the norm before it does the normatively knowable, not only because of the former's greater importance, but also because it aids in the latter's realization.

[Norm and normatively knowable are the first two of Gautama's sixteen categories of thought.][125] The fourteen others

—doubt, relevance, example, tenet, syllogism, conjecture, demonstrated conclusion, discussion, sophistical disputation, polemic, paralogism, quibbling, specious reasoning and fallacies—are treated as the main categories' specific variants or constituents.

However, this does not contravene Gautama's sixteenfold classification. For through combination and separation implicit in such [additional] attributes as incongruity and error, it is possible to indicate a lessening or diminution in the number of categories. It will also be difficult to determine whether a procedure of this kind is useful or not. Such is undoubtedly Gautama's intent also.

[It needs to be determined first of all whether a norm of knowledge exists. However,] "there is indeed a norm." This sentence certifies the existence of the royal road of all activity, whether of common sense or of scientific inquiry. If that postulate is not respected, scientific inquiry itself, being void of a basis, will be unable to arise.

Activity in the world always needs a basis [in this case, the ascertainment of whether a norm exists or not. But in the world of common sense] this basis is not known except in a general sense. Here we are inquiring into the reason why [norms exist]. When the meaning is ascertained in a general sense, there is a desire to know it more specifically. And it is proper to institute an inquiry which explicates the character of one's chosen norm.

ŚRĪ NIVĀSA

The opponent who maintains that it has not been decided whether a norm exists or not has to be asked if this is so because

1. There is no norm to justify anything.
2. There is a norm to justify everything.
3. Norms and non-norms are mutally abrogative.
4. Everything is uncertain.

VEDĀNTA DEŚIKA

Invalidation of the First Two Alternatives

1. It cannot be that there is no norm for anything, because that would destroy your position.

2. It cannot be that there is a norm for everything, because that would also destroy your position, though for another reason.

ŚRĪ NIVĀSA

. . . If there is no justification for anything . . . there is no justification for your proposition to that effect, so you will have destroyed your position through your own postulates . . . If there is a justification for everything, there will be justification for our own proposition that "your theory is unjustified," so you will have destroyed your position through your opponent's postulates . . .

VEDĀNTA DEŚIKA

Whether your position is proved or not, the commonsensible always is. And whether the commonsensible is proved or not, yours never is.

ŚRĪ NIVĀSA

. . . If your position "the polarity between norm and non-norm is non-existent" is proved, then that proposition is valid [hence, it is a norm] and the counter-proposition is invalid [hence, it is a non-norm: in other words, you really accept the polarity]. The commonsensible position is thus verified. If your position is not proved, then denial of the polarity [which it embodies] is not proved, and hence the existence of the polarity will be assured.

In the same way whether the commonsensible position is proved or not, your own position is not . . . If the polarity between valid and invalid [or norm and non-norm] is proved, then your theory, which denies it, is not. If it is not proved, then the polarity between your own valid proposition and the opponent's invalid one will not be either, so your own position will be justified even less . . .

VEDĀNTA DEŚIKA

Invalidation of the Third Alternative

3. The abrogation of a norm by a norm is destroyed by its

own inconsistency. As for the abrogation of a norm by a non-norm: why can it not realize the latter's abrogation too?

ŚRĪ NIVĀSA

The opponent who says that "the polarity between norm and non-norm is non-existent, because it is mutually abrogative," must be asked if (a) norm abrogates norm, or (b) non-norm abrogates norm. If (a), the abrogated norm will also abrogate the abrogating norm; hence the abrogation of the norm [thus neutralized] will not be proved. If (b), why cannot the abrogating non-norm abrogate the non-norm as well, since there is no difference [or polarity] between norm and non-norm?

. . . 'It is easy to confront your theory also with such options. Any disputant who upholds the existence of a norm must be asked if that norm is proved through (a) a non-norm, or (b) a norm. If through (a), a non-norm certifying a norm's existence would be able to certify a non-norm's existence too. As there is no difference between norm and non-norm, it would not necessarily establish the former to the exclusion of the latter. If through (b), is a norm's self-normativeness proved through that norm itself, or through another? Self-proof is impossible, as a thing cannot function in itself. Proof through another norm [means that the other would itself need to be justified—by the very norm it is justifying; this] would result in mutual apprehension of validity and thus in circular reasoning. If there were to be no apprehension of validity, our intent would be proved' . . .

VEDĀNTA DEŚIKA

The norm is not equally justified by a non-norm as by a norm, since it is justified by a norm alone—through a justification that secures both itself and the thing it justifies.

ŚRĪ NIVĀSA

. . . Norm alone justifies norm . . . it also apprehends its own normative character. Knowledge is self-illuminant [and self-validating]. As will be explained later, when dealing with the perception of self-validity, validity, immanent in itself, can without inconvenience be self-apprehending. Your argument is therefore implausible. Thus, when any validity is established, its correlative invalidity is logically abrogated.

. . . 'The polarity between abrogation and non-abrogation can also be established on the basis of non-norm abrogating norm, hence the polarity you advocate [that of norm abrogating non-norm only; in other words, of *normative abrogation*, as opposed to the *mutual abrogation* we support] is implausible.'

To this argument Vedānta Deśika replies:

VEDĀNTA DEŚIKA

The polarity of abrogation and non-abrogation is on the basis of normative abrogation [alone], because that is established. Otherwise the polarity you hold would be no polarity at all; that is established too.

ŚRĪ NIVĀSA

. . . If, while not accepting the polarity of *normative* abrogation, you are led, by your position on the polarity of *mutual* abrogation, to affirm that "the polarity of the normative kind is *nowhere* ascertained" [you will be adopting the very kind of polarity you wish to put an end to, with its one-way abrogation. For you intend by that proposition to abrogate your opponent's, and not to be abrogated in turn. Since you have accepted his ideas to give significance to yours], your position will have been abrogated by your opponent's . . .

VEDĀNTA DEŚIKA

Invalidation of the Fourth Alternative

4. As there is no certainty anywhere, there is none as to whether doubt arises or is experienced. Wherever options embodying doubt are affirmed, certainty exists: hence certainty can exist in other cases too.

ŚRĪ NIVĀSA

. . . As certainty is the cause of the doubt embodied in the options [as, for instance, "Is this mountain fiery or not?" or

"Is this erect object a man or a post?"—to that extent] doubt is non-existent. If, in one case, the certain existence of the two options determining doubt ["fiery or not"] is accepted, as well as the certain existence of their subject ["the mountain"] —certainty, by reason of parity, can be accepted in other cases too.

VEDĀNTA DEŚIKA

In the above ascertainment the doubt, embodying the options inherently common to their subject, expressed itself in "this or this" ["This erect object is either man or post"; "This mountain is either fiery or not"].

Not everyone, everywhere, is seen to doubt. "Everything is doubtful"—that is your certainty, you clever man!

ŚRĪ NIVĀSA

. . . The doubt which you refer to and which embraces everything—is it dubious or not? If it is, then the total doubt you experience is not verified. If it is not dubious, it will follow that there is a certainty comprehending all doubt, and your Monism of doubt [to the total exclusion of certainty] will be wrecked . . .

VEDĀNTA DEŚIKA

The votary of the Monism of doubt is not doubtful about doubt. You cannot keep certainty away from your doubt, no matter how far you go.

ŚRĪ NIVĀSA

. . . 'When I say, "All is doubtful," I imply that that proposition is doubtful also: in this way, I accept doubt on the all-embracing doubt itself.'

Then you cannot avoid admitting that the cause for your *accepting* such a doubt [and not rejecting it] is your *certainty* about it; so, no matter how many hiding places you run into, certainty does not let go of you.

Vedānta Deśika closes this general discussion of the difference between norm and non-norm. Next, to understand what a norm is, he proceeds to resolve the doubt whether a particular norm is really a norm or not. The resolution of this doubt is his motive for defining "norm" [next].

—*The Purification of Logic*[126]

XIX. INNATE DIFFERENCE-IN-IDENTITY, or *SVĀBHĀVIKABHEDĀBHEDA*

See Scheme 30

The theology of Majesty outlined in the Pāñcarātra corpus was developed with consummate intellectual finesse by Qualified Nondualism and the Dualist Vedanta (School VI). But there was an even greater Vaiṣṇava scripture, the *Bhāgavata Purāṇa,* the Bible of Kṛṣṇaism, which outlines a theology of Sweetness—the implications of which begin to unfold in the system of Nimbārka (thirteenth century), the creator of the first Vedantic theology of Kṛṣṇa.

In its metaphysics Nimbārka's school professes, like Rāmānuja's, to go back to the Ancient Vedanta, to the thought of the three sages whose views Bādarāyaṇa quotes with respect—Āśmarathya, Kāśakṛtsna and Auḍulomi—and whom it believes to have been the protagonists of the Difference-in-Identity doctrine. Unlike other schools professing the doctrine, it emphasizes not just Identity, but Difference and Identity equally. On this principle Nimbārka erects an imposing system, mostly Pāñcaratra in character (see Scheme 30). For his basic bipolarity he borrows the scheme of Madhva dependent–independent (see Scheme 19) —a scheme, as one would have thought, uncongenial to any doctrine except that of Difference.

Nimbārka himself wrote very summarily, formulating his entire theology in ten verses (Selection 77). He had three illustrious followers: Śrī Nivāsa (late thirteenth century), chief interpreter of his thought, who develops the concept of God as the sole object of theology (Selection 78) with the concision and comprehensiveness proper to his school; Puruṣottama Prasāda, of uncertain date, and Keśava Kāśmīrin (Selection 79).

77

NIMBĀRKA

Sum of the Theology of Innate Difference-in-Identity

1. *The Soul.* [The texts of Revelation and the great sages] declare the infinitesimal soul to be in essence knowledge, dependent on God, unitable with and separable from the body, distinct in each body, actively knowing and eternal.

2. Through God's grace [the followers of the Vedic tradition] know the soul to be invested by the beginningless Mirific Power. [The Vaiṣṇavas] must understand it to be free and bound, and to be particularized by the subdivisions of free and bound.

3. *The Inconscient.* The Inconscient is conceived to be immaterial, material and temporal. [The material is] described by the terms "Mirific Power" and "Prime Matter." The distinctions of white [red and black, signifying Matter's triple Attributes] are all found in it.

4. *The Absolute as Energizer: Kṛṣṇa.* Let us meditate on Kṛṣṇa, the Brahman—by nature excluding all imperfection, the one mass of all noble qualities, the embodier of the Theophanies, the supremely desirable being, Viṣṇu, the lotus-eyed.

5. *The Absolute as Energy: Lakṣmī or Rādhā.* Let us always call to mind Vṛṣabha's younger sister, all radiant with joy at Kṛṣṇa's left, endowed with a loveliness that reflects His nature, always surrounded by thousands of attendant companion maids, the Goddess gratifying every desire.

6. *Brahman, the Adored.* With all one's heart and at all times must Kṛṣṇa be worshiped by men [seeking salvation], so that the influx of the darkness of ignorance may cease. This was declared by sages like Sanandana to the noble Nārada, witness to all the truth.

7. *Identity of the Adorer and the Adored.* The knowledge

of all things derived from the texts of Revelation and Tradition is therefore wholly true, because it is in essence the Brahman itself. This is what the knowers of the Vedas believe. But the Triad [of categories—the Absolute as the Brahman, the Conscient or soul, and the Inconscient] is also established by Revelation and by Bādarāyaṇa's aphorisms.

8. *Dependence on God.* No goal can one perceive besides Kṛṣṇa's lotus feet, praised by gods like Brahmā and Śiva; besides Kṛṣṇa's forms, so agreeable to the fancy and so quick to reveal themselves at the devotees' desire; and besides the God's transcendent power of incomprehensible meaning.

9. *Devotion to God.* His grace is born in a person united with Himself through helplessness, whence grows a particular love for that Great Soul Who has no one for His master. This is devotion of the highest kind. But there is another sort, the one that conduces to liberation.

10. *The Supreme Goal.* These [then] are the five themes that the good must meditate on: (1) the nature of the adored Being [Kṛṣṇa]; (2) the nature of the adorer [the soul]; (3) the effect of God's grace; also (4) the supreme savor of devotion; and (5) the nature of the [two] factors hindering the realization of God.

—*The Decade of Verses*[127]

78

ŚRĪ NIVĀSA

God, the One Object of Revelation

The whole of the Veda refers only to the Brahman.

A portion of it is no doubt connected, after a fashion, with ritual activity, but in its total implication it relates to none other than the Brahman.

The portion consisting of the Upaniṣads bears on the Brahman immediately, as it is directly concerned with elucidating His nature and all else relevant to His intelligibleness. Such, for instance, are the proclamations of *Difference,* which refer to the Brahman in so far as they indicate the three fundamental categories—conscious being, unconscious being and the Brahman; those of *Non-difference,* as signifying the Brahman nature of all things; those on His *cosmic acts,* like creation, as bearing upon such of His attributes as the causality of the world; those of *attributelessness,* as negating in Him the three Attributes of the Mirific Power; those on *attributefulness,* as referring to His essential attributes; and those declaring His *quantitative illimitability,* as is evinced in scriptural statements like:

> The being unmanifested by speech, but manifesting speech, know that to be the Brahman, and not the thing which people adore.[128]

There are also those statements on necessary and optional duties, referable to the Brahman alone, in so far as they bring about the purification of the aspirant's nature, and thus aid the rise of the Brahman knowledge; statements on optional duties implying that the delight afforded even by sense objects is only a portion of the Brahman joy, as the scriptural assertion "other beings live only on a small portion of that joy"[129] suggests; statements on optional duties again, as those that treat of bodies, pure as those belonging to gods eligible for liberation, which thus imply Brahman knowledge [to be the sole means to release and to a glorious state].

Further there are the statements which are based on the principle of the connection and separation between optional and necessary. Through scriptural passages like "one who wants sense objects to enjoy must sacrifice with curds" and others like "he sacrifices with curds," evince that just as a necessary act like sacrificing with curds can procure enjoyable sense objects, so acts that help realize heaven can also promote the rise of knowledge [which had the Brahman for its end]. And there are texts like "He has a golden beard, golden hair, and is all gold, to the tips of his nails"[130] which refer to Him through alluding to His glorious body.

Finally, as the whole assemblage of things is of the Brahman nature, the assemblage of words which describes it must directly refer to the Brahman. It is thus established that the entire Veda refers to Kṛṣṇa, the all-knowing, the God endowed by His nature with infinite and ineffable powers, the Brahman, the Supreme Person and the Reality both identical and different from conscious and unconscious beings.

—*Kaustubha Jewel of the Vedanta*[131]

79
KEŚAVA KĀŚMĪRIN
Liberation: The Attainment of God's State

Through the experience of the glorious Lord's essence and attributes unconstrained, dawns the state of liberation—heralded by the manifestation of "this great Being, endless and limitless, concentrated knowledge itself,"[132] of the Essence that is the condensation of knowledge endowed with qualities such as the repellence of evil. Such is the doctrine of the Bādarāyaṇa, the noble Aphorismer. Thus no revealed statement is contradicted. The words of Revelation—

> Now that tranquil being, emerging from this body, reaches the highest light: that is the Self[133]

—speak of the category of the Brahman's state, the unrestrained experience of the Brahman, enduring as long as the soul lasts. The soul reaches the august Supreme Person, Who is the Highest Brahman itself, and directly perceives Him through his own selfhood, and in his own form, as well as in the form of an uninhibited experience of His essence and attributes, and then abides in His essence: this is the import of Revelation.

> When the seer sees the golden creator, the lord, the person emanant from the Brahman, then the wise man shakes off merit and demerit, and, free from passion, attains the supreme equilibrium.[134]

These revealed words describe the equilibrium as a state. Similarity to the divine essence and attributes is what this supreme equilibrium is.

The varying texts on the divine state may be harmonized in this way: one attains a similarity of essence through the essence of knowledge, and similarity of attributes through the quality of a knowledge that is unrestricted. The essence of the divine state lies in being other than God, while being participant in most of His attributes—that is, being distinct from the

Brahman, through lacking His sovereignty and independence, yet being in possession of attributes like omniscience and repellence of all evil. This is confirmed by the "Omniscience" Scripture:

> He who sees this does not see death, illness or suffering, He who sees this sees everything, and obtains everything everywhere.[135]

'But this conflicts with Revelation [which seems to imply a participation in God's independence also] as in the following passage:

> He who sees, reflects on and understands this—the Self becomes his passion, his caresses, his orgasm and his ecstasy, and he becomes master of himself.'[136]

[I answer that] there is no conflict whatever, because God's essential transcendence is not found in that communion. Communion means "being in union with"; it signifies an inseparable connectedness; and the meaning of divine *state* is precisely an inseparable connectedness with God.

'"Communion" can only mean "identity."'

You are wrong: communion never has the sense of identity.

'Then you are again at odds with Revelation, as with the following passage:

> Rivers, flowing, disappear into the sea, divesting themselves of conceptual and corporeal distinctions: so too, the wise man, divesting himself of those very distinctions, goes to the divine Person, who transcends the highest.'[137]

Of course I am not at odds with Revelation, for difference persists there too. Water to which more water has been added does not become one in essence with it: it only acquires the relation of inseparable connectedness as exists between the parts of a divisible substance. Rivers, for instance, are seen to increase and diminish with changes of rainy and other seasons.

'But we see no increase and diminution in the sea: it is ever the same.'

The sea, too, is a divisible substance; so on the analogy of the rivers we can infer that it undergoes increase and diminution also. Besides, we see difference in it in the form of waves. The only sense that we can extract from the metaphor of the sea is *sameness* [not identity], as we notice in another passage:

> As pure water poured into pure water remains the same, so, Gautama, does the self of the sage who knows.[138]

I have dwelt at length on the import of Revelation on this topic in my commentary on the *Gītā*, the *Illuminatrix of the Truth.* I refer my reader to it.

'Your doctrine conflicts in part with Revelation, when the latter declares:

> He who knows the Highest Brahman, becomes the Brahman in truth.'[139]

On the contrary, those words described the divine state very well, as happening through union with God's great quality of knowledge. If you do not admit this, you too will be in conflict with Revelation, which says:

> The knower of the Brahman attains the highest[140]

and thus propounds the distinction [not identity] between action [attainment of the highest] and agent [knower of the Brahman].

'But Kṛṣṇa's words in the *Gītā*—

> Arjuna, only through devotion to Me can one know and see Me as I really am, or enter into Me, valiant hero[141]

—speak of an "entry into," and one who has entered into cannot be seen as different: entry into God then proves nondifference.'

Hardly. What Kṛṣṇa is referring to there is entry into His cosmomorphic body. One can only enter something different from oneself. As the words from the divine Mouth itself witness:

> Arjuna, see the whole world of stable and moving things centered as one here in My body.[142]

And the words accompanying the experience of His listener, Arjuna:

> My God, I see gods in Your body, multitudes of all kinds of beings, the lord Brahmā on his lotus throne, the sages, and all the divine snakes![143]

This is what it all means. Entry occurs when God's own universe of conscious and unconscious beings, inherently of the Brahman nature, subsists in the cosmomorphic God as His energies, coincident with an experience [on the part of conscious souls] of His inbeing—in accordance with the revealed pronouncement "that subtle essence is the inbeing of all this universe."[144] The cosmomorphic Brahman, the august Supreme Person Himself, is the foundation of the world, and the world reposes in Him, because the universe comprises His higher and lower energies. This is indisputable; it is guaranteed by the words from the divine Mouth itself:

> This is My lower Matter. But you must know that I have another, higher Matter, which has become all living beings.[145]

In the same way all the controllers of cosmic functions, as well as their controlling energies, have Him as their sole end, and so repose only in Him. At the time of creation, certain meritorious beings become competent to exercise cosmic control, certain extraordinary souls worthy of rising to the status of the creator Brahmā and the destroyer Śiva: these He conjoins to His extraordinary energies capable of creating and destroying the world, constituted of a variety of elemental and partial effects. And at the time of dissolution He disjoins the cosmic controllers, Brahmā and others, from His energies. But these energies [directed to cosmic actions]—eternally subsistent as they are in God's being—abide indissolubly with those other interior energies, such as His innate everlastingness. As the *Viṣṇudharmottara Purāṇa* says:

> Brahmā, Śiva, the sun, the moon, Indra and other gods, and yet other beings are conjoined with Viṣṇu's energy. They are disjoined from it when the world's creation concludes.

In the same way it is plausible to suppose that the liberated, indifferentiable as they are from His energies, abide in the cosmomorphic God through an everlasting experience of Him, which begins when His essential nature as such is revealed.

—*The Radiance of the "Kaustubha Jewel of the Vedanta"*[146]

XX. PURE NONDUALISM, or *ŚUDDHĀDVAITA*

See Scheme 31

With Vaiṣṇava ideas now integral to the Vedantic framework, and with the *Bhāgavata* set up as a norm virtually equal to the Vedas, theology could turn its attention to exploring the specifically Tantric character of the Vaiṣṇava religion, without being preoccupied with presenting it entirely in Vedic terms.

Basic to Kṛṣṇa devotion is the stress on joy, and Vallabha (1481–1533) is the creator of a theology of joy in all its phases—as expressed in the pretty delights of children's frolics, in the range of adult affections, but especially in the pleasures of Eros—all these embodied in the dark-blue form of the Cowherd Kṛṣṇa, sporting with cowherdesses in a bucolic paradise.

A Christian theology of joy was formulated in the seventeenth century by thinkers like François de Sales (1567–1622) and Nicolas de Malebranche (1638–1715). Declares the latter:

> I know of only two principles which of themselves directly determine the movements of our love—light and delight: light which discloses to us our various good things, and delight which makes us savor them.[147]

Each of these principles has a corresponding grace. The Grace of Light was effective before man's Fall, because he was not then swayed by concupiscence; now that he is, the Grace of Light is less effective than the Grace of Delight:

> But since the Fall, besides Light, the Grace of Delight has been necessary for man to resist the movements of concupiscence. For as man invincibly desires to be happy, it is not possible for him to sacrifice his pleasure to his light unceasingly: his pleasure, which makes him happy in fact, and which inheres in him in spite of all his resistance—to his light, which does not inhere except by a painful ap-

> plication of the spirit, which is dissipated by the presence of the least factual pleasure, and which does not promise a secure happiness except after death, an event that appears to the imagination as a real extinction.[148]

Vallabha proceeds to construct his theology of joy with the following principles. First, that of Difference-in-Identity. Vallabha restates it to mean that greatness consists in being a substrate of contrary attributes, and greatness is God's inalienable characteristic. Second, manifestation and non-manifestation. God manifesting Himself is existence, not manifesting Himself is non-existence. He is unmodifiable in essence, but all that exists has Him as its material cause. So what appears to be a modification of the divine substance is only the same substance diversely *manifested*. Third, the definition of God accepted by the Vedantic schools—being, consciousness and joy. These aspects are capable of manifestation and non-manifestation (or concealment). When they are all manifested, we have God as the Inner Controller; when joy is concealed, we have the conscious beings or souls; when consciousness is concealed, we have the inconscient beings; and when being is concealed we have non-existence.

Joy, then, manifests the deepest essence of God. Concealment of it is bondage, and its disclosure, liberation, both actions indulged in motivelessly from God's innate playfulness (Selection 82). In so far as this motiveless impulse binds, it is known as the Mirific Power; in so far as it liberates, it is known as Grace. Through the impulse of this Grace, the love of self expands into the love of the cosmic God, through a process that is known as the Way of Fullness.

Here we have a system perhaps even more imposing than Qualified Nondualism, but with lighter and more graceful contours. Vallabha summarizes it in the first chapter of his *The Lamp of the Meaning of the Truth* (Selection 80). In Vallabha's view all the knowledge we have of God is derived from Word alone—an idea echoed in our times with more dogmatic fervor than intellectual cogency by the proponents of the so-called Theology of the Word, for whom Revelation is the exclusive source of our knowledge of God. Many other ideas of these latter theologians have Hindu prototypes, such as the tripartite scheme of theology itself (see above, p. 35, and Scheme 2), suggested by Uddālaka, and followed by Barth in his celebrated systematization of Calvinist dogmatics

(God in Himself, as Creator, as Reconciler). However, these and other similarities, as the theologians of the Word believe with a serene faith, have little significance—but might have had more if Uddālaka, before formulating his scheme, had taken the precaution of reading his Bible.

Vallabha did not create his theology of joy in a vacuum, but based his structure on the theory of aesthetics, which originates in the work of Bharata, the *Treatise on the Dance*, given its present shape by the fourth century A.D. Following on its insights, writers on poetics created theories on significant emotion and aesthetic delight. These theories were integrated into theology by the great Abhinava Gupta (School XXIII), and ultimately refined by a thinker of Vallabha's school, Jagannātha Paṇḍitarāja (fl. 1620–65), principally a poet and an aesthetic philosopher. No Indic school was so dominated by its founder as Pure Nondualism by Vallabha, most of its prominent representatives being the founder's own descendants. One of them was the poet and theologian Hari Rāya (1591–1716), author of an exposition, in simple and vivid language, of Vallabha's doctrine of divine playfulness (Selection 82).

Yet, notwithstanding Vallabha's importance in the school, it did not remain monolithically one, but divided into two schools, one emphasizing the study of the norms of knowledge, and the other, the objects of knowledge, chiefly Grace. A prominent theologian of the Norm School is that marvel of learning Puruṣottama Pītāmbara (1668–1781), and of the Grace School, Gokula Nātha (1552–1641), besides Hari Rāya himself.

80
VALLABHA

Principles of the Theology of Pure Nondualism

PROLOGUE

1. Adoration to God Kṛṣṇa, wonderful in His deeds, Who

plays with, and is Himself, the corporeal and conceptual divergence of the universe!

2. The sublime devotees of God, the aspirants to liberation, born to their last life in the transmigratory world—it is for them that this inquiry is begun.

3. [The knowledge the inquiry embodies is gained] by a knowledge of the science of God, the sacred Vaiṣṇava teaching, by constant reflection on it, and by appreciation of what God said for dispelling doubt.

4. There is only one Teaching, that proclaimed in song [the *Gītā*] by Kṛṣṇa, Devakī's Son. There is only one God, that same Son. Only one mantra, His names. Only one work, His service.

5. Keeping this constantly in mind, I shall develop three themes [giving a chapter to each]—"The Import of Kṛṣṇa's Teaching," "The Ascertainment of All Wisdom," and "The Exposition of the *Bhāgavata*."

6. The terms for the Absolute in the Vedanta, Tradition and the *Bhāgavata* are, respectively, "the Brahman," "the Supreme Self" and "God." In my three chapters, I shall speak of these terms in their order.

7. The Vedas, Kṛṣṇa's words, Vyāsa's [Bādarāyaṇa's] aphorisms, and Vyāsa's meditation language [in the *Bhāgavata*]—this is the fourfold source of all authoritative teaching.

8. Of these sources, each one that follows is for clearing its antecessor's doubtful points. All that does not conflict with this fourfold norm is valid authority, not otherwise. All that conflicts with it has no authority at all.

9. Else—God being manifest in all meaning, as differentiated through concept and play—all sacred writings have authority, except for those portions in conflict with the fourfold norm.

10. At the beginning of the Dvāpara age [the era of confusion], religious Observance, being twofold [Vedic and traditional], the rules of faith were also twofold. As with inconsistent texts [explained consistently by commentators] so also with their ascertainments [expounded differently by different systems, consistently by each].

11. In the first section of Revelation [the Vedas] God is Sacrifice, in the second [the Upaniṣads] He is the Brahman, and in the *Bhāgavata,* the Incarnate.

12. In the Brahman section, God, invested with forms like those of the sun, is proclaimed as knowledge. In all the

puranic texts of Tradition, He asssumes the forms of a multitude of gods.

13. If one strives for the goal of knowledge, one should worship the Brahman in all His forms. But if one desires union with God, only His primordial form, Kṛṣṇa, is to be adored.

14. From Kṛṣṇa is unqualified liberation, from other gods, the qualified. Knowledge brings on perfect liberation or liberation in this life. The man aiming at liberation through knowledge, and who worships Kṛṣṇa, has no superior.

15. In our own days, God has become incarnate as the Buddha. In obedience to His will the gods, appearing among Brahmins, have taught them various doctrines, bringing them into confusion, and so frustrating the worship of Kṛṣṇa in any way they can.

16. This is the great delusion, this the great scandal—that men of wisdom, of deep learning in the sciences, and of great energy should not be worshipers of Kṛṣṇa! Living as they do for ritual actions alone, transmigration will be their sole reward.

17. The perfection of knowledge is ascertained when a person becomes omnipotent; the perfection of ritual activity, when the mind is pleased; the perfection of devotion, when Kṛṣṇa is pleased.

18. Without these perfections, then, there is no realization of any kind. This is my firm belief. And it is through the salvific disciplines that the perfections themselves are realized, not through flights of verbal fancy.

19. This triple way leads to results if one follows the methods proper to each. But all propriety has vanished today, in this Kali age. Yet if one serves Kṛṣṇa with devotion, even the Kali age will be fruitful.

20. This, and only this, is the primary sense of the Vedic sentences and of Kṛṣṇa's words. Anything else is fiction excogitated by other systems of thought.

21. Those who proclaim the meaning of the Vedic doctrine in Kṛṣṇa's words are said to be God's devotees; they are the Pure Nondualists [professors of the "Pure Brahman" Doctrine].

22. Not aware of this orthodox teaching, even these chosen souls, following other systems of thought, do not serve God. It is for their sake that this work has been begun.

I. THE BRAHMAN AS BEING: CREATION AND LIBERATION

23. An effect of God, the world is His nature, and emanates through His Mirific Power. Through Ignorance, His energy, the soul becomes involved in transmigratory existence.

24. It is transmigration that dissolves at the time of release, not the world. The world's dissolution is for Kṛṣṇa's delight, and brings relief to all living things.

25. All-pervading like the sky, the Brahman is enveloped by Its mode, the Mirific Power. "With feet, hands and fingertips everywhere, everywhere eyes, heads and mouths;

26. Everywhere ears, it stands encompassing all things in creation."[149] Infinite in Its forms, the Brahman is indivisible, though seeming divided.

27. "Let me be many; let me generate!" The vision expressed in these divine words proved fruitful. Then, consubstantial with the Brahman, and from God's will alone, emanated the particle intelligences [the souls].

28. In the beginning of creation [from God's Consciousness], through His will, emerged the souls, formless [emptied of their connaturally divine form], like sparks from a fire. Also, from His Being, the unconscious beings emerged.

29. From the substance of His Joy came all the Inner Controller forms. In His modes of Being, Consciousness and Joy, each antecedent is implied in its consequent.

30. Hence, with the aspect of Joy suppressed, the first two categories of being [the unconscious and the souls] are said to be formless [devoid of God's intrinsic form, joy]. The pragmatic distinction [in God's undivided being] is thus threefold —unconscious, soul and Inner Self.

31. Knowledge and Ignorance are God's powers, projected only by the Mirific Power. They belong to none but the soul: so do sorrow and powerlessness.

32. [Of the five members of Ignorance] one is said to be the ignorance of one's own nature, and the others the fourfold superposition of body, senses, breath and the Inner Faculty.

33. Ignorance is five-membered. Through it the bound soul transmigrates. When knowledge destroys Ignorance, it will be liberated.

34. The body, senses and breath are all cleared of su-

perposition in one liberated in this life—but do not disappear all at once.

35. Through service to God—the Mouth [source of the Fiery Word]—the divine condition of the senses leads to their own dissolution, and the Brahman nature of the soul to its own.

36. When the aspect of Joy is revealed, the Brahman nature is attained. Then union with God results; if not, there is resolution into the Inconscient. Both Brahman nature and union arise from service to God. Sometimes He Himself, the increate, accomplishes all this.

37. Sometimes through Spirit [as the puranas say], sometimes through other causes [the Four Theophanies, as the Pāñcarātras tell], sometimes as All-Soul, does Kṛṣṇa come to be the universe.

38. Sometimes, through the Mirific Power, God creates everything as one vast web of illusion. Then such things as knowledge exist only as words, not realities.

39. Sometimes, Viṣṇu diverts Himself by creating the universe as the sky and then entering it in the dual form of the Inner Controller and soul.

40. All this is possible to One Whose energies are limitless. Hence Revelation declares the variances of creation to be manifold.

41. In one manner or another, His greatness is extolled, and the statements of Revelation, like "You are It"[150] are made only to assure His worship.

42. A love unshakable and superabundant, accompanied by a knowledge of God's greatness—such is devotion. Through it alone is liberation and through no other way.

43. Fivefold that He was, God assumed twelve, ten, a hundred, a thousand—more, innumerable forms. He is one, equal, repellent of all imperfection, plenary in His qualities, and the exemplar of innumerable things,

44. Immaculate, the embodiment of qualities in their plenitude, the self-dependent, devoid of the characteristics of the innately unconscious body. Pure delight are His limbs—as hands, feet, mouth and stomach. Everywhere He is untouched by the triple divergence [unconscious, soul and Inner Controller].

45. Isolation is reached through knowing Him and eschewing ignorance. So is dispassion, Sankhya discrimination, yogic discipline, asceticism and devotion to Kṛṣṇa.

46. This is the fivefold knowledge through which the wise man enters God. Ready for emancipation are those divine souls born in a glorious other-worldly existence.

47. The liberation that occurs, even in a sacred place, at some time and of some one—is only of someone furnished with Kṛṣṇa's grace, not of anyone else. Such is my firm belief.

48. Sometimes, somewhere, Kṛṣṇa will mercifully free His servant. Hallowed by events such as these, the holy place is given praise.

49. So, abandoning all, firm in his trust, let a man praise God through the salvific disciplines—listening, reflecting and meditating—and by that knowledge he will be freed.

50. Those who have entered the Brahman Joy experience it in their nature, their faculties having dissolved. But the devotees, in a special manner,

51. Are able to experience it in all their senses, their Inner Faculty and their nature as well. Possessed as they are of the Brahman nature, even the devotees' home life excels.

52. When the mind is cleared of the filth from the doctrines that only precipitate delusion, people repose their trust in the sacred Vaiṣṇava teaching, and salutary results are produced.

II. THE BRAHMAN AS CONSCIOUSNESS: THE SOUL

53. Tiny as the point of an awl, the soul is nonetheless different [in that it is not constricted by space], like perfume [which pervades more space than its flower]. However, the "All-pervasiveness" Scripture ["the eternal, the omnipresent, the all-pervading . . . source of all things"][151] is applicable to the soul only in its innate divinity.

54. When the aspect of Joy unfolds in the soul, millions of worlds rise into vision. Limitation and illimitability thus appertain to the soul.

55. That conscious Luminance shines in its brightness.

56. Material senses cannot grasp it and no light exists that can illuminate it. But it is disclosed to yogic perception, to God's insight and to the divine eye.

57. In this way, and in no other, is the soul an appearance and a reflection of the Brahman. With the Brahman's Joy concealed, He appears as the soul; with the Joy revealed, the soul appears as the Brahman.

58. Concealed by the curtain of Illusion, the soul cannot be reflected anywhere. Revelation condemns Reflectionism—in

texts like those on the Two Birds and on the Entry into the Cave—and so do Kṛṣṇa's words in the *Gītā*.

[*The two birds:* Two birds, constant companions, perch on the same tree. One of them eats the sweet fig. The other does not eat but looks on.[152]

The cave: The two drink the reward of their good deeds in the world; they enter the cave on the highest peak. The Brahman knowers call them light and shade.[153]

Kṛṣṇa's words: In the world of the living, a particle of Me, eternal, becomes the soul, drawing to itself the five senses derived from Matter.[154]

Whether he emerges from the body or remains in it, or whether, through contact with the body, he undergoes experience, fools do not perceive him. Only those who possess the wisdom-eye do.][155]

59. [In Reflectionism] liberation is the disappearance of the soul. Liberation in this life is rendered impossible, as it is found to exist in the Subtle Body and in Ignorance itself.

[*Comment.* For Reflectionism the soul is only the Brahman reflected in Ignorance. Reflectedness in ignorance is by definition bondage; the disappearance of the reflection is liberation. To remove the reflection is thus to remove the soul. Liberation "in this life"—needing both the reflection, to make "this life" possible, and its absence, to assure liberation—is therefore self-contradictory.]

60. Its controller eliminated, the body cannot move. The fact that his inchoate karmas remain will not make a sleeper walk.

61. However subtly one interprets the statement "You are It,"[156] it cannot be made to produce knowledge. Its import is quite another—

62. The differentiated assertion of the Brahman's omniformed essence, because such a supernatural object of knowledge cannot be attained through reason.

63. In the age of Truth [the first aeon in the world's history] a man could with great trouble acquire knowledge—through asceticism, through the reasons furnished by Revelation, and through the grace of the Supreme Lord.

64. Omniscience and an unworldly splendor were his characteristics, which, when attained, did not bring about libera-

tion, since ignorance and knowledge succeed each other as do the sleeping and waking states. Thus devotion is everywhere believed to be the best means.

III. THE BRAHMAN AS JOY

65. The Brahman is intrinsically Being, Consciousness and Joy; all-pervading, imperishable, omniscient, independent, all-knowing and free from Matter's Attributes.

66. Devoid of variances—homogeneous [the souls], heterogeneous [unconscious beings] and intrinsic [the Inner Controllers]—it is forever furnished with myriads of natural qualities, like truth, purity, mercy and patience.

67. Supporter of all things, Controller of the Mirific Power, the Brahman is the form of Joy, the Supreme, distinct from all objects in phenomenal existence.

68. As He is the world's material cause as well as its efficient cause, He sometimes diverts Himself joyously within His inner being, and sometimes within the phenomenal world.

69. "When, by Him, from Him, of Him, to Him, whatever, as and when—all this will be God, Who is directly Matter, Spirit and Supreme Lord."[157]

70. Immanent in things everywhere, He is untouched by them; hence the body He penetrates and illumines does not know Him. Unfavorable to all doctrines, He is yet complaisant with all.

71. Of infinite forms, the Brahman is immovable and moving, the repository of discordant attributes, and beyond the range of reason.

72. He fascinates through His multiple forms, manifested and concealed. Invisible to the powers of the sense, He becomes visible through His will.

73. As the pure Brightness in God's form of Joy comes to fulfillment, the Joy, as it reveals itself, glows with an emerald luster [the color of Kṛṣṇa's body].

74. In the four ages of the world, God assumed a variety of forms, and the form of contingent Time is reflected in the Brahman.

75. Else, the Brahman, the impenetrable, appears to mundane vision like emptiness or the sky. Sight is otherwise unable to reach Him.

76. As the world is the creation of Himself, there is no

injustice or cruelty in it. In other doctrines, there is karma to justify such acts, but karma is itself determined by Him.

77. He alone is the universe's Creator, but He is not Attributeful [the three Attributes of Matter do not belong to His nature as Creator. The triad of gods, Brahmā, Viṣṇu and Śiva] who assume these Attributes are His parts; it is they who are known to be Atttributeful. The Creator is independent, and hence incompatible with the Attributes.

IV. CRITIQUE OF DISSENTIENT DOCTRINES

78. Some thinkers of excessively clear minds depart from the sense of Revelation, and reject Viṣṇu's material causality of the world.

79. They say that the real cause is the Brahman bound by beginningless Ignorance; that He transmigrates because of His ignorance, and that liberation is attained through instruction by an imagined teacher [all individuals in the world being fictions of the mind].

80. Such a scandalous teaching, destructive of all greatness in God, must be spurned by His devotees, contrary as it is to Revelation and to Tradition. It enjoys great respect in this Kali age, but, averse to God that it is, its fruit is darkness.

81. If you say that all this talk about illusion is only to show that the world can be obliterated by knowledge, the contrary has been established in Revelation, in the texts that explain knowledge and ignorance [as: "knowledge and ignorance—one knows Him through both. Through ignorance one goes beyond death; through knowledge one tastes immortality"].[158]

82. The talk about illusion in the puranas is to set forth the theory of the phantasmagorial nature of variety in creation [and so to foster dispassion]. It is also, to be sure, the exposition of unorthodox doctrine. On the other hand, in the texts of Revelation, as we know them, there is no mention of such illusion anywhere.

83. The "Verbality" statements of Revelation ["The changes (in clay) are only verbal, a mere matter of name: only clay is the reality"][159] are intended to teach the Brahman's non-difference from the world, and not the world's falsehood. This we accept because of Vyāsa's [Bādarāyaṇa's] unequaled authority [and Bādarāyaṇa explicitly states that

"The Brahman is not different from the world, as the words of Revelation declare the verbal nature of the effect"].[160]

84. 'Can it be that Revelation's teachings on acts like creation are merely expressions of appreciation, helping to promote liberative knowledge?'

No; this doctrine is unacceptable. It does not help one to follow scriptural injunctions or to know God's greatness.

85. 'Cannot one believe that the ascription of creatorship to God denotes nothing real, but that it is only in the manner of an exception [proving the rule of the Brahman's qualitylessness] to assure that one will have a firm knowledge of the Brahman?'

This is also untenable.

86. The primary sense of Revelation's words is not abrogated because one experiences the reality of God's effect, the world. However, even on the hypothesis that it is illusory, we can say that God is a creator in the manner of an actor [who identifies himself with his roles illusorily].

87. In the Illusionist hypothesis, liberation will be entirely dissipated, like an elephant in a dream. Revelation and Bādarāyaṇa's *Aphorisms* repudiate the causality of Illusion or of the souls.

88. In the passages where the Sacred Teaching asserts that God is not a creator, it does so to proclaim His greatness [by denying Him causality in a mundane sense. Greatness being something in which contrary qualities abide] the appreciation of contrary qualities is not logically possible if one suppresses any of them [by declaring it unreal].

89. The puranas preach the illusoriness of the world to incite detachment from it. Hence Illusionism of a rigorous kind only serves to delude.

90. " 'The world is devoid of reality,' they say, 'it has no Ground, no ruling Lord. It does not come to be by interacting causes. How then does it arise? Through desire alone.' "[161]

91. Only when undifferenced nonduality is revealed does everything seem to be the Brahman. Knowledge puts an end to the awareness of difference, not to that of its underlying unique essence.

92. No difference is possible in so far as the Brahman is the [indivisible] material cause of things. Purely verbal as it is, through what cause can a supervening difference arise?

93. There are many Sankhya systems: only one is valid for

the good—the one where the twenty-eight categories have God for their essence.

94. The other systems are condemned in Bādarāyaṇa's *Aphorisms.* There is also only one Yoga that the good respect —the one where the contemplation, even when Seedless, of God, gives rise to a knowledge of the soul.

95. Worshiping God through renunciation, knowledge, Yoga, love and asceticism—or through one of these solid means—a man can attain liberation.

96. Many are the means propounded for dissolving the world through knowledge, but only one—accordant with the Sankhya—for assuring purity of mind.

97. Purity of mind can also be assured through realizing the divinity of the senses, and this realization itself through service to Kṛṣṇa, the Cowherd and the Mouth—and through no other way.

98. Through knowledge of the soul's nonduality arises dispassion, because of which one leaves home. It is furthered by the dissolution of speech in the mind.

99. These dissolutions are only mental experiences: there is no total dissolution of the objective world. That is why there is sometimes talk of the world being a mental fiction.

100. If men professing other doctrines worship and believe in accordance with the path of devotion, their worship is not repulsed. But its fruit is not assured, because of the inconsequence of their behavior [sometimes accordant with true devotion, sometimes with their own false principles].

EPILOGUE

101. "All things are from Him, all things are He." A man who with this thought in mind serves God through the discipline of knowledge, with love and by means of the salvific disciplines—listening, reflection and meditation—is the highest kind of devotee.

102. If he is lacking in love, he will be of the middling kind; if lacking in knowledge, of the lowest; if lacking in both, at least the destruction of sin will follow from the salvific disciplines.

103. With asceticism and dispassion conjoined, his knowledge will bear fruit. Conjunction with Yoga will generate love. Without these paths all that is left to do is to praise God.

104. God is ever determining this doctrine in a felicitous

manner [in the *Gītā*] through all the Vedic utterances, and through the words of the Rāmāyaṇas, the *Mahābhārata,* the Pāñcarātras, the pronouncements of the other sacred sciences [the texts of Tradition] and the aphorisms of truth [those of Ritualism].

—*The Lamp of the Meaning of the Truth*[162]

81

JAGANNĀTHA PAṆḌITARĀJA

The Nature and Divinity of Aesthetic Emotion

The power of a singular intuition, rendered delightful through the choiceness and grace of its Integrants, and aided by the percipient's aesthetic sensibility—this power combines the Elements signified as supramundane Causes, Effects and Concomitants [with the Basic Emotion], and by reason of them [the merely contingent factors like] Duśyanta's personality and such like things melt away. These Elements comprise heroes or heroines like Śakuntalā, which are the *Personalities* [the "sustaining" Causes]; enchanting objects like the moon, the *Excitants* [the "illuminant" Causes]; actions, like the shedding of tears, the *Effects;* or like sudden anxious thoughts, the *Concomitants.*

From this combination a supramundane activity emerges in the sensitive percipient; the veiling Ignorance is at that moment dispelled by his joyous nature, and all limitations like restricted perception are torn away. Then the inerrant percipient, through his self-luminant nature and substantially innate joy, brings to light a conceptual latency, such as that of Erotic Passion, that had previously been implanted in the mind. This is what we know as Sentiment. Hence it is said [by Mammaṭa]:

> The Basic Emotion, manifested by the Elements, such as the Causes, is what is known as Sentiment.[163]

"Manifested" means made the object of manifestation. And manifestation itself is the Consciousness bereft of its Veil. A lamp may be hidden under a potsherd, but with the potsherd taken away, it reveals the objects around it and is itself revealed. Similarly Self-Consciousness reveals emotions like Erotic Passion, invested in the Causes and the other Elements, since qualities [like emotions] are capable of being illuminated by the Witness. This Witness can without contradiction equally illuminate illusory objects like horses seen in a dream, and real ones like solid metal silver. The ruminative savoring of the Elements, such as the Causes, can lead to the destruction or to the restoration of the covering Veil, but both events subserve Sentiment; as, for instance, with sound. Eternal though it is, it stands in relation to the revealing function of vocal areas like the palate, which emit the sounds that form the word *cow* [the sounds *c o w* are eternal, but are concealed in the vocal areas, and reveal their meaning in time, when all of them have been put together by the pronouncing voice]. In the same way, though the covering Veil is [partially] destroyed, the Light behind it is still [partially] concealed. Hence the Basic Emotion, though existent, does not reveal itself, until the savoring of all the Elements, such as the Causes, has been completed.

To put it in another way, the power of the savoring of the Elements, such as the Causes, awakened by the impact of the aesthetic percipient's sensibility—or efformed by the innate joy linked with the various types of Basic Emotion—generates a mental state comparable to that of the yogi during concentration. This joy has nothing in common with mundane happiness, because it has the form of the Inner Faculty. It is certain, on the authority of Abhinava Gupta, Mammaṭa and others, that Sentiment is nothing but the Consciousness deprived of its Veil. In fact it is on the evidence of Revelation, to be alluded to presently, that we know Sentiment to be none but the unveiled Consciousness qualified by the Basic Emotions like Erotic Passion. At all times do we perceive the qualifier and the qualified reality of the essentially qualified Consciousness. In so far as it is Consciousness, the Sentiment's eternity and self-luminance are established; in so far as it is Erotic Passion, its transience and illuminability.

As was said before, ruminative savoring is nothing but the removal of the Veil over Consciousness, or a mental state efformed of the latter. Sentiment, however, is different from yogic concentration, since it possesses the savor of the Supreme Brahman, and is sustained by the joy of Consciousness affected by the Elements, such as the Causes, and apprehensible only by the action of poetry.

'Is there any proof that the Brahman's joyous aspect is revealed in Sentiment?'

Well, is there any proof that it is revealed during yogic concentration? This is an equally valid counter question. As is said:

> An absolute joy is one which exceeds anything the senses can grasp.

'We have the authority of Revelation for yogic concentration.'

We have it for Sentiment too:

> He is truly Savor itself. One who relishes this Savor is filled with joy.[164]

These are the words of Revelation; there is also the experience of sensitive persons: we thus have a twofold proof. The experience of the sensitive is essentially a mental state efformed by the Consciousness, and is explained as the ruminative savoring of Sentiment. Since it is apprehended through the use of words, it is verbal; as it is sustained by intuitively apprehended joy, it is essentially intuitive. As the great Abhinava Gupta said, the truth is like intelligence generated by words.

—*The Bearer of the Ganges of Sentiment*[165]

82

HARI RĀYA

The Motivelessness of Divine Play

'If, as you say, the souls are naturally a part of God, how can they be divided into divine and devilish?'

Understand that the division is for play, through His will. Consequently, when the final goal is realized, adoration finds its reward by virtue of the soul's inferior state. If this were not to be so, the autonomous Way of Devotion would be null. As there is a natural inferiority in the souls, so is there a superiority above all things in the Brahman.

'But how can there be the relation of inferior to superior, since all are really parts of the same Brahman?'

To this I say: the Lord [as cause] reveals Himself [as effect] in the form of the world, for play. This is how things may be explained: the Brahman is being, consciousness and joy, and those aspects are possessed by the triple-formed Imperishable Being. Its consciousness-particles are the souls, formed by His will for play. Were the diversity to be absent, the play would be non-existent. Hence, in [the three categories] the Inconscient, the Conscious and the Inner Controller, there is a concealment of one or another of these aspects [or no concealment at all: concealment of the aspects of consciousness and joy in the Inconscient, of joy in the Conscious, and of nothing in the Inner Controller] according to His will. The division of His integral form is consequently for play, and the play, in God's basic essence, consists in bondage and liberation alone. To prove then that play is eternal, we must postulate bondage and liberation to be eternal also—all of which explains why the divine and the devilish are different.

'What then is this divinity and devilhood?'

I reply that this is how they are to be discriminated: at the time of creation, the Energy separates from the divine Essence; the assumption [of beings] by this separated Energy is devilhood, while the assumption by the Essence itself is divinity. It is true that the devils are parts of God, but as they have been assumed by the separated Energy for delusion's sake at the time of the world's creation, they can never enter God again—just as a jewel, fallen out of a jewel box and into the hands of thieves, cannot be recovered even by a thousand stratagems. But the entry of the gods into God is like a jewel taken out of the jewel box by one's own hand and put back into the box again. The creation of the devils is therefore the work of the Mirific Power distinct from God [in His essentially blissful inbeing]. Because of the delusion produced by this Power, the effects of the two energies of knowledge and devotion are non-existent in them, so union with God [realized through those energies alone] is impossible to attain.

And this is why the Lord has said:

> Implanted in devilish wombs, deluded in birth after birth, they never attain Me, Arjuna, and go down to the lowest way.[166]

That is because those two causes of realizing Him [knowledge and devotion] are absent in the devilish souls. So then, as a part of a man, his sperm—once it has entered a woman's womb and established itself there, it permits no other man's sperm to enter—so too those demons never enter God. In human things, as in divine ones, the case is as that of a son [especially favored over someone who is not], even when we postulate that all beings are parts of God. Therefore, this characteristic of being God's part has been described as true in a relative sense, brought about as it is through connection with Matter.

'But, even so, Matter [or the Mirific Power] is God's energy and indistinct from him, and hence is intrinsically joy; those entering it must therefore decidedly possess joy. How then can they not attain God?'

They cannot, because God does not *manifest* His joyous essence to the demons. Understand, then, that as the form of joy is not manifested, the demons do not feel even a puff of it—else when God reveals His joy form to His devotees, the demons would experience its joy too. [As they do not] we must suppose that the joy form is not manifested to them. The Lord says:

> This divine Mirific Power of Mine, formed of the Attributes, is difficult to transcend.[167]

And:

> They embrace a deluding Matter which is monstrous and devilish.[168]

These two statements disclose the demons' connection with Matter and their lack of any connection with God, and describe the difference between the divine and devilish varieties of the Mirific Power. In both cases also delusion is diversified through a differentiation in effects—in the one case for the sake of liberation, in the other for that of bondage.

And it is precisely to signify the evil variety of the Mirific Power that "devilishness" has been referred to, to bring out the cruelty of the demons. Innately cruel as they are, Vallabha defines them as lacking in compassion in his *Commentary on the "Bhāgavata Purāṇa."* The purana itself describes them in the following manner [expressing their thoughts in the words of the king (Parīkṣit) who opens its tenth book]:

> What man can attain to passionlessness without the massacre of animals—which has been celebrated by ascetics freed from their desires, is a medicine for transmigration, a delight to the ears and to the mind, and whose qualities have been echoed in the best poetry?[169]

Also, the word "delusiveness" has been used to exclude [from the definition of demons] any divine effect that is lacking in that quality.

'At the time of dissolution, Matter is dissolved in God, and the demons are thereby dissolved in Him also; in consequence, they are united to God: they cannot then fail to experience joy, can they?'

They can indeed. For even though they are united with God at dissolution, an obstruction is placed to their experience of joy—else there would be no difference between dissolution and release. And if release were dissolution, the effort to practice the salvific disciplines would be in vain. No sensible person engages in strenuous effort for his own destruction [or dissolution, but he does engage in that effort for his salvation]. So release, whose essence is the experience of joy, is quite distinct from dissolution. The latter is like what happens to worms in a belly: they experience the objects proper to themselves, but they do not thereby experience joy [as does the person in whose belly they are].

This is because joy is realized by devotion alone. Devotion is in essence affection, and is therefore an abiding in the heart of God. That is why the Lady Glory and the devotees abide in that heart. It has been said:

> The good are My heart; I am the heart of the good. Besides Me they know nothing; and I know nothing besides them, no, not for a moment.

And Jayadeva says:

> Keeping Rādhā in His heart, Kṛṣṇa, king Kaṁsa's foe, abandoned the lovely cowherdesses.[170]

So in dissolution, as in sleep, the troubles caused by numerous births are not dispelled. Hence everything is clear.

—*The Doctrine of the Brahman*[171]

XXI. INEFFABLE DIFFERENCE-IN-IDENTITY or *ACINTYABHEDĀBHEDA*

See Scheme 32

Vallabha's system is a theology of Sweetness, but a relatively sober Sweetness. In the last of the great Vaiṣṇava systems, founded by that most ecstatic of mystics, Caitanya (1486–1533), a younger contemporary of Vallabha, the Sweetness becomes inebriant.

Caitanya was no theologian, but he founded a school which was fortunate in having two theologians of genius to organize its doctrines, Rūpa (fl. 1495–1550) and Jīva (fl. 1555–1600) Gosvāmī. For the Gosvāmīs the *Bhāgavata Purāṇa* is almost the exclusive norm of sacred knowledge, and theology but a commentary on the *Bhāgavata.* As theologies of Difference-in-Identity, those of Rūpa and Jīva are founded on the concept of an eternally existent divine play—its sublimest moment the love between Kṛṣṇa and the cowherdesses of that divine Arcadia, Vṛndāvana, culminating in the ecstatic Passion Dance (the Rāsa) on a night of the full moon.

Here then is a theology of liberation through joy, realized, not in another world, but now, through mystic participation in Kṛṣṇa's play. In clarifying the nature of this participation, Rūpa Gosvāmī employs the concepts of the aesthetic philosophers on sentiment, and thus develops a refined mystical theology of Passion (Selection 83). Through its ecstatic techniques one is enabled to live the delights of the idyllic Paradise of Vṛndāvana, situated in Vraja land, delights visibly manifested at a moment in time, but now invisible to the eyes of all except devotees (Selection 84). Indeed, the Vṛndāvana Garden and all its components are formed of the subtlest spiritual essence, as is the form of Kṛṣṇa the Cowherd which supremely ennobles it. Reality's most exalted level is Kṛṣṇa's human form, and its humblest the undifferenced and impersonal Brahman.

Thus the triumph of devotion (with its craving for the visible and tangible) over knowledge (with its penchant for the abstract) is complete. So is the triumph of the human-faced Sweetness, distinctive of the new Vaiṣṇava schools, over the divinely visaged Majesty, characteristic of the older: a theme developed by the last great theologian of Difference-in-Identity, Baladeva Vidyābhūṣaṇa (1720–90; Selection 85).

83

RŪPA GOSVĀMĪ

The Mystical Theology of Passion

1. Manifested gloriously among the dwellers of Vraja land is Passion-Souled Devotion, upon which follows the Passion-Sequent.

2. I shall first explain the Passion-Souled variety to ensure a clear comprehension of the Passion-Sequent.

I. PASSION-SOULED DEVOTION

3. Passion is a spontaneous and total engrossment in one's chosen deity. Absorbing devotion is here affirmed to be Passion-Souled.

4. This devotion is of two kinds, erotic and associatory.

5. In the seventh canto of the *Bhāgavata,* the sage Nārada tells king Yudhiṣṭhira: "Many have fixed their minds on the Supreme Lord, through devotion, expressed as passion, hate, fear, affection, have freed themselves of sin and have reached liberation—

6. The cowherdesses through passion, king Kaṁsa through fear, the Cedi princes through hate, the Yādava tribesmen through companionship, you, king Yudhiṣṭhira, through affection, and I myself through devotion."[172]

7. I have left out fear and hate as being contrary to the agreeable nature of devotion. As affection connotes [passionless] friendship, I have classed it under Injunctional Devotion.

8. Also, when love is only a means to an end, it does not

help realize Passion-Souled Devotion. Nārada's words "and I myself through devotion" clearly evince a devotion of an Injunctional kind.

9. If God's enemies and friends are said to have the identical goal, then the Brahman and Kṛṣṇa are one, comparably with a ray and the sun.

10. Viṣṇu's enemies are generally dissolved into the Brahman. Some arrive at a semblance of similarity with him, but subside into the qualityless Brahman bliss.

11. As the *Brahmāṇḍa Purāṇa* says: "Beyond darkness are the worlds of the blessed. There live the blessed, and the fiends that Viṣṇu killed, immersed in the Brahman-bliss."

12. Sprayed with the nectar of His lotus feet, God's dear devotees, the very embodiments of love, go worshiping Him with intense attachment.

13. In the tenth canto of the *Bhāgavata* the goddesses of Revelation, hymning Kṛṣṇa, exclaim: "The Brahman—Whom the sages worship through firm control of their hidden breaths, their minds and their senses—Your enemies attain through recollection, and Your women through intentiveness on Your pleasure-giving arms lovely like the body of the serpent king. We are alike and share their feelings, absorbing the nectar of Your lotus feet."[173]

14. *Erotic Passion-Souled Devotion.* Next, is Passion-Souled Devotion of the erotic kind. Erotic-Souled passion—functioning solely for Kṛṣṇa's delight—is what reduces the appetite for pleasure to a subsistent state.

15. It is among the goddesses of Vraja that this type of devotion is perpetually refulgent. Their singular love has acquired an unwonted sweetness. Inciting as it does amorous play, the wise call it Eros.

16. As the *Tantra* says: "It is only the love of the cowherds' beautiful wives that has come to be celebrated as passion."

17. So Uddhava and others dear to God have come to envy that love.

18. It is thought that [the hunchback woman] Kubjā's amorous urges are very like the Passion described above.

19. *Associatory Passion-Souled Devotion.* Next is Associatory Passion-Souled Devotion. Associatory Devotion is the belief of oneself as linked with Kṛṣṇa in a relationship like the parental, a relation which the Yādava cowherds, by implica-

tion, share. [In their relations with Kṛṣṇa,] the knowledge of His divine sovereignty is absent and Passion predominates.

20. The two types of Passion-Souled Devotion, having pure love as their essence and implanted in Kṛṣṇa's eternal associates, are not discussed here in detail.

II. PASSION-SEQUENT DEVOTION

21. Passion-Souled Devotion being twofold, Passion-Sequent Devotion is twofold too, and admitted to have two forms—the Erotic-Sequent and the Associatory-Sequent.

22. *Eligibles for Passion-Sequent Devotion.* As for the eligibles of these two types—those burning to experience the emotions of people like the dwellers of Vraja, undeviating in their Passion-Souled love, are eligible for Passion-Sequent Devotion.

23. The rise of this burning desire is discernible when the mind is intent only on hearing of the sweetness of the emotions [and of all else to do with Kṛṣṇa and His associates], and where neither sacred science nor reasoning has any place.

24. The sacred sciences and reasoning are right for those eligible for Injunctional Devotion—until the emotions described manifest themselves.

25. The followers of Passion-Sequent Devotion should live only in Vraja, thinking always of their beloved Kṛṣṇa and of those dear to Him, listening to talk about Him being their only delight.

26. One eager to experience those emotions—as a beginner or as a perfect master—must serve God in accordance with the practice of Vraja's eternal inhabitants.

27. The practices of Injunctional Devotion described above —as listening to recitals of Kṛṣṇa's delights, the celebration of His praises—are also useful here, as the wise should know.

28. *Erotic-Sequent Devotion.* Next is Erotic-Sequent Devotion, an appetite for pleasure patterned on that of Passion-Souled Devotion.

29. It is of two kinds—avidity for the joys of divine sex and of divine amorous feelings.

30. Avidity for the joys of divine sex has lascivious play in mind; avidity for divine amorous feelings is a craze for sweet emotional experience.

31. Those who contemplate the sweetness of His august image, who listen to recitals of His playful exploits and who

crave to experience the emotions of the Vraja women—they are the ones eligible for the two kinds of Passion-Sequent Devotion. Men also qualify, as one hears from the *Padma Purāṇa* accounts.

32. In the following one, for instance: "Once all the great ṛṣis [rishis] living in the Daṇḍaka forest saw Viṣṇu incarnate as Rama and yearned to enjoy His beautiful body.

33. Becoming women, they were all born in Gokula, where they espoused Viṣṇu with passion, becoming thereby saved from the ocean of transmigration."

34. Anyone, desirous of divine sex-play, who serves the Beloved in accordance with the way of Injunctional Devotion only, will become one of Kṛṣṇa's queens in Dvārakā city.

35. As the great *Kūrma Purāṇa* says: "Through ascetic practices the fire-god's sons acquired both womanliness and a husband in Vāsudeva's Son Kṛṣṇa—the increate, the all-pervading, the source of the universe."

36. *Associatory Sequent Devotion.* Next is Associatory Sequent Devotion. It consists, as the wise say, in assuming or imagining oneself in the role of Kṛṣṇa's parent or friend.

37. Aspirants drawn to such emotions as parental tenderness should practice a devotion replicating the feelings of Nanda, the Vraja chieftain [Kṛṣṇa's foster father] and Suvala [Kṛṣṇa's friend].

38. The sacred books tell us of an old carpenter who lived in Hastināpura. On Nārada's advice he worshiped the image of Nanda's Son, with the feelings of a father for his son, and so succeeded in having Kṛṣṇa become his Son in fact.

39. The *Hymn to Nārāyaṇa's Theophanies* says: "Those who always think of Viṣṇu as Husband, Son, Companion, Brother, Father and Friend with alacrity—reverence to them!"

40. Passion-Sequent Devotion is the one which aims only to attain the compassion of Kṛṣṇa and His devotees. Some [like Vallabha] call it the Way of Fullness.

—*The Ocean of the Ambrosial Sap of Devotion,* wave 2[174]

84
JĪVA GOSVĀMĪ
The Delights of Kṛṣṇa

We have thus shown the connection between Kṛṣṇa's delights in their hidden and in their manifest forms. These two delights have been described in the words "enjoyment" and "delight" in the second half of the *Padma Purāṇa:*

> Enjoyment is an eternal state: He sometimes brings its delight into focus.

These words mean that delight is what is [enjoyment] sometimes brought into focus. Though both kinds of delight [the hidden and the manifest] are in their deepest essence one, yet the experience that accompanies the manifest type is superior, because it abounds in the play of various emotions, like love in union and in separation. This is why one pursues it absorbedly.

Yes! This is indeed the Lord we know as Kṛṣṇa, ever the master of ourselves who live for no one else! Only now is He able to procure for [His clansmen] the Yādavas, obsessed with the knowledge of His majesty, the wonder of intense joy, through the nectarine torrents of all kinds of delights. It was in the house of His father that He satiated His people—of His father, Vāsudeva, that jewel of the Yādava clan, eternally endowed with the virtues of fatherhood!

And then the Supreme Lord, greatest of friends, the realizer of the principal and varied acts of our sacrifice, delight, stands radiant before our sight—as we adopt our various roles of devotion—in His most exalted and inaccessible abode, Mathurā or Dvārakā, closely attended by His mistresses, excellers in all the arts of sweetness, and also by Brahmā and the other gods!

Only now in the noble Vṛndāvana Garden has this Love burst into view—the Love that forges the bonds between His very own people, the dwellers of Vraja land, who live solely by the dictates of love!

Yes, He is the One, the lovely glow of the accumulated fortunes of the Gokula clan, a particle of the mole of Whose foot lustrates the mass of living beings, Who is the Tree of Desire surpassing the yearnings of desire, the Sapphire from the great mine of the mighty Vṛndāvana Wood—He is the one who revealed Himself to one so humble as me!

Yes, it is He Who, afflicted as He was by the hordes of demons, like Pūtanā, whom Kaṁsa had dispatched all at once—it is He Who, while proceeding to their destruction, was Himself as though benignly bestowed upon us, like the moon to the partridges!

Yes, it was He Who, with the gods and sages delighted by the multitude of His endowments—through a certain power he had received, and also of a sudden, paying no heed to the afflictions to Himself arising from the mass of adversity, it was He Who came to our rescue!

Yes, it was He Who, with the loveliness of His nature and form, His qualities, His disclosing of His hidden affection—by these delights dexterously combined, it was He Who filled us with satiation!

Yes, it was He Who, with the merest glimmer of His perfections, obtained for us the fullness of joy and caused the miracle of His marvelous sweetness to flash in every particle of the delights that people like myself yearned for, or of more transcendent joys!

Yes, it is He Who, to protect all good people, made public His relationship with the Yādava clan, and through that also entered their city Himself, in order to destroy the gang of crowned demons!

Yes, it was He Who suddenly consoled Uddhava, ourselves and others, long waiting in loneliness and separation, and whose minds had been struck with sorrow!

Yes, it is He Who, His multiple forms drawing a myriad sighs, came, on the pretense of making a pilgrimage, to us who had voyaged to Kurukṣetra, and who seemed to have nothing left but sighs—where we found Him as if He were a sea of ambrosia!

Yes, it is He Who, when we in His presence were in the state described, had, with the highest family feeling, passed some months joyously with His haughty Yādavas—it was He Who made us, as we thronged around him, a secret sign of love, and with the suggestion "I am all yours," set us all on fire!

Yes, it is He Who, realizing that the noble Vṛndāvana is of all things the most desirable, reassured Himself and us with solemn vows, and trusting to His quick return, persistently dispatched messengers to us!

And He is the one Who, not suspecting that if He were to fail to come, the lassitude resulting from the release of a myriad sighs would start to appear in us, quickly came Himself to Vṛndāvana, His appointed tasks still undone, as though issuing from the mouth of the ferocious tiger of His own separation, and He now drenches us with the nectarine stream of His glances!

And then, at each moment does He endear Himself to us, solely through the fullness of an affection that constantly renews itself, and which is His own distinctive natural endowment, equaled by none. Then, too, does He endear Himself to us through amassing the abundance of the ambrosial form of His innate loveliness. Then, too, does He endear Himself to us by fully enjoying Himself with flowers, adornments and great fortune; by bearing the special load of the sweetness of sport; by the intellectual pleasure of the dazzle of joy in the exercise of His multiple gifts; by the graceful pastimes of cattle rearing, the summoning of cows, childish pranks and winning ways, by the play of His magic flute and other like deeds. Then, too, by such delights as leaving Gokula and coming back to it again. Then also, by the depth of His affection for His loved ones shown by His exercising those particular sportive arts that properly fascinate them. By these and other acts does He endear Himself to us, because of which we are unable to perceive how time comes and goes.

—*Collection on the Lord*[175]

85

BALADEVA VIDYĀBHŪṢAṆA

The Knowledges of Majesty and Sweetness

As the Godhead is dual in nature, formed of Majesty and Sweetness, it will now be shown that knowledge and devotion, which have the Godhead as their object, are also twofold. In the words of Kṛṣṇa to His parents:

> I have shown you that form of Mine to remind you of My past births. Not otherwise does knowledge born of Me arise in mortal form.[176]

Or, in His words to Arjuna:

> See my power as Lord![177]

In the case of Sweetness, human frolic is never transgressed, whether or not the supreme Majesty is revealed. As, for instance, in the killing of the demoness Pūtanā, where the actions were those of a human baby, the sucking of the breasts[178]; in the upsetting of the cart, very hard and bulky, which was realized by a stroke of Kṛṣṇa's foot, soft as a leaf[179]; [in the shaking loose from the mortar] by Kṛṣṇa's showing an infant's helplessness and fear to its mother, even though no rope, however long, could have secured Him[180]; in the sport of [a herdboy] taking his calves to pasture, notwithstanding His omniscience, in the affair of the perplexity of the god Brahmā[181]; and though possessing the supreme Majesty itself, in His not manifesting it, as in His stealing of the butter, and His infatuation with the girls of Vraja.

However, in one's experience of God, because of the palpitation of the heart caused by reverential awe, the knowledge of Majesty has the peculiar quality of benumbing one's disposition, as is expressed in the words of Kṛṣṇa's father Vasudeva;

> You are not our sons, but are directly Matter, Spirit and the Lord.[182]

or in Arjuna's words to Kṛṣṇa:

> If in careless presumption, or even in friendliness, I said, "Kṛṣṇa, son of Yadu, my friend!" this I did unconscious of Your greatness.
>
> And if in irreverence I was disrespectful—when alone or with others—I made a jest of You at games, or while resting, or at a feast, forgive me in Your mercy, immeasurable God![183]

Here there is a numbing of the nature of the affections of tenderness and friendliness. But even in the experience of the supreme Majesty, the knowledge of Sweetness is a peculiar quality fortifying the natural dispositions, as the tremors of the heart never appear, if ever so slightly. This is seen in the words of Suta:

> He recognized Viṣṇu—the Lord whose greatness is sung by the Triad of Vedas, by the Upaniṣads, and by the Sankhya, Yoga and Pāñcarātra systems—as his very own Son.[184]

Or, as the cowherdesses sang:

> His admirers, the company of gods, surrounding Him, offered tributes in the way of songs and instrumental music. The darling of the cows, upholder of the mountain, He was reverenced on His way by old men. At sunset, He drove His cows, His fame celebrated by His followers with songs and flute music.[185]

Here, notwithstanding intimacy with the supreme Majesty, there is no benumbing of the feelings of tenderness and of warm passion.

In the souls devoted to Sweetness, the knowledge of Majesty exists in latent fashion—like the river Sarasvatī[186] at the confluence of the three streams—because of the absence of reverential awe, the cause of the tremors of the heart. That does not inhibit emotion, but rather foments it, since there is the joy expressed in the words "my Son, my Friend, my Beloved, is Lord of all things." In mundane life, too, when one's son or lover is the lord of the earth, one's tenderness for him increases. The same happens here. The moment of its appearance is at the time of wonder, separation or distress, like the sudden appearance of the Sarasvatī.

Like the knowledge of Majesty, that of Sweetness also has the qualities of the Brahman, and the knowledge that is its object is none other than Brahman-knowledge. The characteristics of the Brahman nature apply to Kṛṣṇa's two-armed form, just as they do to His [majestic] thousand-headed one,[187] as is attested by Revelation and Tradition. In the words of the *Gopāla-pūrva-tāpinī Upaniṣad:*

> I worship the two-armed Lord, with His lovely lotus eyes, His rain-cloud hue, His lightning-colored ves-

> ture, rich in His attitude of silence and garlanded with forest flowers.[188]

Or in those of the *Viṣṇu Purāṇa:*

> A man, listening to the Lord Who holds the flute, is freed from all his sins. For Kṛṣṇa, as He is known, has become incarnate, Kṛṣṇa, the supreme Brahman in the form of a man.

Or:

> The mysterious supreme Brahman, in man's form[189]

and in other such passages. In this way, both kinds of knowledge being true, Tradition bears witness to the devotion of the knowers of sweetness, Brahmā, Uddhava and others, a devotion that makes them proud of being as the dust to Viṣṇu's feet.

—*The Jewel of Orthodoxy*[190]

XXII. MONIST PASTORALISM, or *LĀKULĪŚAPĀŚUPATA DARŚANA*

See Scheme 33

A marvel or organization, Monist Pastoralism is a "theology of a counterculture," perhaps the only one ever to be formulated. Salvation, it believes, is attained by shocking the respectable (*épater les bourgeois*), through flouting the trivial practices they so highly respect. The adherents of the modern counterculture seem to follow the Pastoralists even in details like wearing flowers, being ragged and hairy, seeming unconcerned about nudity, disliking commerce, adopting a boisterous and carefree behavior, and in cultivating the knack of inviting violence from the infuriated bourgeois (Selection 94), while practicing non-violence themselves (Selection 89). Common to both is the insistence on uncomplicated, even uncomfortable living (Selections 88 and 97), and eroticism—seriously pursued, as it seems, in the contemporary movement, but only affected in the ancient one (Selection 95). Early Franciscanism, especially as described in the *Fioretti,* shares features from both movements.

All in all, Monist Pastoralism may be described as a dionysiac religion of joy (Selection 93), cultivated through disdain for the habits of the respectable and through indifference to their hostility. This attitude seems to have prevailed among the Determinists, or Ājīvikas, in the sixth century B.C.—an attitude which the Greek Diogenes (413–324?), who lived in a tub, might have appreciated—and to have been practiced by their founder Makkali Gosāla. It was followed by the Dualist Pastoralists, the first theologians of Śaivism, of whose work nothing seems to have survived.

Pastoralism seems to have been transformed into a Monist doctrine around the second century A.D. by Lakulīśa, the "lord holding the club" (Selections 86 and 87). The Dualist and Monist Pastoralisms have the same five categories (see Scheme 33), only the first two, Cause and Effect, are different in the older school, and different-and-identical in the newer. Lakulīśa founded a line of teachers, the sixteenth of them being Kauṇḍinya (fourth–fifth century ? A.D.), the main interpreter of Lakulīśa's thought (Selections 88–97). Lakulīśa's Monist interpretation of Śaivism served to prepare the way for the even grander interpretation of Triadism.

Dionysiac religion easily turns violent, and we have another Śaiva school, with the same metaphysics as the Pastoralist, but with wholly different practices—the school of the Skullmen, or Kāpālikas, who seem not to have written theological tracts, as they were engaged in far more exciting things:

> We offer [says a Skullman in a play] great fire oblations of flesh filled with brains, intestines and fat, and we relish quaffing liquors especially prepared in skulls from Brahmin corpses. We worship the Great Terrifier god with sacrifices of human victims—sacrifices fearful and brilliant with the pure blood pouring from their firmly fleshed throats just slit.[191]

86

LAKULĪŚA

The Pastoral Way

1. Now then, we shall explain the Pastor's pastoral union and ritual.

2. Let a man perform the three ablutions [of dawn, noon, and sunset] by bathing in ashes.

3. Let him lie in ashes.

4. and bathe again in ashes,

5. wear garlands,

6. bear Śiva's symbol,

7. live in temples,

8. worship with laughter, song, dance, boisterous noises, salutations, prayers and offerings,

9. standing to the left of Śiva's image,

10. wearing a single cloth

11. or no cloth at all.
12. Let him not look at urine or stool,
13. not talk to woman or low-caste.
14. But if he has looked at such or talked to them
15. or touched them,
16. Let him—exercising breath control—
17. recite the incantations to Śiva the Fearful, to the sun and to Śiva the Many-formed.
18. To one of unsullied mind
19. who wanders
20. Yoga accrues.
21. He gains the power of hearing, conceiving and knowing things from afar,
22. omniscience,
23. swiftness of thought,
24. the capacity to assume forms at will,
25. power without organs
26. and special power.
27. All these come under his control;
28. None of them control him.
29. He takes possession of them all
30. and none of them possess him.
31. He can undo them.
32. They cannot unmake him.
33. Fearless,
34. indestructible,
35. ageless,
36. immortal,
37. he moves unimpededly everywhere,
38. and furnished with these qualities becomes the great leader of the Great Lord's hosts.
39. Let him intone "Brahman";
40. "I fall at the feet of Śiva the Suddenly Born";
41. "Adoration to Śiva the Suddenly Born";
42. "Adoration to Śiva in the world of flux, not beyond it."
43. Worship Me
44. The source of flux.

—*The Pastoralist Aphorisms*[192]

87

LAKULĪŚA

Secret Virtue, Apparent Vice

1. The austerity of knowledge, kept secret, lights the way to infinity.

2. Let a man's vows be kept secret,

3. his virtuous language be kept secret.

4. Let him shut all the doors

5. with his mind.

6. Let him walk among people like someone mad . . .

8. People will think him mad and a fool.

9. Of all moral practices, the abandoning of pride is said to be the best . . .

12. Through pretended [disreputable] actions, well performed, Indra [the first practitioner of the Pastoral Way] achieved his ends.

13. Censure is no censure, hence

14. let a man wander enduring blame—

15. while performing blameless actions.

16. This [Pastoral] Way is the most excellent of all.

17. The pure Way.

18. All other ways are bad.

—*The Pastoralist Aphorisms*[193]

88

KAUṆḌINYA

Ashes

[Ash is fire, ash is water, ash is earth, everything is ash. Ether is ash, the mind, the eyes and other senses are ash.][194]

Here ash is stuff given to Śiva, and produced from the union of fire and fuel. Earthly food produced for others from it is splendorous. One must procure ashes as alms from villages and other places, and use them as aids in observing the precepts of bathing, of lying in ash, and of re-bathing in ash. They stand for freedom from property and for non-violence. They are the noblest substance and pure, and must be liberally used as means for achieving salvation.

89
KAUṆḌINYA
Non-violence

Violence is of three sorts—the causing of pain, the breaking of eggs, and the taking of life.

The causing of pain is of various sorts, such as the use of hard words, threats, beating and abuse. One must not injure any of the four classes of living creatures [born of wombs, eggs, sprouts and sweat] by mind, word or deed. From this, non-violence to beings follows.

As for the breaking of eggs, to avoid danger to them from burning, heat and smoke, one should not place them on a flame, not take or give them, or replace them or set them on fire. Nor should one have others do any of these things.

As for the taking of life, one should constantly and carefully examine one's clothes, hangers, vessel for ashes and begging bowl. And why? Because living creatures of minute forms are quickly destroyed. Hence constantly use fine strainers, filters of deer or yak hair and of palmyra leaves, or of cloth: use flowing water. Let this be done on green grass, not on wet soil. Let a mendicant travel the eight months of spring, summer and early winter. For kindness towards all creatures let him stay in one place during the rains.

90
KAUṆḌINYA
The Universal Range of Knowledge

In consequence, the knowable being limitless, the knowing faculty is applied in manifold fashion. In other words, like the sunlight on crystal, it radiates everywhere.

91
KAUṆḌINYA
God's Glory in His Effects

LAKULĪŚA'S APHORISM

His abode is formed.

The Lord's abode is "formed," that is, adorned and vibrant—as the sky with stars—by the triple effect of knowledge, faculty and soul, which He alone provides with origin, support and dissolution.

92
KAUṆḌINYA
God, One with His Effects

Now, the abode. Hence, the immortal and imperishable Lord, at His pleasure, abides in His effect, which itself abides in His energy. Hence both effect and cause are said to be abode-inclosed.

Says the objector:

'The fault in your theory lies in commingling the natures of cause and effect, as the milk of a cow, a goat, a sheep and a buffalo. [You cannot tell them apart when they are mixed].'

No, I say. There is no commingling at all, as in the instance of a fingertip and the form to which it points. Again, there is no commingling, like the light in the lamp and in the sun, and the ray that strikes the eye.

The objector insists:

'In case there is commingling, there is indistinction, which is a fault, for the components—God, the soul and knowledge—will be like the stuff of a beehive.'

I reply that if the Principles are so ordered that one is higher than the other, as container and contained, the fault of indistinction will not apply. In sequence, the container is the Principle, God; the contained are Spirit and the rest of the twenty-five Principles [according to the doctrine of the Sankhya].

93
KAUṆḌINYA
Joyfulness

Joyfulness is love, satiation and delight in divine things illumined by virtue born of precept . . .

'But what are the marks of this attribute?' you may ask.

I answer, the ones that make for the purity of effect and instrument. Purity of *effect* is as follows: When the divine body sees itself flaming and refulgent in the heavens, on earth and in the air, and upraised like a staff of gold, then arise the effect's three qualities—the power to diminish size, to lighten weight and to expand one's dimensions.

Purity of *instrument* is as follows. Through the power of increasing weight at will, the qualities of greatness, mental effort, desire, perceptiveness and the capacity of controlling objects in distance come into existence on earth, by means of the outer organs and through the Inner Faculty as well.

Also the power to attain the unattainable through the senses, the possession of an unthwarted will, the capacity to impose one's power on objects, an independence from the Attributes, and the fulfillment of all desires—these five attributes of the instrument also come into being. In this way what others know as the eight qualities, such as the capacity to diminish form, the sovereignty that results from the qualities of the sixty-four fancies, is what our own teaching designates as joyfulness.

94
KAUṆḌINYA

Salvation through Opprobrium and Injury

LAKULĪŚA'S APHORISM

Let him wander, enduring assault.

Assault is the laying on with sticks and blows, something to do with the body, in other words . . . We must see such an assault as the poor man's coronation. It must be for him as a stone for testing gold or as the Mandara mountain [used by the gods for churning nectar out of the sea]. The words "Let him wander" imply that he becomes as one who is entitled to his earnings. What they signify is that the man must wander, under the obloquy of false accusation, being censured for earning merit and for performing his duty.

The objector asks, 'Does the despised man, who wanders enduring assault, only find rest from his sorrows, or does he also acquire purity?'

Answer: He does that too. Hence the aphorism:

LAKULĪŚA'S APHORISM

With his sins destroyed.

. . . Sins are of two sorts, those qualified by pleasure or by pain.

LAKULĪŚA'S APHORISM

Hence,

Because of the injury, like humiliation, inflicted by evil sinners, one attains purity, and with the attraction of the merit of others to oneself, prosperity is assured. "Hence," through the attainment of a supernatural body, organs and objects, one arrives at the final and absolute nearness to Śiva, an attainment without question infinite.

LAKULĪŚA'S APHORISM

Let him wander like a ghost.

Like a madman, a pauper smeared with ashes, his body covered with dirt, with beard, nails and hair all grown, he must live like one who has shunned all decency. In this way his association with the castes and states is severed, and his dedication to asceticism grows. And it is through ignominy that such an end is accomplished.

LAKULĪŚA'S APHORISM

Let him also pretend to snore.

Now, when he has acquired knowledge, rid himself of his sins, has been given his discharge as a pupil, he should then leave his teacher and approach a cemetery, or enter a town, where a concourse of people is found. There he should install himself, not too far and not too near, in such a way as not to be out of their range of sight. Taking care to avoid the paths of elephants, horses and chariots, he should sit, and engage himself in such acts as seeming to be asleep, and of nodding and yawning. Unslumbering, he should there act as though he were asleep. Then, as he snoringly exhales, he should make rasping sounds in his throat. The people will then say, either to themselves or aloud, "This fellow is asleep, is he?" and so come near him and thump him. By that assault, falsely induced, all their merit will attach to him, and all his sins go to them. In this way affected snoring is a purificatory act.

95
KAUṆḌINYA
Merit through Pretended Seduction

LAKULĪŚA'S APHORISM

Let him also play the profligate.

A man should, without molestation, stand not too far from a crowd of women and not too near, always within their range of sight. Making one young and lovely woman the object of his attentions, he should ogle, solicit, importune, swagger and indulge in similar actions. Though making eyes at a woman is not proper, he should show signs of his passion such as acting as though he was holding the woman by the hair. Then the men, women and eunuchs, who have been talking among themselves, will say, "This fellow is a sex maniac and a womanizer." By that false accusation all their merit will decidedly attach to him, and all his sins to them.

96
KAUṆḌINYA
Life's Goal: Union with God, not Liberation

LAKULĪŚA'S APHORISM

That is what Śiva said.

. . . When the Sankhya and Yoga say that those endowed with detachment from mundane things are liberated and have attained peace, their doctrine is vitiated, like the impaired eyesight which sees the moon [as two moons]. And the wholesome teaching, it must be noted, is that one is *united,* not liberated.

LAKULĪŚA'S APHORISM

The yogi, constant in God.

Stillness prevails in one who, through study and meditation, is engrossed in God. In spite of slight interruptions, there is an unintermitted attainment of a discipline that is beyond Yoga.

'But how is engrossment in God to be recognized?'

I answer, in the control of the senses.

97
KAUṆḌINYA
The Life of a Cow or Deer

LAKULĪŚA'S APHORISM

The yogi should be like a cow or a deer.

These animals, it is true, have many differing qualities, but let us take the one they share in common: the ability to tolerate contraries, mental or otherwise.

—*Commentary of the Five Categories*, on Lakulīśa's *The Pastoralist Aphorisms*[195]

XXIII. TRIADISM, or *TRIKA*

See Schemes 34 and 35

We now come to what seems to be the greatest and most consistent of the Difference-in-Identity theologies (see Selection 100). The highest perfection, Triadism seems to suggest, is paradoxically inclusive of imperfection. Two of the highest perfections, inseparable from the ultimate Reality, are Consciousness and Freedom. Consciousness, or Light, is unique—which is a perfection; but it needs to conceive multiple ideas—an imperfection. If it does not do so, it will be obtuse insentience.

Similarly Freedom or independence is incapacity to be conditioned by external limitants, and is therefore plenitude—a perfection. But Freedom implies a capacity to be what one wishes, even what one is not. So it must be possible for the ultimate Reality to empty itself of its plenitude and unity—again an imperfection.

The supreme Reality, in consequence, is a unity that needs to be multiple; its Identity pole is inconceivable without its Difference pole. For Triadism, Consciousness is not the inert Witness that it is for the Sankhya and most other Hindu theologies, but is a vibrant Self-Awareness. This Vibrancy (see Selection 103) precipitates the undifferenced unity of Consciousness into the multiplicity of the universe, realized through self-obscuration and the self-emptying of plenitude; the Vibrancy also reinstates the Consciousness to its primordial unity. Through this Vibrancy, again, the texture of Consciousness becomes penetrated with—indeed constituted of—wonder. Wonder, then, is the essence of Consciousness, and the absence of wonder is insentience.

Everything is of the nature of everything else, and everything is of the Śiva nature (Selection 99). Śiva is Himself light and Vibrancy, at once Consciousness and Self-Awareness. The Vibrancy, again, is the Divine Feminine, multiplied into those goddesses of fire and dissolution, the Consuming Energies or Kālīs (see Scheme 35). The wonder that is innate to Consciousness, in its fully luminous state, is liberation; as shining through the veil of self-obscuration, is aesthetic delight. In this way, the philosophy of aesthetics, developing independently from Bharata's days, was integrated into the sublime Triadic system by Abhinava Gupta, the Sun King of Hindu theology (c. 993–1015).

Abhinava's century and the next produced two other mystical theologies of Light, that of Symeon the New Theologian (949?–1022) in the Christian world, and that of Al-Suhrawardy (1153/55–91) in the Islamic. The idea of the supreme Reality as the undifferenced Light is echoed in the words of the divine Dante himself:

> *Nel suo profondo vidi che s'interna*
> *Legato con amore in un volume*
> *Ciò che per l'universo si squaderna:*
> *Sustanze e accidenti e lor costume*
> *Quasi conflati insieme per tal modo*
> *Che ciò ch'io dico è un semplice lume.*[196]

> I saw that the Light contains within its abyss, bound by Love in one volume, all that is scattered [like pages] in the universe—substance, accidents, and the connection between them, so what I speak of is one simple Light.

Triadism contains many themes echoed in Christian and modern Western thought. First, that of self-emptying, or *kenosis,* proclaimed by St. Paul well before Abhinava Gupta's time:

> Let your bearing towards one another arise out of your life in Christ Jesus. For the divine nature was his from the first; yet he did not think to snatch at equality with God, but made himself nothing, assuming the nature of a slave.[197]

A theology of Difference, like the Catholic, for which God is, so to speak, a unipolar substance and wholly immutable, cannot permit self-emptying within that substance—for that would annihilate It—but only in the exterior manifestations of Its glory. This is what happens in the Incarnation, by Christ concealing this glory. Says Bossuet:

> It is a truth sufficiently astonishing, but nonetheless indubitable, that among the infinite means God

> has to establish His glory, the most efficacious of all is found to be necessarily connected with lowness. He can overturn all nature, He can make man see His power by a thousand new miracles; but through a marvelous secret, He cannot bear His grandeur higher except when He lowers and humiliates Himself.[198]

As it is a Difference-in-Identity theology, Triadism can allow self-emptying or self-humiliation in the divine substance—in the Difference, not in the Identity, pole. This self-emptying helps it to realize its capacity to be the multiple world of creatures, and thus find its plenitude. Catholic theology echoes this idea, for it maintains that God's infinity is inconceivable without His creatures. The inexhaustibility of the divine perfections consists in the incapacity of the beings, created in imitation of those perfections, of ever equaling them, however their own perfection be increased or the number of beings itself be multiplied. None besides God, intuiting His essence, is able to penetrate the infinite "emanables" that are latent in It—which is why the Beatific Vision of every being except God is limited. Says the great Suárez:

> in order to comprehend a thing it is not enough to know all that is *formally* existent in it, but to know all of it in such a way that, by reason of that manner of knowing, everything that can and does *emanate* from it is comprehended. And this is what it means to know a thing, not only as a whole, but also *wholly* . . .[199]

God, therefore, realizes His infinity through His creatures.

In our own days the Triadic concepts of the concealment, disclosure and wonder of being are echoed in the metaphysics of Heidegger, and the vibrancy innate to reality is almost identical with Bergson's *élan vital,* or vital impetus—the inexhaustible source from which all spiritual and material beings, in their perennial flux, originate.

Triadism can be viewed as the theology of the rediscovery of one's Śiva nature through four Ways—the Individual, the Energic, the Divine and the Null (explained in Selections 98 and 102). Of these, the first is the least important; of the others, each forms the basis of a school. Triadism thus has three schools:

a. The Family (of Energies) School, *Kula,* founded in Assam by Ardha Tryambaka towards the end of the fourth century A.D., based on the Individual and Divine Ways, and accenting Śiva's infinity and freedom.

b. The Gradation School, *Krama,* apparently founded by Śivānanda Nātha, perhaps towards the end of the seventh century and the beginning of the eighth. It is based on the Energic Way, and emphasizes the Divine Feminine, especially as embodied in the Wheel of Energies. Like the Family School, it has ritual sex as a salvific means.

c. The Vibration School, *Spanda,* also known as the Self-Awareness School, *Pratyabhijña,* founded by Vasu Gupta (c. 825–850; Selection 98), and elaborated by Somānanda (c. 850; Selection 99). Theologically it is the most important of the three schools, is based on the Null Way, and stresses Śiva's nonduality. All these schools were synthesized by Abhinava Gupta (Selections 100–2). The integrated school is represented by Kṣema Rāja (second quarter of the eleventh century; Selection 103), and Maheśvarānanda (twelfth century), who sums up the doctrines of Triadism in language of great poetic beauty (Selection 104).

98
VASU GUPTA

The Śaiva Mysteries

I. THE DIVINE WAY

1. The Consciousness, Śiva, is the soul of the world.

2. Restricted knowledge [or ignorance] is bondage.

3. Bondage also includes the Principles originating from the Womb [the Mirific Power], as well as those whose essence is activity.

4. The Mother of the Universe [the primordial goddess of sound] is the support of [restricted] knowledge.

5. The inner Impulse is the God of Terror.

6. Union with the Wheel of Energies causes the world's destruction.

7. The joy of the fourth [or undifferenced] state is generated in the states of wakefulness, sleep and dreamless slumber.

8. Knowledge is the waking state.

9. Imagination is sleep.

10. Lack of discrimination, the Mirific Power, is dreamless slumber.

11. The Lord of the Senses enjoys the three states.

12. The yogic stages are all wonder.

13. The Energy of Will is the Virgin Umā.

14. The visible world is the body.

15. With the mind concentrated on the heart, the visible and the dreamlike are revealed.

16. Contemplating on the Pure Principle [the Supreme Śiva], one sheds the energy of the Beast state.

17. Meditation ["I am Śiva, the Self of the Universe"] is the knowledge of the Self.

18. The joy of Totality is the joy of unmoved concentration.

19. From the meditation on Energy [the Virgin Umā] originates the body [of one's desire].

20. From the meditation on Energy, too, one realizes a pleasurable union with the realities of sense, or separation from them, as well as a true knowledge of the universe [of space and time].

21. From the meditation on Energy, further, pure knowledge ["I am all things"] arises, and one becomes Lord of the Wheel of Energies.

22. Immersion in the great pool of Supreme Energy makes one experience the potency of the mystic incantations.

II. THE ENERGIC WAY

1. Intelligence [of the supreme truth] is the Mystic Incantation [the revelation of mystery].

2. Effort is the means of achieving it.

3. The secret of the Mystic Incantation is the essence of embodied knowledge.

4. The expansion of Intelligence, restricted knowledge, and the dream all unfold in the Womb, Ignorance.

5. With knowledge spontaneously welling the Śiva state emerges—the state of the Sky-Roaming Goddess.

6. The means of achieving the knowledge of the Mystic Seal and Incantation is the Teacher.

7. From the Teacher, one obtains the knowledge of the Wheel of the Mothers [the goddesses of the phonemes].

8. [For one who knows this wheel] the body is sacrificial food.

9. Knowledge also is food.

10. With [restricted] knowledge dissolved, one sees the dream that rose from it.

III. THE INDIVIDUAL WAY

1. Intelligence is the infinitesimal soul.

2. Restricted knowledge is bondage.

3. Confusion about the Principles—those that begin with Aptitude—is Illusion [or the Mirific Power].

4. These Principles are consumed with the body.

5. The yogis must experience the stoppage of the arteries, the subjection of the elements, and separation and freedom from them.

6. Supranormal power results from concealment by Illusion.

7. Through the overpowering by Illusion being endlessly extended, one arrives at the triumph of spontaneous wisdom.

8. With this wisdom attained one awakens [with Energy] the Second [to the supreme Śiva] as his radiance.

9. The Self is an actor.

10. His stage is the inner Self.

11. The faculties are his audience.

12. The control of the investigative faculty gives rise to bright activity.

13. Through this activity [the yogi's] independence is realized.

14. As in the yogi's body, so also elsewhere.

15. He must concentrate on the Seed [the cause of the universe, the essence of luminousness, the Supreme Energy].

16. Secure in his yogic posture, he sinks with ease into the pool [of immortality].

17. He creates and manifests a part of himself.

18. With wisdom indestructible, there is destruction of birth.

19. In the class of gutturals, the presiding goddesses are the

Mothers of the Beasts, such as the Great Queen [the Supreme Word].

20. In the three states—waking, sleep and dreamless slumber—one must inject the fourth [the undifferenced state] like oil [drop by drop].

21. Immersed in the Supreme, let a man sink into it with his own intelligence [and not with more commonplace yogic methods].

22. His breath moving slowly, he attains to a knowledge of evenness.

23. In the middle a lower state is born.

24. With knowledge not united to objects, the lost steadiness is recovered.

25. The yogi becomes equal to Śiva.

26. His bodily acts are worship.

27. His talk is prayer.

28. His gift is the knowledge of the Self.

29. He who protects Beasts is cause of knowledge.

30. The world is filled with his energies.

31. So are maintenance and destruction.

32. Even when these states persist, he does not lapse from his state as knower.

33. He has thought of pleasure and pain and of things outside himself.

34. Liberated from them, one is Isolated.

35. One overcome by delusion is a karma-ridden soul.

36. With difference eliminated, one acquires the power for another creation.

37. The power to cause [another creation] is proved, because it is experienced.

38. Living at the root of the three states [creation, maintenance and dissolution, the yogi should animate his existence].

39. The accompaniment of the three states by the fourth should be practiced in the body, organs and objects, as it is in the fixation of the intelligence.

40. Through desire the soul's transmigration goes out.

41. With the consciousness fixed on it, with desire eliminated, the soul is destroyed.

42. The yogi, sheathed in the contingent, becomes, when liberated, almost like the Master himself, the Supreme.

43. The connection with the breath is natural.

44. With the control of the middle of the nostril's interior

attained, in the right, left and middle arteries, what is left to be done?

45. There will again be reabsorption with the Consciousness.

—*Aphorisms on Śiva*[200]

99

SOMĀNANDA

The Śiva Nature of All Things

1. May the Śiva impenetrated into my limited self through His Energy, offer worship to the Śiva of the expansive Self—the concealer of Himself by himself!

2. Śiva is the Self shining in all things, the all-pervasive Self-Quiescent Consciousness, unimpeded in the procession of His Will, of processional Knowledge and Activity.

3. When He exists as exclusive absorption into the experience of His consciousness-joy, in proportional manner does His Will, and so do His Knowledge and Activity.

4. This Triad of Energies most subtle then subsists in coalescence. Then the Supreme is undifferentiated, supreme in His consciousness-natured beatitude.

5. This condition of coalescence abides not only in Śiva's supreme state, but also at the time of contact with the knower, before the rise of all differentiated knowledge.

6. [That is the moment before the innately vibrant, and unreposeful, act of knowledge is precipitated.] The condition of coalescence is then experienced as inherent in repose. It is experienced similarly at the termination of that knowledge [when the acquisition of it brings fulfillment, and repose]. At no time, then, is there separation from the Triad of Energies—

7. On part of the Self-Quiescent Consciousness, whether in a state of undifferentiatedness or of differentiation.

But when, by a dilatation of wonder at the epiphanies that form the essence of Consciousness,

8. There springs an impulse, which is none other than the

same Consciousness, towards plunging into the creation of manifold effects of diversified design—that is the first movement of the Will.

9. The impulse is perceived in the heart, when we remember something we had to do, hear joyful news, are confronted with fear,

10. When of a sudden see something we had not seen for long, are about to discharge semen, exclaim as we discharge it, or when we read or run in a hurry—

11. In situations like these all our energies commingle [or coalesce].

'But how can the Exalted have an impulse to the vile [how can God, quiescent in His connatural joy, have an urge to transform Himself into imperfect things]?'

12. His five activities—creation, conservation, dissolution, graciousness and obscuration—are all intrinsically Śiva-natured: so Śiva, engaging in them out of delight at His natural impulse, is not deserving of blame.

13. Why then should we demand other motives on His part?

As water, once calm, becomes restless with waves;

14. If we turn our gaze to it in the beginning, we perceive the impetus [latent in it, a slight tremor]. We also first notice the tremor as the hand is about to be clenched into a fist.

15. The desire of the Self-Quiescent Consciousness for creation, the initial expansion in the direction of that activity, is what we know as Impulse.

16. Some prominent theologians [like Bhaṭṭa Pradyumna] call Impulse "a kind of swelling." Its effect is the Will [in the inchoate state]; by means of it Śiva becomes Will-endowed.

17. The gross [or palpable] experience of this Impulse is Will in its developed state. However, involvement in this Impulse does not make Śiva participant in that grossness.

18. As milk falls from the cow's udders, it changes thereby. But we do not at that moment remark, "That is not milk!"

19. The fact that Śiva wills to know and act implies an action connected with the Will. We must postulate two parts in that Will, an anterior and a consequent one. The first [or anterior] Will—

20. Is the realization of the desire for *activity,* its Impulse and its expansion. The second [or consequent] Will is the ca-

pacity for intuiting the knowledge of [the terminus of the activity,] the *effect*.

21. This is the Energy of Knowledge. For its sake is the gross effort [or experience, mentioned above]. Thus arises the Energy of Activity. In this way the whole world is stabilized.

22. Thus, when all things come into existence, the inherence of the Triad of Energies is not dissolved.

23. If any of these were to be lacking, the effect would never emerge. The coalescent identity of all the categories is therefore confirmed.

24. [Here is an instance of how Will, Knowledge and Activity are inseparably linked.] At the time one knows a pot, the differentiated knowledge expressed in the words "He knows a pot" is a sequential action. So the *knowledge* embodied in the "He knows" is here present as an *activity*. And no one lacking a *will* is able to know.

25. [And here is how Impulse, desire and consciousness are linked.] In the absence of Impulse, differentiated knowledge ceases. Without desire, one is unable to deal with the hateable [to free oneself of it]. And one cannot know without consciousness.

26. [Sankhya objector] 'How can there be understanding without Instinct [or "understanding stuff"]? Instinct is the offspring of Matter. And there can be no bond between Śiva and Matter, can there?'

It is only in the lower state [of the Reality that is Śiva, occurring when He obscures Himself, that there is this differentiating knowledge, and]

27. That such understanding exists. On the other hand, the subtle all-pervading knowledge, replete with consciousness, is always connatural to Śiva.

28. This doctrine cannot be compared to that of the Logicists. The mind [or knowledge], they maintain, is an attribute of the self, is formed of Matter. Such cannot be postulated of the Supreme Intelligence [that Śiva is].

29. The same reasoning can obviously apply to the will [which the Atomists hold to be an attribute of the mind].

So God emanates in the following way. Sometimes He assumes the form of absolute Energy

30. Through the Will; sometimes out of abundance, of the Ever Beneficent, through the Energy of Knowledge; sometimes, through enjoying the Energy of Activity,

31. The state of the Supreme Lord. Sometimes, through

gross knowledge [of Impulse], He assumes the forms of Pure Wisdom, the Wisdom Lords, the Incantations and the Incantation Lords;

32. Sometimes, indulging in the play of self-obscuration, the form of the Mirific Power. In this way He assumes the forms of the thirty-six categories,

33. Some lastingly, some occasionally, in a process that continues until the gross phenomenon of the unconscious, the earthy mass, is compacted.

34. In the same way He creates various bodies and the worlds [they inhabit] and then assumes the forms of exalted, middling and low [that is, of gods, men and animals].

35. Assuming bodies suitable to place, and conceptual latencies suitable to bodies, He Himself is taken for each of the forms assumed.

36. The bodies of the workers of evil, suffering torment, and experiencing the fruit of their evil, dwelling in the depths of the oceans of hell—

37. These the Supreme Lord assumes out of playfulness. As a sovereign monarch, exhilarated by the delights of power,

38. Plays, by reason of that pleasure, at being a common soldier—so too the Lord, the embodiment of delight, plays in the guise of various beings.

39. Hence Śiva, the plenitude of knowledge, is Himself supreme desire. Desire becomes transformed into Impulse, and Impulse into Will, Knowledge and Activity.

40. He, the Blessed Lord, alone originates the universe of living beings, from the Energy-embodied [like the Wisdom Lords] down to the damned, from His own consciousness, down to the compact of the earth.

41. Thus, through these categories, His inbeing is subsistent everywhere.

Sometimes, as though ignoring His [omniformed] Śiva nature, He comes to be described as Beast [as Śaiva Orthodoxy terms the soul].

42. Sometimes He sees Himself in His Śiva nature, but as quiescent [the inert Brahman of some Vedantins]. At other times merely as the Supreme Lord [of the Atomists and Logicists]; at still other times as nothing but Śiva [as Śaiva Orthodoxy conceives Him].

43. Sometimes, unawakened and bereft of sense faculties, He appears as the Dissolution-Deconditioned Soul. At other

times, He awakens to His Self, and still free of sense faculties, appears as the Intelligence-Deconditioned Soul.

44. As yogis, merely by willing, can produce things of great variety, needing no assistance [in the way of material and other causes] besides the will of the Lord,

45. So also, through God's will alone, the universe unfolds in its variety. Through His will again, we truly perceive a variety of things, connected with emotions like fear [desire, sorrow and madness; we also see robbers in dreams].

46. [Buddhist Objector] 'Are they not all unreal then [especially the robbers]?'

I shall prove below that they are real. Thus, as in all things this Śiva nature;

47. So also, formlessness, desire, the link with the Triad of Energies, and consciousness—all these endure eternally, as will also be explained below.

48. Thus the Śiva nature abides in all things equally. The distinctions of higher and lower states have been ascribed to it by the credulous.

49. In this way the Śiva Principle, innately diversified [through the vibrations of Impulse, not by credulity] is everlasting and infinite. And because it so persists, reality belongs to its manifold forms too.

—*Vision of Śiva*[201]

100
ABHINAVA GUPTA
An All-inclusive Nondualism

This Light is one only, in no way diversified. There is consequently no difference which can divide the great Nondual Lord, lovely with radiance and blessedness.

'Can it be that factors like space, time, form, knowledge, attributes, contingencies, and distance, held to be diversifiers, become manifest in this Light?'

—Yes, but what so appears is nothing but Light. If the Light were not such, this nonduality would be nothing. Difference is no more than sound emanating from that Light.

Let the conception of Difference also be something generated by that Light. According to what we have said, it can only be based on nonduality. Ideas expressed in statements like "This is a pot," "And this is a cloth," are distinct among themselves, from other knowing subjects and even from me. Hence there is but one Light, which has such conceptualizing as its nature.

'But how can you call this position Nondualism? You must confess that Difference exists: in opposing it, are you really not resisting it?'

This is like giving a vocal and instrumental concert before an audience of the deaf! The nondual we speak of is not of the kind which bars the entry of duality. To do so would be to fall into your way of thinking, and we would have a duality of a most unambiguous kind. True nonduality exists when expressions such as "This is duality, this is nonduality, this is both duality and nonduality," occur simultaneously.

'But this is exactly what Difference is!'

We are in no mood for word games! Let it be as you say. Unlike you, we have nothing to reject and nothing to receive.

—*Commentary on "The Triumph of the Engarlanded Goddess"*[202]

101
ABHINAVA GUPTA

Delight, the Agitation of Force

All that enters through the inner and outer senses is in the form of breath and of intelligence; located in the central artery, it enlivens the whole body, and goes by the name of Force. This same Force, which invigorates all the body's members, and is inseparable in potency from them, again enters as a nourishing infusion through the faculties of sight and hearing, as color and sound. Because of its invigorating power, it kindles the fire of love, itself an Agitation of Force. Such a kindling, as someone said, arises "through a song, by a touch of the members."

Since everything is of the essence of everything else, anything that has been richly invigorated by this Force has the capacity to cause the Agitation—itself the cause of all things—by means of one or other object of the senses, as, for instance, color. Such an Agitation can rise through a memory, or from a differentiating concept, caused as it is by the enrichment of sense impressions like sound, infinite in number, that are stored in the omniformed mind. But only the Great Force constituted of all things, in its plenary intenseness, is capable of invigoration and creativity, and not the force that is unfledged or diminished, as in infants and in the old. With this Agitation of Force—a Force which is our own selves and also indivisible—Freedom becomes the source of happiness. It is a Freedom that is the plenary Consciousness, the Tremendous God Himself; it is none but the exalted Self-Awareness saturated with Vibrancy, untouched by the measure of space and time, and overflowing with the Energy of Joy. The color that strikes the eye is itself a source of joy, but only in so far as it separates itself from the great Emission, essentially a stirring of the same Force; the same can happen to the ears, through occurrences like sweet songs. In the other senses, however, all that enters does not enjoy a like creative fullness, as it stays contained within itself.

But there are those unaffected by this invigoration, who are ignorant of the joy of the Eros of the stirring of the Force, and who are thus like stones. The form of the loveliest of girls and the sweet and soft music echoing from the throats of curvaceous damsels causes them no delight. As such experiences do not stir them, their sense of wonder is to that extent limited. A total lack of this sense of wonder is of course unconsciousness itself. But an infusion of a greater feeling of wonder, in essence the stirring of the Force, is what is known as aesthetic sensitivity. Only one who has a heart transfigured by this infinitely invigorating Force, only one constantly engaged in enjoying such experiences—only such a one has this superior sense of wonder.

Such a sense exists in sorrow too, for sorrow is only a special kind of wonder. It consists of the *force* of an inner joy in a loved woman or son; and of *agitation* awakened by a memory, the sight of someone alike [the lost loved ones], by a cry and such like things. It matures with the realization that what was will nevermore be. As Somānanda says:

> Śiva is resplendent in sorrow too.[203]

When all the breaths have been concentrated into the arteries of the senses, when the central region of the spinal cord has been permeated, an identity with the Vibration of one's own energies is attained. Then duality begins everywhere to fall away, and one plunges into the wonder of the I, which is the very plenitude of Self-Awareness charged with all Its energies. Then too—as one interfuses with that fullness of Emission and joy, Śiva coupling with His Energy, through falling away from the Emission which is the potency of the great Incantation—there stands revealed the God of the Unmoved State, the Waveless Lord, the Exalted-Above-The Family, the Tremendous God Himself.

An example is the moment of orgasm, which anyone can experience for himself. As one is tumescent with the force of the semen's impulse, in a state of oneness with the central artery and free of all sense of otherness, one feels a tactile thrill, brought about by the agitation of the semen as it yearns to be discharged.

Moreover, it is not only through attachment to this imagined body of ours, but also through recollection and instruction, that one can achieve ingress into the Unmoved State—a state realized [as we saw] by the falling away from the Emission that the Great Incantation is. It is in essence the Supreme Goddess Herself, Who is joy, freedom and the union of Śiva and His Energy constituted of the highest Brahman. As will be said later on:

> By fourteen prayerful mutterings, by flowers, and by yogic postures must a man sacrifice to the Emission.[204]

And as was remarked earlier;

> The great banyan, puissant with its energies, is latent in the banyan seed; so is the world of the movable and the unmoving latent in the seed of the Heart.[205]

And in still another place:

> This is how one enjoys the results of the Incantation; this is Śiva coupled with His Energy; this, through effort, is fulfillment, and the realization of omniscience.[206]

In another book it is said:

> Goddess, the intense recalling to mind the pleasure a woman has given with her tongue-play and caresses, produces a torrent of joy, even if the energy is absent.[207]

In other words, the delightful contact, intensely recalled and reflected in the central artery—which is physically uncaused and is identical with the Supreme Energy—produces of itself, without contact with a woman, an agitation of force in the erotic region, consisting of a sensation that is interior, tactile and womanly. As was said above

> The excitement of union with Energy brings about Her possession. The joy of the reality of the Brahman is a reality abiding in ourselves.[208]

And elsewhere:

> Through love, let him seek the Way of the Family.

Even that great hero, the revered Vyāsa, has sung:

> The Great Brahman is a womb to me. I plant My seed in it and from it all beings arise.[209]

—*Commentary on "The Highest Trigesimal"*[210]

102
ABHINAVA GUPTA

The Principles of Triadism

OPENING PAEANS

1. The Great Mother, splendorous with Her newest creation, Her substance the purest portion of the moon;
The Father, embodied plenitude, His glory hidden by His five faces—
Proceeding from Their union may my heart, palpitant

and emissional in its essence, and my body, sublime and immortal, flame with coruscation!

2. Not all can fathom my *Light of the Tantras.* Listen then to this straightforwardly written *Essence of the Tantras.*

3. To worship Śiva, the Great God, pluck this lotus of Abhinava Gupta's heart, opened by the rays fallen from the sun, Śambhu Nātha [great teacher of arcane Tantric lore]!

PROLOGUE: BONDAGE, RELEASE AND REVELATION

Knowledge is here the cause of release, because it dispels ignorance, the cause of bondage. Ignorance is of two kinds, mental and personal. The mental consists either in a lack of conviction, or in a conviction contrary to the truth. The personal, on the other hand, is in essence dualizing thought, and is formed of contracted intelligence. It is this ignorance that is the root cause of transmigration, as we shall see when we come to discuss the pollution of the soul [in chapter 8 below]. Personal ignorance, it is true, can be dispelled by Initiation. But Initiation is not possible in the case of mental ignorance, innately lacking as it is in application. Initiation itself is preceded by a conviction as to what should be desired or shunned, and consists of the purification of the Principles and of union with Śiva.

Of prime importance, then, is the innately applicative knowledge implanted in the mind. When exercised, it dispels even the personal ignorance, because, in the final analysis, the exercise of dualistic perception is interiorly vacuous of dualizing thought. The Self-Consciousness uncontracted by this dualizing thought, luminance in essence, consubstantial with Śiva—such is the knowledge of veracious conviction that we must seek, a knowledge implanted in every way in all things.

Such a knowledge presupposes the Sacred Doctrine. The doctrine enunciated by Śiva, the Supreme Lord, is the sole norm of knowledge, because the teachings that other systems of doctrine enunciate are found stated in it with discernment, for it describes, in assured terms, the reasonings [illuminative of those teachings, but] which transcend the intelligence of those systems. Hence the knowledge enunciated by the other sacred traditions liberates from bondage limitedly and not wholly; only the Supreme Lord's doctrine is wholly liberative. It has five streams [issuing from Śiva's five mouths. His five heads are the following: the Master, at the top, the Original Spirit to the east, the Suddenly Born to the west, the Lovely Lord to the north and the Non-Terrifying to the south]. It is separated into ten, eighteen and sixty-four divisions. Quintessence of the whole Sacred Doctrine are the scriptures of Triadism, [chief] among them *The Triumph of the Engarlanded Goddess.*

A compedious explanation of the meaning they contain exceeds possibility. Still, unless the truth of things is described, no liberation is possible, nor the power to liberate: such a power belongs to pure knowledge alone. Hence, as man's supreme goal depends on such knowledge well applied, I begin this work to help realize that goal.

> Ignorance is said to be the cause of bondage, and is known in scripture as Pollution. It is extirpated when the moon of full knowledge rises. The dawn of Self-Consciousness, dissolvent of all pollution, leads to release. In this science, therefore, I shall make clear all the truth that needs to be known [to realize that release].

CHAPTER 1: THE FOUR WAYS TO RELEASE

Here, then, the supreme desirable is the Essence Itself. It is of the nature of Light in all things, because what is vacuous of Light is also empty of Essence. It is also not manifold, as Light, unable to impenetrate [or identify with] an Essence diverse from Itself, is void of differentiations in the Essence. Nor are place and time Its differentiators, for they too have as their Essence that identical Light.

There is therefore only one Light, and It is Consciousness. The fact that Consciousness is innately illuminant of objects is a fact that no one disputes. That Light is not dependent [that is, not lacking in Freedom], because illuminability is the only lack of Freedom. Such illuminability stands in need of another light [in order to be illumined]. But there is no other Light. There is therefore but one Light, sovereignly free. In virtue of Its Freedom, It is untouched by the limitations of space, time and shape, and is omnipresent, eternal, omniformed and formless in Its being. Its sovereign Freedom is the Energy of Joy; Its wonder, the Energy of Will; Its subsistent luminosity, the Energy of Consciousness; Its self-reflective hypostasis, the Energy of Knowledge; and Its omniform potential, the Energy of Action. Thus, endowed as It is with these prepotent Energies, this unmitigated Light, imbued with the Energies of Will, Knowledge and Action, and reposing in Its own blessedness, is the Śiva Essence Itself.

The same Light, manifesting Itself through Its sovereign Freedom as contracted, is called the infinitesimal soul [or the individual]. And again, through Its Freedom, It reveals Itself, being then manifest in truth as the unmitigated Light of the Śiva Essence. Then also—again through Its Freedom—It reveals Itself either as unattainable through any Way whatever [or, to so put it, as "attainable" through the Null Way], or as attainable through some Ways. In the latter case, as attainable through Will, Knowledge and Action, by reason of which there exist three types of Śiva-impenetration—the Śiva Way [or the Divine Way], the Energic Way, and the Individual Way. This fourfold Way will now be explained in order.

> The Self is embodied Light, and is Śiva, the sovereignly free. Impelled by the exhilaration of His Freedom, He obscures His essence, and then discloses It in plenitude—with or without sequence, or in triple phasis . . .

CHAPTER 2: THE FIRST, OR NULL, WAY

I shall now explain the Null Way. When a man, struck by an intense Energic Fulmination, deliberates to himself in a manner I shall presently indicate—when he has pondered but once on his teacher's words—his impenetration into Śiva, free of all Ways, originates from within.

'Deliberation is one of the members of Yoga [which is not a null, but a positive, Way]. How then can a follower of the Null Way be said to deliberate?'

I answer [that this is how he deliberates]: "That Supreme Lord is our very own substantially self-luminant soul—of what use are Ways with regard to Him? They cannot help attain His Essence, because it is eternally inexistent in all; nor His knowledge, because He is self-illuminated; nor a removal of veils [occluding His luminosity], for such veils cannot exist; nor an impenetration of Him, because [an impenetrator needs to be distinct from the impenetrated, and] no distinct impenetrator can be found. And what, pray, can this Way be? For a Way also, distinct as it must be from Himself, the Goal, is impossible.

All this is therefore one Reality—a Reality undivided by time, unconfined by space, unenfeebled by accidents, unconstrained by configurations, unexpressed by words and unmanifested by norms of knowledge. It is the cause, at Its own will and pleasure, of the attainment of the essences of these things, from time to the norms. It is the sovereignly free Reality, the concentration of beatitude. And I am absolutely It—there, within me, is reflected the universe!"

One who deliberates thus with resolution, impenetrates Śiva eternally and without recourse to any Way, constrained by no need for incantations, acts of worship, meditations and disciplinary rules.

> "The complex of Ways do not illumine Śiva: does the sun, aureoled in a myriad rays, shine with a radiance derived from a pot?" Deliberating this, a man of exalted vision enters at once into Śiva, the self-luminant.
>
> "Wherever coruscation flames, there the whole Supreme Lord shines pure within me." For one who, with the insight of the absolute truth, knows Him to be none other than the soul, no more remains to be done.

CHAPTER 3: THE SECOND, OR DIVINE, WAY

When one is unable to impenetrate that infrangible orb, the substantially luminous Śiva Principle just described, one then perceives the energy of Freedom to be predominant, experiencing thereby an impenetration of the Tremendous God that is unmitigated by dualizing thought.

The following is the teaching with regard to such a person. The whole complex of existents is a mere reflection on the sky of Consciousness, because the existents are endowed with the character of reflections. This is how a reflection may be defined: something incapable of appearing as different, manifesting itself as commingled with other things—like a face in a mirror, taste in saliva, odor in the odoriferous, the copulatory touch in the organ of joy, the touch of a trident or spear in the internal tactile sense, and an echo in the ether.

That taste, however, is not the original taste, because it is not seen to produce the latter's proper effects, such as the healing of illness. And that smell and touch are not the original smell or touch, because if the person experiencing them were to be absent, they would never occur; besides, they are unable to give rise to a sequence of effects. But neither is that smell or touch unreal, because we see bodies grow pallid [at the sight of wounds] and the emission of semen [from tactile thrills in sex]. Neither is that sound the original sound, for the speaker hears the echo of his voice as though it were another person speaking.

In this way, as all this appears reflected, so does the universe in the light of the Supreme Lord.

'Now, what can this reflection be?'

Nothing at all.

'You mean to say that it has no cause?'

Oh, it is a question of cause, is it? What becomes of your point on the reflection, then? [To answer your question] the cause is none but the Supreme Lord's Energy, known as Freedom. The Lord holds within Himself the reflection of the universe, so He is its constitutive principle. For the universe is Consciousness in essence, and the place where the Intelligence discloses Itself. And that very universe is the reflection, so the latter's sustainment pertains to God. Being the constitutive principle of all things is the Supreme Lord's essence, an essence not void of conceptualization, for everything that is Consciousness by nature cannot avoid conceptualizing its own essence. Were it to be lacking in such conception, it would in truth be obtuse insentience.

This conception is not conventional [that is, it is not conception in its limited and phenomenal form], but is none other than the Being Which has pure Consciousness as Its essence, and is known as the Supreme Repository of Sound. And the Supreme Lord's configuration of Energies is conceptual exactly to the extent that it is creative of the universe.

The three principal Energies of the Supreme Lord are the Supreme, Will and Expansion. These are the three conceptions *a, i, u*. It is from this triad that the whole complex of energies proceeds: Joy is the repose in the Supreme; Domination is repose in the Will; and the Wave, repose in Expansion. And these are the three conceptions *ā, ī, ū*. The first three of these conceptions possess a portion of Light by nature, and are solar in essence; the last three conceptions, in which Joy, the essence of repose, prevails, are lunar in essence . . .

In this way, God reveals Himself as Lord of the Family

[of Divine Energies] in the Supreme Energy itself, and in this aspect, has but one energy, Emission—which generates the Family. And when Śiva, through that energy, vibrates from the form of Joy to that of the external principles [such as the earth], the conceptions, represented by the classes of sounds, also finally attain the shape of the identical exterior principles . . .

That Emission is again threefold—the *infinitesimal,* a repose in the limited intelligence [of Śiva limited by self-obscuration]; the *energic,* an awakening of that limited intelligence; and the *divine,* a dissolution of that same limited intelligence. Thus Emission alone is God's energy for generating the universe . . .

In this way, one who perceives his self as the only point of repose of all the conceptions, where the differences of all the Principles, the beings and the worlds are reflected—he becomes the Liberated in Life, through divine impenetration and freedom from dualizing thought . . .

—*The Essence of the Tantras*[211]

103
KṢEMA RĀJA

The Cosmic Vibrations of Divine Energy

VASU GUPTA

The opening and shutting of His eyes form the world's creation and dissolution. We worship Him, Śiva, the Circle of Energies' fountain of glory!

KṢEMA RĀJA

We worship the "cause of happiness," Śiva, who is our very own nature! He causes the happiness in the form of a favor—an expansive recognition of the consciousness that is indivisibly one with the supreme joy, a joy extinguishing all pain. While meditating on Him as transcending the world, we sink the condition of imagined experiencer that He Himself produced in us, and so plunge into His being. It is this plunging, the fruit of Liberation during Life, that will be explained in this treatise. The use of "we" [instead of "I"] is to express the identity of all the recipients of the favor, those on whom the favoring Glance has fallen. Vasu Gupta's first sentence "The opening and shutting of His eyes form the world's creation and dissolution," suggests what is uniquely Śiva's. This is explicated in the second sentence, "We worship Him, Śiva, the Circle of Energies' fountain of glory!"

Here, then, is the Supreme Lord, the Great God Whose substance is light. He is the essence of the self-apprehension of plenary Selfhood, formed of the ultimate import of the complex of sounds: He is therefore the sempiternal nature of the plenary Freedom indivisible from the Supreme Energy, itself the fire stick of the two emissions of concentrated joy and conscious Vibrancy.

Then there is the Energy of Freedom of the august God, Who is Himself unmoving. Indivisible though She is from Him, She projects, by virtue of Her essential consciousness, the sequence of all the cosmic acts, as creation and dissolution, on the wall that is Herself, like a city reflected in a mirror—a sequence which, as will later be proved, seems to transgress the limits of the divine being, while not doing so in fact. This Energy is described by the word "Vibrancy," itself derived from a word signifying "a slight tremulousness." God is therefore eternally consubstantial with His Vibrancy, and never Vibrancy-bereft, though there are some who say that the ultimate Reality is devoid of that Vibrancy. If that were true, the universe, being inactive in nature, would be vacuous of the sovereign essence of deity.

This sacred science, appropriately called the "Science of Vibrancy," was originated by the great teacher Vasu Gupta, to disclose to us our own nature, which is Śiva Himself—Śiva endowed with the Energy of Vibrancy, the substance of the apprehension of the pulsating Consciousness. This science will be developed below.

And this is what the Energy of Vibrancy is: Her substance is the joy aroused at the wonder of the concentered Selfhood which enwombs creations and dissolutions without number; it is also the totality of immaculate and polluted things. She is consubstantial with the appearance of the contraction and expansion of knowers and objects known. She is the Goddess Whom the Upaniṣads adore, and is at once the opening and shutting of Śiva's eyes.

To explain: She Who is the dissolutive "eye-closing" [or concealing] state of the complex of principles previously created, starting with Śiva and ending with the earth; She alone, in connection with the beings about to rise, is their creative "eye-opening" [or disclosing] stage. Thus the stage of universal reversion to quiescence, the basis for the immersion into concentrated Consciousness, is also the state of universal awakening. As the Sacred Tradition declares:

> The Goddess Ever-Lambent [always relishing delight] shines unceasingly in plenitude. She is the wave on the ocean of awakening, She is the Lord's Energy of Will.

For His part, the august Great God, through His Energy of Freedom, assumes the state of *knower*—comprising [the seven Hierarchies of conscious beings] Śiva, the Great Incantation Lords, the Incantation Lords, the Incantations, the Intelligence-Deconditioned Souls, the Dissolution-Deconditioned Souls, and the Conditioned souls. He also assumes the state of the *known* as well. Then His playfulness to conceal His own inner essence becomes the background [as it were, of the emanations soon to rise]. On this background, in the order of *descent* [from the summit of perfection], He successively conceals the anteriorly subsistent emanations and discloses the ones posteriorly originated. On the other hand, in the order of *ascent* [from the nadir of imperfection], He successively conceals the posterior emanations, and—in the yogis endowed with knowledge—discloses the forms of those anterior. Thus it is that the Great God, abandoning the contractional nature in each posterior emanation, discloses in it each anterior one in its expansiveness; on the other hand, He sinks the expansive nature in each anterior emanation, revealing it as each posterior one in its contractedness. In this way everything is permeated by everything, and all this perception of difference is only through the contractions made manifest by Himself. It is to deracinate this difference that my treatise has been composed.

—*The Ascertainment of Vibrancy*[212]

104

MAHEŚVARĀNANDA

Résumé of the Truths of Triadism

I. THE PRIMORDIAL UNITY OF LIGHT AND SELF-AWARENESS

1. Prostrating at the feet, ever pure, of the teacher Mahā Prakāśa, [the Great Light], Maheśvarānanda [he whose joy is the Great Lord Śiva] arranges this fragrant *Bouquet of Great Meaning.*

2. May Mahā Prakāśa, the Great Light, radiant with the vibrant and motionless brilliance of Self-Awareness, ever prosper [or increase]! The sacred sciences are intent only with defining the excellence of his name.

3. The Self is assuredly the root of the universe. No one asks that it be proved: is anyone immersed in the Ganges flood ever thirsty?

4. The dull [cowherds], yes, even the stupid water-carrying women, recognize Him, the Lord of Energy—to Whom alone adoration! To what person, then, is He not manifest?

5. Experience is handicapped; so is inference—which derives from it. Only the glory of the lamp of Revelation emblazes His greatness somewhat.

6. Some imagine the nature of the Self as definable in distinction from the Lord Himself. May those who are thus turned away from the Self, be in error when distinguishing those capable of liberation [from those who are not].

7. "Where attraction is, there is precept; where attraction is not, there is prohibition." This is discrimination—for those who, like ourselves, believe the sacred sciences to be only the Heart's vibration.

8. A man whose heart resists looking into the Self, the essence of Reality, such a man is overpowered by fear of rebirths, as though impelled by the force of the poison of doubt.

9. The finest of rubies is as if wrapped in the halo of its

own rays. Likewise the Self, even though it shines most manifestly to the world, is as though not manifest at all.

10. Exalted shines the Light, lamp of auspiciousness to the worlds that are and to those that are not. The flow of oil, with its clutter of impurities, burns at the top of the wick of Self-Awareness.

11. Only the Light of the Heart is real, and is the cause of the world's creation. Reposeful, it is the Self-Awareness of creation; agitated, it is the expansion of the universe.

II. SEPARATION OF LIGHT FROM SELF-AWARENESS: THE EMANATION OF THE PRINCIPLES

12. In the contraction of the world [lowest of the Principles] and of Śiva [exalted above all Principles], both have Light as their transcendent essence. One is differentiated from the other by the Heart's awakening Self-Awareness.

13. The concentration of the myriads of energies everywhere perceived is Śiva, the supremely independent, His essence the impulse of His Heart.

14. When ready to will, know and create the universe, Śiva is the expansion, delightful and strong, of the triangle of the Heart, said to have Energy as its essence.

15. Energy is of two kinds, Knowledge and Action. The awakening of the first is the Ever Beneficent god. Through the efformation of the second rises the second god, the Supreme Lord.

16. The Self is the knower, and universal activity the knowable. When knower and knowable are fused into a uniflavored essence, that in truth is the immaculate Wisdom.

17. From this uniflavored essence arise the artifices of differentiated knowledge. Their authoress is the Mirific Power, the deluding energy of the supremely independent Lord of the Universe.

18. There are the five [sheathing] energies: because of them the Lord—omnipotent, all-knowing, perfect, eternal and unlimited—is as though inversely transformed.

19. The benevolent Śiva, the Pure Witness, the actor in the world drama, becomes an infinitesimal soul [or Spirit], His business the assumption of multiple roles.

20. In their state of indifferentiation the three Attributes, Knowledge, Action and Magic—whose essence is Brightness, Passion and Darkness—form the Principle Matter, an energy of the Lord.

21. The three Inner Faculties [Instinct, Egoism and Mind] are buoyed on the waves of the ocean of the Heart. They attract to themselves now thisness [the object], now I-ness [the subject].

22. With the lamps of the five knowing faculties, unfailingly focused on their respective spheres, the Lord, abiding in the Heart, perceives objects without obstacle.

23. Five indeed are the faculties of the Lord of the worlds, made principally for action. And man, different as he is from unconscious beings, acts with them as he pleases.

24. The Dandy of the three worlds amuses Himself, sniffing at the perfume of the five aromatic flowers blossoming in the garden of the world. The first of them is Odor [the others, Sight, Sound, Taste and Touch].

25. Like balls of molasses gradually coagulating from sugarcane juice and never losing their sweetness, so also the Five Elements of the Śiva Light [solidify from it and never lose its brightness].

III. THE RETURN TO THE PRIMORDIAL UNITY

26. Śiva's Great Energy, charged with the impetus of Self-Awareness, comes into view, as though She were the rope making for the smooth motion of the wheel of the worlds.

27. There are six Orbits: half their number signifies Light, or Meaning; half, Self-Awareness, or Word. Such is the delight of Śiva's conjugal union.

28. As in the distinctive art form which figures both elephant and bull at once, we here conceive, in the same reality, Śiva's difference from Energy.

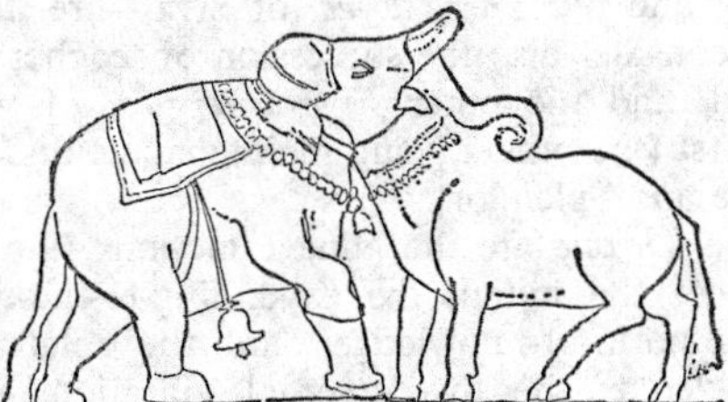

From the Virappa Nayaka Temple,
Krishnapuram, Tirunelveli District

29. Consider how great Energy is even in an insect, whose body is no larger than a sesame seed. What must She not be in the body of the universe glorious in its independence!

30. What the Spiritual Master's expansive force is at the moment of the world's awakening, it is also in its embryonic state, at the moment of the world's falling asleep.

31. This All is in fact triply structured [as knower, known and knowledge]. It is equal in the knower and the known. The solid knot uniting both, the activity of knowledge, produces three worlds one in essence.

32. What real difference is there between a flower [on earth] and a flower in the sky, since the world is consubstantial with the vibrant Consciousness, and this Consciousness the same in all?

33. The illusion of difference between being and non-being —as that between a ruby and an emerald [where the color of each, reflected in the other, makes both seem the same]—is eliminated by the uniform relationship established between them by the vibrant Consciousness.

IV. THE ENERGIC WAY

34. Resplendent are the goddesses of the faculties on the throne of the body, the world-egg. In their midst blazes the Supreme Śiva, abode of all knowledge.

35. It is there that one must adore Him—with flowers and fragrant perfumes of Self-Awareness, with the strong drink of the nectar of the knowable offered in cups of the intellect.

36. Consider the Wheels of Totality—the divine *Throne* [of the energies, the human body], the *Five Waves* [of the five highest Energies—of Consciousness, Joy, Will, Knowledge and Action], and the *Three Eyes* [of Śiva—fire, the sun and the moon]; consider also the succession of teachers [or *Spiritual Masters*], and the other *Five Energies*, of which creation is the first [the others being maintenance, dissolution, the Inexpressible and Splendor].

37. On the *Throne* are the Nine Functions [the four internal vibrations: the initial, the expanding-to-the-cosmos, the related-to-the-norm-of-knowledge, and the related-to-the-objects-of-knowledge; the five external vibrations, comprising the five elements]; on the *Fivefold Wave* only five; on *the Eye of the forehead* [the Eye of Fire], seventeen [ten igneous in the Eye's interior, seven tongues of flame of the

Vedas]; and *the other two Eyes,* twelve [in the right Eye, the Eye of the sun, consisting of the functions of Instinct, Mind, the five perceptual and the five motor faculties], and sixteen [in the left Eye, the Eye of the moon, comprising the five gross and the five subtle elements, the five Breaths, and the Immortal Function, where the essence of the elements and the Breaths resides].

38. In the Wheel of Totality, where five sections are seen [each having one Spiritual Master], there are [in addition] sixty-four types of *Spiritual Masters.* In the circle there is no restriction on the number of Spiritual Masters who have transcended all restriction.

39. [As to the *Five Energies,*] there are ten functions in creation [the superior five; Consciousness, Joy, Will, Knowledge and Action; the inferior five; creation, maintenance, dissolution, the Inexpressible and Splendor]; twenty-two energies in *maintenance* [those found in the four Masters of the Cosmic Cycles, the twelve Princely Initiates, and the six Controllers of Virility]; eleven energies in *destruction* [latent in the five perceptual and the five motor faculties, and in Egoism]; and thirteen energies in the *Inexpressible* [comprising the Supreme Kālī, who vomits twelve other Kālīs, goddesses presiding over the three states of creation, maintenance and dissolution, each multiplied with itself, the other two and with the undifferenced state].

40. In the divine *Splendor,* with the one unstained Beauty all radiant, the differentiating concepts do not appear. When She reveals herself in reflections in the sixteen functions [comprising the four states of creation, maintenance, dissolution and the Inexpressible, each multiplied with itself and the other three], the Goddess then transcends them.

41. The unenlightened imagine a division when they say that Splendor is the fifth function of the whole which comprises creation [preservation, absorption and the Inexpressible]. In fact Splendor is the root bulb of creation, and creation the foliage of Splendor.

42. The perception of one's power is worship, a worship difficult to realize in this world. The worship of the Lord of the universe [requires only] wines, betel leaves, perfumes and flowers—all easy to procure.

43. To become aware of one's being—whether it is evolving towards effects or is in a state of tranquillity—one must real-

ize that outward events are to be excluded and the breath controlled.

44. Desiccation in bodies is the destruction of Pollution; the latter's combustion is the extirpation of conceptual latencies; its dousing, the creation of purity with the sprinkling of the nectar of knowledge.

45. The rites purifying the body of the mass of differentiating concepts consist of undifferenced Awareness; the libation water is the play of the knowable; and the flowers, the essences that nourish the Essence.

46. Turning to plenary Selfhood and throwing away the sprouts of differentiating concepts, purifying oneself by reciting the mystic incantations—in this, I say, the full satisfaction to Śiva and to His Energy lies.

47. Deep attachment to a thing transforms it in very truth into a deity. Images to which one is deeply attached bring the desired object to fruition.

48. A picture does not paint a picture; it is the painter who sees and paints it. Say then to which of the two [the author or the work] one ought to attribute the notion of divinity?

V. THE DIVINE WAY

49. This is what Mystic Incantation means: a certain intuition that comprises "reflection" on one's exalted state, and "protection" as regards the fear of one's mundane constriction: it is an insight that devours all differentiating concepts.

50. Displayed Word is Activity, the Interjacent is Knowledge, and the Visioning is Will, a subtle force and a function common to all.

51. Radiant with joy, Beauty, Who is the abatement of the fascination of the eight grand powers of Yoga, is perceived on that occasion [of God's delight]—She Who alone is God's universal Seal.

52. The wishing tree of Self-Awareness, with its mighty branches, standing full-grown in the region of the Heart, has the loveliness of experience for its flowers, and the festive splendor of unimpaired joy for its fruits.

53. There is no succession in God: how, then, can He be touched by the pollution of time? What obstacle to liberation can there be to one Who lives eternally free of obstacles?

54. All that exists—in whatever form or place—it still ex-

sts, does it not? The Self is therefore eternal and unchangea-le, becoming changeable only with the destruction of the in-tant.

55. Does not Revelation tell us that the love of all things is lue to the love of the Self? Hence every soul is in essence joy, ree or bound though it be.

56. If one has the desire to ascertain the eternal and spot-ess expansion of one's Heart, one has to explode the Center f divisible duration, where the sun and moon have set.

57. Even among the most coarse elements, consider how ure the state of the sky is. Of what kind will the Supreme iva, the Moon-Lord, not be, He Who is far above the Thirty-Six Principles?

58. Abandoning themselves to the delight of the Great Ban-quet, where they drink the intoxicating quintessence of nectar rom the pots of undifferenced Energy—the revelers make old to masticate the sprouts of differentiating concepts.

59. Let a face be reflected in a mirror [the eyeball], and let hat mirror further throw its reflection into another mirror consciousness]. The [second] mirror in which the reflection is —that is the one to know.

60. The jay's wings are alike on both sides: where, then, loes this idea of introvert and extrovert yogis arise?

61. On the single thread of Self-Awareness of yogi strings he sequent states of waking, sleep, dreamless slumber and undifferenced awareness—as though he were stringing a neck-ace of many-colored gems.

62. His heart atremble with the inebriatingly sweet taste of he ambrosial wine of beatitude, the yogi now yearns for the our tamarind savor of the world's festive flurry.

63. The faculties through which the yogi senses the world's leasures, and which are capable of pouring out his heart—it s through them that he fills the world with a conscious ibrancy.

VI. THE NULL WAY AND REALIZATION

64. "Stay where you are and have no care,"[213] for the end s assured. In this discrimination lies: who other than the Self can teach it and to whom?

65. How wonderful is the unitive realization of Śiva's yogis, where the blemishes of mental affliction have been obliter-ated. How abundant is their joy in the midst of the trans-

migratory flux, how easy their happiness on the Way of Lib-eration!

66. Though touched for but a moment by that Realit whose essence is nectar, the All that transcends all obtains a glory that always endures.

67. He is more hidden than the hidden; more evident tha evidence itself. When the glance of the Spiritual Master fal on the lucky ones, the first alternative ceases to exist fc them.

68. Away with all other knowledge! This God, the Terrify-ing Churner, churns this Truth abounding in nectar, as H churned the oceans of the four torrents.

69. Yes, we have proclaimed the Mystery. So, fools, do nc drift from one womb hollow to another. Examine this Hear so near to you, examine its vibrant impulse!

70. This is the Great Truth that Kṛṣṇa himself, the god ar-rayed in sixteen thousand energies, taught Arjuna, Pāṇḍu son, at the start of the battle. Peace!

—*The Bouquet of Great Meaning*[21]

XXIV. ŚAIVA NONDUALISM, or *ŚIVĀDVAITA*

Śaivism finally capitulated to the Vedanta around the thirteenth century, in Śrī Kaṇṭha. It underwent the same process as Vaiṣṇavism with Yāmuna and Rāmānuja—the demonstration of the accord of the Śaiva scriptures with the Vedic, and the substitution of as many Vedantic terms as possible for those traditional in Śaiva theology. Śrī Kaṇṭha based his system on the first Vaiṣṇava Vedanta, Qualified Nondualism, so that his doctrine came to be called, alternatively, Qualified Śaiva Nondualism. One important point of contact between the Vedanta and Śaiva theologies is the concept of the divine as destructive—in the expression of which Śaivism excels all other schools of thought—interpreted by Śrī Kaṇṭha with elegance and Vedantic learning (Selection 105).

105

ŚRĪ KAṆṬHA

The Compassion and Pitilessness of Divine Terror

BĀDARĀYAṆA'S APHORISM

The Brahman is the eater, because He devours the movable and the unmoving.

Who knows where He is—the God for whom both the Brahmin and the warrior are rice, and Death the sauce?[215]

This text of Revelation introduces the topic. The doubt here is whether the eater of the morsel of the universe of conscious and unconscious beings—implied by the words Brahmin and warrior—spiced with the sauce of Death, is the Supreme Lord or somebody else.

DISSENTIENT VIEW

It is not proper to ascribe the act of devouring all things to the Favorer of all, the supremely compassionate Lord. The taking of another's life is essentially violence. Anger is the shoot from which the impulse to violence springs, and the root bulb of anger, that baneful quality, is delusion. The stuff of delusion is darkness, the primary cause of all destruction. Hence a destroyer is a tenebrous being. Tenebrousness is a quenching of illumination through the concealment of knowledge. In saying that the Brahman is the destroyer of everything, one would be confounding baneful qualities like those of dark ignorance, delusion and anger with the eternally pure reality, the source of limitless beneficence, the Being untouched by the stain of transmigration. All those qualities like omniscience and eternal contentment, established as being His innate characteristics, would become void of meaning. Therefore someone other than the Brahman has those qualities and is the destroyer. Such is the unorthodox position.

ORTHODOX JUDGEMENT

The orthodox teaching is that Revelation declares the Brahman to be the All-Destroyer. And why? "Because He devours the movable and the unmoving." The devouring of the entire universe of movable and unmoving things, which you say is not proper on the part of the Brahman, is the characteristic of the Brahman alone, and not of the soul. Limited as the latter is, he lacks the capacity to destroy all movable and unmoving things. In the words of the *Atharvaśiras*—

> To the Destroyer, the Great Devourer, adoration![216]

Revelation proclaims the Supreme Lord, and not any mere soul, to be the All-Destroyer. And from its words:

> He who offers all these worlds in sacrifice,[217]

we understand the Brahman's nature as sacrificer of the holocaust of the universe in the fire of His own radiance. This cannot be true of the soul, who is only one among the myriads of the holocaust offerings. When the Supreme Lord has absorbed into His being everything other than Himself, movable and unmoving, conscious and unconscious: then—with the distinctions of time, as between night and day, obliterated by the quenching of the light of the moon, the sun, and other luminaries; with the mundane diversities, such as those between gross and subtle, gods and men, annulled through the effacement of the polarities of the conceptual–corporeal complex—all this survives only as Darkness. Nothing then remains besides that one Supreme Lord, unconstrained in His splendor, the Witness of all. Hence Revelation declares:

> When there is darkness, there is no day or night, no being or non-being. Only Śiva.[218]

The words "no being or non-being" do not deny the essence of reality to Beast and Bond, identified respectively with that being and non-being, but only a gross form characterized by the diversities of the conceptual and corporeal complex.

'When the Supreme Brahman, Śiva, the eternally radiant, exists, how can the world be a mass of darkness?'

How is Śiva, the self-illuminant, the Witness of all, affected, I ask. As the souls are then bereft of organs, bodies and powers, the complex of the conceptual and the corporeal is a void, and objects can no longer be grasped—these souls have no perception of the universe. As for their faculties of knowledge, they too are fogged by Pollution, and, as before, have no vision of Śiva, the self-illuminant in essence. Therefore that august state, the supreme Dreamless Slumber in its amplitude, where all knowledge of specific objects has been expunged, is what is known as Darkness. In the words of Tradition:

> All this existed reduced to Darkness, unperceived, undefined.[219]

Śiva is called the Isolated Being, marked as He is with the subtle energies of the universe of the conscious and unconscious, and not marred by the polarities of the conceptual and corporeal complex. Then at the time of creation, preceded by the first vibrations of His energies—solely through an impulse of will, independently of any material cause, and out of His own substance—He creates, that is, manifests, the totality of conscious and unconscious things, endowing them earlier with their particular names. There is a felicitous passage in this regard:

> Like a yogi, God, innately consciousness itself, flashes outside Himself the things existent within, without any material cause, by a mere impulse of will.

'But Revelation asserts that the Mirific Power and Spirit are the world's material cause, in texts like:

> Know the Mirific Power to be the material cause, and the Supreme Lord as the wielder of that Power.[220]

> From him the Cosmic Soul was born.[221]

How can you then say that there is no material cause?'

You are right. In the production of a pot, for instance, the material cause, the lump of clay, is seen to be distinct from the potter's body. But material causes like the Mirific Power are not distinct from the Supreme Lord, because the world emerges from Him Who is intrinsically that same Mirific Power. There is no contradiction then. Hence the material cause is said to be the Supreme Lord Himself—as the Mirific Power and Spirit in subtle form, existing inseparably from that very Lord's essence. As the *Atharvaśikhā* says:

> The Lord must be meditated on and worshiped. All this creation emanates from Him, gods like Brahmā, Viṣṇu and Rudra, and all the faculties and elements. He is not a cause, but the creator of causes. He is the thinker, while the cause is the object of thought. In the middle of the sky is the beneficent Śiva, the Lord of all, to whom all supremacy belongs.

Hence, where the dissolution of all things is, there indeed is their origin; where the absorption of beings without end, there only—in Śiva, brimming with energies without end—is their continuance. Therefore the word "Brahman" stands only for Śiva, the Destroyer of all.

Your objection—that destruction, being essentially violence, would ally the Brahman with the baneful qualities, such as anger, that derive from violence—is nothing but a thoughtless play of words, since it is to Matter alone that the Attribute of Darkness, the root of all anger, belongs. Divine Revelation itself is our authority for the fact that the Supreme Lord is beyond all Darkness. In the passage which begins with the words:

> The Master, attended by the Goddess Umā, the Supreme Lord,

there is the following line

> The Witness of all, beyond darkness.[222]

The voice of puranic Tradition also declares the Supreme Lord to be eternally implicated in qualities like knowledge which dispel ignorance, in passages such as:

> Knowledge, passionlessness, power, heat, truth, forgiveness, constancy, creative causality, knowledge of the Self and superintendence—these ten imperishable qualities abide eternally in Śiva.

> A passionate youth is Śiva, tumescent with the pure and infallible apprehension of all things, full of ecstatic delight in the taste of the nectar of his own powers.

Unconstrained in His brilliance, the Supreme Lord is all ready to discharge [His power into creation, when]

> He yearns to be many,[223]

joins His Energy of Will, the Mirific Power, in an intimate embrace with Himself, the receptacle of many worlds. [Then]

> He becomes charged with heat.[224]

Through His energy, which in essence is heat and knowledge, He pauses to reflect on the aggregation of bodies to be formed in accordance with the karma of all the individual souls. After His reflection, employing His Energy of Action, devoid of all conceivable organs

> He creates all this.[225]

In this way, on the wall of His Energy of Will, He unfolds the picture of the whole world. And according to the words:

He created it, and entered it,[226]

He associates Himself with the triple energies [of Knowledge, Will and Action], enters into the total agglomerate of effects, and emerges as the universe, comprising the triad of deities [Viṣṇu, Brahmā and Rudra], identical with the Attributes, and other beings. Who can comprehend the greatness of Śiva, the all-powerful and the all-knowing?

It is clear then that the Supreme Lord is the All-Destroyer.

—*Commentary on the "Aphorisms on the Brahman"*[227]

XXV. ENERGY-QUALIFIED NONDUALISM, or *HERO-ŚAIVISM*, or *ŚAKTIVIŚIṢṬĀDVAITA*, or *VĪRA-ŚAIVA DARŚANA*

See Schemes 36 and 37

We now come to the most complex of the Indic systems, the synthesis of all previous Śaiva theologies—Energy-Qualified Nondualism, the theology of the Vīra-Śaiva (Hero-Śaivism) or Liṅgāyata (Symbol-Bearing) denomination. Founded by Basava (1131–67), it seems to have been furnished with a theology by his brilliant nephew Cenna Basava (see Scheme 37). Śaivism, by Basava's time, had compromised with the Vedic castes and states. Basava, in ridding his faith from the latter, sought to restore it to its pristine Tantric purity. In creating a theology for Hero-Śaivism, Cenna Basava chose for its ultimate category the All Void of the Buddhist Vacuists (or Mādhyamikas), a concept that most Hindu theologians had viewed with horror. From this All Void emanates the ultimate Repository, and from the latter, the six Repositories and the six Symbols. A contemporary avatar of this archetype seems to be Tillich's idea of God as the Ground of all being, with finite beings as symbols of that Ground.

Basava and his immediate followers did not use Sanskrit, the sacred tongue of Vedism, but Kannaḍa, the spoken language of their region. Their compositions came to be called sayings or *vacanas*. But it soon became necessary for the new theology to come to terms with the invincible Vedic tradition—which it could only do by using the latter's theological idiom and language. The Sanskritization of Hero-Śaivism seems to have been achieved by Śivayogi, of uncertain date, but subsequent to Basava; and its Vedantization by Śrī Pati (fourteenth century) through the usual process—a commentary on Bādarāyaṇa's *Aphorisms*. There, among other things, he develops the notion of Grace as Śiva's Energic Fulmination (Selection 106), a concept borrowed from Triadism and Śaiva Orthodoxy (School VII). The theological structure of Hero-Śaivism was finally elaborated—without any reference to the Buddhist All Void, by the fifteenth-century theologian Māyi Deva (Selections 107 and 108).

106

ŚRĪ PATI

The Energic Fulmination

The omniscience of the soul is concealed at the time of dissolution through union with the Energy of Knowledge, and through Śiva becoming manifest as Bond in the form of Dreamless Slumber. Discriminant percipients must therefore strive to realize at once the two knowledges, florescent and radical, which eradicate the sense of "I" and "mine," and also the knowledge of Śiva that eradicates the knowledge of self—for that is what the Vedas and the Vedanta proclaim.

Revelation, in passages like the following:

> A man who has a teacher, knows.[228]

And:

> Let a man who is beyond the four states of life suppress all his senses, salute his teacher with devotion . . .[229]
>
> Let him take fuel in his hand and approach a learned teacher who lives entirely in the Brahman.[230]

In these passages and others Revelation speaks of the release of the soul from the body, achieved by means of the Energic Fulmination, obtained through the good works reflected in the Supreme Śiva. The occurrence of the Energic Fulmination is referred to in the scriptures of the Śaiva Sacred Tradition, in words such as the following:

> Let the good teacher, from concern for his pupil, spark off the Energic Fulmination—the cause that blots out the Pollution of the matured Great Bond. Through that Fulmination, the soul comes to enjoy the Brahman nature. For everyone, the Fulmination is unconditioned and undecaying; it is both the cause and the motive of supreme joy; and it has severe and mild varieties, O Queen of the gods! It is celebrated as being sixfold, according as it is found in the six Repositories [emanant from the Ultimate Repository]—those of the Devotee, the Great Master, Clearness, Breath, the Suppliant, and Oneness.

Energic Fulmination can therefore be defined as the cause that blots out the matured Pollution in the soul. It is the motive whereby an unexcelled and limitless joy is manifested in the soul in the form of the Supreme Śiva, Who is the Brahman Itself. The Energic Fulmination in its severe and mild forms is [as I said] sixfold, found in the Repositories from that of the Devotee to that of Oneness. Through the sequence of the salvific disciplines, listening, reflection and meditation, prescribed in the Vedanta, the Vedas and the texts of Tradition—a sequence which emblazes the supreme mystery of the Master, Beast and Bond—the Great God Principle, eternal, consummated and blissful in essence, is manifested in the mental concept generated by the indivisibly formed Word.

The *first* manifestation is pointed out in the Devotee Repository. It is the vision of the Ever Beneficent Principle—condensed consciousness, conspicuous and stainless in its being—showering dust into the hollow bowl of ignorance.

The *second* is revealed in the Great Master Repository. Through the practice of Śiva Yoga, assisted by the Serpentine Energy [situated in the body's midpoint], it moves along the spinal cord and breaks through the six plexuses to the optic thalamus. It consists of the union of Śiva with His Energy.

The *third* is pointed out in the Clearness Repository. Through an exceeding favor to his disciple, the teacher abandons his own body and enters that of his student. There, by purifying the student's veins, he passes, by means of the latter's Serpentine Energy, through the seven plexuses in a form invisibly manifest, like Śiva, moving through all the worlds.

The *fourth* is signified in the Breath Repository. By means of contact with the Breaths, Ascendent, Descendent and Vital, he finds an abundant beneficence whose substance is the Consciousness Energy flashing in the middle of the spinal cord. And he attains the eight yogic powers—the capacity to contract the body, and to dilate it, to levitate, to attain the unattainable through the senses, the possession of an unthwarted will, of a capacity to impose his power on objects, an independence from the Attributes of Matter, and the fulfillment of all desires.

The *fifth* is spoken of as occurring in the Suppliant Repository. Through experiencing the vision of the plenary Śiva Principle, in the form of the supreme sky—unexcelled, spotless, unmodified and impartible—like a lamp of camphor, its flame unmoved by wind and unflickering, flung into torrid sunshine—one's state of being is dispelled, and one arrives at an ecstatic dissolutive state devoid of all knowledge of objects external and internal, of body, senses, mind and breath.

The *sixth* is referred to in the Oneness state. In this way, by means of Energic Fulmination—explainable by the metaphors of ant, monkey, bird, cow, fish and tortoise—the Śiva nature is realized in its highest state, through the cessation of one's natural selfhood: this is what liberation is. It is therefore indisputable that the soul depends on God, and that God projects the states of waking, sleep and dreamless slumber.

—*The Giver-of-Good Fortune Commentary on the "Aphorisms on the Brahman"*[231]

107

MĀYI DEVA

Categories of the Theology of Energy-Qualified Nondualism

I. THE REPOSITORY

1. I shall now explain the Repository teaching from the start, as the God of gods taught it, succinctly, to preserve its mystery.

2. There is but one Supreme Brahman, the Śiva Principle signified by Being, Consciousness and Joy. The teachers of Śiva call it the Repository, out of respect.

3. It is the abode of all the Principles—like the Prodigious—and is the place in which they all dissolve. That is why it is known as the Repository.

4. It is the place where, in the beginning, the world of Matter and Spirit is sustained; where, at the end, it is dissolved. That is why it is called the Repository [*sthala*].

5. Of the two syllables of the Sanskrit word for "repository" *stha* and *la, stha* denotes "place" [*sthāna*] and *la,* "dissolution" [*laya*]. Since it is the cause of both, it is called *sthala.*

6. The substratum of everything that is stable and mobile, the source of the world's reality—that is known as the Repository.

7. The principle which is the support of all energies, all luminaries, and all souls—that is what the wise proclaim as the Repository.

8. The Supreme Brahman, the abode of all beings, worlds, and of every excellence: they call It the imperishable Repository.

9. The paramount state of those secure in perfect liberation: the nondual Repository—so it is called by those resolved on the knowledge of Śiva alone.

II. THE SYMBOL AND THE BODY

10. Through its energy being agitated the unique Repository becomes two—the one called the Symbol Repository, and Body Repository the other.

11. The Repository, divided in two by the two conditionings—Symbol and Body—is the Supreme Principle itself, known by the names of Śiva, Rudra and other gods.

12. Known through the differentiations of Symbol and Body, the Repository is the Supreme Principle, giving its name to Śiva, Rudra and other gods.

13. Dichotomized into worshiper and worshiped, the Repository, as Symbol, becomes the worshiped, and, as Body, the worshiper.

14. Worshiper or worshiped, it is still the Supreme Śiva, subsistent in His unfailing essence through His spontaneous cosmic play.

15. Simultaneously and in succession, in His own person and by His own power, Śiva attains the state of worshiper and worshiped. Millions of rebirths cannot qualify someone who is not Śiva for Śiva worship.

16. The worship of Śiva is by Śiva only: so Revelation guarantees in several places. The Repository, signified by qualities like the truth, is evidently the supreme Consciousness itself in all its purity.

17. The Repository subsists in the dichotomy of Symbol and Body, Śiva and soul. In its Self-nature as Śiva, it is called pure Consciousness.

18. In its Symbol and Body forms it is known simply as the Repository. The Respository, of course, is pure Consciousness too, and the Symbol is Śiva Himself.

19. The Body is the Soul: this is the highest Śaiva teaching.

III. THE TWO ENERGIES

As the Repository becomes two, so does the Energy abiding in it.

20. Energy, the incomparable, is really participant in Śiva's qualities [is Śiva's feminine Partner]. She is the Witness, the plenitude of truth, the undifferentiated, the Sovereign Queen.

21. Śiva enjoys that twofold Energy through the vigor of His independence. The Goddess, tender to Her devotees, is dichotomized in Her qualitied equality with Her Lord.

22. One part of Her inheres in the Symbol, the other in the Body. The part inherent in the Symbol is proclaimed as Aptitude.

23. The part inherent in the Body is Devotion, the dispeller of transmigration. [Though one, Energy is] like the light of a great conflagration breaking up [into many flames].

24. So, as the Sovereign Queen, Energy, the dichotomized, Devotion in essence, is tenebrous glory; She is the shining One, the beautifully radiant.

25. Energy therefore possesses conceptual latencies; Devotion is free of them. Devotion is mighty, pure, most subtle, of supreme loveliness.

26. Being, Consciousness and Joy in essence, She bestows the fruits of experience and liberation—She, Energy known as Devotion; She, Devotion who is Energy always.

27. When truth in its absolute state is reflected on, there is

no difference between Energy and Devotion. Energy is termed action, and Devotion, quiescence.

28. Energy promotes creation, and Devotion, dissolution. Energy's manifoldness leads form even to formlessness.

29. Devotion's manifoldness also leads form to formlessness. Energy, through innate quality, tends to the world's progress.

30. Through innate quality, Devotion tends to the world's dissolution. Energy's face is turned downwards, Devotion's upwards.

31. Energy is furnished with the Mirific Power, Devotion is free of it. Logic and other norms show Devotion to surpass Energy in qualities.

32. Energy is the worshiped, Devotion the worshiper. Thus Energy inheres in the Symbol, Devotion in the Body.

IV. IDENTITY OF SYMBOL AND BODY

33. The Symbol is Śiva Himself, the Body the soul. Symbol and Body are one, Śiva and soul are one.

34. He who knows this tears the knots of ignorance apart. This is the orthodox teaching on Śiva; it is Śiva-Nondualism; it is the state of blessedness [Śiva].

108

MĀYI DEVA

Symbols and Energies

I. THE MEANING OF SYMBOL

1. I shall now declare the teaching on the Symbol, concisely or at length, just as Śiva once proclaimed it.

2. Śiva is Himself the Symbol: such is the Symbol's greatness. The Symbol has nothing else for its symbol, all else being fabricated from it.

3. Those who know the truth of the Symbol [*liṅga*] call it that, because it is where everything is dissolved [*līyate,* a word beginning with *li,* the first syllable of *liṅ-ga*], and where every-

thing is originated [*gamyate,* a word beginning with *ga,* second syllable of *liṅ-ga*].

4. As He is the cause of the dissolution and rise of embodied beings, Śiva, the partite and impartite, is called the Symbol [*liṅga*].

II. THE SIX SYMBOLS

5. The Symbol is described as triple. Its divisions are as follows. First is the Faith Symbol. The Breath Symbol is second.

6. The Desired Symbol is third. In this way Symbol is threefold. The Faith Symbol, in its higher and lower states, is impartite, and is apprehended by Faith.

7. As men of great wisdom attest, the Faith Symbol is pure existence. The Breath Symbol is grasped by the mind, and is partite and impartite.

8. Revelation calls it the Symbol within the mind of living beings. The great Desired Symbol is a Repository that can be grasped entire in space and time.

9. It realizes desired objects at once, and repels the undesired. Its worship is ever desired; the desired is worshiped in reverence.

10. The worshipers of the Symbol call it the Desired Symbol. It promotes its devotees' ends at all times.

11. Therefore Revelation, in the *Atharva Veda,* calls it the Desired Symbol. The Faith Symbol is Being, the Breath Symbol, Consciousness.

12. The Desired Symbol is Joy in essence. In the great scriptural declaration of oneness, "You are It,"[232] the word "are" stands for the Faith Symbol, "You" for the Breath Symbol.

13. And "It" for the Desired Symbol: this is how the three words are to be interpreted. The Faith Symbol is the supreme principle. The Breath Symbol is the most subtle.

14. The Desired Symbol is gross: such is the triad of Symbols. The gross is said to be external, and the subtle, internal.

15. What is both external and internal is termed the supreme principle. In the forms of body, breath and soul, of activity, implements and purpose,

16. Of Nucleus, Sound and Aptitude—it is in these forms that the triad of symbols is explained. Through manifold function, each Repository is frequently duplicated.

17. As men of great wisdom say, the Faith Symbol becomes double, double the Breath Symbol, and double the Desired Symbol too.

18. Determined by its own experience, the Faith Symbol becomes a double Repository—the Great Symbol, and the Symbol known as Brightness.

19. The Breath Symbol becomes the Motion Symbol and the Śiva Symbol. This is an undoubted tenet of the Symbol doctrine.

20. The Desired Symbol, for its part, becomes the Teacher Symbol and the Observance Symbol. What I say is the truth.

21. The Great Symbol, the Brightness Symbol, the Motion Symbol, and Śiva Symbol, the Teacher Symbol and

22. The Observance Symbol—this is how Symbol is explained as sixfold. In this sextuple form, the Symbol is the supreme cause.

III. THE SIX ENERGIES

23. Arising from His power, His independence, and His cosmic play, are the sixfold Energies, known to be implanted in the six Repositories.

24. The real nature of these energies will now be described in order. The Energy of Consciousness is named the Totally Elevated-Above-Tranquillity.

25. The Supreme Energy is the Elevated-Above-Tranquillity; the Primordial Energy is called Tranquillity itself. The Energy of Will is Wisdom, the Energy of Knowledge, Stability.

26. The Energy of Activity is Quiescence: this is how the Energies are synonymously linked. The Energy of Consciousness, the Supreme Energy, the Primordial Energy,

27. The Energies of Will, Knowledge and Activity, are the six Energies so-called. I shall now, in order, separately explain the essential characteristics of the six Repositories as furnished with their respective Energies.

IV. NATURE OF THE SIX SYMBOLS

28. They call the Śiva Principle the Great Symbol. It is devoid of beginning and end, it is the spotless, the abounding, the unique, the subtle, the higher than the highest, the innocuous, the immeasurable, attainable by faith alone, untouched

by insentience, the fulguration of the Energy of Consciousness.

29. They call it the Integral Brightness Symbol. It is ignescent, constant, infrangible, beyond the grasp of the senses, attainable by knowledge, the germ of transformation, the Ever Beneficent Principle itself, brought into being by the Supreme Energy, void of all conditioning.

30. Sages of fulfilled minds call it the Motion Symbol. It is possessed of exteriority and interiority, it is the formless principle, the spirit exalted even above the Imperishable, created by Śiva's innate Primordial Energy. It must always be meditated on in the mind.

31. What they call the Śiva Symbol is radiant with the form fashioned by Wisdom and Aptitude, the single-faced, the tranquil, the formed principle disseminated with His Energy of Will, established in Matter's evolute Egoism.

32. What is known as the Teacher Symbol originates from the power of Śiva's Energy of Knowledge. It is founded on all instruction, injunction and corpus of Doctrine. It is the abode of splendor, the ocean of the fullest joy. It is fixed in Matter's evolute Instinct.

33. What the knowers of the Veda call the Observance Symbol is the symbol that has become the substrate of all the Principles through its active essence. It is unmoving through its Activity Energy, and has ascended the path of liberation.

34. In this way, I have described the Six Repositories—starting with the Great Symbol and proceeding in order—as to their essence and their characteristics.

V. EVOLUTION OF THE SIX SYMBOLS

35. I shall now describe the manifestation of these Repositories. Through His Consciousness Energy, Śiva Himself becomes the Great Symbol.

36. Then, as worshiper, He becomes the great Oneness Repository. Next, through the Supreme Energy's fulguration in the exalted Great Symbol—

37. The eminent Repository, known as the Brightness Symbol, emerges, and is transformed, as worshiper, into the Suppliant Repository.

38. Then, in the Brightness Symbol, through the Primordial Energy's power, arises the unsurpassed Repository known as the Motion Symbol.

39. As worshiper, the Motion Symbol becomes the Breath Repository. From the Motion Symbol emanates that radiant mass of flame—

40. The Śiva Symbol, it emanates directly through the power of the Energy of Will. As worshiper, it becomes the Clearness Repository.

41. Next, in the Śiva Symbol, through the flash of the Energy of Knowledge, arises, as cause, the Repository known as the Teacher Symbol.

42. As worshiper it becomes the Great Master Repository. Then, in the Repository of the Teaching Symbol, through the power of the Energy of Action—

43. Proceeds the beautiful Repository known as the Observance Symbol, which, as worshiper, becomes the Devotee Repository.

44. So the Great Symbol, the Brightness Symbol, the Motion Symbol, and the Teacher Symbol, too,

45. And, finally, the Observance Symbol. This is the order of their creation. Thus the sextet of Symbols and Repositories has been briefly described. In each of these Repositories other divisions and subdivisions exist.

46. He who knows this tears the knot of ignorance apart. This is the orthodox teaching on Śiva; this is Śiva Nondualism; this is the state of blessedness.

—*Aphorisms on the Experience of Śiva*[233]

XXVI. ENERGICISM, or *ŚĀKTA DARŚANA*

See Scheme 38

A distinctive characteristic of Tantric Hinduism is the belief that the masculine–feminine principle pervades the universe (see Selection 26), thus accenting the feminine element neglected by the Vedic tradition. In Christianity the feminine principle is exalted in the person of the Madonna by the older and Apostolic churches, but the more recent Christian sects show less enthusiasm about her whom the Orthodox Church calls the All-Holy. The consensus of the older churches on the Madonna is strikingly expressed by Vieira:

> *Dous tronos há no céu mais sublimes que todos: o de Deus e o de sua Mãe . . .*
>
> There are two thrones in heaven more sublime than all the others: those of God and His Mother. The throne of God is infinitely higher than that of His Mother; the throne of His Mother is almost infinitely higher than the thrones of all the other creatures. But the greater glory of Mary does not lie in the fact that her throne transcends the thrones of all the created hierarchies—but in having a Son Whose throne infinitely transcends her own.[234]

The Lady is still excelled by her Son: but in Energicism (a theology never fully systematized), the Goddess transcends all Her "sons," becoming Herself the Supreme Principle (Selection 109), with the Divine Feminine becoming thereby exalted above the Divine Masculine.

109

NĪLAKAṆṬHA THE ŚĀKTA

The Goddess, the Supreme Divinity

'Why is it that the sacred sciences refer to the Goddess in words such as the "Mirific Power"? Instead, why do they not signify Her through words like "the Brahman," so as to avoid the flaw of ambiguous implication, and to ensure definiteness of meaning?'

Listen. The absolute Being of the Brahman has four epiphanies—the Male Power, the Golden Embryo, the Unevolved and the [Supreme] Brahman. The problem is: through which of these epiphanies is one to adore the Goddess?

As Revelation in the *Maitrāyaṇi Upaniṣad* says:

> [In the beginning this was one Darkness, existing in the Supreme Being. Impelled by that Being, it lost its equilibrium. It then became Passion. Then Passion too lost its equilibrium, and took the form of Brightness . . . Students! The part of Him that belongs to Darkness is Rudra (or Śiva). The part which belongs to Passion is Brahmā, and the part which belongs to Brightness is Viṣṇu. He who is one, became three . . .][235]

these Three Lords—the Male Power, the Golden Embryo and the Unevolved, who are Brahmā, Viṣṇu and Śiva—are each invested with only one of Matter's three Attributes. When these Attributes are in equilibrium, the Mirific Power is signified through words like "Matter." We are then to understand that the object in the adoration of the Goddess is none but the Supreme Brahman signified by the word "Mirific Power" [in its transcendent meaning]. It is therefore to declare this exalted truth that words such as the "Mirific Power" have been employed.

—*Exposition of the Goddess' Greatness,* Introduction[236]

Part Three
SCHEMES

Scheme 1

TEMPLE OF HINDU THEOLOGY

Both Hindu temple and theology are bipartite. The temple has antechamber and shrine; the theology, Norm and Objects of Knowledge. In both, the first part is a preparation for the second. We can thus, appositely, consider the Norm as the antechamber, and the shrine as the Object. I have selected sixty-seven from among the topics of Hindu theology, which I have found to be common to most schools. I shall first list them serially, and then show them as interconnected—in the structure of the Temple of Hindu Theology.

1. Norms of knowledge (*pramāṇa*)
2. Experience (*pratyakṣa*)
3. Sense experience (*laukika pratyakṣa*)
4. Supranormal experience (*alaukika pratyakṣa*)
5. Aesthetic experience (*rasa*)
6. Yogic experience (*yoga*)
7. Undifferentiated awareness (*turīya*)
8. Divine vision (*sālokya*)
9. Inference (*anumāna*)
10. Word (*śabda*)
11. Revelation proper (*śabda*)
12. Scriptures (*śruti*)
13. Tradition (*smṛti*)
14. Theology (*brahmavidyā*)
15. Objects of knowledge (*prameya*)
16. The Transcendent (*paratattva*)
17. God in Himself (*brahmasvarūpa*)
18. Divine essence and attributes (*guṇaguṇībhāva*)
19. The divine powers (*śaktiśaktimadhāva*)
20. Personal God and Impersonal Absolute (*pauruṣeyāpauruṣeyabhāva* ?)
21. The divine unmanifest and manifest (*vyaktāvyaktabhāva*)
22. Transcendent-Phenomenal Relationship
23. Man's supreme end (*puruṣārtha, phala*)
24. Beatific and Non-Beatific Liberation
25. Personal and Impersonal Liberation

26. Circumstances of Glory
27. The Ultimate Cause (*kāraṇa*)
28. God, the Gracious
29. God, the Cause of Bondage
30. God the Creator
31. God, the Efficient Cause (*nimitta*)
32. Divine material causality (*upādāna*)
33. God the Preserver
34. God the Destroyer
35. Trichotomous Relationship
36. Difference (*bheda*)
37. Difference-in-Identity (*bhedābheda*)
38. Identity (*abheda*)
39. The phenomenal (*aparatattva*)
40. The Phenomenal-Transcendent Relationship
41. Causality of the Phenomenal (*kāraṇa*)
42. Man, agent of self-liberation
43. The path of Devotion (*bhaktimārga*)
44. The path of Knowledge (*jñānamārga*)
45. The path of Works (*karmamārga*)
46. Man, perpetuator of self-transmigration
47. Man's causal activities
48. Goals of phenomenal existence (*puruṣārtha*)
49. Social behavior (*dharma*)
50. Self-interest (*artha*)
51. Love life (*kāma*)
52. The essence of the phenomenal
53. Conscious beings (*cit, ajaḍa*)
54. Free beings (*mukta*)
55. The eternally free (*nityamukta*)
56. The liberated (*mukta*)
57. Aspirants of liberation (*mumukṣu*)
58. The bound (*baddha*)
59. Inconscient beings (*acit, jaḍa*)
60. Eternal insentients
61. Eternal and temporal insentients
62. Time (*kāla*)
63. Matter (*prakṛti*)
64. Ignorance (*avidyā*)
65. Misery (*duḥka*)
66. Karma
67. Temporal insentients

तत्त्वसंख्यानमन्दिरम्

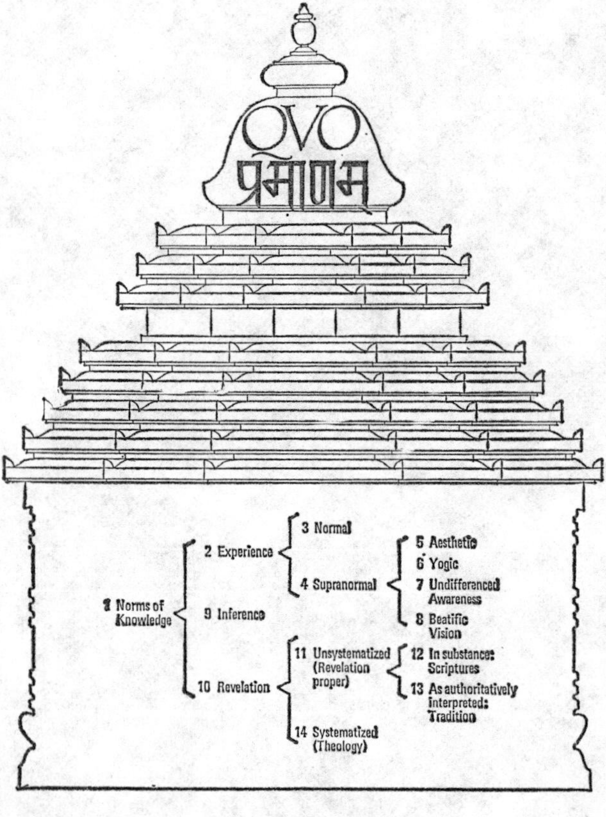
OVO
प्रमाणम्
1 Norms of Knowledge
2 Experience
3 Normal
4 Supranormal
5 Aesthetic
6 Yogic
7 Undifferenced Awareness
8 Beatific Vision
9 Inference
10 Revelation
11 Unsystematized (Revelation proper)
12 In substance: Scriptures
13 As authoritatively interpreted: Tradition
14 Systematized (Theology)

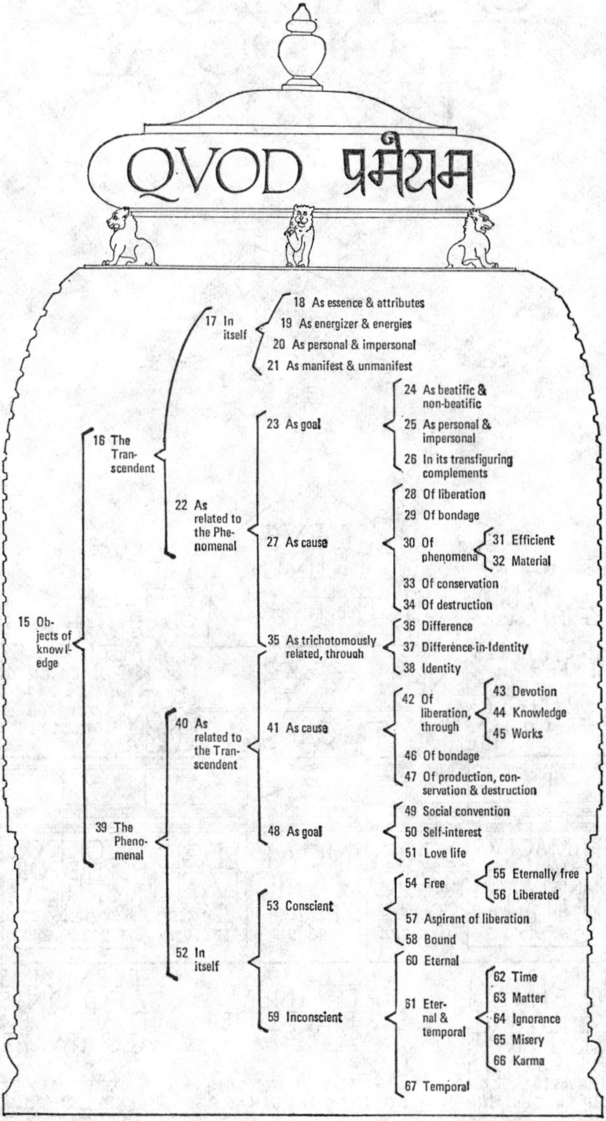
QVOD प्रमेयम्
15 Objects of knowledge
16 The Transcendent
17 In itself
18 As essence & attributes
19 As energizer & energies
20 As personal & impersonal
21 As manifest & unmanifest
22 As related to the Phenomenal
23 As goal
24 As beatific & non-beatific
25 As personal & impersonal
26 In its transfiguring complements
27 As cause
28 Of liberation
29 Of bondage
30 Of phenomena
31 Efficient
32 Material
33 Of conservation
34 Of destruction
35 As trichotomously related, through
36 Difference
37 Difference-in-Identity
38 Identity
39 The Phenomenal
40 As related to the Transcendent
41 As cause
42 Of liberation, through
43 Devotion
44 Knowledge
45 Works
46 Of bondage
47 Of production, conservation & destruction
48 As goal
49 Social convention
50 Self-interest
51 Love life
52 In itself
53 Conscient
54 Free
55 Eternally free
56 Liberated
57 Aspirant of liberation
58 Bound
59 Inconscient
60 Eternal
61 Eternal & temporal
62 Time
63 Matter
64 Ignorance
65 Misery
66 Karma
67 Temporal

CATHOLICAE THEOLOGIAE TEMPLVM

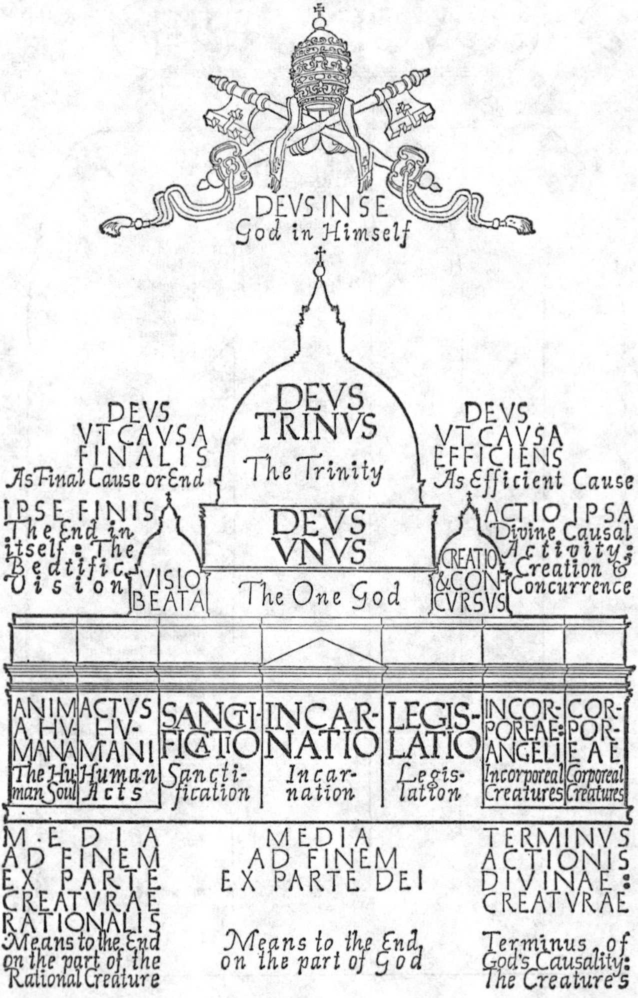

DEVS IN SE
God in Himself
DEVS TRINVS
The Trinity
DEVS VT CAVSA FINALIS
As Final Cause or End
DEVS VT CAVSA EFFICIENS
As Efficient Cause
IPSE FINIS
The End in itself: The Beatific Vision
VISIO BEATA
DEVS VNVS
The One God
CREATIO & CONCVRSVS
ACTIO IPSA
Divine Causal Activity: Creation & Concurrence
ANIMA HVMANA
The Human Soul
ACTVS HVMANI
Human Acts
SANCTIFICATIO
Sanctification
INCARNATIO
Incarnation
LEGISLATIO
Legislation
INCORPOREAE: ANGELI
Incorporeal Creatures
CORPOREAE
Corporeal Creatures
MEDIA AD FINEM EX PARTE CREATVRAE RATIONALIS
Means to the End on the part of the Rational Creature
MEDIA AD FINEM EX PARTE DEI
Means to the End on the part of God
TERMINVS ACTIONIS DIVINAE: CREATVRAE
Terminus of God's Causality: The Creatures

SCHEME 2

CATHEDRAL OF CATHOLIC THEOLOGY

Comparable in monumentality to Hindu theology is the Catholic Scholastic, based on the tripartite scheme first suggested by Uddālaka (see above pp. 35, 316). This scheme is clearly articulated by Greek thinkers like Proclus: (1) The Divine Being in Itself; (2) The procession of the creatures from that Being πρόοδος; (3) The return of the creatures to that Being ἐπιστροφὴ. Aquinas employs the scheme as the basis of his systematization of Catholic doctrine. The scheme was brought to perfection by Francisco Suárez, the colossus of Baroque theology, and the contemporary of two other of Catholicism's architectural master-minds, Michelangelo and Bernini, designers of St. Peter's. In its bares outline Suárez's systematization of Catholic thought has the following plan:

1. GOD IN HIMSELF
   - As three
   - As one
2. GOD IN RELATION TO HIS CREATURES AS EFFICIENT CAUSE
   - The Causality in itself
     - Creation
     - Conservation
   - The Terminus of the Causality: the creatures
     - Corporeal: human and other beings
     - Incorporeal: angels
3. GOD IN RELATION TO HIS CREATURES AS FINAL CAUSE (OR END OF THE RATIONAL CREATURE)
   - The end in itself (the Beatific Vision)
   - The means to the end
     - On part of God
       - Incarnation (and Redemption)
       - Sanctification (Grace)
       - Legislation
     - On part of the creature
       - Basis of human action: the human soul
       - Human acts

दर्शनराजीवः

DUALIST VEDANTA
DIFFERENTISM
SAIVA ORTHODOXY
SONIC ABSOLUTISM
NONDUALISM
ENERGICISM
SANKHYA
YOGA
RITUALISM
DUALIST PASTORALISM
ATOMISM
LOGICISM
ENERGY-QUALIFIED NONDUALISM
ANCIENT VEDANTA
CONDITIONED DIFFERENCE IN IDENTITY
INDIVISIBLE NONDUALISM
PAÑCARĀTRA
QUALIFIED NONDUALISM
INNATE DIFFERENCE IN IDENTITY
PURE NONDUALISM
INEFFABLE DIFFERENCE IN IDENTITY
MONIST PASTORALISM
TRIADISM
ŚAIVA NONDUALISM
BUDDHIST DOCTRINE
VACUISM
BUDDHIST IDEALISM
DETERMINISM
JAIN THEOLOGY
MATERIALISM

SCHEME 3

LOTUS OF INDIC THEOLOGIES

Of the four rows of the petals of the lotus, the two inner ones represent the non-Hindu systems, and the two outer ones the Hindu. The innermost row represents the systems now forgotten. Below are some of the non-Hindu systems; the Hindu ones are listed in Scheme 4.

I. MATERIALISM (*Cārvāka darśana*) of Bṛhaspati, systematized by Jayarāśi

II. DETERMINISM (*Ājīvika*) of Makkali Gosāla

III. JAIN THEOLOGY. Jainism has two sects (the Sky-Clad, *digambara*, and the White-Clad, *śvetāmbara*), but both have basically the same theology, systematized by the White-Clad monk Hemacandra

IV. BUDDHIST THEOLOGIES

- A. Buddhist (Higher) Doctrine (*Abhidharma*) or Scriptural Theology
  1. Presbyterism or Elder School (*Theravāda*), systematized by Buddhaghoṣa
  2. Omniexistentialism (*Sarvāstivāda*), systematized by Vimalamitra
  3. Canonicalism (*Sautrāntika*), systematized by Vasubandhu
- B. Vacuism or Mediatism (*Śūnyavāda* or *Mādhyamika*)
  1. Undivided School of Nāgārjuna
  2. Reductionism (*Prāsaṅgika*) of Buddhapālita
  3. Independentism (*Svātantrika*) of Bhāvaviveka
- C. Idealism (*Vijñānavāda* or *Yogācāra*)
  1. Formless Idealism (*Nirākāravijñānavāda*) of Asaṅga
  2. Formed Idealism, or Critical School (*Sākāravijñānavāda* or *Pramāṇa*) of Dinnāga

वैदिकतान्त्रिकदर्शनचक्रम्

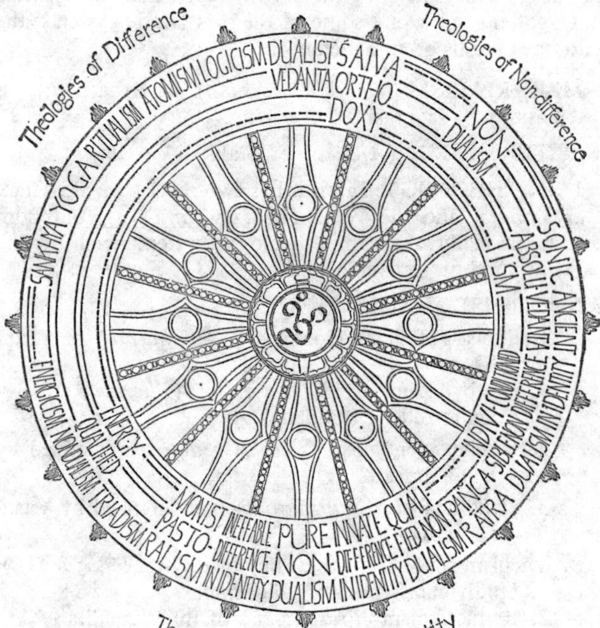

SCHEME 4

WHEEL OF THE HINDU SYSTEMS

This is a list of all the schools I have been able to trace. Only the important ones appear in the drawing opposite. The schools and their affiliates are shown in Roman capitals, their sub-schools in large and small letters, and the Sanskrit names in italics. A question mark after a Sanskrit name indicates that it is not traditional.

I. Schools of Difference

1. SANKHYA, OR DISCRIMINATIONISM (*Sāṅkhya*)
2. YOGA, OR SELF-INTUITIONISM (*Yoga*)
3. RITUALISM (*Mīmāṁsā*)
   - Vericist (*Prābhākara-Mīmāṁsā*)
   - Contrarist (*Bhāṭṭa-Mīmāṁsā*)
4. DUALIST PASTORALISM (*Pāśupata darśana*)
5. ATOMISM (*Vaiśeṣika*)
6. LOGICISM (*Nyāya*)
7. DUALIST VEDANTA (*Dvaita Vedānta*)
8. DIFFERENTISM (*Bhedavāda*)
9. ŚAIVA ORTHODOXY (*Śaiva Siddhānta*)
   - Gnostic Śaiva Orthodoxy (*Jnāñasādhana Śaivasiddhānta* ?)
   - Devotional (or Tamilian) Śaiva Orthodoxy (*Bhaktisādhana Śaivasiddhānta* ?)

II. Schools of Identity, or Non-Difference

1. UNDIVIDED NONDUALISM (*Purātanādvaita* ?)
2. LIMITATIONISM (*Avacchedavāda*)
3. REFLECTIONISM (*Pratibimbavāda*)
4. APPARITIONALISM (*Ābhāsavāda*)
5. IDEALISM (*Dṛṣtiśṛṣṭivāda*)
6. SYNCRETIC NONDUALISM (*Saṁyuktādvaita* ?)
   - GAṆEŚA DOCTRINE (*Gāṇapatya darśana* ?)

III. Schools of Difference-in-Identity

A. *Non-Vedantic Vedic Schools*

1. SONIC ABSOLUTISM (*Śabdabrahmavāda*)

B. *Non-denominational Vedanta*
   2. ANCIENT VEDANTA (*Puratāna Vedānta* ?)
   3. CONDITIONED DIFFERENCE-IN-IDENTITY (*Aupādhikabhedābheda*)
   4. INDIVISIBLE NONDUALISM (*Avibhāgādvaita*)

C. *Vaiṣṇava Theologies, mostly Vedantic*
   5. PĀÑCARĀTRA
   6. CONSCIOUSNESS NONDUALISM (*Cidādvaita* ?)
   7. QUALIFIED NONDUALISM (*Viśiṣṭādvaita*)
      Passivist or Southern School (*Tengalai*), Cat School
      Activist or Northern School (*Vadagalai*), Monkey School
      RĀMĀNANDA SCHOOL (*Rāmānanda Siddhānta*)
      SVĀMĪ NĀRĀYAṆA SCHOOL (*Akṣarabrahmaparabrahmavāda*)
   8. INNATE DIFFERENCE-IN-IDENTITY (*Svābhāvikabhedābheda*)
      COMPANIONISM (*Sakhisampradāya*)
   9. IMMACULATE NONDUALISM (*Viśuddhādvaita*)
   10. PURE NONDUALISM (*Śuddhādvaita*)
      Norm School (*Pramāṇa*)
      Grace School (*Prameya*)
   11. INEFFABLE DIFFERENCE-IN-IDENTITY (*Acintyabhedābheda*)
   12. RĀDHĀVALLABHA SCHOOL OR ESTABLISHED NONDUALISM (*Rādhāvallabha Siddhānta* or *Siddhādvaita*)

D. Saiva Theologies
   13. MONIST PASTORALISM (*Lākulīśapāśupata darśana*)
   14. NANDIKEŚVARA ŚAIVISM (*Nandikeśvara darśana* ?)
   15. TRIADISM (*Trika*)
      Family School (*Kula*)
      Gradation School (*Krama*)
      Vibration or Self-Awareness School (*Spanda* or *Pratyabhijña*)
   16. ŚAIVA NONDUALISM (*Śivādvaita*)
   17. ENERGY-QUALIFIED NONDUALISM (*Śaktiviśiṣṭādvaita*)

E. Śākta Theologies.
   18. ENERGICISM (*Śākta darśana*)

La rose des théologies catholiques

Scheme 5

ROSE WINDOW OF CATHOLIC THEOLOGIES

Catholic theology also compares with the Hindu for variety of systems. The following are some Catholic systems from the ninth to the eighteenth centuries. A number of the earlier ones were reorganized with greater symmetry in the Baroque period—the age par excellence of theological architectonics—by theologians whose names are indicated below those of the systems' founders.

1. Eriugenism John Scotus Eriugena (c. 810/15–77)
2. Anselmianism Anselm of Canterbury (1033–1109)
   José Saenz de Aguirre (d. 1699)
3. Bernardism Bernard of Clairvaux, *Doctor Mellifluus* (1090–1153)
4. Bonaventurianism Bonaventura, *Doctor Seraphicus* (1221–74)
   Gaudenzio Bontempi (1612–72)
5. Thomism Thomas Aquinas, *Doctor Angelicus* (1225–74)
   Cajetan (1468–1534)
   João de Santo Tomás (1589–1644)
   Salmanticenses (1631–1717), especially Juan de la Anunciación (1633–1701)
6. Egidianism Egidio Colonna, *Doctor Fundatissimus* (1243/47–1316)
   Federico Niccola Gavardi (1639–1715)
7. Scotism John Duns Scotus, *Doctor Subtilis* (c. 1265–1308)
   Mastrio de Meldola (1602–73)
8. Baconianism John Bacon, *Doctor Resolutus* (end 13th cent.–1346)
   Giuseppe Zagaglia (d. 1711)
9. Nominalism William of Ockham (1295/1300–49/50)
10. Suarezianism Francisco Suárez, *Doctor Eximius* (1548–1617)
11. Cartesianism (René Descartes, 1596–1650) Nicolas de Malebranche (1638–1715)
12. Norisianism Henri Noris (1631–1704)
    Gianlorenzo Berti (1696–1766)

वेदान्तप्रदीपः

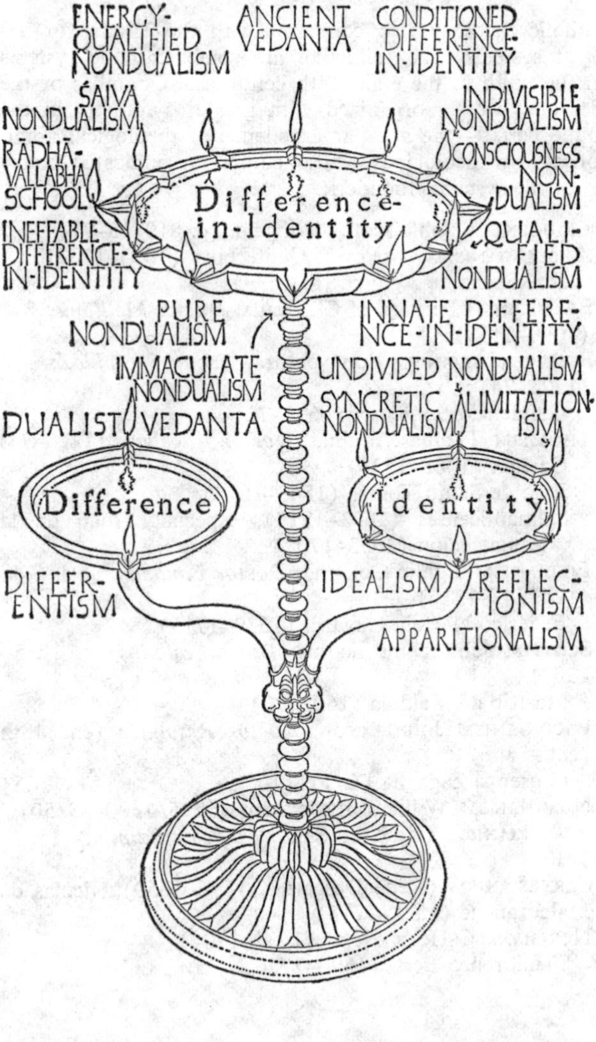
ENERGY-QUALIFIED NONDUALISM
ANCIENT VEDANTA
CONDITIONED DIFFERENCE-IN-IDENTITY
ŚAIVA NONDUALISM
INDIVISIBLE NONDUALISM
RĀDHĀ-VALLABHA SCHOOL
CONSCIOUSNESS NON-DUALISM
Difference-in-Identity
INEFFABLE DIFFERENCE-IN-IDENTITY
QUALI-FIED NONDUALISM
PURE NONDUALISM
INNATE DIFFERE-NCE-IN-IDENTITY
IMMACULATE NONDUALISM
UNDIVIDED NONDUALISM
SYNCRETIC NONDUALISM
LIMITATION-ISM
DUALIST VEDANTA
Difference
Identity
DIFFER-ENTISM
IDEALISM
REFLEC-TIONISM
APPARITIONALISM

SCHEME 6

LAMP OF THE VEDANTA

The affiliated schools have not been shown in the drawing. Wicks without flame indicate extinct schools.

I. Schools of Difference

1. DUALIST VEDANTA (*Dvaita Vedānta*) of Madhva
2. DIFFERENTISM (*Bhedavāda*) of Śuka

II. Schools of Identity, or Non-Difference

1. UNDIVIDED NONDUALISM (*Purātanādvaita* ?) of *Gauḍa Pāda*
2. LIMITATIONISM (*Avacchedavāda*) of Maṇḍana or Vācaspati Miśra
3. REFLECTIONISM (*Pratibimbavāda*) of Padma Pāda
4. APPARITIONALISM (*Ābhāsavada*) of Sureśvara
5. IDEALISM (*Dṛṣṭisṛṣṭivāda*) of Prakāśānanda
6. SYNCRETIC NONDUALISM (*Saṁyuktādvaita* ?) of Madhusūdana Sarasvatī
   GANESA DOCTRINE (*Gāṇapatya darṣana* ?) *of Nīla*kaṇṭha

III. Schools of Difference-in-Identity

1. ANCIENT VEDANTA (*Purātana Vedānta* ?) of Bādarāyaṇa
2. CONDITIONED DIFFERENCE-IN-IDENTITY (*Aupādhikabhedābheda*) of Bhāskara
3. INDIVISIBLE NONDUALISM (*Avibhāgādvaita*) of Vijñāna Bhikṣu
4. CONSCIOUSNESS NONDUALISM (*Cidādvaita* ?) of Yādava Prakāśa
5. QUALIFIED NONDUALISM (*Viśiṣṭādvaita*) of Yāmuna
   Passivist or Southern School (*Tengalai*), Cat School
   Activist or Northern School (*Vadagalai*), Monkey School
   RĀMĀNANDA SCHOOL (*Rāmānanda Siddhānta*)
   SVĀMĪ NĀRĀYAṆA SCHOOL (*Akṣarabrahmaparabrahmavāda*)
6. INNATE DIFFERENCE-IN-IDENTITY (*Svābhāvikabhedābheda*) of Nimbārka
   COMPANIONISM (*Sakhisampradāya*) of Hari Dāsa

7. Immaculate Nondualism (*Viśuddhādvaita*) of Viṣṇu Svāmin
8. Pure Nondualism (*Śuddhādvaita*) of Vallabha
   Norm School (*Pramāṇa*)
   Grace School (*Prameya*)
9. Ineffable Difference-in-Identity (*Acintyabhedābheda*) of Caitanya
10. Rādhāvallabha School or Established Nondualism (*Rādhāvallabha Siddhānta* or *Siddhādvaita*) of Hita Harivaṁśa
11. Śaiva Nondualism (*Śivādvaita*) of Śrī Kaṇṭha
12. Energy-Qualified Nondualism (*Śaktiviśiṣṭādvaita*) of Basava

वैष्णवदर्शनकमलाकरः

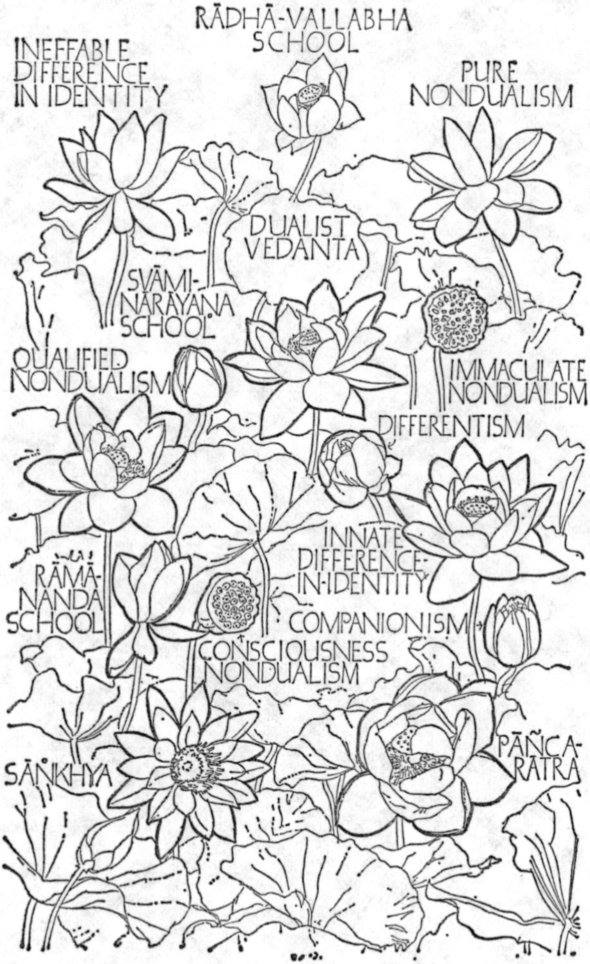

Scheme 7

LOTUS POOL OF VAIṢṆAVA THEOLOGIES

The lotus is prominent among Viṣṇu's symbols. Lotuses (*nelumbo*) show schools that retain Vaiṣṇava mythology; water-lilies (*nymphaea*) demythologized schools. Buds indicate affiliated schools; their evolution to maturity is shown by the different stages of bloom. Pods represent extinct schools. Subschools are not shown.

I. Schools of Difference

1. Sankhya, or Discriminationism (*Sāṅkhya*) of Kapila
2. Dualist Vedanta (*Dvaita Vedānta*) of Madhva
3. Differentism (*Bhedavāda*) of Śuka

(II. Schools of Identity, or Non-Difference

No Identity School is denominationally Vaiṣṇava, but the Syncretic Nondualism of Madhusūdana Sarasvatī is pronouncedly Kṛṣṇaite.)

III. Schools of Difference-in-Identity

1. Pāñcarātra
2. Consciousness Nondualism (*Cidādvaita* ?) of Yādava Prakāśa
3. Qualified Nondualism (*Viśiṣṭādvaita*) of Yāmuna
   - Passivist or Southern School (*Tengalai*), Cat School
   - Activist or Northern School (*Vadagalai*), Monkey School
   - rāmānanda school (*Rāmānanda Siddhānta*) of Rāmānanda
   - svāmī nārāyaṇa school (*Akṣarabrahmaparabrahmavāda*) of Śvamī Nārāyaṇa
4. Innate Difference-in-Identity (*Svābhāvikabhedābheda*) of Nimbārka
   - companionism (*Sakhiśampradāya*) of Hari Dāsa
5. Immaculate Nondualism (*Viśuddhādvaita*) of Viṣṇu Svāmin
6. Pure Nondualism (*Śuddhādvaita*) of Vallabha
   - Norm School (*Pramāṇa*)
   - Grace School (*Prameya*)

7. Ineffable Difference-in-Identity (*Acintyabhedābheda*) of Caitanya
8. Rādhāvallabha School (*Rādhāvallabha Siddhānta*) of Hita Harivaṁśa

माहेश्वरदर्शनत्रिशूलसंहतिः

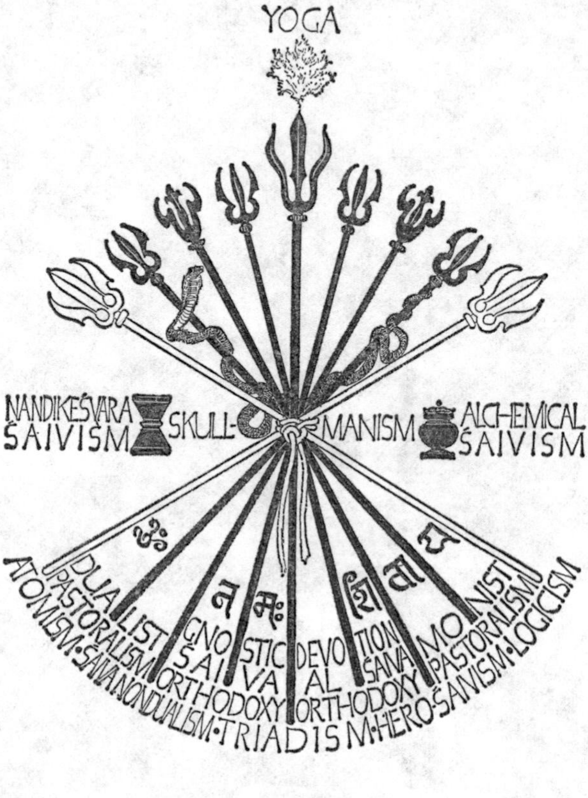

SCHEME 8

TRIDENT CLUSTER OF ŚAIVA THEOLOGIES

Śiva is the god of the trident, and of the drum, serpent and fire. Black objects are mythologically Śaiva; the white are demythologized.

I. Schools of Difference

1. YOGA, OR SELF-INTUITIONISM (*Yoga*) of Patañjali
2. DUALIST PASTORALISM (*Pāśupata darśana*) of uncertain foundation
   SKULLMANISM (*Kāpālika*); founder uncertain
3. ATOMISM (*Vaiśeṣika*) of Kaṇāda
4. LOGICISM (*Nyāya*) of Gautama
5. ŚAIVA ORTHODOXY: GNOSTIC (*Jñānasādhana Śaivasiddhānta* ?) of Sadyojyoti ?
6. ŚAIVA ORTHODOXY: DEVOTIONAL OR TAMILIAN (*Bhaktisādhana Śaivasiddhānta* ?) of Meykanta Tevar

(II. Schools of Identity, or Non-Difference

No Identity school is denominationally Śaiva, but the Gaṇeṣa Doctrine, or *Gāṇapatya darśana,* is associated with Śaivism, since Gaṇeśa is Śiva's son.)

III. Schools of Difference-in-Identity

1. MONIST PASTORALISM (*Lākulīśapāśupata darśana*) of Lakulīśa
2. NANDIKEŚVARA ŚAIVISM (*Nandikeśvara darśana*) of Nandikeśvara
3. TRIADISM (*Trika*)
   Family School (*Kula*) of Ardha Tryambaka
   Gradation School (*Krama*) of Śivānanda Nātha ?
   Vibration or Self-Awareness School (*Spanda* or *Pratyabhijña*) of Vasu Gupta
4. ŚAIVA NONDUALISM (*Śivādvaita*) of Śrī Kaṇṭha
5. ENERGY-QUALIFIED NONDUALISM (*Śaktiviśiṣṭādvaita*) of Basava

(6. ENERGICISM (*Śākta darśana*), an associated school, since the Goddess is conceived as Śiva's Energy.)

Also shown, as a vase of elixir, is Alchemical Śaivism (or *Raseśvara darśana*).

वेदान्तसमन्वयद्वारम्

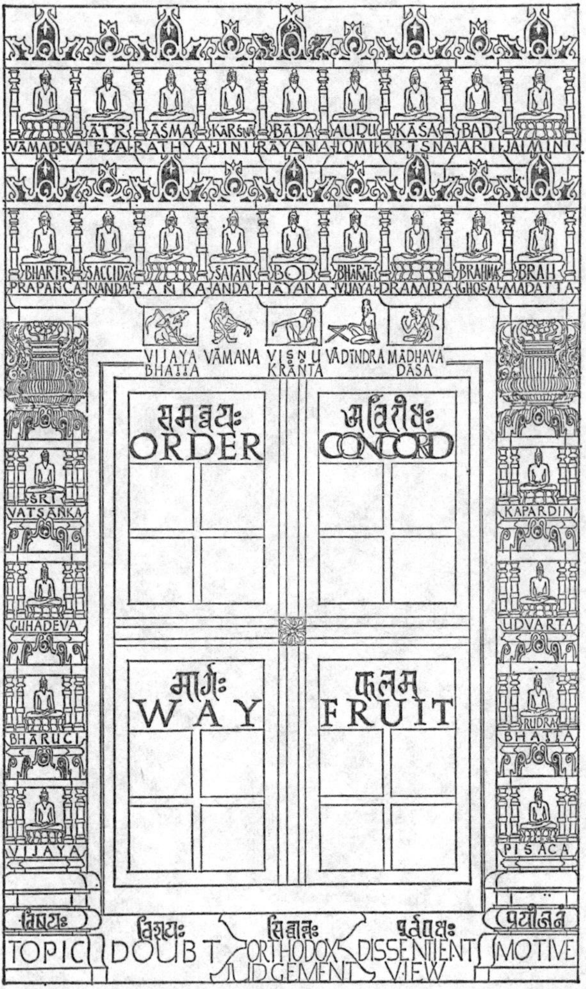

Scheme 9

PORTAL OF THE VEDANTA SYNTHESIS

Bādarāyaṇa's systematization of Vedanta theology—the *Aphorisms on the Brahman*—comprises four chapters, each divided into four sections (shown in the drawing as four quadripartite panels on the door of the shrine of the great temple of the Vedanta). The Vedantic schools all seem unanimous on the significance of the chapters, but not on that of the sections. The four chapters deal with God, the Absolute or the Brahman—the first two as He is in Himself, and the last two as the Goal of human existence.

More precisely, Chapter 1 ("Correlation" or ORDER, *Samanvaya*), correlates all the texts that deal with the Brahman, and classifies them topic-wise.

Chapter 2 ("Non-contradiction" or CONCORD, *Avirodha*) harmonizes the apparent discord among them and rebuts the attacks against the Vedanta by hostile systems.

Chapter 3 ("Salvific Means" or WAY, *Sādhana*) proceeds to discuss the means of attaining the Brahman thus established.

Chapter 4 ("Result" or FRUIT, *Phalam*) describes the attainment itself.

The method of discussing the above topics—shown as the five sections of the step before the portal—is fivefold:

1. *THEME* (*viṣaya*), the statement of the thesis
2. *DOUBT* (*viśaya*), problems that the thesis raises
3. *DISSENTIENT VIEWS* (*pūrvapakṣa*), arguments against the thesis
4. *ORTHODOX JUDGEMENT* (*siddhānta*), arguments establishing the thesis
5. *RELEVANCE* (*prayojaña*), theological significance of the thesis

Bādarāyaṇa's system, like all great works, was not formed out of a vacuum. It was preceded by the partial syntheses of thinkers whom Bādarāyaṇa mentions in his *Aphorisms*. These are shown in the niched compartments of the top register of the overdoor. They may all have been Bādarāyaṇa's contemporaries—except for the Vedic sage Vāmadeva. The *Aphorisms* inspired numerous theological works, nearly all lost, either as creative commentaries (*bhāṣyas*) or explanatory glosses (*vṛttis*). The major commentators are shown in the niched compartments of the bottom register of the overdoor; those who seem to have been minor commentators, on the pilasters flanking the door; and those who appear to have written glosses, on the small panels beneath the niched compartments of the bottom register of the overdoor.

शब्दायतनम्

LITERATURE
THEOLOGY
ETHICS
POLITICO-ECONOMICS
SEXOLOGY
TANTRAS
EPICS
PURANAS
ŚĀKTA
ŚAIVA
VAIṢṆAVA
MAHĀBHĀRATA
GĪTĀ
RĀMĀYAṆA
VAIṢṆAVA
ŚAIVA
ŚAKTA
PARIŚIṢṬA
VEDĀNGAS
UPANIṢADS
ĀRAṆYAKAS
BRĀHMANAS
VEDAS

Scheme 10

SHRINE OF HINDU LEARNING
DE LOCIS THEOLOGICIS

The shrine has four parts: the podium, the shrine proper, the superstructure and the finial, with the following correspondences:

I. *The Podium*. THE VEDIC REVELATION AND IMMEDIATELY CONNECTED DISCIPLINES
1. The Four *Vedas,* Inspired hymns
2. The *Brāhmaṇas,* Ritual texts
3. The *Āraṇyakas,* Forest books; transition from ritual to theology
4. The *Upaniṣads,* Secret teachings
5. The *Vedāṅgas,* Disciplines for the study of Revelation
6. The *Pariśiṣṭa,* Vedic appendix

II. *The Shrine Proper*. TEXTS OF TRADITION, principally Tantric, in three groups:
1. The *Epics*
   a. The *Mahābhārata,* epic of the Great Indian War. In the heart of the Epic is the *Gītā,* gem of the Hindu scriptures, accepted by all the Hindu traditions, Vedic and Tantric
   b. The *Rāmāyaṇa,* epic of Rāma's war on the demons
2. The *Purāṇas,* encyclopedic mythological poems or cosmic histories, in three groups:
   a. Vaiṣṇava Purāṇas
   b. Śaiva Purāṇas
   c. Śākta Purāṇas
3. The *Tantras* proper, texts of arcane and mystical knowledge, also in three groups
   a. Vaiṣṇava Tantras
   b. Śaiva Tantras
   c. Śākta Tantras

III. *The Superstructure*. SCIENCES OF THE FOUR GOALS OF LIFE AND RELATED SCIENCES
The turrets of the central bay are the sciences of the

Four Goals; the turrets of the side bays, the innumerable related sciences

1. Science of Delight and Sex (*Kāmaśāstra*), sexology
2. Science of Politics and Economics (*Arthaśātra*), politico-economics
3. Science of Social Behavior (*Dharmaśāstra*), ethics
4. Science of Liberation or the Brahman (*Śāstra, Brahmavidyā*), theology

IV. *Finial.* LITERATURE (*Kāvya*), the Culmination of the Sciences

ब्रह्मविद्यासम्प्रदायकर्तारः

AGHAMARṢAṆA
BRAHMAṆASPATI
DĪRGHATAMAS
NĀRĀYAṆA
HIRAṆYAGARBHA
VIŚVAKARMĀ
MAHIDĀSA AITAREYA
ŚĀṆDILYA
SATYAKĀMA JĀBĀLA
GĀRGYĀYAṆA
PRATARDANA
UDDĀLAKA
VARUṆA
YĀJÑAVALKYA
ASURI
BHARADVĀJA
NACIKETAS

Scheme 11

FATHERS OF HINDU THEOLOGY

See Benimadhab Barua, *A History of Pre-Buddhistic Indian Philosophy*, 1921 and 1970. We might call them the archetypes of religious speculation, some indicated after their names below. They span a period from about 1300 B.C. to about 800 B.C., which may be divided into three epochs:

I. *Initiation*

1. AGHAMARṢAṆA. Probably the world's first theologian. Doctrine of Time as the ultimate, and Warmth and the creative, principle.
2. "BRAHMAṆASPATI." Water as the fundamental principle. Emanation.
3. DĪRGHATAMAS. Sun the ultimate principle. Agnosticism.
4. "NĀRĀYAṆA." The four castes formed out of the Primeval Man.
5. "HIRAṆYAGARBHA." Inchoative conception of the One God.
6. "VIŚVAKARMĀ." Abstract and metaphysical concept of God.

II. *Organization*

1. MAHĪDĀSA AITAREYA. "Father of Indian Philosophy." First comprehensive treatment of the problems of theology and philosophy.
2. ŚAṆḌILYA. Identity of the soul and the Brahman.
3. SATYAKĀMA JĀBĀLA. The Brahman as light. Man a corporeal being inhabited by an incorporeal principle.
4. GĀRGYĀYAṆA. Accent on immortality. Idealism: ideas as existent things.
5. PRATARDANA. Psychology as autonomous discipline. The soul as unifying the functions of the senses.

III. *Systematization*

1. UDDĀLAKA. Beginnings of systematic theology, and its tripartite division. Monism: Matter and Mind aspects of the Deity. Emanation doctrine articulated.

2. VARUṆA. Joy as goal of all human activities; the five sheaths (food, breath, mind, intelligence and joy).
3. YĀJÑAVALKYA. Apophatic theology. Doctrine of the Self. God as pure thought. The three states of soul (waking, dream, sleep).
4. ASURI. Derivation of male and female principles from the soul.
5. BHARADVĀJA. Theology as the divine science. Knowability of God.
6. NACIKETAS. Beginnings of Yoga.

अनुमानस्वरूपम्

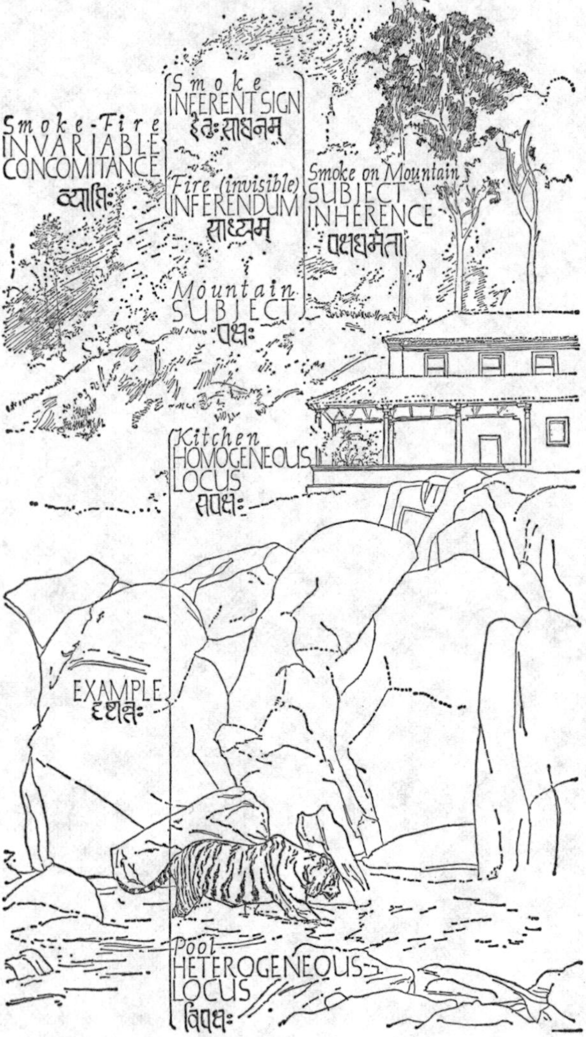

Smoke-Fire
INVARIABLE
CONCOMITANCE
व्याप्तिः
Smoke
INFERENT SIGN
हेतुः साधनम्
Fire (invisible)
INFERENDUM
साध्यम्
Smoke on Mountain
SUBJECT
INHERENCE
पक्षधर्मता
Mountain
SUBJECT
पक्षः
Kitchen
HOMOGENEOUS
LOCUS
सपक्षः
EXAMPLE
दृष्टान्तः
Pool
HETEROGENEOUS
LOCUS
विपक्षः

Scheme 12

THE NYĀYA SYLLOGISM

The Nyāya syllogism has two forms, the extended, in five members, and the abbreviated, in three. The latter is the former with the last two members dropped. The standard example of the Nyāya syllogism in its extended form is as follows:

1. PROPOSITION. The mountain has fire.
2. REASON. Because it has smoke.
3. EXAMPLE. As in a kitchen.
4. APPLICATION. Whatever has smoke has fire.
5. CONCLUSION. Therefore the mountain has fire.

It will be noticed that the Aristotelian syllogism omits members 1 and 3, and rearranges the rest in the following order: 4–2–5. Also, the Aristotelian syllogism is only deductive, while the Nyāya is deductive and inductive both. The principle of the Nyāya syllogism is that an *invariable concomitance* exists between an attribute or *inferent sign* (smoke) with the attribute's possessor, or *inferendum* (fire).

However, most Hindu theologians employ the three-membered syllogism, with the following constituents, all necessary for a valid argument.

1. PROPOSITION
   a. *Subject,* mountain.
   b. *Inferendum,* fire.
2. REASON
   a. *Subject-inherence,* the inherence of the *inferent sign* (smoke) in the *subject* (mountain).
   b. *Existence in a homogeneous locus,* a locus possessing both fire and smoke together: a kitchen.
   c. *Non-existence in a heterogeneous locus,* a locus possessing neither fire nor smoke: a pond.
3. EXAMPLE
   a. *Presential concomitances:* in all examples where smoke is, fire is.
   b. *Absential concomitances:* in all examples where smoke is not, fire is not.

SCHEME 13

SANKHYA, OR DISCRIMINATIONISM 1: CATEGORIES

Īśvara Kṛṣṇa

Ultimate categories

SPIRIT (*puruṣa*)

MATTER (*prakṛti*), also known as the UNEVOLVED (*avyakta*). Has two features:

- Attribute Triad (*guṇatrayam*)
  - Brightness (*sattva*)
  - Passion (*rajas*)
  - Darkness (*tamas*)
- Evolutes, also known as the EVOLVED (*vyakta*)
  - a. Instinct or the Prodigious (*buddhi* "Mind," or *mahat*)
  - b. Egoism, the Ego Principle or the Individuator (*ahaṅkāra*)

Subclassifications

a. INSTINCT, OR THE PRODIGIOUS

- Four Bright Forms
  - Virtue (*dharma*)
  - Knowledge (*jñāna*)
  - Detachment (*virāga*) or dispassion
  - Power (*aiśvarya*)
- Four Dark Forms
  - Vice (*adharma*)
  - Ignorance (*ajñāna*)
  - Attachment (*rāga*)
  - Weakness (*anaiśvarya*)

b. EGOISM (*ahaṅkāra*)

- Bright or Modified forms (*sāttvikarūpa* or *vaikṛta*)
  - Inner Faculty, Mind, or sensus communis (*manas*)
  - Five Perceptual Faculties, also called Faculties of Knowledge (*buddhīndriyāṇi*): eye (*cakṣu*), ear (*śrotra*), nose (*ghrāṇa*), tongue (*rasana*) and skin (*tvak*)
  - Five Motor or Active Faculties, or Faculties of Action

(*karmendriyāṇi*): voice (*vāk*), hands (*pāṇi*), feet (*pāda*), anus (*pāyu*) and genitals (*upastha*)

Fiery forms (*taijasarūpa*): comprise the Bright Eleven (Mind and the Ten Faculties, perceptual and motor) and the Subtle Elements.

Dark or Elemental forms (*tāmasarūpa*):

Five Subtle Elements: sound (*śabda*), touch, (*sparśa*), color (*rūpa*), taste (*rasa*), and smell (*gandha*)

Five Gross Elements (*mahābhūta*): ether (*ākāśa*), wind (*vāyu*), fire (*tejas*), water (*āp*) and earth (*prithivī*)

SCHEME 14

SANKHYA, OR DISCRIMINATIONISM 2: EVOLUTION OF THE UNIVERSE

Īśvara Kṛṣṇa and Sankhya commentators

Main categories

EVOLUTION (*sarga*)

Subjective or Mental (*pratyayasarga*). The "Fifty Divisions" (*pañcāṣaḍbhedāḥ:* Error, five; Incapacity, twenty-eight; Contentment, nine; Success, eight):

a. Error (*viparyaya*)
b. Incapacity (*aśakti*)
c. Contentment (*tuṣṭi*)
d. Success (*siddhi*)

Objective, Material or Elemental (*tanmātrāsarga*). Fourteen divisions (divine, eight; human, one; subhuman, five):

e. Divine (*daiva*)
Human (*mānuṣa*)
f. Subhuman (*tairyakyonayaḥ*)

Subclassifications

a. ERROR (*viparyaya*): five divisions, sixty-two subdivisions:

Ignorance, Darkness (*avidyā, tamas*), eight varieties

Egoism, Delusion (*asmitā, moha*), eight varieties (occult powers)

Desire, Extreme Delusion (*rāga, mahāmoha*), ten varieties (objects of sense)

Aversion, Thick Darkness (*dveṣa, tāmisra*), eighteen varieties (eight occult powers and ten objects of sense)

Attachment, Total Darkness (*abhiniveśa, andhatāmisra*), eighteen varieties (as in Aversion)

b. INCAPACITY (*aśakti*): two divisions, twenty-eight subdivisions:

From injuries to Instinct (*buddhivadha;* seventeen varieties, arising from the frustrations of):

The nine varieties of Contentment (*tuṣṭibhedavaiparītyena*)

The eight varieties of Success (*siddhibhedavaiparītyena*)

From injuries to the Eleven Faculties (*ekādaśendriya-vadha*):
Madness (*unmāda*), frustration of mind
Deafness (*bādhiryam*), of hearing
Blindness (*andhatā*), of sight
Paralysis (*prasupti*), of skin
Loss of taste (*upajihvikā*)
Loss of smell (*ghrāṇapāka*)
Dumbness (*mūkatā*), of speech
Mutilation (*kuṇitvam*), of hand
Lameness (*khāñjyam*), of foot
Constipation (*guḍāvarta*), of anus
Impotence (*klaibyam*), of genitals

c. CONTENTMENT (*tuṣṭi*): two divisions, nine subdivisions:
Internal (*adhyātmikā*): four varieties. Contentment arising from:
Nature (*prakṛti*)
Means (*upādāna*)
Time (*kāla*)
Luck (*bhāgya*)
External (*bāhyā*). Contentment derived from:
Sound (*śabda*)
Touch (*sparśa*)
Color (*rūpa*)
Taste (*rasa*)
Smell (*gandha*)

d. SUCCESS (*siddhi*): two divisions, eight subdivisions:
Primary (*mukhya*): three varieties:
Internal (*adhyātmika*)
External (*ādhibhautika*)
Superhuman (*ādhidaivika*)
Secondary (*gauṇya*): five varieties. Success arising from:
Study (*adhyayanam*)
Teaching (*śabda*)
Investigation (*ūha*)
Acquisition of friends (*suhṛtprāpti*)
Generosity (*dānam*)

e. DIVINE BEINGS: The Eight Hierarchies:
The chief creator god (*Brahmā*)
The Lords of Creatures (*prājāpatya*)
The Celestial King (*aindra*)

Ancestors (*paitra*)
Celestial godlings (*yakṣa*)
Fiends (*rākṣasa*)
Goblins (*paiśāca*)

f. SUBHUMAN BEINGS:

Five varieties: cattle, wild beasts, birds, reptiles and immovable objects

SCHEME 15

YOGA OR SELF-INTUITIONISM: CATEGORIES

Vijñāna Bhikṣu

Main categories

NATURE OF YOGA (*yogasvarūpam*)
- Generic (*sāmānyam*)
  - Suppression of mental states (*cittavṛttinirodha*)
  - a. Suppressible mental states (*niroddhavyāscittavṛttayaḥ*)
- Specific (*viśeṣa*)
  - b. Undifferenced awareness (*asamprajñātayoga*)
  - c. Unifocal awareness (*samprajñātayoga*)
- Consequent (*phala*), effects of
  - d. Undifferenced awareness (*asamprajñātayoga*)
  - e. Unifocal awareness (*samprajñātayoga*)

STAGES OF YOGIC ATTAINMENT (*yogasādhanāni, yogādhikāriṇaḥ*)
- Supreme Stage: the Highest Aspirants (*uttamādhikāriṇaḥ*)
  - f. Dispassion (*vairāgyam*)
  - g. Application, practice or catharsis (*abhyāsa*)
- Intermediary Stage: the Middling Aspirants (*madhyamādhikāriṇaḥ*)
  - Dispassion (*vairāgyam*)
  - Application (*abhyāsa*)
  - h. Yogic discipline (*kriyāyoga*)
- Incipient Stage: Novices (*mandādhikāriṇaḥ*)
  - Application (*abhyāsa*)
  - i. Yogic Discipline or Members of Yoga (*kriyāyoga, yogāṅgāni*)

Subclassifications

a. SUPPRESSIBLE MENTAL STATES (*niroddhavyāscittavṛttayaḥ*)
- Norms of knowledge (*pramāṇa*), experience, inference, Word
  - Error (*viparyaya*)
  - Verbal fiction (*vikalpa*)
  - Sleep (*nidrā*)
  - Memory (*smṛti*)

b. UNDIFFERENCED AWARENESS (*asamprajñātayoga*)
Natally induced (*bhavapratyaya*), as in the highest gods
Practically induced (*upāyapratyaya*)
Realization (*prajñā*)
Concentration (*samādhi*)
Contemplation (*smṛti*)
Consideration (*vīrya*)
Love of Yoga (*śraddhā*)

c. UNIFOCAL AWARENESS (*samprajñātayoga*)
Apperceptive (*asmitānugata*) Transconceptual Stage (*atikrāntabhāvanīya*)
Rapturous (*ānandānugata*)
Introspective (*vicārānugata*)
Incomposite (*nirvicāra*) Wisdom-Fire Stage (*prajñā-jyoti*)
Composite (*savicāra*)
Percipient (*vitarkānugata*)
Non-notional (*nirvitarka*) Mellifluent Stage (*madhubhūmika*)
Notional (*savitarka*) Incipient Stage (*prathamakalpika*)

d. EFFECTS OF UNDIFFERENCED AWARENESS (*asamprajñātayogaphalam*)
Invisible (*adṛṣṭa*). Liberation at will (*svecchayā mokṣaḥ*)
Visible (*dṛṣṭa*). Suppression of mental states and the pain consequent on them (*vṛttinirodhena, vṛttyutthaduḥkabhoganivṛttiḥ*)

e. EFFECTS OF UNIFOCAL AWARENESS (*samprajñātayogaphalam*)
Invisible. Liberation on destruction of mental ills (*avidyāvikleśanivṛttyā mokṣaḥ*)
Visible. As in (d)

f. DISPASSION IN THE SUPREME YOGIC STATE (*vairāgyam*)
Superior (*param*)
Inferior (*aparam*)
Total control (*vaśīkārasaṁjñā*)
Absorption into Inner Faculty (*ekendriyasaṁjñā*)
Ascertainment of achieved control (*vyatirekasaṁjñā*)
Preliminary effort (*yatamānasaṁjñā*)

g. APPLICATION OR CATHARSIS (*abhyāsasādhanam parikarma*)

Contemplation of Chosen Deity (*yathābhimatadhyānam*)
Contemplation of dream and deep sleep experience (*svapnanidrānyatarajñānacintanam*)
Contemplation of the minds of the dispassionate (*viraktacittacintanam*)
The Painless Radiant State (*viśokā jyotiṣmatī*)
Intuition of Spirit (*viviktapuruṣasākṣātkāra*)
Intuition of Instinct (*buddhisākṣātkāra*)
Object Oriented Reflection (*viṣayavatīpravṛtti*)
Peace of mind (*cittaprasāda*)

h. YOGIC DISCIPLINE (OF THE INTERMEDIARY STAGE) (*kriyāyoga*)
Dedication of self to God (*īśvarapraṇidhāna*)
Scriptural study and prayer (*svādhyāya*)
Austerity (*tapa*)

i. YOGIC DISCIPLINE (OF THE INCIPIENT STATE): MEMBERS OF YOGA (*kriyāyoga, yogāṅgāni*)
Inner members (*antaraṅgāni*)
Concentration (*samādhi*)
Contemplation (*dhyānam*)
Consideration (*dhāraṇā*)
Outer members (*bahiraṅgāni*)
Abstraction (*pratyāhāra*)
Breath Regulation (*prāṇāyāma*)
Postures (*āsana*)
Spiritual precepts (*niyama*)
Disciplinary precepts (*yama*)

Scheme 16

RITUALISM: CATEGORIES

Nārāyaṇa (Kumārila or Contrarist School)

Main categories

NORMS OF KNOWLEDGE (*māna, pramāṇa*)

- Experience (*pratyakṣa*)
- Inference (*anumāna*)
- Word (*śabda*)
- Analogy (*upamāna*)
- Hypothesis (*arthāpatti*), presumption, circumstantial evidence

OBJECTS OF KNOWLEDGE (*meya, prameya*)

- a. Substance (*dravyam*)
  Genus (*jāti*)
- b. Quality (*guṇa*)
- c. Action (*karma*)
- d. Non-existence (*abhāva*)

Subclassifications

a. SUBSTANCE (*dravyam*), eleven varieties:

1. Sound (*śabda*)
2. Mind (*manas*)
3. Soul (*ātman*)
4. Space (*dik*)
5. Time (*kāla*)
6. Ether (*ākāśa*)
7. Darkness (*tamas*)
8. Air (*vāyu*)
9. Fire (*tejas*)
10. Water (*āp*)
11. Earth (*pṛthivī*)

b. QUALITY (*guṇa*), twenty-four varieties:

1. Potency (*śakti*): Vedic and worldly
2. Manifestness (*prākaṭya*)
3. Audible sound (*dhvani*)
4. Impression (*saṁskāra*): Vedic and worldly (possessing the attributes of elasticity, residue in soul, and velocity)
5. Endeavor (*prayatna*)

6. Desire (*icchā*)
7. Aversion (*dveṣa*)
8. Happiness (*sukha*): liberative, celestial and worldly
9. Misery (*duḥka*): infernal and worldly
10. Knowledge (*buddhi*)
11. Viscidity (*sneha*)
12. Fluidity (*dravatva*)
13. Weight (*gurutva*)
14. Distance (*paratva*)
15. Proximity (*aparatva*)
16. Conjunction (*saṁyoga*)
17. Disjunction (*vibhāga*)
18. Distinctness (*pṛthaktva*)
19. Size (*parimāṇa*)
20. Number (*saṅkhyā*)
21. Touch (*sparśa*)
22. Smell (*gandha*)
23. Taste (*rasa*)
24. Color (*rūpa*)

c. ACTION (*karma*), five varieties:
1. Upward propulsion (*utkṣepaṇam*)
2. Downward propulsion (*apakṣepaṇam*)
3. Contraction (*ākuñcanam*)
4. Expansion (*prasāraṇam*)
5. Motion (*gamanam*)

d. NON-EXISTENCE (*abhāva*)
Mutual (*anyonyābhāva*)
Connectional (*saṁsargābhāva*)
  Total (*atyantābhāva*)
  Subsequent (*dhvaṁsābhāva*)
  Prior (*prāgabhāva*)

Scheme 17

ATOMISM: CATEGORIES

Chiefly Praśasta Pāda

The Seven Categories of Atomism are shown in numbers after each category.

Main categories

REAL BEINGS

a. Substance (*dravyam*) 1.
b. Quality (*guṇa*) 2.
c. Activity (*karma*) 3.

INTELLECTUAL CONSTRUCTS

d. Generality (*sāmānyam*) 4.
Particularity (*viśeṣa*) 5.
Inherence (*samavāya*) 6.
Non-existence (*abhāva*) 7.

Subclassifications

a. VARIETIES OF SUBSTANCE: nine varieties:
Interior (*antardravyam*)
1. Mind (*manas*)
2. Soul (*ātman*)
3. Space (*dik*)
4. Time (*kāla*)
5. Ether (*ākāśa*)

Exterior (*bahirdravyam*)
1. Air (*vāyu*)
2. Fire (*tejas*)
3. Water (*āp*)
4. Earth (*pṛthivī*)

b. VARIETIES OF QUALITY: twenty-four varieties:
Universal
1. Speed (*saṁskāra, vega*)
2. Weight (*gurutva*)
3. Distance (*paratva*)
4. Proximity (*aparatva*)
5. Conjunction (*saṁyoga*)
6. Disjunction (*vibhāga*)
7. Distinctness (*pṛthaktvam*)

8. Size (*parimāṇa*)
9. Number (*saṅkhyā*)
10a. Fluidity—contrived (*naimittikadravatvam*)

Particular

10b. Fluidity—natural (*sāṁsiddhikadravatvam*)
11. Sound (*śabda*)
12. Merit (*dharma*)
13. Demerit (*adharma*)
14. Viscidity (*sneha*)
15. Endeavor (*prayatna*)
16. Desire (*icchā*)
17. Aversion (*dveṣa*)
18. Happiness (*sukha*)
19. Misery (*duḥka*)
20. Knowledge (*buddhi*)
21. Touch (*sparśa*)
22. Smell (*gandha*)
23. Taste (*rasa*)
24. Color (*rūpa*)

c. VARIETIES OF ACTIVITY: five varieties:
1. Upward propulsion (*utkṣepaṇam*)
2. Downward propulsion (*apakṣepaṇam*)
3. Contraction (*ākuñcanam*)
4. Expansion (*prasāraṇam*)
5. Motion (*gamanam*)

d. VARIETIES OF GENERALITY
Higher (*para*): Being
Lower (*apara*): The Seven Categories

SCHEME 18

LOGICISM: CATEGORIES

Umesh Misra, *History of Indian Philosophy,* vol. 2, and other sources

Main categories

I. BEING (*sat*)
 Norms of knowledge (*pramāṇa*)
  Experience (*pratyakṣa*)
 a. Inference (*anumāna*)
  Testimony or Word (*śabda*)
  Analogy (*upamāna*)
 Normatively knowables
 b. The Desirable: the soul (*upādeya; ātman*)
 c. The Undesirable: conditioners and states of the soul (*heya; upādhayaḥ*)

II. NON-BEING (*asat*)

Subclassifications

a. VARIETIES OF INFERENCE
 1. Doubt (*saṁśaya*)
 2. Relevance (*prayojana*)
 3. Example (*dṛṣṭānta*)
 4. Tenet (*siddhānta*)
 5. Syllogism (*avayava*)
 6. Conjecture (*tarka*)
 7. Demonstrated conclusion (*nirṇaya*)
 8. Discussion (*vāda*)
 9. Sophistical disputation (*jalpa*)
 10. Polemic (*vitaṇḍā*)
 11. Paralogism (*hetvābhāsa*)
 12. Quibbling (*cala*)
 13. Specious reasoning (*jāti*)
 14. Fallacy (twenty-four varieties) (*nigrahasthāna*)

b. THE DESIRABLE: THE SOUL (*ātman: upādeya*)
 1. Free from the undesirable (*heyarahita*): liberated souls
  The Supreme Lord: untouched by transmigration (*īśvara*)

Inferior souls: freed from transmigration (*muktajīvātman*)

2. Not free from the undesirable: bound souls (*baddhajīvātman*)

c. THE UNDESIRABLE: CONDITIONERS AND STATES OF THE SOUL (*heya; upādhayaḥ*)

1. Body (*śarīra*)
2. Faculties (*indriyāṇi*)
3. Objects of experience (*artha*)
4. Experience (*bhoga*)
5. Mind (*manas*)
6. Activity (*pravṛtti*)
   Leading to knowledge
   Leading to action
7. Imperfection (*doṣa*)
   Attachment (*rāga*)
   Hate (*dveśa*)
   Ignorance (*moha*)
8. Afterlife (*pretyabhāva*)
9. Fruition (*phalam*)
10. Suffering (*duḥkam*)

SCHEME 19

DUALIST VEDANTA: CATEGORIES

Madhva

Ultimate categories

INDEPENDENT: VIṢṆU, THE BRAHMAN (*svatantra*)
DEPENDENT (*paratantra*)
  Being (*bhāva*)
    a. Conscious (*cetana*)
    b. Unconscious (*acetana*)
  Non-being (*abhāva*)
      Antecedent (*prāgabhāva*)
      Consequent (*dhvaṁsābhava*)
      Total (*atyantābhāva*)

Subclassifications

a. CONSCIOUS DEPENDENT BEING (*cetana*)
  Impassible: Lady Glory, or Lakṣmī (*duḥkāspṛṣṭa, Lakṣmī*)
  Passible (*duḥkaspṛṣṭa*)
    Liberated (*vimukta*)
      Gods (*deva*)
      Sages (*ṛṣi*)
      Ancestors (*pitṛ*)
      Men (*nara*)
    Inveterate in misery (*duḥkasaṁstha*)
      Capable of liberation (*muktiyogya*)
        Gods (*deva*)
        Sages (*ṛṣi*)
        Ancestors (*pitṛ*)
        Men (*nara*)
      Incapable of Liberation (*muktyayogya*)
        Eternally transmigrant (*nityasaṁsārin*)
        The damned (*tamoyogya*)
        Immoral men (*martyādhama*)
        Goblins (*piśāca*)
        Fiends (*rakṣa*)
        Devils (*daitya*)

b. UNCONSCIOUS DEPENDENT BEINGS (*acetana*)
  Eternal (*nitya*)
    The Vedas (*veda*)

The castes (*varṇa*)
The unmanifest ether (*avyākṛtākāśa*)
Eternal and transient (*nityānitya*)
Time (*kāla*)
Matter (*prakṛti*)
The Mirific Power (*māyā*)
Ignorance (*avidyā*)
The Purāṇas (*purāṇa*)
Transient (*anitya*)
Incomposite (*asaṁsṛṣṭa*)
Composite (*saṁsṛṣṭa*)

The Fivefold Difference or the Universe of Beings (pañcavidho bheda; prapañca)

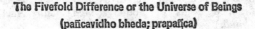

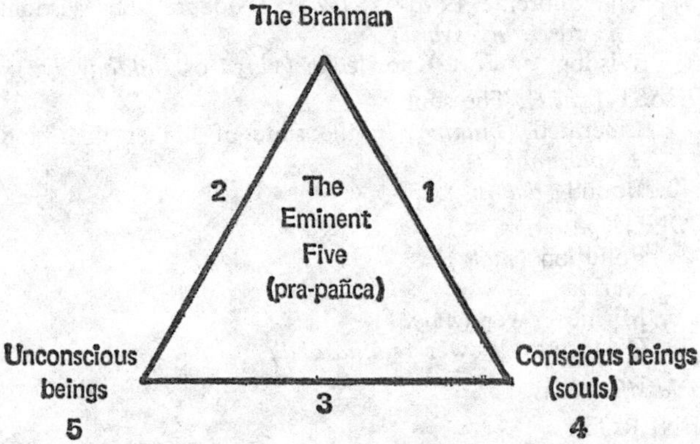

1 The Brahman and the souls
2 The Brahman and unconscious beings
3 The souls and the unconscious beings
4 Souls among themselves
5 Unconscious beings among themselves

Scheme 20

ŚAIVA ORTHODOXY: GNOSTIC SCHOOL: CATEGORIES

Bhoja and Śrī Kumāra

Three ultimate categories: Master, Beast, Bond

MASTER (*pati*). The Five Pure Principles (*śuddhatattva*):
- Śiva
- a. Energy (*śakti*)
- The Ever Beneficent (*sadāśiva*): abode of the Conditioned Souls of Sound (*nāda*) and Nucleus (*bindu*)
- The Supreme Lord (*īśvara*): abode of the Wisdom Lords (*vidyeśvara*)
- Wisdom or Pure Knowledge (*vidyā* or *śuddhavidyā*)

BEAST (*paśu*). The soul:
- Liberated (*mukta*); in the state of higher liberation (*paramokṣa*)
- b. Bound (*baddha*)

BOND (*pāśam*):
- Pollution (*mala*)
- Karma
- c. Mirific Power (*māyā*)
- Obstruction Power (*rodhaśakti*)

Subclassifications

a. ENERGY:

Activities	*Correspondence to Śiva's Five Heads*	*Correspondence to Śiva's Body*
Creation (*sṛṣṭi*)	Master (*īśāna*)	Head (*mastaka*)
Conservation (*sthiti*)	The Original Spirit (*tatpuruṣa*)	Face (*vaktra*)
Destruction (*saṁhāra*)	The Non-Terrifying (*aghora*)	Heart (*hṛdaya*)
Obscuration (*tirobhāva*)	The Lovely God (*vāmadeva*)	Genitals (*guhya*)
Grace (*anugraha*)	The Suddenly-Born (*sadyojāta*)	Foot (*pāda*)

b. BOUND BEASTS (*baddha paśu*)

Intelligence-Deconditioned Souls (*vijñānākala*), Contamination-Liquidated Beasts (*samāptakaluṣa*), the eight Wisdom Lords (*aṣṭavidyeśvarāḥ*), all in the state of lower liberation (*aparamokṣa*). The names of the Wisdom Lords are as follows:

Ananta, Sūkṣma, Śivottama, Ekanetra, Ekarudra, Trimūrtika, Śrī Kaṇṭha and Śikhaṇḍī.

Doomsday-Deconditioned Souls (*pralayākala*), Contamination-Unliquidated Beasts (*asamāptakaluṣa*)

Beasts whose Pollution and Karma have matured (*pakvamalakarma*): Sphere Lords (*bhuvanapati*)

Beasts whose Pollution and Karma have not matured (*apakvamalakarma*): transmigrants (*janmabhāk*)

Conditioned Souls (*sakala*)

Beasts whose Pollution has matured (*pakvakalmaṣa*) 118 Incantation Lords (8 Circle Lords; 8 gods, comprising Krodha and others; Vireśa and Śrī Kaṇṭha; and 100 Rudras)

Beasts whose Pollution has not matured (*apakvakalmaṣa*)

c. THE MIRIFIC POWER (*māyā*)

The Five Pure–Impure Principles (*śuddhāśuddhatattva*)

Time (*kāla*)
Necessity (*niyati*)
Aptitude (*kalā*)
Knowledge (*vidyā*)
Attachment (*rāga*)

The Seven Impure Principles (*aśuddhatattva*)

The Unevolved (*avyakta*)
The Attributes (*guṇa*)
Instinct (*buddhi*)
Egoism (*ahaṅkāra*)
Inner Faculty (*manas*)
The outer faculties (*indriyāṇi*)
Gross body (*sthūlaśarīra*)

SCHEME 21

ŚAIVA ORTHODOXY: SOUTHERN OR DEVOTIONAL SCHOOL: CATEGORIES

Manavacakam Katantar, derived from M. Dhavamony, *Love of God According to Śaiva Siddhānta*

Numbers after the categories indicate the thirty-six categories of Triadism (Scheme 34). Tamil, not Sanskrit, terms.

Main Categories: The Triad

I. MASTER (*pati*)
II. BEAST (*paśu*)
III. BOND (*malam, pāśam*)
Cause of obscuration
Cause of action (*karman*)
Matter as entangling and obscuring (*māyai*)
  a. Śiva (*civa* or *cutta tattuvam*)
  b. Knowledge (*vittiyā tattuvam*)
  c. Self (*attuma tattuvam*)

Subclassifications

a. ŚIVA (*civa tattuvam*), the Five Pure Principles
  Wisdom (*civam*), deity's male energy 1.
  Energy (*catti*), deity's female energy 2.
  The Ever Beneficent (*catācivam*), Illuminator 3.
  The Supreme Lord (*makēcuram*), Obscurer 4.
  Pure Wisdom (*cuttavittai*), Destroyer, Reproducer, Conserver 5.

b. KNOWLEDGE (*vittiyā tattuvam*), essential for transmigration
  Time (*kālam*) 6.
  Karmic Law (*niyati*) 7.
  Dispeller of obscuration (*āṇavam, kalai*) 8.
  Thought (*vittai*) 9.
  Desire (*irākam*) 10.
  Spirit (*puruṭan*) 11.
  Matter (*māyai*) 12.

c. SELF (*āttuma,* or *acutta, tattuvam, pōkkiya kāṇṭṭam*), essential for man's intellectual and animal existence

The four intellectual and organic faculties (*antakkaranam*)

Understanding (*manam*) 13.
Judgement (*putti*) 14.
Egoism (*akaṅkāram*) 15.
Will (*cittam*) 16.
The Five Perceptual Organs (*ñānēntiriyam*) 17–21.
The Five Motor Organs (*kanmentiriyam*) 22–26.
The Five Subtle Elements (*aimpulan*) 27–31.
The Five Gross Elements (*pūtam*) 32–36.

SCHEME 22

NONDUALISM 1: CATEGORIES

Vidyāraṇya and Sadānanda

Two Main Categories, one ultimate

I. REALITY, THE BRAHMAN (*vastu*)

II. UNREALITY, MATTER (*avastu, prakṛti*), with its three Attributes, Brightness, Passion and Darkness
   - a. Illusion (*māyā*), where Brightness is pure. Reality conditioned by Illusion gives rise to the Supreme Lord (*īśvara*).
   - b. Ignorance (*avidyā*), where Brightness is sullied. Reality conditioned by Ignorance produces the Intelligent (*prajñā*), known also as the soul (*jīva*) and the Causal Body (*kāraṇaśarīra*).
   - c. The Phenomenal Universe, (where Darkness prevails ?); also known as the Effectual Body (*kārya-śarīra*).

Subclassifications

a. THE SUPREME LORD, THE BRAHMAN CONDITIONED BY ILLUSION
   The Golden Embryo (*hiraṇyagarbha*), related to the totality of Subtle Bodies
   The Universal Fire (*agni vaiśvānara*), related to the totality of Gross Bodies

b. THE INTELLIGENT SELF, THE BRAHMAN CONDITIONED BY IGNORANCE
   The Fiery (*taijasa*), related to individual Subtle Bodies
   The Universal (*viśva*), related to individual Gross Bodies

c. THE PHENOMENAL UNIVERSE
   Brightness aspect: the Five Perceptual Faculties, Mind and Instinct
   Passion aspect: The Five Motor Faculties, and the Five Breaths. From the Brightness and Passion Aspects rises the Subtle Body
   Darkness aspect: from whence the Cosmic Egg, source of the Gross Body

Scheme 23

NONDUALISM 2: EVOLUTION OF THE UNIVERSE

Sureśvara and Vidyāraṇya

STAGE 1: THE UNMANIFEST OR UNEVOLVED

I. THE BRAHMAN, Absolute Reality, Pure Being, qualityless (*nirguṇa*)

II. IGNORANCE, neither Being nor Non-Being (*avidyā, sadasadbhinnā*)

Potencies of Ignorance (*avidyāyā śaktayaḥ*)
Desire (*kāmanā*)
Karma

STAGE 2: SUBTLE CREATION

Ignorance superimposed on the Brahman gives rise to the following differentiations:

III. MACROCOSMIC CREATION (*samaṣṭirūpā sṛṣṭi*)

Potency of Knowledge (*jñānaśakti*). The Golden Embryo (*hiraṇyagarbha*)

Potency of Action (*kriyāśakti*). The Thread (*sūtra*)

IV. MICROCOSMIC CREATION (*vyaṣṭirūpā sṛṣṭi*)

Potency of Knowledge (*jñānaśakti*), or The Inner Faculty (*antaḥkaraṇa*); gives rise to two types of knowing faculty: ascertaining (*niścayātmikā*) and critical (*vimarśarūpam*), the former is Instinct (*buddhi*) and the latter, Mind (*manas*).

Potency of Action (*kriyāśakti*), or The Breath (*prāṇa*); is fivefold: circulating (*vyāna*), upward (*udāna*), uniform (*samāna*), downward (*apāna*), and vital (*prāṇa*).

From the combination of the modes of the Inner Faculty and Breath:

V. THE GENESIS OF THE PRINCIPLES

The following is the order of evolution: Five Simple Elements, Five Perceptual Faculties, Five Motor Faculties, the Subtle Body.

Elements (*bhūtādi*)	*Perceptual Faculties* (*jñānendriyāṇi*)	*Motor Faculties* (*karmendriyāṇi*)
Ether (*ākāśa*)	Hearing (*śrotra*)	Speech (*vāk*) speech
Wind (*vāyu*)	Touch (*tvak*)	Handling (*pāṇi*) hand
Fire (*tejas*)	Seeing (*akṣi*)	Walking (*pāda*) foot
Water (*āp*)	Taste (*rasana*)	Excretion (*pāyu*) anus
Earth (*prithivī*)	Smell (*ghrāṇa*)	Procreation (*upastha*) genitals

From the Five Simple Elements rise the Five Composite Elements, each comprising one half of one simple element, and four portions each of one eighth of the other Simple Elements.

STAGE 3: GROSS CREATION
The principles are then amassed, giving rise to:

VI. THE COSMIC EGG (*brahmāṇḍa*)
From which the physical universe proceeds. [Compare Scheme 28.]

Scheme 24

ANCIENT VEDANTA: CATEGORIES

Bhartṛ Prapañca (according to Hiriyanna)

Bhartṛ Prapañca's categories can be classified as the Eight States or the Three Groups. The number of the state is shown after the category.

I. THE EIGHT STATES

Single ultimate category

THE BRAHMAN

Supreme (*para*). Essence, basis of the untransformed, homogeneous

Lower (*apara*). States, modes, transformed, heterogeneous:

a. Spiritual: macrocosmic creation (*samaṣṭisṛṣṭi*)

b. Material: microcosmic creation (*vyaṣṭisṛṣṭi*)

Subclassifications

a. SPIRITUAL REALITY: MACROCOSMIC CREATION

Limiter ignorance (*paricchetṛ*)

The Inner Controller (*antaryāmin*) 1.

Limiter and modifier ignorance (*paricchetṛ* and *vikartṛ*)

Soul (*jīva*) 2.

Cosmic: the all-commanding Fire (*agni vaiśvānara*)

Individual

b. MATERIAL REALITY: MICROCOSMIC CREATION

Cosmic level

Subtle material of the universe (*avyākrta*) 3.

Instrument of Subtle-to-Gross transformation (*sūtra*) 4.

Gross material of the universe (*virāj*) 5.

Organs of the Cosmic Spirit (*devatā*) 6.

Non-cosmic level

Created types of universe (*jāti*) 7.

Created individuals of the universe (*piṇḍa*) 8.

II. THE THREE GROUPS (*rāśayaḥ*)
(*co-ordinated with the Eight States*)

I. GROUP OF THE SUPREME SELF (*paramātmarāśi*)

The Supreme Brahman

The Inner Controller 1.

II. GROUP OF THE SOUL (*jīvarāśi*)
Soul, or Spirit 2.
Cosmic Spirit—the Golden Embryo, the all-commanding Fire
The Individual Soul

III. GROUP OF THE EMBODIED AND BODILESS (*mūrtāmūrtarāśi*)
Subtle material of the universe 3.
Instrument of transformation 4.
Gross material of the universe 5.
Organs of the Cosmic Spirit 6.
Created types of the universe 7.
Created individuals of the universe 8.

SCHEME 25

CONDITIONED DIFFERENCE-IN-IDENTITY: CATEGORIES

Bhāskara, derived from Dasgupta,
History of Indian Philosophy, vol. 3

Single ultimate category

THE BRAHMAN

In Himself, transcending the world (*niṣprapañca*): the Inner Controller (*antaryāmin*)

In His Energies, constituting the world (*saprapañca* ?)

Experiencer-Energy (*bhoktṛśakti*): the souls:

Liberated: by desire for the Brahman

Bound: by desire for worldly objects

Experienced-Energy (*bhogyaśakti*): Matter:

Includes three limiters, ignorance (*avidyā*), desire (*kāma*) and activity (*karma*), which are dissolved by a combination of knowledge (*jñāna*) and action (*karma*).

SCHEME 26

INDIVISIBLE NONDUALISM 1: CATEGORIES

Vijñāna Bhikṣu

Single ultimate category

THE BRAHMAN

Unlimited (*anaupādhika*)

Limited (*aupādhika*)

Through causal limiter: the Supreme Self, the Supreme Lord, the Subtle Body, and Immutable Potency (*kāraṇopādhi, paramātman, īśvara, liṅgaśarīra, apariṇāminī śakti*)

Through effectual limiter, and mutable potency. Gross body (*kāryopādhi, pariṇāminīśakti, sthūlaśarīra*)

Subclassifications

MODIFICATIONS OF THE MUTABLE POTENCY

1. Spirit (*puruṣa*)
2. Matter (*prakṛti*). Both conjoined by the Supreme Self, give rise to:
3. Instinct or the Prodigious (*buddhi, mahat*), which has three varieties, each presided by a deity:
   —Bright (*sāttvika*) Viṣṇu
   —Passional (*rājasika*) Brahmā
   —Dark (*tāmasika*) Śiva
4. Egoism, or the Ego Principle (*ahaṅkāra*); also has three varieties:
   —Bright (*sāttvika*) Mind
   —Passional (*rājasika*) The Ten Faculties, perceptual and motor
   —Dark (*tāmasika*) The Ten Elements, subtle and gross

Scheme 27

INDIVISIBLE NONDUALISM 2: EVOLUTION OF THE UNIVERSE

Vijñāna Bhikṣu

I. EVOLUTION OF (UNIQUE) SUBTLE BODY, from which follows partition into innumerable subtle bodies.

II. EVOLUTION OF GROSS BODY, from which is the following sequence of evolutes:

Instinct
Egoism
Ether
Air
Fire
Water
Earth
The Cosmic Egg
The creator god, Brahmā
Creation of the physical universe

Scheme 28

PĀÑCARĀTRA THEOLOGY: EVOLUTION OF THE UNIVERSE

Vaiṣṇava Saṁhitās and Tantras, according to F. O. Schrader, *Introduction to the Pāñcarātra and Ahirbudhnya Saṁhitā*

The universe evolves in four stages:

1. Pure Creation: the Theophanies

2. Impure Creation 1: Intermediate creation. The emergence of Prime Matter

3. Impure Creation 2: the Genesis of the Principles

4. Impure Creation 3: Materialization of the World

STAGE 1: PURE CREATION: THE THEOPHANIES (śuddhasṛṣṭi)

Single ultimate category

THE SUPREME ULTIMATE REALITY (*paratattva*), which is bipolar: Viṣṇu, the Supreme Brahman (*parabrahma, Nārāyaṇa, puruṣa*) Lakṣmī, Lady Glory, the Divine Energy (*śakti*), also bipolar:

Energy of Action (*kriyāśakti*)

Energy of Becoming (*bhūtiśakti*)

a. The Empyrean (*paravyoma*)

b. Primary Pure Emanations, or Theophanies (*vyūha*)

c. Manifestations, or Incarnations (*vibhava, avatāra*)

Subclassifications

a. THE EMPYREAN. Divine emanations embodied in a spiritual Matter. Comprises the heavenly abode Vaikuṇṭha and its inhabitants.

The Supreme Vāsudeva (*paravāsudeva*)

Divine Energies (*śaktayaḥ*)

Spirits or souls (*jīvāḥ*)

Celestials (*nityāḥ, sūrayaḥ*)

The liberated or blessed (*muktāḥ*)

Accessories of glory (*bhogakaraṇāni*)

b. PRIMARY PURE EMANATIONS, OR THEOPHANIES (*vyūha*). Embodiments of the Six Glorious Attributes—knowledge, sovereignty, energy, power, vigor and refulgence

Vāsudeva

Saṅkarṣaṇa, Germ of the Impure Creation (to follow in Stage 2)

Pradyumna, Principle of the emergence of Duality (Stage 2)

Aniruddha, Principle of the development of Duality

From these four Theophanies emanate the twenty-four Numina (*caturviṁśatimūrtayaḥ*), three from each Theophany. They comprise:

Twelve Secondary Pure Emanations (*vyūhāntara*)

Thirteen Lords of Wisdom (*vidyeśvara*)

c. MANIFESTATIONS OR INCARNATIONS. Embodiments of the Pure Emanations

Principal (*mukhya*), thirty-nine in all, including the Ten Avatars

Secondary (*gauṇa*)

The Inner Controller, Aniruddha (*antaryāmin*)

STAGE 2: IMPURE CREATION 1: INTERMEDIATE CREATION. THE EMERGENCE OF PRIME MATTER. From Saṅkarṣaṇa emerge (a) Pradyumna and (b) Aniruddha

a. EMANATIONS OF PRADYUMNA, Principle of the emergence of Duality:

Spirit (*puruṣa*), the aggregate of souls, from which emerge:

The four Superhuman Couples, or the eight Manus. They descend the long line of categories that will emerge from Aniruddha until these categories are fully materialized.

Matter (*prakṛti*), from which emerge the Attributes (*guṇa*) and Fate (*niyati*) and Time (*kāla*)

b. EMANATIONS OF ANIRUDDHA, in the following order:

1. Potency (*śakti*)
2. Fate (*niyati*)
3. (Subtle) Time (*kāla*)

4. Body of Triple Attributes (*guṇamayavapu*) of Brightness, Passion and Darkness. From them emerges the Sheath of Generation (*prasūtikoṣa*), comprising the Three Divine Couples. The correspondence between the Body and the Sheath is as follows:
   Brightness: Viṣṇu and Lakṣmī
   Passion: Brahmā and Sarasvatī
   Darkness: Śiva and Pārvatī. From this Body emerges:
5. Prime Matter (*mūlaprakṛti*) or the Unmanifest (*avyakta*)

STAGE 3: IMPURE CREATION 2: THE GENESIS OF THE PRINCIPLES. From Prime Matter evolve (a) the Prodigious, or Cosmic Breath (*mahat*), and (b) Egoism, or the Ego Principle (*ahaṅkāra*). Concomitant with these evolutes is (c) the descent of the Superhuman Couples or Manus into the evolutes and their modes.

a. MODES OF THE PRODIGIOUS, OR THE COSMIC BREATH (*mahat*)

Bright (*sāttvika*): Mind (*buddhi*)
Passionate or Energetic (*rājasika*): Breath (*prāṇa*)
Dark (*tāmasika*): Time (*kāla*)

b. MODES OF EGOISM OR THE EGO PRINCIPLE (*ahaṅkāra*)

Transforming or Bright (*vaikārika* or *sāttvika*)
  The Five Perceptual Faculties (*jñānendriyāṇi*)
  The Five Motor Faculties (*karmendriyāṇi*)
Fiery of Passionate (*taijasa* or *rājasika*)
Elemental or Dark (*bhūtādi* or *tāmasika*)
  The Five Subtle Elements (*tanmātrā*)
  The Five Gross Elements (*mahābhūtā*)

c. CONTINUED DESCENT OF THE MANUS. When the Couples have descended into the above modes, the following evolution takes place:

The Couples become furnished with all organs.
They then generate the Manu children, or Mānavas, who themselves generate the Manu grandchildren, the Mānavamānavas.
Then there is a fall from knowledge (*jñānabhraṁśa*), in consequence of which there is
The establishment of religion.

STAGE 4: IMPURE CREATION 3: MATERIALIZATION OF THE WORLD. In the following order:

The massing of the Principles (*saṁhati*)
Generation of the Cosmic Egg (*brahmāṇḍa*)
Birth of the god Brahmā from lotus emergent from Cosmic Egg
Brahmā's three creations: (a) the Four Youths: Sana, Sanaka, Sanatkumāra and Sanandana, (b) the Androgynous Śiva, from whom emerge the major and minor Rudras, and (c) the Ten Lords of Created Beings (*prajāpataya*), producers of moving (*cara*) and unmoving (*acara*) beings.

Scheme 29

QUALIFIED NONDUALISM: CATEGORIES

A. RĀMĀNUJA'S SCHEME (*see Selection 72*)

I. SOUL: The Brahman

II. BODY: The Universe of Conscious and Unconscious beings

  Soul: Conscious beings

  Body: Unconscious beings

B. SCHEME OF VEDĀNTA DEŚIKA AND ŚRĪ NIVĀSA

Main Categories

I. NORMS OF KNOWLEDGE (*pramāṇa*)

  Experience (*pratyakṣa*)

  Inference (*anumāna*)

  Word (*śabda*)

II. NORMATIVELY KNOWABLES (*prameya*)

  Substance (*dravya*)

    Conscious (*ajaḍa*)

      a. Intrinsic (*pratyak*)

      b. Extrinsic (*parāk*)

    Unconscious (*jaḍa*)

      c. Matter (*prakṛti*)

      d. Time (*kāla*)

  Accident (*adravya*)

    The Three Attributes, Brightness, Passion, Darkness (*triguṇa: sattva, rajas, tamas*)

    The Five Sensations: sound, touch, color, taste, smell (*pañcatanmātrā: śabda, sparśa, rūpa, rasa, gandha*)

    Relation (*saṁyoga*)

    Potency (*śakti*)

Subclassifications

a. INTRINSICALLY OR SUBSTANTIALLY CONSCIOUS SUBSTANCES (*pratyak*)

  God (*Īśvara*)

    The Embodied (*śarīrin*)

      Supreme Form (*para*)

      Theophanies (*vyūha*)

      Incarnations (*vibhava*)

Inner Controller (*antaryāmin*)
Iconic Embodiments (*arcā*)
Self-manifested (*svayaṁvyakta*)
Consecrated by gods (*daiva*)
Consecrated by sages (*saiddha*)
Consecrated by men (*mānuṣa*)
The Body (*śarīra*)
Efficient cause (*nimitta kāraṇa*)
Auxiliary cause (*sahakāri kāraṇa*)
Material cause (*pradhāna kāraṇa*)
Souls (*jīva*)
The eternally free (*nitya*)
The liberated (*mukta*)
The bound (*baddha*)
Religiously docile (*śāstravaśya*)
Liberation seekers (*mumukṣu*)
Experience seekers (*bubhukṣu*)
Religiously indocile (*śāstrāvaśya*)

b. EXTRINSIC CONSCIOUS SUBSTANCES (*parāk*)
Eternal manifestations (*nityavibhūti*)
Objects of delight: the bodies of the blessed (*bhogyam*)
Accessories of delight (*bhogopakaraṇāni*)
Abodes of delight (*bhogasthānāni*)
Qualitative (as opposed to substantial) Consciousness (*dharmabhūtajñāna*)

c. MATTER (*prakṛti*)
Unmanifest (*avyakta*)
Manifest (*vyakta*), from which emerge the following evolutes:
Instinct, or the Prodigious (*buddhi* or *mahat*)
Egoism (*ahaṅkāra*), in its three modes
Mind (*manas*)
The Ten Faculties (five perceptual and five motor)
The Ten Elements (five subtle and five gross).

d. Time (*kāla*)
Indivisible (*akhaṇḍa*)
Divisible (*khaṇḍa*)

Scheme 30

INNATE DIFFERENCE-IN-IDENTITY: CATEGORIES

Nimbārka, Puruṣottama Prasāda, Giridhara Prapanna and secondary sources

Single ultimate category

THE BRAHMAN, OR REALITY (*sattā*)
- Independent (*svatantra*)
  - a. Nature (*svarūpa, bhāva*)
  - b. Forms (*rūpa*)
- Dependent (*paratantra*)
  - c. Conscious: souls (*cetanātmaka; jīva*)
  - d. Unconscious: Matter (*acetanātmikā; prakṛti*)

Subclassifications

a. NATURE OF THE BRAHMAN (*brahmaṇaḥ svarūpam*)
- Energizer (*śaktimat*): Kṛṣṇa
  - Incommunicable attributes
    - Infinity, all-pervasiveness and independence
    - The Three Cosmic Activities: creation, conservation and destruction
  - Communicable attributes
    - Primary: being, consciousness and joy
    - Secondary: freedom from sin, aging, death, pain, hunger, thirst; and capacity to fulfill all desires
- Energy (*śakti*): Rādhā

b. FORMS OF THE BRAHMAN (*brahmaṇaḥ rūpāṇi*)
- Theophanies (*vyūha*)
  - God as attributeless (*nirguṇa*): Vāsudeva
  - God as Inner Controller (*antaryāmin*): Kṣetrajña or Saṅkarṣaṇa
  - God as the mind of all beings: Pradyumna
  - God as controller of cause and effect: Aniruddha
- Incarnations (*avatāra*)
  - Sportive incarnations (*līlāvatāra*): manifestations of being, consciousness and joy:
    - Essential (*svarūpāvatāra*)

Plenary (*pūrṇarūpa*)
Partial (*aṁśarūpa*)
Assumed (*āveśāvatāra*)
Assumed by the divinity itself (*svāṁśāveśa*)
Assumed by the divine energies (*śaktyaṁśāveśa*)
"Spirit" incarnations (*puruṣāvatāra*)
God, controller of Matter (*prakṛtiniyantā*)
God, controller of macrocosmic creation (*samaṣṭiniyantā*)
God, controller of microcosmic creation (*vyaṣṭiniyantā*)
"Attribute" Incarnations (*guṇāvatāra*)
God creator (*sraṣṭā*)
God conserver (*pālayitā*)
God destroyer (*saṁhartā*)

c. CONSCIOUS BEINGS OR SOULS (*jīva*)
Free (*mukta*)
Eternally free (*nityamukta*)
Divine adornments (*ānantarya*)
Divine attendants (*pārṣada*)
Liberated (*mukta*)
Realizers of God's true nature (*bhagavadbhāvāpattilakṣaṇamuktivantaḥ*)
Realizers of own nature (*svabhāvānandamātreṇa santuṣṭā*)
Bound (*baddha*)
Seekers of liberation (*mumukṣavaḥ*)
Desirous of realizing God's nature (*bhagavadbhāvāpattimuktikāmāḥ*)
Desirous of realizing own nature (*svabhāvāpattikāmāḥ*)
Seekers of experience (*bubhukṣavaḥ*)
Predestined to happiness (*bhāviśreyaskāḥ*)
Eternally transmigrant (*nityasaṁsāriṇaḥ, nityabaddhāḥ*)

d. UNCONSCIOUS BEING OR MATTER (*prakṛti*)
Immaterial (*aprākṛta*)
Material (*prākṛta*), the cause of
The Subtle Body (*liṅgaśarīra*)
The Gross Body (*sthūlaśarīa*)
Eternal (*nitya*)

- Body of God
- Bodies of the liberated

Non-eternal (*anitya*)

- Not caused by karma (*akarmaja*)
- Caused by karma (*karmaja*)

Time (*kāla*)

SCHEME 31

PURE NONDUALISM: CATEGORIES

A. VALLABHA'S SCHEME (*see Selection 80*)

Single ultimate category

THE BRAHMAN: JOY, CONSCIOUSNESS AND BEING

1. All characteristics unconcealed	THE INNER CONTROLLER
2. Joy concealed	SOULS
3. Joy and Consciousness concealed	INCONSCIENT BEINGS
(4. All characteristics concealed	NON-EXISTENCE)

B. SCHEME OF PURUṢOTTAMA PĪTĀMBARA, Prasthānaratnākara (?). From description by J. G. Shah, *Srimad Vallabhacharya: His Philosophy and Religion,* chap. 2. The scheme will need to be revised.

Single ultimate category

THE BRAHMAN
Essence (*svarūpam*)
Kṛṣṇa, the Supreme Person (*puruṣottama*)
a. The Imperishable (*akṣara*)
The Inner Controller (*antaryāmin*)
Cause (*kāraṇa*)
Material (*pradhāna*), without inherence (*samavāya*), through unmodified modification (*avikṛtapariṇāma*)
Final (*prayojana*): motiveless cosmic play (*līlā*)
b. Efficient (*nimitta*)
Effect (*kārya*)
c. Conscious beings, or souls (*cit, jīva*)
Inconscient beings (*acit*): Matter (*prakṛti*): the evolutes of Sankhya (see Scheme 13)

Subclassifications

a. THE IMPERISHABLE (*akṣara*)
Time (*kāla*)

        Superhuman (*ādhidaivika*)
        Internal (*adhyātmika*)
        External (*ādhibhautika*)
    Action (*kriyā*)
    Nature
        Manifestation (*āvirbhāva*)
        Concealment (*tirobhāva*) or non-manifestation

b. GOD, EFFICIENT CAUSE (*nimittakāraṇa*)
    Of bondage (*bandha*)
    Of liberation (*mokṣa*)
    Of other activities: incarnational, supracosmic, cosmic

c. CONSCIOUS BEINGS, OR SOULS (*cit, jīva*)
    Liberated (*mukta*)
        Liberated in life (*jivanmukta*)
        Liberated after death (*pretyamukta*)
    Unliberated (*muktetara*)
        Deific (*daiva*)
            Following the Way of Fullness (*puṣṭimārga*)
            Following the Way of Injunction (*maryādāmārga*)
        Demonic or transmigrant (*āsura* or *prāvāhi*)
            Ignorant (*ajña*)
            Malicious (*durjña*)

Scheme 32

INEFFABLE DIFFERENCE-IN-IDENTITY, OR PARADISAL KṚṢṆAISM: CATEGORIES

Jīva Gosvāmi, derived from S. K. De,
Early History of the Vaisnava Faith and Movement in Bengal, chap. 5

Single ultimate category

THE NONDUAL (*advaya*), in three aspects, each with an Energizer and an Energy:

a. God (*bhagavat*) or Kṛṣṇa, and the Internal Energy (*antaraṅgā śakti*), also known as the Supreme, Essential, Joyful or Intelligential Energy (*parā, svarupa, ānanda,* and *cit śakti*)

b. The Supreme Soul (*paramātman*), and the Peripheral Energy (*taṭasthā śakti*), also known as the Soul or Field-Knower, Energy (*jīva* or *kṣetrajñā śakti*)

c. The Brahman, and the External Energy (*bahiraṅgā śakti*), also known as the Ignorance Energy (*avidyā śakti*) or the Mirific Power (*māyā*)

Subclassifications

a. God or Kṛṣṇa, and the Internal, Supreme, Essential, Joyful, or Intelligential Energy
 Essence (*svarūpa*)
  The Beatific Energy (*hlādinī śakti*)
  The Conscious Energy (*saṁvit śakti*)
  The Existential Energy (*sandhinī śakti*)
 Essential Glory (*svarūpa vaibhava*)
  Kṛṣṇa's adornments
  Kṛṣṇa's abodes (*dhāman*)
   Vṛndāvana or Goloka, the Supreme Paradise, the divine Arcadia
   Mathurā
   Dvārakā
  Kṛṣṇa's Associates
   In Vṛndāvana: the cowherds and cowherdesses, chief among them Rādhā

In Mathurā and Dvārakā: members of the Yādava tribe

b. THE SUPREME SOUL, AND THE PERIPHERAL, SOUL, OR FIELD-KNOWER, ENERGY

Spirit (*puruṣa*)
- Incarnations (*avatāra*)
  - Spirit incarnations (*puruṣāvatāra*): the last three Theophanies of Pāñcarātra (see Scheme 28)
  - Attribute incarnations (*guṇāvatāra*)
    - Viṣṇu (embodiment of Brightness)
    - Brahmā (of Passion)
    - Śiva (of Darkness)
  - Sportive incarnations (*līlāvatāra*), including the Ten Avatars
- Souls (*jīva*)
  - God-inclined (*bhagavatsammukha*)
  - God-averse (*bhagavanvimukha*)

Soul Energy or Efficient Energy (*jīva* or *nimitta māyā*),
- Its motive or final cause
  - Knowledge (*vidyā*), cause of liberation
  - Ignorance (*avidyā*), cause of bondage
- As efficient causal power (*nimitta māyā*), producing Time (*kāla*), occasioner of imbalance in Matter's Attributes
  - Karma, cause of the imbalance
  - Fate (*daiva*), effects of karma
  - Nature (*svabhāva*), conceptual latencies
- As material causal power (*guṇa māyā*), producing
  - Subtle elements (*bhūtasūkṣma*) or substance (*dravya*)
  - Matter (*prakṛti*) or Field (*kṣetra*)
  - Breath (*prāṇa*) or vital principle
  - Egoism (*ahaṅkāra*) or soul (*ātman*)
  - Five Faculties and Five Gross Elements or Modifications (*vikāra*)

c. THE BRAHMAN, AND THE EXTERNAL ENERGY. Best described by the Nondualists (see Schemes 22 and 23).

SCHEME 33

MONIST PASTORALISM: CATEGORIES

Bhāsarvajña, *Gaṇakārikā*

The main categories comprise two groups, the Teaching (five categories) and the Teacher (nine categories):

I. THE TEACHING

1. CAUSE (*kāraṇa*). Author of creation, destruction and grace
2. EFFECT (*kārya*)
   a. Sentiency (*vidyā*)
   b. The Sentient, or Beast (*paśu*)
   c. The Insentient (*kalā*)
3. UNION (*yoga*). Conjunction of the soul with God through intellect
   Arising from cessation of activity (*kriyoparamalakṣaṇa*)
   Arising from activity (*kriyālakṣaṇa*)
4. RITUAL BEHAVIOR (*vidhi*)
   d. Principal (*pradhānabhūta*)
   Subsidiary (*guṇabhūta*): purificatory ablutions
5. CESSATION OF PAIN (*duḥkānta*)
   e. Personal (*sātmaka*)
   Impersonal (*anātmaka*): total extirpation of pain

Subclassifications

a. SENTIENCY (*vidyā*)
Cognitive (*bodhasvabhāvā*)
Proceeding with discrimination (*vivekapravṛtti*)
Proceeding without discrimination (*avivekapravṛtti*)
Incognitive (*abodhātmikā*)

b. THE SENTIENT, or BEAST (*paśu*)
Non-appetent (*nirañjana*)
Appetent (*sāñjana*)

c. THE INSENTIENT (*kalā*)
Causal (*kāraṇākhyā*)
The Three Internal Faculties (*antaḥkaraṇatrayam*)
Intellect (*adhyavasāya*)
Egoism (*abhimāna*)

- Cogitant Principle (*saṅkalpa*)
- The Five Perceptual Faculties (*jñānendriyapañcakam*)
- The Five Motor Faculties (*karmendriyanpañcakam*)

Effectual (*kāryākhyā*)
- The Five Subtle Elements (*pañcaguṇāḥ; tanmātrā*)
- The Five Gross Elements (*pañcamahābhūtāḥ*)

d. PRINCIPAL RITUAL BEHAVIOR (*pradhānabhūtavidhi*)

Acts of piety (*vratam*)
- Perambulation (*pradakṣiṇā*)
- Pious muttering (*japa*)
- Oblations (*upahāra*)
  - Pious ejaculation (*japya*)
  - Adoration (*namaskāra*)
  - Sacred gabble (*huḍukkāra*)
  - Dance (*nṛtyam*)
  - Song (*gītam*)
  - Laughter (*hasitam*)
- Bathing or lying in ashes (*bhasmasnānaśayanam*)

Postures (*dvārāṇi*)
- Talking nonsensically (*avitadbhāṣaṇam*)
- Acting absurdly (*avitatkaraṇam*)
- Affected wooing (*śṛṅgāraṇam*)
- Affected limping (*mandanam*)
- Affected trembling (*spandanam*)
- Affected snoring (*krāthanam*)

e. CESSATION OF PAIN, PERSONAL (*sātmaka duḥkānta*)

Visual power (*dṛkśakti*)
- Omniscience (*sarvajñatvam*)
- Discrimination (*vijñanam*)
- Reflection (*mananam*)
- Audition (*śravaṇam*)
- Vision (*darśanam*)

Active power (*kriyāśakti*)
- Power of independence from organs (*vikaraṇadharmitvam*)
- Power of assuming forms (*kāmarūpitvam*)
- Swiftness of thought (*manojavitvam*)

II. THE TEACHER

The Nine Groups

(Eight Pentads and one Triad)

1. ACQUISITIONS (*lābha*): knowledge (*jñānam*), penance (*tapa*), permanence of the body (*nityatvam*), constancy (*sthiti*) and purity (*śuddhi*).
2. POLLUTIONS (*mala, paśutvamūlam, heya*): false knowledge (*mithyājñānam*), demerit (*adharma*), attachment (*śakti*), interestedness (*hetu*) and lapse (*cyuti*).
3. EXPEDIENTS (*upāya*): use of habitation (*vāsacaryā*), pious muttering (*japa*), meditation (*dhyānam*), recollection of Śiva (*sadā Rudrasmṛti*) and apprehension (*prapatti*).
4. CONTACTS (*deśa*): spiritual teacher (*gurujana*), caverns (*guhā*), special place (*deśa*), burning ground (*śmaśāna*) and Rudra (*Śiva*) only (*Rudra eva*).
5. PERSEVERANCES (*avasthā*): differenced (*vyakta*), undifferenced (*avyakta*), muttering (*japa*), acceptance (*dānam*) and devotion (*niṣṭhā*).
6. PURIFICATIONS (*viśuddhayaḥ*—abrogation of the Pollutions of category 2): loss of false knowledge, loss of demerit, loss of attachment, loss of interestedness and loss of lapse.
7. INITIATIONS (*dīkṣā*): the material (*dravyam*), the proper time (*kāla*), the rite (*kriyā*), the image (*mūrti*) and the spiritual guide (*guru*).
8. POWERS (*bālāni*): devotion to teacher (*gurubhakti*), clarity of mind (*prasāda*), conquest of pleasure and pain (*dvandvajaya*), merit (*dharma*) and carefulness (*apramāda*).
9. THREE MODES OF EARNING SUSTENANCE (*annārjayopāyā vṛttayaḥ*): mendicancy (*bhaikṣya*), living on alms (*utsṛṣṭa*) and living on chance supplies (*yathālabdhābhidhā*).

Scheme 34

TRIADISM 1: CATEGORIES

Abhinava Gupta and secondary sources

The thirty-six categories of Triadism are indicated by numbers after the categories. The categories are thirty-seven if the Trans-universal, which transcends categories, is included among them. Categories 12–36 are those of Sankhya (see Scheme 13).

Single ultimate category

CONSCIOUSNESS, INTELLIGENCE OR LIGHT (*cit, prakāśa*)

Trans-universal, inconceptualizable (*viśvottīrṇa, anuttara*): the Supreme Śiva (*paramaśiva*)

Universal, conceptualizable (*viśvamaya*)

a. Macrocosmic, the "Pure Way" (*śuddhādhva*)

b. Microcosmic, the "Impure Way" (*aśuddhādhva*). The Pure and the Impure Ways unfold the elements of the conception innate in the Consciousness, expressible in the sentence "I am this (unmanifested) universe," and constituted of subject and object.

Subclassifications

a. MACROCOSMIC CONSCIOUSNESS: THE PURE WAY: THE FIVE ENERGIES

Subject

ŚIVA. Energy of Consciousness (*cicchakti*). "I am this unmanifested universe." 1.

ENERGY (*śakti*). Energy of Joy (*ānandaśakti*). "I." 2.

THE EVER BENEFICENT (*sadāśiva*). Energy of Will (*icchā-śakti*). Incipient experience of phenomenal being. "I am this" ("I" emphasized). 3.

Object

THE SUPREME LORD (*īśvara*). Energy of Knowledge (*jñānaśakti*). Crystallized experience of phenomenal being. "I am THIS" ("I" not emphasized). 4.

Subject and Object

PURE WISDOM (*śuddhavidyā*). Energy of Action (*kriyāśakti*). "I am THIS" ("I" re-emphasized). 5.

b. MICROCOSMIC CONSCIOUSNESS: THE IMPURE WAY

Subject

SELF-OBSCURATION (*māyā*) 6.

THE FIVE SHEATHS (*kañcuka*)

Aptitude (*kalā*) 7.

Knowledge (*vidyā*) 8.

Desire (*rāga*) 9.

Time (*kāla*) 10.

Fate (*niyati*) 11.

SPIRIT (*puruṣa*) 12.

Object

MATTER (*prakṛti*) 13.

INSTINCT (*buddhi*) 14.

EGOISM (*ahaṅkāra*) 15.

Mind (*manas*) 16.

The Ten Faculties (*indriya*)

Five Perceptual (*jnāñendriya*) 17–21.

Five Motor (*karmendriya*) 22–26.

The Ten Elements (*bhūtādi*)

Five Subtle (*tanmātrā*) 27–31.

Five Gross (*mahābhūta*) 32–36.

SCHEME 35

TRIADISM 2: THE TWELVE CONSUMING ENERGIES, OR KĀLĪS

Abhinava Gupta and Jayaratha

There are four Kālīs of creation, maintenance, destruction and ineffability, in each of the three groups of knowable, norm and knower. While Scheme 34 shows the procession of multiplicity from the unity of the undifferenced Supreme Śiva, this one shows the regress to that unity.

I. *The Kālīs of the Knowable*

1. KĀLĪ OF CREATION (*Sṛṣṭikālī*). Function, creation of objects.
2. KĀLĪ OF BLOOD (*Raktakālī*). Experience of objects.
3. KĀLĪ OF THE DESTRUCTION OF STABILITY (*Sthitināśakālī*). Termination of the experience of objects.
4. KĀLĪ OF THE DEATH GOD (*Yamakālī*). Doubt about the experience of the object.

II. *The Kālīs of the Norm*

5. KĀLĪ OF DESTRUCTION (*Saṁhārakālī*). Dissociation of objects from external norms, making the subject able to grasp them within itself.
6. KĀLĪ OF DEATH (*Mṛtyukālī*). Total merging of object in subject.
7. FEARFUL KĀLĪ (*Rudrakālī*). Object momentarily reinstated (to be finally dissolved).
8. KĀLĪ OF THE SUN (*Mārtaṇḍakālī*). Merging of the twelve Faculties (Instinct, Mind, the Five Perceptual and the Five Motor, Faculties, categories 14, 16–26) into Egoism (category 15).

III. *Kālīs of the Knower*

9. KĀLĪ OF THE SUPREME SUN (*Paramārkakālī*). Merging of Egoism into the limited subject or Spirit (category 12).
10. KĀLĪ OF THE FIRE OF DOOM (*Kālānalarudrakālī*): Merges Spirit with Pure Widsom (category 5).

11. KĀLĪ OF THE GREAT DEATH GOD (*Mahākālakālī*): Merges Pure Wisdom into Energy (category 2).

12. FURIOUS, VIOLENT AND TERRIFYING KĀLĪ OF THE GREAT TREMENDOUS GOD (*Mahābhairavacaṇḍograghorakālī*). Merging of Energy into Śiva (category 1; perhaps into the Supreme Śiva Himself, transcendent above the categories ?).

Scheme 36

ENERGY-QUALIFIED NONDUALISM 1: CATEGORIES

Māyi Deva and secondary sources

Single Ultimate Category

THE ULTIMATE REPOSITORY (*sthala*) which has the following emanations:

Śiva, or Energizer (*śaktimat*)
- a. Symbol (*liṅga*)
- b. Body (*aṅga*)

Energy (*śakti*)
- c. Potency or Aptitude (*śakti, kalā*)
- d. Devotion (*bhakti*)

Subclassifications

a. SYMBOL (*liṅga*)
- Faith Symbol (*bhāvaliṅga*)
  - Great Symbol (*mahāliṅga*)
  - Brightness Symbol (*prasādaliṅga*)
- Life Symbol (*prāṇaliṅga*)
  - Motion Symbol (*caraliṅga*)
  - Śiva Symbol (*śivaliṅga*)
- Desired Symbol (*iṣṭaliṅga*)
  - Teacher Symbol (*guruliṅga*)
  - Observance Symbol (*ācāraliṅga*)

b. BODY (*aṅga*)
- Union Body (*yogāṅga, prājña*)
  - Oneness Repository (*aikyasthala*)
  - Suppliant Repository (*śaraṇasthala*)
- Experience Body (*bhogāṅga, taijasa*)
  - Breath Repository (*prāṇasthala*)
  - Clearness Repository (*prasādisthala*)
- Renunciation Body (*tyāgāṅga, viśva*)
  - Great Master Repository (*māheśvarasthala*)
  - Devotee Repository (*bhaktasthala*)

c. POTENCY OR APTITUDE (*śakti, kalā*)
- Illumination (*prakāśana*)

Consciousness Energy: The "Totally Elevated-Above-Tranquillity" (*cicchakti, śāntyatītottarā*)
Supreme Energy: The "Elevated-Above-Tranquillity" (*parāśakti, śāntyatītā*)
Reflection (*vimarśana*)
Primordial Energy: "Tranquillity" (*ādiśakti, śānti*)
Volition Energy: "Knowledge" (*icchāśakti, vidyā*)
Manifestation (*ābhāsana*)
Knowledge Energy: "Stability" (*jñānaśakti, pratiṣṭhā*)
Activity Energy: "Quiescence" (*kriyāśakti*)

d. DEVOTION (*bhakti*)
Purity (*viśuddhabhakti*)
Even-flavored Devotion (*samarasabhakti*)
Joy Devotion (*ānandabhakti*)
Preparation (*vicārabhakti*)
Experience Devotion (*anubhavabhakti*)
Attention Devotion (*avadhānabhakti*)
Submission (*vidheyabhakti*)
Firm-Faith Devotion (*niṣṭhābhakti*)
Divine-Faith Devotion (*śraddhābhakti*)

Scheme 37

ENERGY-QUALIFIED NONDUALISM 2: EVOLUTION OF THE UNIVERSE

Cenna Basava

The following comprises the Ultimate Repository and the Emanations from it:

1. REPOSITORY OF THE SELF-SUBSISTENT ALL-VOID
2. REPOSITORY OF THE VOID SYMBOL (*śūnyaliṅgasthala*)
3. REPOSITORY OF THE IMPARTITE SYMBOL (*niṣkalaliṅgasthala*)
4. REPOSITORY OF THE GREAT SYMBOL (*mahāliṅgasthala, paraśiva*)

   Enwombs within itself the Five Pentads:

   a. The Five Energies (*śakti*): Supreme (*parā*), Primordial (*ādi*), Volition (*icchā*), Knowledge (*jñāna*) and Activity (*kriyā*).

   b. The Five Lusters (*sādākhya*): of Deity (*śiva*), Formlessness (*amūrta*), Form (*mūrta*), Agent (*kartṛ*) and Action (*karma*).

   c. The Five States (*kalā*): The Elevated-Above-Tranquillity (*śāntyatīta*), Tranquillity (*śānti*), Knowledge (*vidyā*), Stability (*pratiṣṭhā*) and Cessation (*nivṛtti*).

   d. The Five Syllables of the Śaiva Mystic Incantation (*pañcākṣara*): NA-MAḤ ŚI-VĀ-YA! "Adoration to Śiva!"

   e. The Five Elements (*bhūta*): ether (*ākāśa*), air (*vāyu*), fire (*tejas*), water (*āp*) and earth (*prithivī*).

   Gives rise to Consciousness, from which emerge the three syllables of the sacred monosyllable of Hinduism:

   a. A, or Sound (*nāda*)
   b. U, or Nucleus (*bindu*)
   c. M, or Function (*kalā*)

These combine to form the mystic monosyllable AUM, or OM.

5. BIFURCATION OF BIPOLARITY OF SYMBOL AND BODY, ENERGIZER AND ENERGY: There follow the emanations outlined in Scheme 36.

Scheme 38

ENERGICISM: CATEGORIES

Bhāskararāya, *Commentary on "Lalitasahasranāma,"* verse 8

Single Ultimate Category

THE BRAHMAN
- Impartite
- Partite
  - Ruler of Universe
    - Brahmā, creator
    - Viṣṇu, protector
    - Rudra, destroyer
  - Universe
    - Stable objects
    - Moving objects
      - Divine beings: the Golden Embryo, etc.
      - Men and animals

NOTES

INTRODUCTION

1. William Jones, quoted in W. Theodore de Bary, *Sources of Indian Tradition* (New York: Columbia University Press, 1958), vol. 2, p. 38.

PART ONE: AN OVERVIEW OF HINDU THEOLOGY

1. In his *The Story of Philosophy,* written in the full twentieth century, Will Durant leaps from Aristotle and Greek science in his second chapter, to Francis Bacon in his third.
2. Tertullian, *De prescriptionibus.* Migne, *Patrologia Latina,* vol. 2, cols. 22–23.
3. Victor Cousin, quoted by Henri de Lubac, *Rencontre du Boudhisme et de l'Occident* (Paris: Aubier, 1952), p. 156.
4. See Etienne Gilson, *The Christian Philosophy of St. Thomas Aquinas* (New York: Random House, 1956), pt. 1, chap. 4, "Haec sublimis veritas," pp. 84 sqq.
5. Galileo, letter written in 1638, quoted by Edward Conze in *Buddhism: Its Essence and Development,* 3rd ed. (New York: Harper, 1959), chap. 1, p. 49.
6. Conze, loc. cit.
7. Jean Jacques Rousseau, *Les rêveries du promeneur solitaire, cinquième promenade.*
8. *Bṛhadāraṇyaka Upaniṣad* 2:3:1.
9. Schubert M. Ogden, "The Reality of God," in Ewert H. Cousins, ed., *Process Theology* (New York: Newman Press, 1971), pp. 119–34, especially p. 124.
10. Friedrich Engels, *Dialectics of Nature,* trans. Clemens Dutt, Marxist Library, vol. 27 (New York, 1940), chap. 7, p. 241. "Nothing is eternal but eternally changing, eternally moving matter and the laws according to which it moves and changes" (chap. 1, p. 24).
11. R. C. Zaehner, ed., *The Concise Encyclopedia of Living Faiths,* (New York: Hawthorn Bks., 1959), pp. 406–12.
12. Ibid., p. 403.
13. *Ṛgveda* 1:164:46.
14. Nicolaus de Cusa, *De pace fidei* I, ed. R. Klibansky and H. Bascour, O.S.B. (London: Warburg Press, 1956), pp. 7 and 10.
15. Gerard Manley Hopkins, *The Wreck of the Deutschland,* v. 7.
16. Juan de la Cruz, *Llama de amor viva,* stanza 2, no. 5.

17. Jacques Bénigne Bossuet, *Instruction faite aux Religieuses sur le silence, troisieme point, Oeuvres oratoires de Bossuet,* ed. J. Lebarq (Paris: Hachette, 1914–1926), vol. 6, p. 378.

18. Augustine, *Epistola 102,* quaest. 2: "De tempore christianae religionis."

19. See *Gītā* 18:64.

20. *Kaṭha Upaniṣad* 2:23.

21. See School XXIII. (References to "Schools" are to headings listed by roman numerals in Contents.)

22. Madhva, *Viṣṇutattvanirṇaya,* quoted by B. N. K. Sharma, *Madhva's Teachings in his own Words* (Bombay: Bharatiya Vidya Bhavan, 1970), p. 73.

23. Bhāskara. See Selection 65. References to "Selections" are to Selected Writings listed by arabic numerals in Contents.

24. *"Contradictoria coincidunt in natura uniali."* Pico della Mirandola, *Conclusiones paradoxae numero LXXI,* n. 15.

25. Engels, op. cit., chap. 7, p. 183.

26. Concilium Lateranense IV, cap. 2. Denzinger, *Enchiridion Symbolorum,* ed. 31, n. 432.

27. Francisco Suárez, *Disputationes Metaphysicae,* disp. 30, sect. 10, n. 8.

28. Juan de la Cruz, *Subida del Monte Carmelo,* lib. 1, cap. 4, nn. 3–4.

29. Spinoza, *Ethica,* pars 1, prop. 15 et Scholium.

30. R. C. Zaehner, *Mysticism Sacred and Profane* (Oxford: Clarendon Press, 1957), pp. 159–60.

31. Jaya Tīrtha, *Nyāyasudhā,* quoted by B. N. K. Sharma, *Philosophy of Śrī Madhvacarya* (Bombay: Bharatiya Vidya Bhavan, 1962), p. 172.

32. Karl H. Potter, *Bibliography of Indian Philosophies* (Delhi: Motilal Banarsidass), 1970. I have derived most of my dates from Potter and from A. K. Warder, *Outline of Indian Philosophy,* also published by Motilal, in 1971.

33. Bādarāyaṇa, *Brahmasūtrāṇi* 1:1:19. Translated by S. Radhakrishnan in his *The Brahma Sūtra. The Philosophy of Spiritual Life* (New York: Harper, 1960), p. 26.

34. Longus, *Daphnis and Chloë,* bk. 2, nos. 33 and 35.

35. Bossuet, *Sermon sur l'unité de l'Église, premier point. Oeuvres oratoires,* vol. 6, p. 118.

PART TWO: SELECTED WRITINGS

THEOLOGIES OF DIFFERENCE

1. Thomas Merton, *New Seeds of Contemplation,* (London, 1962), pp. 5–6. Quoted by R. C. Zaehner, *Concordant Discord* (Oxford: Clarendon Press, 1970), pp. 100–1.

2. Francis Bacon, *De dignitate et augmentis scientiarum*, lib. 2, cap. 2.
3. Īśvara Kṛṣṇa, *Sāṅkhyakārikā*, ed. with commentary of Gauḍa Pāda and trans. T. G. Mainkar, 2nd ed. (Poona: Oriental Book Agency, 1972).
4. *Mahābhārata* 3:30:88.
5. *Hitopadeśa*, book 1, v. 180.
6. *Mahābhārata* 12:231:25 and 12:227:79.
7. Gauḍa Pāda, *Bhāṣya* on the *Sāṅkhyakārikā*, vv. 56–62, pp. 182–93. See n. 3 above.
8. Vācaspati Miśra, *Sāṅkhyatattvakaumudī*, ed. and trans. Ganganatha Jha, revised and re-edited by M. M. Patkar (Poona: Oriental Book Agency, 1965), pp. 2–6.
9. Vijñāna Bhikṣu, *Sāṅkhyapravacanabhāṣyam* on 6:1, ed. Ramshankar Bhattacharya (Varanasi [Benares]: Bharatiya Vidya Prakashan, 1966), p. 238.
10. *Bṛhadāraṇyaka Upaniṣad* 4:3:15.
11. Aniruddha, *Vṛtti* on the *Sankhya Sutras*, ed. Ramshankar Bhattacharya (Varanasi [Benares]: Pracyabharati Prakashan, 1964).
12. *Bṛhadāraṇyaka Upaniṣad* 4:4:19 and *Kaṭha Upaniṣad* 4:1.
13. *Chāndogya Upaniṣad* 8:15:1.
14. Ibid., 4:15:5–6 and 5:10:1.
15. "Kapila," *Sāṅkhyasūtrāṇi, adhyāya* 6, ed. and trans. J. R. Ballantyne in *The Sankhya Aphorisms of Kapila* (London, 1885), pp. 419–60.
16. Vyāsa, *Yogabhāṣya* on 1:21, in Rajaram Sastri Bodas, ed., *Pātañjalasūtrāṇi*, with Vyāsa's *Yogabhāṣya* and Vācaspati Miśra's *Tattvavaiśāradī*, Bombay Sanskrit and Prakrit Series, no. 46 (Bombay, 1887, 1892 and 1915). Both commentaries translated by Rama Prasad in *Sacred Books of the Hindus* 4 (1910) and 7–9 (1924).
17. Vācaspati Miśra, op. cit. on 1:38.
18. Patañjali, *Yogasūtrāṇi, adhyāya* 1. See n. 16 above.
19. Vyāsa, op. cit. on 1:1–4.
20. John Calvin, *Institutes of the Christian Religion*, bk. 1, chap. 7, sect. 2.
21. *Ṛgveda* 1:64:50 and 10:90:16.
22. Śabara, *Mīmāṁsāsūtrabhāṣyam* on 1:1:2, ed. with Prabhākara's *Bṛhati* and Śālika Nātha Miśra's *Ṛjuvimalapañcikā* by K. R. Sastri (Madras: University of Madras, 1934), pp. 20–41. Trans. Ganganatha Jha (Baroda: Oriental Institute, 1933).
23. Jaimini, *Mīmāṁsāsūtrāṇi* 7:1:9.
24. Kumārila Bhaṭṭa, *Tantravārttika, adhyāya* 2, *pāda* 1, *sūtra* 5, ed. Gangadhara Sastri, in Benares Sanskrit Series (Benares, 1903), pp. 365–70. Trans. Ganganatha Jha, *Bibliotheca Indica* 161 (1903–24).

25. This syllogism is given by Udayana himself in his proofs for the existence of God. See Selection 15, argument 6 (b).

26. Śālika Nātha Miśra, *Prakaraṇapañcikā, prakaraṇa* 2, ed. with Jayapuri Nārāyaṇa's *Nyāyasiddhi* by S. Sastri (Varanasi [Benares]: Kāśi Hindū Viśvavidyālaya, 1961), pp. 29–42.

27. Pārtha Sārathi Miśra, *Nyāyaratnamālā.* I have been unable to trace this sentence.

28. Pārtha Sārathi Miśra, *Śāstradīpikā,* commentary on Kumārila Bhaṭṭa's *Ślokavārttika,* ed. R. M. Sastri in *Pandit,* vol. 7 (1885), pp. 145–48. Trans. D. Venkataramiah in *Gaekwad Oriental Series,* vol. 89 (1940).

29. Praśasta Pāda, *Bhāṣya* on Kaṇāda's *Vaiśeṣikasūtrāṇi,* ed. Dhundiraj Sastri with Hindi commentary, in Kashi Sanskrit Series, no. 173 (Benares: Chowkhamba Sanskrit Series Office, 1966), pp. 29–34.

30. Vātsyāyana, *Bhāṣya* on Gautama's *Nyāyasūtrāṇi, adhyāya* 1, *āhnika* 1, *sūtra* 1, ed. Dhundiraj Sastri with Hindi commentary *Prakāśikā* in Kashi Sanskrit Series, no. 43 (Benares: Chowkhamba Sanskrit Series Office, 1960), pp. 1–6.

31. Uddyotakara, *Nyāyavārttika* on Vātsyāyana's *Bhāṣya* on 1:1:1, ed. V. Prasad in Chowkhamba Sanskrit Series (Benares, 1916), pp. 21–22. Trans. Ganganatha Jha in *Indian Thought,* vols. 4–11 (1912–19).

32. Two Brahmin ascetics, who had lived in the Himalayas for fifty years, went on a pilgrimage to the kingdom of Benares, and were looked after by a friend, Māṇḍavya, who built leaf huts for them in a cemetery. A thief, running away with stolen goods, and chased by the owner, flung the goods into one of the huts and escaped. Believing Māṇḍavya to have stolen them, the king had him impaled, and Dīpāyana (who seems to have been that great theologian of many aliases, Kṛṣṇa Dvaipāyana, or Vyāsa himself) kept him company, and his body was darkened with the spurts of Māṇḍavya's blood. Which is why he came to be called Kṛṣṇa, the "dark" or "black." The king may have been looking for a pretext to impale Māṇḍavya for his bold theories. See *The Jataka, or Stories of the Buddha's Former Births,* trans. under the editorship of E. B. Cowell, Cambridge: University Press, 1895–1907, vol. 4, story no. 444.

33. Udayana, *Ātmatattvaviveka, pariccheda* 2, *prakaraṇa* 4, ed. with Nārāyaṇa Ātreya's *Nārāyaṇī* by Dhundiraj Sastri in Chowkhamba Sanskrit Series (Benares, 1936), pp. 248–55.

34. *Gītā* 8:10.

35. Manu, *Manusmṛti,* chap. 12, v. 106.

36. Udayana, *Nyāyakusumāñjali, stabaka* 5, ed. with Haridāsa Nyāyālaṅkāra's *Vyākhyā* and trans. by E. B. Cowell and M. C. Nyāyaratna (Calcutta, 1864), pp. 48–51.

37. Suárez, *Disputationes Metaphysicae,* disp. 1, sect. 1, n. 5.

38. *Bṛhadāraṇyaka Upaniṣad* 2:5:18.
39. *Bhāgavata Purāṇa* 11:19:3.
40. *Taittirīya Āraṇyaka* 3:1:3.
41. *Kaṭha Upaniṣad* 2:22.
42. *Bhāgavata Purāṇa* 2:10:12.
43. *Ṛgveda* 10:112:9.
44. Unidentified citation.
45. *Bṛhadāraṇyaka Upaniṣad* 1:4:8.
46. *Bhāgavata Purāṇa* ?
47. *Bṛhadāraṇyaka Upaniṣad* 1:4:8.
48. *Taittirīya Upaniṣad* 2:1:1.
49. Padmanābha Tīrtha, *Sannyāyaratnāvalī,* quoted by Suzanne Siauve on p. 90 of work quoted in n. 62 below. Padmanābha (fl. 1318–24) is an early theologian of Dvaita Vedanta.
50. *Chāndogya Upaniṣad* 6:8:7.
51. The *Science of the Brahman,* or the *Brahmatarka,* is a lost work that Madhva also calls the *Science of Logic,* or *Tarkaśāstra.*
52. The *Science of the Gods,* or the *Devaśāstra,* is another lost work known to Madhva and Jaya Tīrtha.
53. *Taittirīya Āraṇyaka* 10:1:1.
54. *Mahābhārata* 12:382:35.
55. *Ṛgveda* 1:125:7; *Atharvaveda* 4:30:7.
56. *Ṛgveda* 1:164:36.
57. Ibid., 1:164:39.
58. Ibid.
59. *Taittirīya Āraṇyaka* 10:1:1; *Mahānārāyaṇa Upaniṣad* 1:3.
60. *Taittirīya Āraṇyaka* 1:1:1; *Mahānārāyaṇa Upaniṣad* 1:4.
61. *Taittirīya Āraṇyaka* 10:1:2; *Mahānārāyaṇa Upaniṣad* 1:6.
62. Madhva, *Anuvyākhyāna* on the *Brahma Sūtras* 1:1:1, ed. and trans. into French by Suzanne Siauve in *La voie vers la connaissance de Dieu selon l'Anuvyākhyāna de Madhva* (Pondichery: Institut Français d'Indologie, 1957), pp. 1–25. Copiously annotated and documented.
63. Bādarāyaṇa, op. cit. 2:1:30.
64. Probably a line from the *Bhāgavata Purāṇa.* Bhadrasena was one of Kṛṣṇa's brothers killed by king Kaṁsa.
65. Jaya Tīrtha, *Nyāyasudhā* on Madhva's *Anuvyākhyāna* on 3:2, *adhyāya* 10, ed. with Vidyādhīśa's *Vākyārthacandrikā* by R. G. Savanur (Dharwar, 1938?), vol. 3, pp. 120–22.
66. *Taittirīya Upaniṣad* 2:1.
67. *Bṛhadāraṇyaka Upaniṣad* 4:4:20.
68. *Kaṭha Upaniṣad* 4:14
69. Jaya Tīrtha, op. cit. on 1:2, vol. 2, pp. 19–23.
70. Ibid., on 2:1, *adhikaraṇa* 9, *adhyāya* 6, vol. 2, p. 219.
71. *Praśna Upaniṣad* 3:7.
72. *Kauśītakī Upaniṣad* 3:8.
73. Bādarāyaṇa, op. cit. 2:1:15–21.

74. *Gītā* 9:29.

75. Vyāsa Rāya's commentator says that this verse is from a book called the *Skandatātparya,* chap. 6.

76. *Gītā* 5:18.

77. Vācaspati Miśra, *Bhāmatī.* I have been unable to trace this passage.

78. Sudarśana Sūri, *Tattvaprakāśikā* ?

79. *Ṛgveda* 10:112:9.

80. The words "As a man . . . wooden doll" quoted by Vyāsa Rāya are from an unknown source; the rest are from the *Gītā* 18:61.

81. Bādarāyaṇa, op. cit. 2:1:28.

82. Ibid., 2:130.

83. *Śvetāśvatara Upaniṣad* 6:8.

84. Vyāsa Rāya, *Tātparyacandrikā* on Jaya Tīrtha's *Tattvaprakāśikā* on Madhva's *Brahmaśūtrabhāṣyam* on 2:1:35–37, ed. T. R. Krishnacharya (Bombay: Nirnaya Sagar Press, 1913), pp. 52–56.

85. Vādi Rāja, *Yuktimallikā, saurabha 1* (*Guṇasaurabha*), ed., with commentary by Surottama Tīrtha, by T. R. Krishnacharya (Bombay, 1903), vv. 8–11.

86. *Bṛhadāraṇyaka Upaniṣad* 4:4:19; *Kaṭha Upaniṣad* 4:11.

87. Vyāsa Rāmācārya, *Nyāyāmṛtataraṅgiṇī, pariccheda 1, dvitīyamithyātvavicāra,* ed. Anantakrishna Sastri in *Śrīnyāyāmṛtādvaitasiddhī Taraṅgiṇyādivyākhyopavyākhyāsaptakopete,* Calcutta Sanskrit Series, no. 9 (Calcutta: Metropolitan Printing and Publishing House, 1934), pp. 161–89.

88. *Taittirīya Upaniṣad* 2:4:1.

89. *Praśna Upaniṣad* 5:5.

90. *Kena Upaniṣad* 1:6.

91. Bādarāyaṇa, op. cit. 3:2:76.

92. *Bṛhadāraṇyaka Upaniṣad* 1:4:8.

93. *Kena Upaniṣad* 1:6.

94. *Bṛhadāraṇyaka Upaniṣad* 4:4:19.

95. Vanamāli Miśra, *Madhvamukhālaṅkāra, Īkṣatinyāyavarṇanam,* ed. N. Vardhekar in Prince of Wales Sarasvati Bhavana Texts, no. 68 (Benares, 1936), pp. 104–6.

96. Bhoja, *Tattvaprakāśa,* ed. with Śrī Kumāra's *Tātparyadīpikā,* Trivandrum Sanskrit Series, no. 68 (Trivandrum, 1920). Trans. E. P. Janvier in *Indian Antiquary* 54 (1925), pp. 151–56.

97. *Bṛhadāraṇyaka Upaniṣad* 3:9:28.

98. Ibid., 1:4:3. Śrī Kumāra's version of this passage does not correspond to the text of the standard version.

99. *Manusmṛti.* ch. 1, v. 32.

100. Śrī Kumāra, *Tātaryadīpikā* on Bhoja, op. cit., *pariccheda* 1, v. 3, pp. 13–16.

101. Aghora Śiva, *Tattvaprakāśikāvṛtti* on Bhoja, op. cit., 2:5

(or v. 25), ed. N. Krishnā Sastri in *Aṣṭaprakaraṇa* (Devakottai 1923–25), pp. 24–27.

THEOLOGIES OF IDENTITY OR NON-DIFFERENCE

1. Madeleine Biardeau, *La philosophie de Maṇḍana Miśra vue a partir de la Brahmasiddhi* (Paris: École Française d'Extrême Orient, 1969).

2. P. B. Grenet, *Les 24 thèses thomistes* (Paris: P. Tequi, 1962), p. 37.

3. The Gaṇeśa doctrine or the Gāṇapatya system was outlined by Nīlakaṇṭha in his commentary on the *Gaṇeśagītā,* a poem composed in imitation of the *Gītā*. Ed. and trans. Kiyoshi Yoroi in *Gaṇeśagītā,* The Hague: Mouton, 1968.

4. Gauḍa Pāda, *Kārikās* on the *Māṇḍukya Upaniṣad, prakaraṇa* 1, vv. 14–18. Ed. and trans. R. D. Karmarkar (Poona: Bhandarkar Oriental Research Institute, 1953).

5. *Bṛhadāraṇyaka Upaniṣad* 4:3:9–10.

6. Gauḍa Pāda, op. cit., *prakaraṇa* 2.

7. Ibid., *prakaraṇa* 4, vv. 1–30.

8. *Anugītā* (*Mahābhārata,* book 14), ch. 16, v. 12.

9. Ibid., ch. 19, v. 7.

10. Ibid., ch. 19, v. 1.

11. Ibid., ch. 43, v. 26.

12. *Gītā* 18:66.

13. Ibid., 5:10.

14. Ibid., 5:11.

15. Śaṅkara, *Bhagavadgītābhāṣyam, Upodghāta,* ed. G. S. Sadhale in *The Bhagavad-Gītā with Eleven Commentaries* (Bombay: Gujarat Printing Press, 1935), pp. 2–5.

16. Śaṅkara, *Brahmasūtrabhāṣyam, Upodghāta,* ed. N. R. Acharya (Bombay: Nirnaya Sagar Press, 1948), pp. 1, 2 and 4.

17. *Chāndogya Upaniṣad* 6:2:3–4.

18. *Bṛhadāraṇyaka Upaniṣad* 4:4:20.

19. *Kaṭha Upaniṣad* 2:18.

20. *Śvetāśvatara Upaniṣad* 6:19.

21. *Bṛhadāraṇyaka Upaniṣad* 3:7:3.

22. *Chāndogya Upaniṣad* 3:12:6.

23. *Ṛgveda* 6:47:18, quoted in *Bṛhadāraṇyaka Upaniṣad* 2:5:19.

24. Prakāśātman, *Pañcapādikāvivaraṇam* on Padmapāda's *Pañcapādikā* on Śaṅkara's *Brahmasūtrabhāṣyam,* on 1:1:2, ed., with seven other commentaries, by Anantakrishna Sastri in Calcutta Sanskrit Series, no. 1 (Calcutta, 1933), pp. 908–11.

25. *Bṛhadāraṇyaka Upaniṣad* 4:4:19 and *Kaṭha Upaniṣad* 4:11.

26. Śrī Harṣa, *Khaṇḍanakhaṇḍakhādya, pariccheda* 1, *anuvāda* 9 (*Bhedakhaṇḍanānuvāda*), ed. and trans. into Hindi by C. Sukula (Benares: Acyuta Grantha Mala, Samvat 2018 [A.D. 1940]),

pp. 66–69. English translation in *Indian Thought*, vols. 1–7 (1909–17).

27. *Yogavāsiṣṭha, Upaśamaprakaraṇam* 13.

28. Ibid., *Utpattiprakaraṇam* 3–4.

29. *Bṛhadāraṇyaka Upaniṣad* 4:5:15.

30. *Taittirīya Upaniṣad* 2:6:1.

31. *Kaṭha Upaniṣad* 2:5:15.

32. Prakāśānanda, *Vedāntasiddhāntamuktāvalī*, sections 13 and 14, ed. and trans. A. Venis (Benares, 1922), pp. 51–59.

33. This view is said to be Vācaspati Miśra's in his *Tātparyaṭīkā* on Uddyotakara's *Nyāyavārttika*.

34. Madhusūdana Sarasvatī, *Advaitasiddhi, pariccheda* 1, *prathamamithyātvavicāra,* pp. 91–155. For reference see n. 87 in previous section. Translated by Ganganatha Jha in *Indian Thought,* vols. 6–9 (1916–19).

THEOLOGIES OF DIFFERENCE-IN-IDENTITY

1. Mark of Ephesus, quoted by M. Jugie in "Palamas," *Dictionnaire de théologie catholique,* vol. 11, cols. 1759 sqq.

2. Basil of Caesarea, *Letter 234,* in Yves Courtonne, ed., *Saint Basile, Lettres* (Paris: Société d'Édition "Les Belles Lettres," 1957–66), vol. 3, p. 42.

3. Yāska, *Niruktam* 1:2.

4. Pāṇini, *Aṣṭādhyāyī* 1:1:68.

5. *Ṛgveda* 4:58:3.

6. Bhartṛ Hari, *Vākyapadīya, Brahmakāṇḍa,* ed. and trans. into French by Madeleine Biardeau, with Hari Vṛṣabha's *Vṛtti* (Paris: E. de Boccard, 1964).

7. Hari Vṛṣabha, *Vṛtti* on *Vākyapadīya, Brahmakāṇḍa,* v. 9, in Biardeau, op. cit., p. 40.

8. Damodar Vishnu Garge shows that Jaimini, contemporary of Bādarāyaṇa (perhaps his student), must have belonged to the Śrautasūtra period (c. 500 B.C.), in his *Citations in Śabara Bhāṣya* (Poona: Deccan College Postgraduate and Research Institute: 1952).

9. *Gītā* 13:5.

10. *Bṛhadāraṇyaka Upaniṣad* 4:5.

11. *Taittirīya Upaniṣad* 3:1:1.

12. *Bṛhadāraṇyaka Upaniṣad* 3:9:26.

13. Ibid., 1:6:1.

14. *Kaṭha Upaniṣad* 1:2:15.

15. *Chāndogya Upaniṣad* 6:4:13.

16. *Bṛhadāraṇyaka Upaniṣad* 4:4:15.

17. *Muṇḍaka Upaniṣad* 2:2:5.

18. *Chāndogya Upaniṣad* 6:8:1.

19. *Bṛhadāraṇyaka Upaniṣad* 5:1:1.

20. *Taittirīya Upaniṣad* 2:8:1.

21. Ibid., 2:7.
22. Ibid.
23. Ibid., 2:6.
24. Ibid., 2:1.
25. *Chāndogya Upaniṣad* 1:6:6–7.
26. *Bṛhadāraṇyaka Upaniṣad* 3:7:9.
27. *Chāndogya Upaniṣad* 1:9:1.
28. Ibid., 1:11:4–5.
29. *Ṛgveda* 10:90:3.
30. *Chāndogya Upaniṣad* 3:12:1, 5, 6; 3:13:7.
31. *Kauśītakī Upaniṣad* 3:1:1, 2, 8.
32. *Bṛhadāraṇyaka Upaniṣad* 1:4:10.
33. Bādarāyaṇa, op. cit. 1:1:1–31. I have mostly followed Madhva's interpretation in classifying the names of the Brahman and in translating aphorisms 1–11. I have translated the others according to what I think is a consensus between the Difference-in-Identity schools. I have derived Madhva's interpretation from the following sources: B. N. K. Sharma, *The Brahmasūtras and Their Principal Commentaries (A Critical Exposition)*, vols. 1 and 2 (Bombay: Bharatiya Vidya Bhavan, 1971 and 1974); R. S. Panchamukhi, ed., *Brahmasūtranyāyasaṅgrahādi Prabandhaṣāṭkam* (Mantralaya, Andhra Pradesh: Śrī Rāghavendrasvāmī Vrindavanam Office, 1968); and Rāghavendratīrtha, *Tantradīpikā,* also edited by Panchamukhi (Dharwar: Karnatak Historical Research Society, 1964).
34. *Chāndogya Upaniṣad* 3:14:1.
35. Ibid., 7:26:2.
36. Ibid., 6:1:4.
37. Ibid., 1:6:6.
38. *Muṇḍaka Upaniṣad* 3:1:8.
39. *Bṛhadāraṇyaka Upaniṣad* 2:3:6.
40. *Śvetāśvatara Upaniṣad* 3:8.
41. *Bṛhadāraṇyaka Upaniṣad* 3:8:9.
42. *Chāndogya Upaniṣad* 3:1.
43. The fragments of Ṭaṅka, Dramiḍa and Bodhāyana are all taken from J. A. B. van Buitenen's edition of Rāmānuja's *Vedārthasaṅgraha* (Poona, 1956), pp. 302–8, where they have all been translated by the editor.
44. *Bṛhadāraṇyaka Upaniṣad* 2:3:6.
45. Ibid.
46. Ibid., 5:10:1.
47. Ibid., 4:3:23.
48. Ibid., 4:2:4.
49. Bhartṛ Prapañca, fragments from his *Commentary on the "Bṛhadāraṇyaka Upaniṣad"* in M. Hiriyanna, "Fragments of Bhartṛ-Prapañca," *Proceedings and Transactions of the Third (All India) Oriental Conference* (Madras, 1925), pp. 439–50.
50. *Bṛhadāraṇyaka Upaniṣad* 2:3:6.

51. Dionysius, *On Mystical Theology,* sect. 2, ed. with French translation by J. Vanneste, *Le mystère de Dieu* (Desclée de Brouwer, 1959), p. 228.
52. *Chāndogya Upaniṣad* 6:2:1.
53. Ibid., 6:12:2.
54. Ibid., 6:2:1–2.
55. Bhāskara, *Brahmasūtrabhāṣyam* on 2:1:18, ed. Vindhyesvari Prasad, Chowkhamba Sanskrit Series, no. 185, fasc. 2 (Benares, 1915 ff.), pp. 101–3.
56. *Bṛhadāraṇyaka Upaniṣad* 2:3:6.
57. Ibid., 2:1:20. *Maitrī Upaniṣad* 6:32.
58. Bhāskara is referring to Śaṅkara's *Brahmasūtrabhāṣyam* on 3:2:22.
59. *Taittirīya Upaniṣad* 2:6:1.
60. Bhāskara, op. cit. on 3:2:23, pp. 168–69.
61. *Bṛhadāraṇyaka Upaniṣad* 2:4:5 and 4:5:6.
62. Sureśvara, *Bṛhadāraṇyakabhāṣyavāttikam,* v. 1083.
63. *Gītā* 3:39.
64. *Bṛhadāraṇyaka Upaniṣad* 4:3:22.
65. This *śruti* cannot be traced to any of the *śruti* texts I am acquainted with.
66. *Bṛhadāraṇyaka Upaniṣad* 4:3:7.
67. Ibid., 4:3:16.
68. *Gītā* 3:27.
69. *Viṣṇu Purāṇa* 6:7:22.
70. *Gītā* 16:8.
71. *Mahābhārata, Śānti Parva* 316:2.
72. Ibid., 301:101.
73. Ibid., 210:22.
74. Bādarāyaṇa, op. cit. 2:1:1.
75. Ibid., 2:2:1.
76. Patañjali, *Yogasūtrāṇi* 1:26.
77. *Viṣṇu Purāṇa* 1:17:83.
78. *Padma Purāṇa* 6:263 or 266–75.
79. Vijñāna Bhikṣu, *Vijñānāmṛtabhāṣyam* on *Brahma Sūtras* 2:3:43–50, ed. M. S. Adkar, Chowkhamba Sanskrit Series, no. 8 (Benares, 1901).
80. Ibid., on 2:3:43.
81. Bādarāyaṇa, op. cit., 4:1:3.
82. Vijñāna Bhikṣu, op. cit., on 2:3:46.
83. Vijñāna Bhikṣu, *Sāṅkhyapravacanabhāṣyam,* Introduction, pp. 2–7.
84. "Kapila," *Sāṅkhyasūtrāṇi* 5:66.
85. *Chāndogya Upaniṣad* 6:9:1–2.
86. *Taittirīya Upaniṣad* 3:6:6.
87. *Bṛhadāraṇyaka Upaniṣad* 3:9:28.
88. *Taittirīya Upaniṣad* 3:6:1.
89. *Manusmṛti,* chap. 12, v. 106.

90. *Taittirīya Upaniṣad* 2:4:1.
91. Ibid., 2:8:1.
92. Ibid., 2:5:1.
93. I cannot trace this *śruti* to any of the known *śruti* texts.
94. *Kaṭha Upaniṣad* 3:12.
95. "Kapila," op. cit., 5:67 and 68.
96. *Śruti* untraceable.
97. Bādarāyaṇa, op. cit., 3:3:11.
98. *Chāndogya Upaniṣad* 7:1:3.
99. Ibid., 8:12:1.
100. *Kaṭha Upaniṣad* 2:12.
101. Īśvara Kṛṣṇa, *Sāṅkhyakārikā,* v. 17.
102. *Gītā* 13:20.
103. Vijñāna Bhikṣu, *Vijñānāmṛtabhāṣyam* on 1:1:2.
104. *Gītā* 18:64.
105. Yāmuna, *Āgamaprāmāṇyam,* ed. and trans. J. A. B. van Buitenen, *Yāmuna's Āgama Prāmāṇyam on the Validity of Pāñcarātra,* Ramanuja Research Society, nos. 89, 112 and 115, (Madras, 1971), on pp. 47, 59 and 60–61, respectively.
106. Rāmānuja, *Śrībhāṣyam* on 1:4:27.
107. *Viṣṇu Purāṇa,* bk. 5, chap. 5.
108. Ibid., chap. 6.
109. Ibid.
110. Ibid., chap. 14.
111. Ibid., chap. 9.
112. Ibid., chap. 8.
113. Ibid., chap. 7.
114. Ibid., chap. 16.
115. Ibid., chap. 20.
116. Ibid.
117. Ibid., chaps. 17–19.
118. Ibid., chap. 19.
119. Rāmānuja, *Gītābhāṣyam, Upodghāta,* in Sadhale, *The Bhāgāvād-Gitā with Eleven Commentaries,* pp. 5–6. Abbreviated translation of the *Gītābhāṣyam* by J. A. B. van Buitenen in *Rāmānuja on the Bhagavadgītā* s'-Gravenhage: De Ned. boeken steendrukkerij V/H. H. L. Smits, 1953.
120. Sudarśana Sūri, *Śrutaprakāśikā* on Rāmānuja's *Śrībhāṣyam,* Introduction, in T. Srinivasa Sarma, ed. *Śrībhāṣyam of Śrībhagavad-Rāmānujamuni with the commentary Śrutaprakāśikā . . . Chatussūtri Portion* (Bombay: Nirnaya Sagar Press, 1916), pp. 1–2.
121. *Chāndogya Upaniṣad* 3:14:2.
122. Yāska, *Niruktam* 1:2.
123. The five celestial elements are said to be *parameṣṭin, pumān, viśva, nivṛtti* and *sarva.*
124. Lokācārya, *Arthapañcakam,* ed. and trans. into Hindi and English by Svāmī Srikṛṣṇācārya and Surendranātha Śāstri (Delhi:

Bharati Research Institute; and Indore: Sri Niwas Visistadvaita Grantha Mala, 1972).

125. See Selection 12 for Gautama's categories.

126. Vedānta Deśika, *Nyāyapariśuddhi,* with Śrī Nivāsa's commentary *Nyayasāra, adhyāya* 1 (*pratyakṣādhyāya*), *āhnika* 1, Chowkhamba Sanskrit Series, no. 358 (Benares, 1927).

127. Nimbārka, *Daśaślokī,* ed. Gopa Sastri Nene with Giridhara Prapanna's *Laghumañjuṣa,* Chowkhamba Sanskrit Series, no. 358 (Benares, 1927).

128. *Kena Upaniṣad* 1:5.

129. *Bṛhadāraṇyaka Upaniṣad* 4:3:32.

130. *Chāndogya Upaniṣad* 1:6:6.

131. Śrī Nivāsa, *Vedāntakaustubha* on 1:1:4, in Nityasvarūpa Brahmacarin, ed., Nimbārka, *Vedāntapārijātasaurabha* on *Brahmasūtras,* with Keśava Kāśmīrin's *Vedāntakaustubhaprabhā* and Śrī Nivāsa's *Vedāntakaustubha* (Vṛndāvana, 1904), pp. 67–68.

132. *Bṛhadāraṇyaka Upaniṣad* 2:4:12.

133. *Chāndogya Upaniṣad* 8:3:4.

134. *Muṇḍaka Upaniṣad* 3:1:3.

135. *Chāndogya Upaniṣad* 7:26:2.

136. Ibid., 7:25:2.

137. *Muṇḍaka Upaniṣad* 3:2:8.

138. *Kaṭha Upaniṣad* 1:4:15.

139. *Muṇḍaka Upaniṣad* 3:2:9.

140. *Taittirīya Upaniṣad* 2:1.

141. *Gītā* 1:54.

142. Ibid., 11:7.

143. Ibid., 11:15.

144. *Chāndogya Upaniṣad* 6:4:13.

145. *Gītā* 7:5.

146. Keśava Kāśmīrin, *Vedāntapārijātasaurabha* on 4:4:7, in Vṛndāvana ed. (see n. 131), pp. 1319–21.

147. Malebranche, *Traité de la Nature et de la Grâce,* partie 2, discours 2, article XXXIII.

148. Ibid., article XXXIV.

149. *Gītā* 13:13.

150. *Chāndogya Upaniṣad* 6:8:7.

151. *Muṇḍaka Upaniṣad* 1:1:6.

152. *Śvetāśvatara Upaniṣad* 4:6.

153. *Kaṭha Upaniṣad* 3:1.

154. *Gītā* 15:7.

155. Ibid., 15:10.

156. *Chāndogya Upaniṣad* 6:8:7.

157. Said to be in *Bhāgavata Purāṇa* 10:82.

158. *Īśa Upaniṣad,* v. 11.

159. *Chāndogya Upaniṣad* 6:1:4.

160. Bādarāyaṇa, op. cit., 2:1:14.

161. *Gītā* 16:18.

162. Vallabha, *Tattvārthadīpanibandha, prakaraṇa* 1 (*Śāstrārthaprakaraṇam*), ed. with author's *Prakāśa* and other commentaries, and with translation of Vallabha's verses by Harishankar Onkarji Shastri (Bombay: The Trustees of Sheth Narayandas and Jethanand Asanmal Charity Trust, 1943).

163. Mammaṭa, *Kāvyaprakāśa, ullāsa* 4, v. 28

164. *Taittirīya Upaniṣad* 2:6:1.

165. Jagannātha Paṇḍitarāja, *Rasagaṅgādhara, ānana* 1, ed. Pandit Durgaprasad and W. L. S. Pansikar, 4th ed. (Bombay: Nirnaya Sagar Press, 1930), pp. 21–23.

166. *Gītā* 16:20.

167. Ibid., 7:14.

168. Ibid., 9:12.

169. *Bhāgavata Purāṇa* 10:1:4.

170. Jayadeva, *Gītagovinda, sarga* 3, v. 1.

171. Hari Rāya, *Brahmavāda,* ed. and trans. into Hindi by Pandit Harisankar Sastri in *The Brahmavādasaṅgraha and Śuddhādvaitapariṣkāra,* Kashi Sanskrit Series, no. 61 (Benares, 1928), pp. 21–28.

172. *Bhāgavata Purāṇa* 7:1:29–30.

173. Ibid., 10:87:23.

174. Rūpa Gosvāmī, *Bhaktirasāmṛtasindhu, kallola* 2, vv. 270–309, in Bon Maharaj, ed. and trans., *Śri Rūpa Gosvāmī's Bhakti-Rasāmrta-Sindhu,* vol. 1 (Vrindavan: Institute of Oriental Philosophy, 1965), pp. 270–326.

175. Jīva Gosvāmī, *Śrīkṛṣṇasandarbha,* sect. 182, in Shyamlal Gosvami, ed., *Ṣatsandarbhoparanāma* (Calcutta: Arya Mission Press, 1890), pp. 435–37.

176. *Bhāgavata Purāṇa* 10:3:44.

177. *Gītā* 11.8.

178. *Bhāgavata Purāṇa* 10:6.

179. Ibid., 10:7.

180. Ibid., 10:9.

181. Ibid., 10:13–14.

182. Said to be in ibid., 10.

183. *Gītā* 11:41.

184. Said to be in *Bhāgavata Purāṇa* 10.

185. Ibid., 10:35:21.

186. The river Sarasvatī, once flowing between the rivers Jumna and Indus, started to dry, apparently in the first centuries of the Christian era. But Hindu mythology does not believe it to have disappeared, but only to have sunk underground—to reappear at the confluence of the Ganges and Jumna at Prayāga (Allahabad), which is thus a confluence of three rivers, and so known as the Three Braids (*Triveṇi*).

187. *Ṛgveda* 10:90:1.

188. *Gopālapūrvatāpinī Upaniṣad,* v. 8.
189. Said to be in the *Bhāgavata Purāṇa.*
190. Baladeva Vidyābhūṣaṇa, *Siddhāntaratna, pāda* 2, ed. Gopinath Kaviraj, in Prince of Wales Sarasvati Bhavana Texts, no. 10, part 1 (Benares, 1924), pp. 65–69.
191. Kṛṣṇamiśra, *Prabodhacandrodaya,* act 3, v. 16.
192. Lakulīśa, *Pāśupatasūtrāṇi, adhyāya* 1, in Anantakrishna Sastri, ed., *Pāśupata Sūtra* with *Pañcārthabhāṣya* of Kauṇḍinya, Trivandrum Sanskrit Series, no. 143 (Trivandrum, 1940). Translation by H. Chakaborti (Calcutta: Academic Publishers, 1970).
193. Lakulīśa, op. cit., *adhyāya* 4.
194. *Atharvaśiras Upaniṣad,* no. 67.
195. Kauṇḍinya, *Pañcārthabhāṣyam.* Selection 88 is a commentary on Lakulīśa, op. cit., *adhyāya* 1, *sūtra* 2; Selection 89, on 1:9; Selection 90, on 1:22; Selections 91 and 92, on 2:5; Selection 93, on 2:12; Selection 94, on 3:5, 6, 10, 11, 12; Selection 95, on 3:15; Selection 96, on 5:8; and Selection 97, on 5:18.
196. Dante, *Paradiso* 33:85–90.
197. St. Paul, *Philippians* 2:5–7.
198. Bossuet, *Carême des Minimes. Pour la fête de l'Annonciation, premier point, Oeuvres oratoires,* vol. 3, p. 436.
199. Suárez, *De Deo Uno,* lib. 2, cap. 29, n. 13.
200. Vasu Gupta, *Śivasūtrāṇi,* ed. with Kṣema Rāja's *Vimarṣini* by J. C. Chatterji in Kashmir Series of Texts and Studies, no. 1 (Srinagar, 1911). Translated in *Indian Thought,* vols. 3 and 4.
201. Somānanda, *Śivadṛṣṭi, āhnika* 1, ed. M. S. Kaul, with Utpala's *Vṛtti,* in Kashmir Series of Texts and Studies, no. 54 (1934), pp. 1–35. Translated by Raniero Gnoli in *East and West* 8 (1957).
202. Abhinava Gupta, *Mālinīvijayavārttika,* 1, vv. 620b–630, ed. Madhusudan Kaul Shastri, Kashmir Series of Texts and Studies, no. 32 (Srinagar, 1921). Translated into Italian by Raniero Gnoli, *Essenza dei Tantra* (Turin: Boringhieri, reprint 1968), pp. 41–42.
203. Somānanda, op. cit., *āhnika* 5, v. 9.
204. *Parātṛṁśikā,* v. 29b.
205. Ibid., vv. 24 sqq.
206. Ibid., v. 35.
207. *Vijñānabhairava,* v. 70.
208. Ibid., v. 69.
209. *Gītā* 14:3.
210. Abhinava Gupta, *Parātṛṁśikāvivaraṇa* on v. 1, ed. Mukunda Rama Sastri in Kashmir Series of Texts and Studies, no. 18 (1918), pp. 45–52. Translated into Italian by Raniero Gnoli, op. cit., pp. 321–26.
211. Abhinava Gupta, *Tantrasāra, āhnikas* 1–3, ed. Mukunda Rama Sastri in Kashmir Series of Texts and Studies, no. 17

(1918), pp. 1–19. There is an excellent translation of the whole work by Raniero Gnoli in op. cit., which I have consulted with great profit.

212. Kṣema Rāja, *Spandanirṇaya,* commentary on Vasu Gupta's *Spandakārikās,* v. 1, ed. M. S. Kaul in Kashmir Series of Texts and Studies, no. 42 (1925), pp. 3 and 4. Has English translation.

213. Verse cited by Jayaratha in his commentary on Abhinava Gupta's *Tantrāloka, āhnika* 2, v. 29. Edited by M. R. Sastri and M. S. Kaul in *Kashmir Series of Texts and Studies,* 12 vols. Srinagar 1918–38.

214. Maheśvarānanda, *Mahārthamañjarī,* ed. and trans. into French by Lilian Silburn (Paris: Publications de l'Institut de Civilisation Indienne, 1968).

215. *Kaṭha Upaniṣad* 2:25.

216. *Atharvaśiras Upaniṣad,* no. 3.

217. *Ṛgveda* 8:3:16.

218. *Śvetāśvatara Upaniṣad* 4:18.

219. *Manusmṛti* 1:5.

220. *Śvetāśvatara Upaniṣad* 4:10.

221. Citation unidentified.

222. *Kaivalya Upaniṣad,* v. 7.

223. *Taittirīya Upaniṣad* 2:6. This and the following two texts have been translated in the present tense to accord with the text in which they are quoted.

224. Ibid.

225. Ibid.

226. Ibid.

227. Śrī Kaṇṭha, *Brahmasūtrabhāṣyam* on 1:2:9, ed. H. Halasyanatha Sastri, *The Brahma-Sūtra Bhāṣya of Śrīkaṇṭhāchārya with the commentary Śivārkamaṇi Dīpikā by the famous Appaya Dīkṣita,* 2 vols. (Bombay: Nirnaya Sagar Press, 1908), vol. 1, pp. 335–46. Translated by Roma Chaudhuri (Calcutta, 1959).

228. *Chāndogya Upaniṣad* 6:14:2.

229. *Kaivalya Upaniṣad,* v. 5.

230. *Muṇḍaka Upaniṣad* 1:2:12.

231. Śrī Pati, *Śrikarabhāṣyam* on 3:2:5, ed. S. Hayavadana Rao (Bangalore, 1936), vol. 2, pp. 315–16.

232. *Chāndogya Upaniṣad* 6:8:7.

233. Māyi Deva, *Śivānubhavasūtram, adhikaraṇas* 2 (*Sthalanirdeśa*) and 3 (*Liṅgasthalanirūpaṇa*), in N. P. S. Mahāntasvāmigalu and M. Mahāsvāmigalu, eds., *Māyideva Śivānubhavasūtram Kannaḍa Bhāvārthabodhinīṭīkāsahitam* (Bellary, 1969), pp. 16–45. In Kannaḍa script.

234. António Vieira, *Sermão da Glória de Maria Mãe de Deus em dia da sua Gloriosa Assunção,* sec. V, in Padre Gonçalo Alves, ed., *Obras completas do Padre António Vieira. Sermões* (Lisbon, 1959), tomo 9, p. 443.

235. *Maitrāyaṇī Upaniṣad* 5:2.

236. Nīlakaṇṭha, *Saptaśatyaṅgaṣaṭkavyākhyānam,* a commentary on the *Devīmāhātmya* section of the *Mārkāṇḍeya Purāṇa;* ms. in Royal Asiatic Society of Bengal (see *Descriptive Catalogue of Sanskrit MSS., Royal Asiatic Society,* vol. VIII, nos. 6409–10).

INDEX

Abhinava Gupta, 24, 37, 40, 42
  Nondualism, 187
  Pure Nondualism, 317, 329, 330
  Triadism, 167, 358, 360, 368–78, 496–99
Absolute, the
  Indivisible Nondualism, 268, 276–81
  Innate Difference-in-Identity, 307, 308
  Joy, 276–81
  Nondualism, 187
  Pure Nondualism, 318
  Sonic Absolutism, 223, 224
Acintyabhedābheda. *See* Ineffable Difference-in-Identity
Action
  Nondualism 196–98, 473
  Śaiva Nondualism, 393, 394
  Śaiva Orthodoxy, 167, 170, 470
  Triadism, 375, 382, 384
Activist (Monkey) School, 284
Advaita schools. *See* Nondualism
Āgamas, the, 41
Agglomerative identity (*samudāyaikyam*), 139–40
Aghamarṣaṇa, 446–47
Aghora Śiva, 167, 168, 179–82
Aguirre, José Saenz de, 425
Ājīvikas (Determinism), 105
All Void, 395, 396
Ancient Vedanta (*Purātana Vedānta*), 220, 239–59, 438–40, 475–76
  architectonic aspect, 240
  Bādarāyaṇa, 220, 239–46, 427, 439
  Bhartṛ Prapañca, 239–40, 252–59, 475–76
  Bhāskara, 240
  Bodhāyana, 240, 251
  Brahman, 240–47, 251, 253, 258–59, 475
    equivalent names, 242–46
  categories, 475–76
  Creation, 240, 243, 475
  Destruction, 240
  Dramiḍa, 239, 248–50
  Faculties, 248
  the Gāyatrī, 244, 245
  Gītā, 239
  God, 241, 248–50
    Body of, 248–49
    Compassion of, 249–50
    Omnipotence of, 250
    Power of, 249–50
  Ignorance, 253–55
  Infinity, 243
  Innate Difference-in-Identity and, 306
  Joy, 242–43
  Knowledge, 240–43, 251, 254–57
  Lamp of, 426–27
  Liberation, 250, 258–59
  Matter, 243
  Nondualism and, 259
  norms, 240, 241
  OM, 241

Qualified Nondualism and, 283
Rāmānuja, 240
Reality, 241, 243, 475
Revelation, 239–43, 248–49
Ritual, 247–48
Sacrifice, 247–48
Sankhya and, 243
the Self, 240–44, 252–59, 475
attainment of, 247–48
Soul, 241–44, 253, 258, 475, 476
Ṭaṅka, 239, 247–49
Truth, 252–53
Wheel of systems, 420, 422
Word, 241
Aniruddha, 55, 71–74
Anselm of Canterbury, 425
Anugītā, 198
Aphorisms on the Brahman or *Brahmasūtras* (Bādarāyaṇa), 36, 125–26, 134–35, 149, 151, 153, 186, 239–46, 439
Apophatic (negation) theology, 260, 265–67
Apparitionalism (*Ābhāsavāda*), 189
Lamp of the Vedanta, 426–27
Wheel of systems, 420–21
Aquinas, St. Thomas, 24, 417, 425
Nondualism and, 188
Architecture, 34–37, 417
Ardha Tryambaka, 435
Aristotelian syllogism, 451
Aristotle, 24
Arjuna, 197, 198, 312–13, 343, 388
Asaṅga, 26, 28, 419
Āśmarathya, 306
Asuri, 63, 446, 448
Atharva, 41, 225, 402
Atharvaśikhā, 392
Atharvaśiras Upaniṣad, 390
Atheism, 271
Atomism (*Vaiśesika darśana*), 51, 105–7, 462–63
Ājīvikas, 105
atoms, 105–7
Brahmā, 106, 107
Buddhism and, 105
categories, 462–63
Conditioned Difference-in-Identity and, 263
Creation, 105–7
Destruction, 105–7
God, 105–7
Indivisible Nondualism and, 269–72, 274
Kanāda, 105
karma, 106, 107
Knowledge, 105, 107
Logicism and, 105, 114, 115
Methodizing Mind, 105
Newton, 105
Nondualism and, 194, 199
Praśasta Pāda, 105–7, 462–63
Reality, 105
Soul, 106
Triadism and, 366, 367
Trident Cluster, 434–35
Udayana, 105
Uddālaka, 105
the Universe, 105–7
Wheel of systems, 420–21
Atoms (*anu, paramāṇu*)

Atomism, 105–7
Logicism, 116–18
Attributes (*guṇa*)
Dualist Vedanta, 123
Energy-Qualified Nondualism, 398
Indivisible Nondualism, 270–71
Innate Difference-in-Identity, 307, 309, 310, 486
Nondualism, 199–200, 207–8, 216
Pure Nondualism, 324, 325
Auḍulomi, 306
Augustine, Saint, 33
Aupādhikabhedābheda. See Conditioned Difference-in-Identity
Avibhāgādvaita. See Indivisible Nondualism

Bacon, Francis, 55
Bacon, John, 425
Bādarāyaṇa, 36, 44–45, 84
Ancient Vedanta, 220, 239–46, 427, 439
Conditioned Difference-in-Identity, 261, 264–66
Dualist Vedanta, 122, 125–26, 134–37, 147, 149, 151, 153, 155
Energy-Qualified Nondualism, 396
Indivisible Nondualism, 273, 279
Innate Difference-in-Identity, 306, 308, 310
Madhva and, 186
Nondualism, 186
Pure Nondualism, 318, 325–27
Qualified Nondualism, 283, 291
Śaiva Nondualism, 389
theological synthesis of, 134–35
Baladeva Vidyābhuṣaṇa, 336, 342–45
Barth, Karl, 316–17
Basava, 221, 395, 428, 435
Basil of Caesarea, 219
Bergson, Henri, 359
Berkeley, George, 26
Bernard of Clairvaux, 425
Bernini, Giovanni Lorenzo, 417
Berti, Gianlorenzo, 425
Bhadrasena, 138
Bhāgavata Purāṇa, 54, 282, 306, 315, 318, 335–37
Bharadvāja, 446, 448
Bharata, 317, 358
Bhartṛ Hari, 220, 223–38
Bhartṛ Mitra, 85
Bhartṛ Prapañca, 239–40, 252–59, 475–76
Bhāsarvajña, 493–95
Bhāskara, 38, 220, 427
Ancient Vedanta, 240
Conditioned Difference-in-Identity, 260–67, 477
Bhāskararāya, 504
Bhaṭṭa Pradyumna, 365
Bhāvaviveka, 419
Bhoja Deva, 167–76, 179–82, 468–69
Bhṛgu, 277
Bibliography of Indian Philosophies (Potter), 44
Bodhāyana, 240, 251, 283
Bodhisattva, the, 33
Bonaventura, 425
Bond (*pāśa*)

Energy-Qualified Nondualism, 396, 397
Śaiva Orthodoxy, 166, 168–70, 468, 470
Bontempi, Gaudenzio, 425
Book of Phrases and Words, The, or *Vākyapadīya* (Bhartṛ Hari), 223–38
Bossuet, Jacques Bénigne, 33, 46, 358–59
Bouquet of Great Meaning, The, or *Mahārthamañjarī* (Maheśvarānanda), 381–88
Brahmā, 125, 286, 325, 394, 407
Atomism, 106, 107
Ineffable Difference-in-Identity, 340, 343, 345, 492
Innate Difference-in-Identity, 308, 313
Brahman, 41, 43
Ancient Vedanta, 240–47, 251, 253, 258–59, 475
equivalent names, 242–46
Conditioned Difference-in-Identity, 264–67, 477
Creation, 147
defects of, 151
Dualist Vedanta, 125–47
expressibility of, 162–65
Energicism, 407, 504
Energy-Qualified Nondualism, 396, 397, 399
Ignorance, 187
impartibility of, 205–6
Indivisible Nondualism, 272–81, 478
Ineffable Difference-in-Identity, 335, 337, 344, 345, 491, 492
infinite perfections of, 147
Innate Difference-in-Identity, 307–13, 486
Monist Pastoralism, 348
Nondualism, 186–89, 198, 201–6, 209, 212–16, 472, 473
Pure Nondualism, 318–26, 330, 331, 489
Qualified Nondualism, 287, 289, 484
Ritualism, 84
Śaiva Nondualism, 389–92
Śaiva Orthodoxy, 177
as self-illuminant, 127–28
Sonic Absolutism, 224–26, 235–38
Soul, 136–40
the Specifics, 141–43, 145
transmogrification, 201–6
Triadism, 367, 371, 372
Brahmaṇaspati, 446–47
Brahmāṇḍa Purāṇa, 337
Bṛhadāraṇyaka Upaniṣad, 178, 239
Bṛhaspati, 274, 419
Bruno, Giordano, 219
Buddha (Gautama), 27, 108, 110, 272, 274, 299–300, 312, 319, 435
Moral Law, 133
tranquil aspect of, 32
Buddhaghoṣa, 419
Buddhapālita, 419
Buddhism, 26–34, 43, 122
Atomism and, 105
Christianity and, 33–34
Idealism and, 84–85
Knowledge, 100–1
Logicism and, 108, 112–13
Lotus of, 418–19

Mahāyāna, 33–34
Nondualism and, 185, 189
Reality, 85
the Self, 27
tranquil aspect of, 32
trichotomous theology, 38
Yoga and, 77

Caitanya, 221, 335, 428, 432
Cajetan, 425
Cambridge School, 223
Canonicalism (*Sautrāntika*), 418–19
Carneades, 27
Cataphatic (affirmation) theology, 260
Causality
Conditioned Difference-in-Identity, 260–63
Dualist Vedanta, 122–25, 147–51, 154
Energy-Qualified Nondualism, 397
God, 147–51, 154, 167, 179–82
limitlessness of, 148–49
Innate Difference-in-Identity, 309
Logicism, 117, 118
Nondualism, 187
Pure Nondualism, 316, 324–30, 489, 490
Śaiva Nondualism, 392
Śaiva Orthodoxy, 167, 177, 179–82
Triadism, 377
the Veda on, 151
Cenna Basava, 395, 502–3
Chāndogya Upaniṣad (Uddālaka), 54, 239
Christianity, 38, 46, 85, 188–89, 316–17, 358, 359
bipolarity, 219–20
Buddhism and, 33–34
Cathedral of, 416–17
contemporary vogue in oriental faiths and, 30–34
dogmatic unity of, 42
dramatic aspect of, 32–33
feminine principle in, 406
God, 33–36, 123, 358–59, 406
Joy, 315
Light, 358
pluralism, 31–32
Rose Window (of Catholic theologies), 424–25
tranquil aspect of, 33
Triadism and, 358
yogic interiority, 29
Chu Hsi, 219
Clement of Alexandria, 34
Cogito (Vijñāna Bhikṣu), 70
Colonna, Egidio, 425
Commentary on the "Bhāgavata Purāṇa" (Vallabha), 333
Commentary on "Lalitasahasranāma" (Bhāskararāya), 504
Communism, 28–29
Conditioned Difference-in-Identity (*Aupādhikabhedābheda*), 220, 260–67, 477
apophatic (negation) theology, 260, 265–67
Atomism and, 263
Bādarāyaṇa, 261, 264–66
Bhāskara, 260–67, 477
Brahman, 264–67, 477
cataphatic (affirmation) theology, 260
categories, 477

Causality, 260–63
Consciousness, 265–67
existent effect (*satkāryavāda*), 264
Knowledge, 264, 477
Lamp of the Vedanta, 426–27
logic, 261–64
Nondualism and, 266
non-existent effect (*asatkāryavāda*), 263–64
Reality, 265
Revelation, 262–66
the Self, 265, 266
Soul, 265
Truth, 260, 266
Wheel of systems, 420, 422
Yājñavalkya, 260
Confucianism, 32
Confucius, 25
Connectional Meaning theory, 134
Consciousness
Conditioned Difference-in-Identity, 265–67
Dualist Vedanta, 138–39, 143
Energy-Qualified Nondualism, 398–404, 501
Nondualism, 189, 209, 221
Pure Nondualism, 316, 320–24, 329–31, 489
Śaiva Nondualism, 392
Śaiva Orthodoxy, 168, 176–78, 181
Sonic Absolutism, 227, 231
Triadism, 357, 361, 364–70, 374–79, 384, 385, 496–97
Yoga, 77
Copernicus, Nicolaus, 26
Cosmomorphic God (*viśvarūpabrahma*), 313–14
Creation (*sṛṣṭi*)
Ancient Vedanta, 240, 243, 475
Atomism, 105–7
Brahman, 147
Dualist Vedanta, 135, 147, 148
Indivisible Nondualism, 479
Innate Difference-in-Identity, 309, 313, 486, 487
Nondualism, 193, 196–97, 201–2, 473–74
Pure Nondualism, 320–26, 331
Śaiva Orthodoxy, 169, 471
Triadism, 363, 365, 498

Dante, 358
Daphnis and Chloë (Longus), 45–46
Darwin, Charles, 29, 54
Dasgupta S. N., 477
Democritus, 27, 105
Descartes, René, 23, 24, 425
Destruction
Ancient Vedanta, 240
Atomism, 105–7
Dualist Vedanta, 135
Logicism, 116
Nondualism, 193
Qualified Nondualism, 283
Sacrifice and, 94
Śaiva Nondualism, 389
Śaiva Orthodoxy, 468
Destruction-of-actions theory (*Karmavināśapakṣa*), 93–94

Determinism (Ājīvikas), 105, 346
Lotus of, 418–19
Devadatta, 88
Devotion (*bhakti*)
Energy-Qualified Nondualism, 400–1, 500, 501
Ineffable Difference-in-Identity, 336–39, 342–43
Injunctional (*vaidha bhakti*), 336, 338, 339
Passion-Sequent (*rāgānugā bhakti*), 338–39
Passion-Souled (*rāgātmikā bhakti*), 336–38
Liberation and, 167
Pure Nondualism, 319, 324, 331–33
Qualified Nondualism, 282, 283, 296
Śaiva Orthodoxy, 167–68, 470–71
Dhavamony, M., 470
Difference theologies. *See* Atomism; Dualist Vedanta; Logicism; Ritualism; Śaiva Orthodoxy; Sankhya; Yoga
Difference-in-Identity theologies. *See* Ancient Vedanta; Conditioned Difference-in-Identity; Energicism; Energy-Qualified Nondualism; Indivisible Nondualism; Ineffable Difference-in-Identity; Innate Difference-in-Identity; Monist Pastoralism; Pure Nondualism; Qualified Nondualism; Śaiva Nondualism; Sonic Absolutism; Triadism
Differentism (*Bhedavāda*), 52
Lamp of the Vedanta, 426–27
Lotus Pool, 430–31
Wheel of systems, 420–21
Dinnāga, 84, 105, 419
Diogenes, 346
Dionysius, 260
Dīrghatamas, 446–47
Discriminationism. *See* Sankhya
Divine Feminine, the
Energicism, 406, 407
Triadism, 357, 360
Divine Play (līlā), 317, 330–35
Divine Way (*śāmbhavopāya*), 359–61, 375–78, 386–87
Dramiḍa, 239, 248–50
Dualist Pastoralism (*Pāśupata darśana*), 51, 122, 346
categories, 166
Śaiva Orthodoxy and, 166
Trident Cluster, 434–35
Wheel of systems, 420–21
Dualist Vedanta (*Dvaita Vedānta*), 51, 52, 122–65, 220, 466–67
architectonic model in, 122
Attributes, 123
Bādarāyaṇa, 122, 125–26, 134–37, 147, 149, 151, 153, 155
Brahman, 125–47
expressibility of

(*brahmaṇaḥ vācyatvam*), 162–65
categories, 466–67
Causality, 122–25, 147–51, 154
Connectional Meaning theory, 134
Consciousness, 138–39, 143
Creation, 135, 147, 148
Destruction, 135
Egoism, 148
Essence, 123, 157
Evil, 122, 149–56
Expressed Relation theory, 133, 134
Falsehood, 157–61
the Fivefold Difference (*pra-pañca* or *pañcavidho bheda*), 467
the Gāyatrī, 125–26
Gītā, 151, 152
God, 122–32, 135–40, 147–56
Expressibility of (*brahmaṇaḥ vācyatvam*), 162–65
Happiness, 138, 150, 151
Identity, 122, 128, 138–40
nuances innate to, 141–47
Ignorance, 126–28, 137, 157
inevitability of, 157–61
Instinct, 148
Jaya Tīrtha, 123, 136–49, 164
karma, 149–51, 153
Knowledge, 122, 125–27, 130, 132, 160
Liberation, 126, 135
logic, 134
Logicism and, 123, 155–56
Lotus Pool, 430–31
Madhusūdana Sarasvatī, 124, 158–60
Madhva, 122–48, 153, 156, 466–67
Matter, 148
Moral Law, 133
Nāgārjuna, 124
Nondualism and, 123, 186, 213, 215
critique of, 126–29
norms, 122, 126–27, 131–33, 138, 161
OM, 125, 149
Padmanābha Tīrtha, 132
Pain, 150, 151
pragmatism, 127, 131, 157–59
Reality, 122, 123, 127, 134, 157–61
Revelation, 122, 125, 128–37, 149, 150, 154, 155, 161–65
Ritualism and, 129–32
Sacred Incantation, 125
the Self, 131, 164
Soul, 122, 126, 128, 132, 136–40, 149, 150, 154–55
Specifics, 123, 141–47
as differential equivalence (*bhedapratinidhi*), 141–43
Infinity of, 145–47
proof of, 143–45
theory of divine perfection, 147
Time, 148
total abrogation, 157–61
Tradition, 154, 155
Truth, 132

Vādi Rāja, 124, 156
Vanamāli Miśra, 124, 162–65
Viṣṇu, 126, 135–36, 150
Viṣṇu Nārāyaṇa, 124–25, 134–36
Vyāsa Rāmācārya, 124, 157–61
Vyāsa Rāya, 123, 124, 149–61
Wheel of systems, 420–21
Witness, 122, 126–27
Word, 122, 126, 133
words (human), 129–30, 133–34
Duns Scotus, John, 425
Duśyanta, 328
Dvaita Vedānta. See Dualist Vedanta
Dvārakā, 340, 491, 492

Egidianism, 425
Egoism (*ahaṅkāra*)
Dualist Vedanta, 148
Energy-Qualified Nondualism, 404
Indivisible Nondualism, 270, 478, 479
Qualified Nondualism, 287, 485
Śaiva Orthodoxy, 169, 170, 173, 469, 471
Sankhya, 53, 54, 59, 65, 67, 74, 452–53
Triadism, 383, 497
Elephant Tantra or *Mātaṅga Tantra,* 180
Emanationism, 166, 167
Empiricism, 24
Energic Fulmination (*sáktipāta*), 396–98
Energicism (*Śākta darśana*), 221, 406–7, 504
Bhāskararāya, 504
Brahman, 407, 504
categories, 504
Divine Feminine, 406, 407
Matter, 407
Mirific Power, 407
Nīlakaṇṭha, 407
Revelation, 407
Śiva, 407
Trident Cluster, 434, 436
Viṣṇu, 407
Wheel of systems, 420, 422
Energic Way, (*śāktopāya*), 359–62, 375, 384–86
Energy (*śakti*), 29
Energy-Qualified Nondualism, 396–405, 500, 501
Innate Difference-in-Identity, 307, 486
Pure Nondualism, 331
Śaiva Nondualism, 393
Śaiva Orthodoxy, 171, 176, 181, 468, 470
Sonic Absolutism, 224
Triadism, 357, 361–72, 375–86, 497–99
Wheel of (*śakticakra*), 360, 361
Energy-Qualified Nondualism (*śaktiviśiṣṭādvaita*), 221, 395–405, 500–3
All Void, 395, 396
Attributes, 398
Bādarāyaṇa, 396
Bond, 396, 397
Brahman, 396, 397, 399
categories, 500–1
Causality, 397

Cenna Basava, 395, 502–3
Consciousness, 398–404, 501
Devotion, 400–1, 500, 501
Egoism, 404
Energic Fulmination, 396–98
Energy, 396–405, 500, 501
Essence, 402, 404
Evolution, 404–5
of the Universe, 502–3
God, 398
Grace, 396
Ignorance, 397
Joy, 399, 400, 402
Knowledge, 396, 403–5, 501
Lamp of the Vedanta, 426, 428
logic, 401
Matter, 398, 399
Māyi Deva, 396, 398–405, 500–1
norms, 401
Pati (Śrī), 395–98
Pollution, 397
Repositories, 395–405, 500, 502–3
Revelation, 396, 400, 402
Śaiva Orthodoxy and, 396
the Self, 396
Śiva, 396–405, 500
Śiva Principle, 398, 399, 403
Śivayogi, 395
Soul, 396, 397, 400, 401
Spirit, 399
Symbols, 395, 399–405, 500, 502
Tradition, 396, 397
Triadism and, 396
Trident Cluster, 434–35
Truth, 400–1
Vacuism and, 395
the Vedanta, 396, 397
the Vedas, 396, 397, 404
Wheel of systems, 420, 422
Word, 397
Yoga and, 397, 398
Engels, Friedrich, 25, 38, 219
Enlightened tradition, 23, 26
Eriugena, John Scotus, 425
Essence
Dualist Vedanta, 123, 157
Energy-Qualified Nondualism, 402, 404
Ineffable Difference-in-Identity, 335, 491
Innate Difference-in-Identity, 308, 310
Nondualism, 187, 197, 199, 207, 214, 216
Pure Nondualism, 316, 323, 331, 489
Śaiva Orthodoxy, 177, 180
Triadism, 357, 374, 375, 386
Essence of the Tantras, The or *Tantrasāra* (Abhinava Gupta), 373–78
Established Nondualism (*Siddhādvaita*), 221
Lamp of the Vedanta, 428
Evil
Dualist Vedanta, 122, 149–56
God and, 149–56
Ritualism, 88–89
Evolution, 54
Energy-Qualified Nondualism, 404–5, 502–3

Indivisible Nondualism, 479
Nondualism, 473–74
Sankhya, 53, 58–59, 61–62, 454–56
of the Universe, 473–74 479, 502–3
Pāñcarātra theology, 480–83
Explanation of the "Aphorisms on the Brahman" or *Anuvyākhyāna* (Madhva), 153
Explicative Verses on Sound (Rājānaka Rāmakaṇṭha), 182
Expressed Relation theory, 133, 134

Faculties
Ancient Vedanta, 248
Monist Pastoralism, 352, 494
Pure Nondualism, 322, 329
Śaiva Orthodoxy, 173–74, 469
Triadism, 362, 383, 387, 497
Family (of Energies) School (*kula*), 360, 372, 378
Fecundation, Epoch of, 43, 44
Fire Sacrifice (*agnihotra*), 87, 88, 112
Five Chapters, The or *Pañcapādikā* (Padma Pāda), 213
Five Impure Principles (*aśuddha tattva*), 166, 170, 173–74, 469
Five Mixed Principles (*śuddhāśuddha tattva*), 166, 170, 172–73
Five Pure Principles (*śuddha tattva*), 166–67, 170, 171, 177, 180, 181, 468–70
Flowering, Epoch of, 43, 44
Force, Agitation of (*vīrya-vikṣobha*), 369–72
Freedom (*svātantrya*), 357, 360, 370, 371, 374–80
Full Moon Sacrifice (*pūrṇamāsa*), 90

Galileo, 26
Gaṇakārikā (Bhāsarvajña), 493–95
Gaṇapati, 189–90
Gandhi, Mohandas K., 28
Gaṅgeśa, 43, 109
Gārgyāyaṇa, 446–47
Gauḍa Pāda
Illusionism, 190–93
Nondualism, 185–96, 427
Sankhya, 55, 64–67
Gautama. *See* Buddha
Gavardi, Federico Niccola, 425
Gāyatrī, the or Sacred Incantation
Ancient Vedanta, 244, 245
Dualist Vedanta, 125–26
Nondualism, 206
Śaiva Orthodoxy, 176
Germination, Epoch of, 43, 44
Ghazzali, Al-, 39, 219
Giridhara Prapanna, 486–88
Gītā

Ancient Vedanta, 239
Dualist Vedanta, 151, 152
Indivisible Nondualism, 270, 281
Innate Difference-in-Identity, 312
Nondualism, 197–99
Pure Nondualism, 318, 323, 328
Qualified Nondualism, 282, 283

Gloss on the Lion Tantra or *Mṛgendravṛtti* (Nārāyaṇa Kaṇṭha), 182

Gnostic Śaiva Orthodoxy (*Jñānasādhana Śaiva Siddhānta*), 167, 168, 468–69

God
Ancient Vedanta, 241, 248–50
Body of, 248–49
Compassion of, 249–50
Omnipotence of, 250
Power of, 249–50
Atomism, 105–7
bipolarity, 220
Causality, 147–51, 154, 167, 179–82
limitlessness of, 148–49
Christianity, 33–36, 123, 358–59, 406
cosmomorphic, 313–14
defects of, 150–51, 154
Dualist Vedanta, 122–32, 135–40, 147–56
Expressibility of, 162–65
Energy-Qualified Nondualism, 398
Evil and, 149–56
fivefold activities, 169
impartiality of, 151–53
independence of, 148
Indivisible Nondualism, 271–74
Ineffable Difference-in-Identity, 337, 338, 343, 491
Infinity of, 359
Innate Difference-in-Identity, 306–14, 486–88
Islam, 123
karma and, 149–51
Liberation and, 310–14
Logicism, 108, 155–56
proof of the existence of, 116–21
Monist Pastoralism, 351–52, 355–56, 493
Nondualism, 188, 198
Pure Nondualism, 316–33, 490
Qualified Nondualism, 283–99, 484
Śaiva Orthodoxy, 166–69, 179–82
Sankhya, 66–67
Scholasticism, 123
Soul and, 136–40, 151, 154–55
Triadism, 365–71, 376–80, 386, 498–99
See also names of gods

God-Goddess nature (*devīdevātmatā*), 176–78

Gods, Age of the, 43

Gokula Nātha, 317

Grace (*prasāda*)
Energy-Qualified Nondualism, 396
Pure Nondualism, 316, 317, 323

Gradation School (*Krama*), 360

Grammar, 235–36

greatness of, 225–26
processing of words, 229–30

Happiness
Dualist Vedanta, 138, 150, 151
Knowledge and, 101–2
Logicism, 109
Nondualism, 197, 198
Observance and, 104
Ritualism, 88, 101–2, 104
Śaiva Orthodoxy, 176, 177
Triadism, 378
Hari Dāsa, 221, 427, 431
Hari Rāya, 317, 330–34
Harṣa, Śrī, 185, 206–8
Heaven (*svarga*)
Logicism, 112
Ritualism, 87, 90, 94
Sacrifice and, 90, 94
Hegel, Georg Wilhelm, 25, 29, 219
Idealism, 26–27
Heidegger, Johann Heinrich, 359
Hemacandra, 268, 419
Heraclitus, 27
Hero-Saivism (*Vīraśaiva darśana*. See Energy-Qualified Nondualism
Hindu theology
antiquity of, 17
background data, 42–46
the bipartite (critical) scheme, 35–36
contemporary vogue of, 30–34
dual norm and dual aspect, 40–42
fathers of, 446–48
the language of, 17
parochial complacency in, 21–22
Shrine of Learning, 442–44
significance for the West, 21–30
Temple of, 411–15
theology as the architectonics of religion, 34–37
tranquil aspect of Hinduism, 32
the trichotomy (three basic types) of theology, 37–40
tripartite (dogmatic) scheme, 35, 36
See also names of theological schools
Hiraṇyagarbha or Golden Embryo, 446–47
Hiriyanna, 475
Hita Harivaṁśa, 221, 428, 432
Hume, David, 27
Hymn to Nārāyaṇa's Theophanies or *Nārāyaṇavyūhastava*), 339

Ibn-Arabi, 219
Idealism (*Dṛṣtisṛṣtivāda*)
Buddhism and, 84–85
defined, 26
Hegel, 26–27
Lamp of the Vedanta, 426–27
Lotus of, 418–19
Nondualism and, 185, 189
Wheel of systems, 420–21
Identity
agglomerative

(*samudāyaikyam*), 139–40
Dualist Vedanta, 122, 128, 138–40
nuances innate to, 141–47
Nondualism, 185–90, 206–7
Triadism, 357, 359
Identity (Non-Difference) theology. *See* Nondualism
Ignorance (*avidyā*)
Ancient Vedanta, 253–55
Brahman, 187
Dualist Vedanta, 126–28, 137, 157
Energy-Qualified Nondualism, 397
Indivisible Nondualism, 270
Ineffable Difference-in-Identity, 492
Innate Difference-in-Identity, 307
Nondualism, 187–89, 200, 207, 209, 212, 472, 473
Pure Nondualism, 320, 323–25, 328, 490
Śaiva Nondualism, 393
Triadism, 360, 361, 373, 374
Illuminatrix of the Truth or *Tattvaprakāśikā* (Keśava Kāśmīrin), 312
Illusionism (*Māyāvāda*)
Gauḍa Pāda, 190–93
Indivisible Nondualism and, 274
Nondualism and, 185–93, 199–200, 216, 472
Pure Nondualism and, 325–26
Triadism and, 362
Immaculate Nondualism (*Viśuddhādvaita*), 221
Lamp of the Vedanta, 426, 428
Lotus Pool, 430–31
Wheel of systems, 420, 422
Impersonal Absolute, Age of the, 43–44
Impulse, (*unmukhitā*), 365–67
Incarnation, 284, 298
Inconscient (*acit, jaḍa*), the
Innate Difference-in-Identity, 307, 308
Pure Nondualism, 321
Individual Way (*āṇavopāya*), 359–64, 375
Indivisible Nondualism (*Avibhāgādvaita*), 220, 268–81, 478, 479
the Absolute, 268, 276–81
atheism, 271
Atomism and, 269–72, 274
Attributes, 270–71
Bādarāyaṇa, 273, 279
Brahman, 272–81, 478
categories, 478
complementarist, 268
Creation, 479
Egoism, 270, 478, 479
equivalential, 268
Evolution, 479
Gītā, 270, 281
God, 271–74
gradationist, 268
Hemacandra, 268
Ignorance, 270
Illusionism and, 274
Instinct, 276, 279, 281, 478, 479
Joy, 269, 271, 276–81
Joylessness, 280–81

Knowledge, 268–72, 277, 279, 281
Lamp of the Vedanta, 426–27
Liberation, 270, 276–81
Logicism and, 269–72, 274
Malliṣeṇa, 268
Materialism and, 271, 274
Matter, 270–71, 273, 279, 281, 478
Mirific Power, 279
norms, 272
pragmatism, 270, 271, 275
Reality, 271
Revelation, 269–74, 277, 279
Ritualism and, 272, 274
Sankhya and, 268–75, 280
the Self, 269–71, 275, 277–80, 478
Śiva, 274–75, 279
Sorrow, 269, 276, 278, 280, 281
Soul, 269–70, 274, 275, 278–80
Spirit, 273, 281, 478
Tradition, 269–74, 278
Truth, 268, 269
Vedanta and, 268, 271–75, 281
Vijñāna Bhikṣu, 268–75, 478, 479
Wheel of systems, 420, 422
Yoga and, 268, 271–74
Indra, 245–46
Ineffable Difference-in-Identity (*Acintyabhedābheda*), 221, 335–45, 491–92
Baladeva Vidyābhūṣaṇa, 336, 342–45
Brahmā, 340, 343, 345, 492
Brahman, 335, 337, 344, 345, 491, 492
Caitanya, 221, 335, 428, 432
categories, 491–92
Devotion, 336–39, 342–43
Injunctional (*vaidha bhakti*), 336, 338, 339
Passion-Sequent (*rāgānugā bhakti*), 338–39
Passion-Souled (*rāgātmikā bhakti*), 336–38
Divine Play, 335
Essence 335, 491
God, 337, 338, 343, 491
Ignorance, 492
Jīva Gosvāmī, 221, 335, 340–42, 491
Joy, 335, 340, 491
Knowledge, 336, 340–45, 492
Kṛṣṇa, 335–45, 491
Lamp of the Vedanta, 426, 428
Liberation, 335
Lotus Pool, 430, 432
Matter, 343, 492
Mirific Power, 491
Pāñcarātra, 344
Passion, 335–39
Passion Dance (the Rāsa), 335
Rama, 339
Revelation, 337, 344
Rūpa Gosvāmī, 221, 335–39
Sankhya and, 344
Soul, 492
Spirit, 343, 492
Tradition, 344, 345
transmigration, 339
Uddhava, 337, 341, 345

Viṣṇu, 337, 339, 344, 345
Vraja land, 335–40, 343
Vṛndāvana, 335, 342, 491
Wheel of systems, 420, 422
Yoga and, 344
Inexplicable (*anirvacanīya*), the, 186, 187, 213–16
Infinity
Ancient Vedanta, 243
of divine perfections, 147
of God, 359
of Specifics, 145–47
Triadism, 359, 360
Injunction (*codanā*), 86–87, 89
Injury (*hiṁsā*), 88–89
Innate Difference-in-Identity (*Svābhāvikabhedābheda*), 221, 306–14, 486–88
the Absolute, 307, 308
Ancient Vedanta and, 306
Āśmarathya, 306
Attributes, 307, 309, 310, 486
Auḍulomi, 306
Bādarāyaṇa, 306, 308, 310
bipolarity, 306
Brahmā, 308, 313
Brahman, 307–13, 486
categories, 308, 486–88
Causality, 309
Creation, 309, 313, 486, 487
Energy, 307, 486
Essence, 308, 310
Gītā, 312
God, 306–14, 486–88
Ignorance, 307
the Inconscient, 307, 308
Joy, 309, 486
karma, 488
Kāśakṛtsna, 306
Keśava Kāśmīrin, 306, 310–14
Knowledge, 307–10
Kṛṣṇa, 306–9, 312, 486
Lakṣmī, 307
Lamp of the Vedanta, 426–27
Liberation, 308–14
Lotus Pool, 430–31
Madhva, 306
Matter, 307, 313, 486, 487
Mirific Power, 307, 309
Nimbārka, 221, 306–8, 427, 431, 486–88
Nivāsa (Śrī), 306, 308–9
Pāñcarātra, 306, 344
Puruṣottama Prasāda, 306, 486–88
Rādhā, 307, 486
Reality, 486
Revelation, 307, 308, 310–12
the Self, 310, 311
Śiva, 308, 313
Soul, 307, 308, 310, 487
the Supreme Person, 309, 310, 313
Tradition, 308
the Veda, 308, 309
Viṣṇu, 307
Wheel of systems, 420, 422
Inner Controller (*antaryāmin*), 316, 320, 321, 331, 489
Instinct (*buddhi*)
Dualist Vedanta, 148
Indivisible Nondualism, 276, 279, 281, 478, 479
Śaiva Orthodoxy, 169–73, 469
Sankhya, 53, 57–60, 65, 67, 452

Triadism, 366, 383, 385, 497
Irradiant, The, or *Bhāmatī* (Vācaspati Miśra), 154
Islam, 38–39, 85
biopolarity, 219
God, 123
Light, 358
Īśvara Kṛṣṇa, 54, 56–70, 166, 452–54

Jagannātha Paṇḍitarāja, 317, 328–30
Jaimini, 84, 93, 104, 272, 274
Ritualism, 86–89
Sacrifice, 93
Word, 98
Jainism, 43, 122
Lotus of, 418–19
non-violence, 28
pluralism, 31
skepticism, 27
tranquil aspect of, 32
Jasmine of Logic, The or *Yuktimallikā* (Vādi Rāja), 124, 156
Jayadeva, 334
Jayaratha, 498–99
Jaya Tīrtha, 123, 136–49, 164
Jesus Christ, 33, 358
Jīva Gosvāmī, 221, 335, 340–42, 491
Jñānaśrī Mitra, 112–13
João de Santo Tomás (or John of St. Thomas), 425
Jones, William, 17
Joy (*ānanda*)
the Absolute, 276–81
Ancient Vedanta, 242–43
Christianity, 315
Energy-Qualified Nondualism, 399, 400, 402
Indivisible Nondualism, 269, 271, 276–81
Ineffable Difference-in-Identity, 335, 340, 491
Innate Difference-in-Identity, 309, 486
Monist Pastoralism, 346, 352–53
Pure Nondualism, 315–17, 320–25, 328–33, 489
Śaiva Orthodoxy, 176–78
Triadism, 361, 364, 370–72, 375–78
Joylessness (*asukham*), 280–81
Juan de la Anunciación, 425
Juan de la Cruz, 37, 39
Junayd, Al-, 219
Jung, Carl Gustav, 29

Kālīs or Consuming Energies, 357, 385, 498–99
Kamalásīla, 27
Kaṁsa, 334, 336, 341
Kaṇāda, 105, 272, 274, 435
Kannaḍa, 395
Kant, Immanuel, 27
Kaṇṭha, Śrī, 169, 389–94 428, 435
Kāpālikas, 347
Kapila, 269, 274, 279
Sankhya, 54, 55, 63, 70–76, 431
Karate, 77
Karma
Atomism, 106, 107
Dualist Vedanta, 149–51, 153

God and, 149–51
Innate Difference-in-Identity, 488
Pure Nondualism, 323, 325
Śaiva Orthodoxy, 158–71, 175, 468, 469
Sankhya, 75–76
Sonic Absolutism, 227
Triadism, 363
Yoga, 79–80
Kāśakṛtsna, 306
Kashmir Śaivism (or Triadism), 221
Kauṇḍinya, 347, 349–56
Kempo, 77
Kenosis, doctrine of, 34
Keśava Kāśmīrin, 306, 310–14
Knowledge
Ancient Vedanta, 240–43, 251, 254–57
Atomism, 105, 107
Buddhism, 100–1
Conditioned Difference-in-Identity, 264, 477
Dualist Vedanta, 122, 125–27, 130, 132, 160
Energy-Qualified Nondualism, 396, 403–5, 501
error in, 85
Happiness and, 101–2
Indivisible Nondualism, 268–72, 277, 279, 281
Ineffable Difference-in-Identity, 336, 340–45, 492
Innate Difference-in-Identity, 307–10
as invalid, 100–1
Liberation and, 167
Logicism, 100, 108–14, 117, 119
Mind and, 99–100
Monist Pastoralism, 349–54
Nondualism, 187–90, 196–99, 207–8, 473
Pañca Śikha, 83
Pure Nondualism, 316–27, 331–32
Qualified Nondualism, 284, 289–90, 296, 299, 302, 484
Ritualism, 85, 95–96, 99–104, 460–61
Śaiva Nondualism, 390–94
Śaiva Orthodoxy, 167, 170–72, 179–80, 468–70
Sankhya, 56, 100
Sonic Absolutism, 224–27, 231, 234, 237
Triadism, 360–67, 373–76, 382–86, 496
Word and, 85, 87, 95–96, 103
words (human) and, 103–4
Knowledge, Era of, 44
Kṛṣṇa, 32, 151, 153, 162, 189, 221, 388
Ineffable Difference-in-Identity, 335–45, 491
Innate Difference-in-Identity, 306–9, 312, 486
Nondualism, 197, 198
Pure Nondualism, 315–24, 327, 334, 489
Qualified Nondualism, 284, 293
Kṣema Rāja, 360, 378–80
Kubjā, 337

Kumāra, Śrī, 167, 175–78, 468–69
Kumārila Bhaṭṭa, 85, 89–95
Kūrma Purāṇa, 279, 339

Lady Glory (Śri or Lakṣmī), 283, 288, 293–97, 333
Laksmī, 34, 307
Lakulīśa, 166, 346–56, 435
Lākulīśapāśupata Darśana. *See* Monist Pastoralism
Lamp of the Meaning of the Truth, The, or *Tattvārthadīpanibandha* (Vallabha), 316–28
Lamp of the Vedanta, 426–28
Liberation
  Ancient Vedanta, 250, 258–59
  Devotion and, 167
  Dualist Vedanta, 126, 135
  God and, 310–14
  Indivisible Nondualism, 270, 276–81
  Ineffable Difference-in-Identity, 335
  Innate Difference-in-Identity, 308–14
  Knowledge and, 167
  Logicism, 108–11
  Monist Pastoralism, 355–56
  Nondualism, 196, 197
  Pure Nondualism, 316–26, 331, 490
  Qualified Nondualism, 293, 298
  Śaiva Orthodoxy, 167–71, 175, 176, 468
  Sankhya, 56–57, 63, 70–72, 75
  Sonic Absolutism, 225, 234–35
  Triadism, 358, 363, 378, 379, 388
Light (*prakāśa*)
  Christianity, 358
  Islam, 358
  Triadism, 357, 358, 368–69, 374–77, 381–83, 496
Light on the Principles or *Tattvaprakāśa* (Bhoja Deva), 168–75
Limitationism (*Avacchedavāda*), 188–89
  Lamp of the Vedanta, 426–27
  Wheel of systems, 420–21
Liṅga Purāṇa, 177–78
Logic
  Conditioned Difference-in-Identity, 261–64
  Dualist Vedanta, 134
  Energy-Qualified Nondualism, 401
  Nondualism, 196
  Sonic Absolutism, 226–27, 235–36
Logicism (*Nyāya* or *Naiyāyika darśana*), 51–52, 108–21, 451, 464–65
  Atomism and, 105, 114, 115
  atoms, 116–18
  Buddhism and, 108, 112–13
  categories, 464–65
  Causality, 117, 118
  Destruction, 116

Dualist Vedanta and, 123, 155–56
Gaṅgeśa, 109
God, 108, 155–56
proof of the existence of, 116–21
Happiness, 109
Heaven, 112
Indivisible Nondualism and, 269–72, 274
Knowledge, 100, 108–14, 117, 119
Liberation, 108–11
Methodizing Mind, 118
Nondualism and, 194, 199, 215
norms, 109–11
Nyāya syllogism, 108, 451
Revelation, 108, 116, 119, 120
Ritual Fruits, 112
Sacrifice, 112
Soul, 112, 464–65
Triadism and, 366, 367
Trident Cluster, 434–35
Truth, 109, 111, 112
Udayana, 105, 108, 112–21
Uddyotakara, 108, 111–12
Vātsyāyana, 108–11
Wheel of systems, 420–21
Logic of the Brahman (Brahmatarka-The Science of the Brahman, q.v.), 163, 164
Lokācārya, 283, 284, 291–99
Longus, 45–46
Lotus of Indic theologies, 418–19
Lotus Pool, 430–32

Madhusūdana Sarasvatī
Dualist Vedanta, 124, 158–60
Nondualism, 186, 189, 213–16, 427
Madhva, 24, 37, 52, 220, 427, 431
Bādarāyaṇa and, 186
Dualist Vedanta, 122–48, 153, 156, 466–67
Innate Difference-in-Identity, 306
Mādhyamikas, 395
Madonna, the, 406
Mahābhārata, 119, 135, 328
Mahā Prakāśa, 381
Mahāyāna Buddhism, 33–34
Maheśvarānanda, 360, 381–88
Mahīdāsa Aitareya, 446–47
Maitrāyaṇi Upaniṣad, 407
Makkali Gosāla, 346, 419
Malebranche, Nicolas de, 315, 425
Malliṣeṇa, 268
Mammaṭa, 328, 329
Maṇḍana, 427
Maṇḍana Miśra, 186–89
Māṇḍavya, 114
Maṇḍukya Upaniṣad, 186
Manu, 87, 120–21, 178
Marīci, 196
Mark of Ephesus, 219
Marx, Karl, 29, 54
Master, 166–70, 468, 470
Materialism, 27
Indivisible Nondualism and, 271, 274
Lotus of, 418–19
Mathurā, 340, 491, 492
Matter (*prakṛti*), 53–54
Ancient Vedanta, 243
Dualist Vedanta, 148
Energicism, 407
Energy-Qualified Nondualism, 398, 399

Indivisible Nondualism, 270–71, 273, 279, 281, 478
Ineffable Difference-in-Identity, 343, 492
Innate Difference-in-Identity, 307, 313, 486, 487
Nondualism, 186, 194–97, 472
Pure Nondualism, 324, 325, 332, 333
Qualified Nondualism, 287, 293, 485
Śaiva Nondualism, 393
Śaiva Orthodoxy, 166, 170, 470
Sankhya, 53–58, 62–67, 72–75, 452
Triadism, 366, 382, 497
Yoga, 77, 78
Māyi Deva, 396, 398–405, 500–1
Melodla, Mastrio de, 425
Merton, Thomas, 54
Methodizing Mind (*apekṣābuddhi*)
Atomism, 105
Logicism, 118
Meykanta Tevar, 168, 435
Michelangelo, 417
Mīmāṁsā. See Ritualism
Mind
Knowledge and, 99–100
Pure Nondualism, 319, 322, 325–28
Ritualism, 97–100
Śaiva Orthodoxy, 169, 170, 173, 180
Sankhya, 53, 59
Triadism, 383, 385, 497
Mirific Power (*māyā*)
Energicism, 407
Indivisible Nondualism, 279
Ineffable Difference-in-Identity, 491
Innate Difference-in-Identity, 307, 309
Nondualism, 192, 197
Pure Nondualism, 316, 320, 321, 324, 331–33
Śaiva Nondualism, 392, 393
Śaiva Orthodoxy, 168–74, 177–82, 468, 469
Triadism, 360–62, 367, 382
Mishra, Umesh, 464
Monism, 38, 39, 51–52, 167, 224, 304
Monist Pastoralism (*Lākulīśapāśupata darśana*), 221, 346–56, 493–95
Bhāsarvajña, 493–95
Brahman, 348
categories, 346–47, 493–95
as a counterculture theology, 346
Faculties, 352, 494
God, 351–52, 355–56, 493
Joy, 346, 352–53
Kauṇḍinya, 347, 349–56
Knowledge, 349–54
Lakulīśa, 346–56, 435
Liberation, 355–56
non-violence, 346, 350
Pain, 353, 493–94
Ritual, 493–94
Śaiva Orthodoxy and, 166
Salvation, 346, 350, 353–54
Sankhya and, 352, 355
Śiva, 347–50, 354
Soul, 352, 493

Spirit, 352
Triadism and, 347
Trident Cluster, 434–35
violence, 346, 350
Wheel of systems, 420, 422
Yoga and, 348, 355–56
Moral Law (*dharma*), 133
Muslim. *See* Islam
Mysticism
Nondualism, 185, 197
Qualified Nondualism, 283

Naciketas, 446, 448
Nāgārjuna, 27, 84, 124, 189, 419
Nandikeśvara, 221, 435
Nandikeśvara Śaivism, 221
Trident Cluster, 434–35
Wheel of systems, 420, 422
Nārada, 307, 336, 337, 339
Nārāyaṇa, 197, 272, 289, 446–47
Nārāyaṇa Kaṇṭha, 182
Necessity (*niyati*), 54, 166, 170, 172, 469
Necklace of the Jewels of Logic or *Nyāyaratnamālā* (Pārtha Sārathi Miśra), 103
Nectar of Logic or *Nyāyasudhā* (Jaya Tīrtha), 123, 136–49, 164
New Moon Sacrifice (*darśa*), 90, 91
Newton, Sir Isaac, 105
Nicholas of Cusa, 31
Nietzsche, Friedrich Wilhelm, 25
Nīlakaṇṭha, 190, 221, 407, 427
Nimbārka, 221, 306–8, 427, 431, 486–88
Nivāsa, Śrī
Innate Difference-in-Identity, 306, 308–9
Qualified Nondualism, 299–305
Nominalism, 425
Nondualism (*Adraita*), 185–216, 472–74
Abhinava Gupta, 187
the Absolute, 187
Action, 196–98, 473
Ancient Vedanta and, 259
apparitionalism, 189
Aquinas and, 188
architectonic sense, 187
Atomism and, 194, 199
Attributes, 199–200, 207–8, 216
Bādarāyaṇa, 186
Brahman, 186–89, 198, 201–6, 209, 212–16, 472, 473
Buddhism and, 185, 189
categories, 186, 197, 472
Causality, 187
Conditioned Difference-in-Identity, 266
Consciousness (*Cidādvaita*), 189, 209, 221
Creation, 193, 196–97, 201–2, 473–74
Destruction, 193
Dualist Vedanta and, 123, 186, 213, 215
critique of, 126–29
Essence, 187, 197, 199, 207, 214, 216
Established (*Siddhādvaita*), 221, 428

Gaṇapati, 189–90
Gauḍa Pāda, 185–96, 427
the Gāyatrī, 206
Gītā, 197–99
God, 188, 198
Happiness, 197, 198
Harṣa (Śrī), 185, 206–8
Idealism and, 185, 189
Identity, 185–90, 206–7
Ignorance, 187–89, 200, 207, 209, 212, 472, 473
Illusionism and, 185–93, 199–200, 216, 472
Immaculate (*Viśuddhādvaita*), 221, 420, 422, 426, 428, 430–31
the Inexplicable, 186, 187, 213–16
Knowledge, 187–90, 196–99, 207–8, 473
Kṛṣṇa, 197, 198
Lamp of the Vedanta, 426–28
Liberation, 196, 197
Limitationism and, 188–89
logic, 196
Logicism and, 194, 199, 215
Lotus Pool, 430–31
Madhusūdana Sarasvatī, 186, 189, 213–16, 427
Maṇḍana Miśra, 186–89
Māṇḍukya Upaniṣad, 186
Matter, 186, 194–97, 472
Mirific Power, 192, 197
mysticism, 185, 197,
the non-Self, 186, 200, 210–12
norms, 210–12
Prakāśānanda, 189, 209–13
Prakāśātman, 189, 201–6
Reality, 190, 194–96, 210, 472
Reflectionism and, 189
Revelation, 186, 191, 202, 205–6, 210–12
Ritualism and, 195, 199
Saṅkara, 186, 188, 196–200
Sankhya and, 186, 194
the Self, 185, 186, 191–93, 198, 200, 202, 205
self-evidence of, 209–13
Śiva, 190
six schools of, 188–90
Soul, 187, 190
Spirit, 186
Syncretic (*Saṁyuktādvaita*), 189–90, 420–21, 426–27
transmigration, 198
transmogrification, 187, 201–6
Triadism and, 187, 368–69
Truth, 185, 188, 190, 193
undivided, 188, 420–21, 426–27
the Universe, 189, 472
Evolution of, 473–74
Vacuism and, 185, 189
the Vedas, 196–99
Viṣṇu, 197
Vyāsa Rāya, 186, 213–14
Wheel of systems, 420, 422
See also Energy-Qualified Nondualism; Indivisible Nondualism; Pure Nondualism; Qualified Nondualism; Śaiva Nondualism
Non-Self (*anātman*), the, 186, 200, 210–12
Non-violence, 28

Monist Pastoralism, 346, 350
Noris, Henri, 425
Null Way (*anupāya*), 359, 360, 375–76, 387–88
Nyāya. See Logicism
Nyāya syllogism (*anumāna*), 108, 451

Obscurantist traditions, 23, 26
Obscuring Power (*tirodhāyikā sakti*), 170
Observance (*dharma*), 84, 86, 88, 89, 104
Occult Virtue (*apūrva*), 84, 85, 89–95, 104
Ockham, William of, 425
OM
  Ancient Vedanta, 241
  Dualist Vedanta, 125, 149
  Śaiva Orthodoxy, 169
  Sonic Absolutism, 223–25, 237–38
  Yoga, 80
Omniexistentialism (*Sarvāstivāda*), 418–19

Padmanābha Tīrtha, 132
Padma Pāda, 189, 201, 213, 427
Padma Purāṇa, 274, 339, 340
Pain (*duḥka*)
  Dualist Vedanta, 150, 151
  Monist Pastoralism, 353, 493–94
  Triadism, 363
Pāñcarātra, 54, 220, 328
  evolution of the universe, 480–83
  Ineffable Difference-in-Identity, 344
  Innate Difference-in-Identity, 306, 344
  Lotus Pool, 430–31
  Qualified Nondualism, 282–87
  Śaiva Orthodoxy, 166
  Wheel of systems, 420, 422
Pañca Śikha, 54, 63, 76, 83
Pāṇḍu, 388
Pāṇini, 223, 229
Parāśara, 272
Parāśara Purāna, 272
Parīkṣit, 333
Pārtha Sārathi Miśra, 86, 99–104
Pārvati, 274–75
Passion, 335–39
Passion Dance (the Rāsa), 335
Passivist (Cat) School, 283–84
Patañjali, 78–83, 223, 273, 435
Pati, Śrī, 221, 395–98
Paul, St., 358
Peirce, Charles S., 86
Personal God, Age of the, 43, 44
Phoneme (*akṣara*), the, 224, 225
Pico della Mirandola, Giovanni, 38
Pleasure, 363, 367
Plenitude, 357, 359, 367
Plotinus, 53
Pluralism, 31–32
Pollution (*mala*)
  Energy-Qualified Nondualism, 397
  Śaiva Orthodoxy, 168–70, 468, 469
  Triadism, 386

Potter, Karl, 44
Prabhākara, 85, 95
Pragmatism
  Dualist Vedanta, 127, 131, 157–59
  Indivisible Nondualism, 270, 271, 275
  Pure Nondualism, 320
  Ritualism, 86
Prahlāda, 274
Prakāśānanda, 189, 209–13, 427
Prakāśātman, 189, 201–6
Prásasta Pāda, 105–7, 462–63
Pratardana, 245–46, 446–47
Presbyterism (*Theravāda*), 418–19
Proclus, 417
Proof of the Brahman, The, or *Brahmasiddhi* (Maṇḍana Miśra), 186
Puratāna Vedānta. See Ancient Vedanta
Pure Nondualism (*Śuddhādvaita*), 221, 315–34, 489–90
  Abhinava Gupta, 317, 329, 330
  the Absolute, 318
  Attributes, 324, 325
  Bādarāyaṇa, 318, 325–27
  Brahman, 318–26, 330, 331, 489
  categories, 327, 489–90
  Causality, 316, 324–30, 489, 490
  Consciousness, 316, 320–24, 329–31, 489
  Creation, 320–26, 331
  Devotion, 319, 324, 331–33
  Divine Play, 317, 330–34
  Energy, 331
  Essence, 316, 323, 331, 489
  Faculties, 322, 329
  Gītā, 318, 323, 328
  God, 316–33, 490
  Gokula Nātha, 317
  Grace, 316, 317, 323
  Hari Rāya, 317, 330–34
  Ignorance, 320, 323–25, 328, 490
  Illusionism and, 325–26
  the Inconscient, 321
  Inner Controller, 316, 320, 321, 331, 489
  Jagannātha Paṇḍitarāja, 317, 328–30
  Joy, 315–17, 320–25, 328–33, 489
  karma, 323, 325
  Knowledge, 316–27, 331–32
  Kṛṣṇa, 315–24, 327, 334, 489
  Lady Glory, 333
  Lamp of the Vedanta, 426, 428
  Liberation, 316–26, 331, 490
  Lotus Pool, 430–31
  Mammaṭa, 328, 329
  manifestation, 316, 318, 329, 332, 490
  Matter, 324, 325, 332, 333
  Mind, 319, 322, 325–28
  Mirific Power, 316, 320, 321, 324, 331–33
  non-manifestation, 316
  norms, 317, 318
  pragmatism, 320
  Puruṣottama Pītāmbara, 317, 489–90

Reflectionism and, 322–23
Revelation, 318, 321–26, 330
Ritual, 319
Ritualism and, 326
Sankhya and, 326–27, 489
the Self, 316
Sentiment, 328–30
Śiva, 325
Soul, 316, 320–27, 330, 489, 490
Spirit, 321
the Supreme Person, 489
Time, 324, 489
Tradition, 318–19, 325, 328
transmigration, 319, 320, 325
Truth, 323
Vallabha, 315–28, 333, 489
the Vedanta, 318
the Vedas, 318, 319
Viṣṇu, 321, 325
Vyāsa, 318, 325
Way of Fullness, 316
Wheel of systems, 420, 422
Witness, 329
Word, 316
Yoga and, 327
Puruṣottama Pītāmbara, 317, 489–90
Puruṣottama Prasāda, 306 486–88
Pūtanā, 341, 343
Pyrrho, 27

Qualified Nondualism (*Viśiṣṭādvaita*), 220, 282–305, 484–85
Activist (Monkey) School, 284
Ancient Vedanta and, 283
Bādarāyaṇa, 283, 291
Bodhāyana, 283
Brahman, 287, 289, 484
categories, 484–85
Destruction, 283
Devotion, 282, 283, 296
Egoism, 287, 485
Gītā, 282, 283
God, 283–99, 484
incarnation, 284, 298
Knowledge, 284, 289–90, 296, 299, 302, 484
Kṛṣṇa, 284, 293
Lady Glory, 283, 288, 293–97
Lamp of the Vedanta, 426–27
Liberation, 293, 298
Lokācārya, 283, 284, 291–99
Lotus Pool, 430–31
Matter, 287, 293, 485
Monism and, 304
mysticism, 283
Nivāsa (Śrī), 299–305
norms, 299–305, 484
Pāñcarātra, 282–87
Passivist (Cat) School, 283–84
Rama, 284, 293
Rāmānuja, 282–84, 287–91, 484
Revelation, 285, 290
Ritual, 295, 296
Sacrifice, 295
Sáiva Nondualism and, 389
Salvation, 284
the Self, 291–94
Soul, 292–93, 298, 484, 485
Spirit, 293

the Supreme Person, 283
Svāmī Nārāyaṇa, 284
Triadism and, 283
Truth, 286–87, 298, 299
the Universe, 283
Vallabha, 284
Vedānta Deśika, 284, 299–305
Viṣṇu, 284, 297, 298
Wheel of systems, 420, 422
Yāmuna, 282–87
Quran, the, 39

Rādhā, 307, 334, 486
Rādhāvallabha School, 221
Lotus Pool, 430, 432
Rājānaka Rāmakaṇṭha, 182
Rāja Yoga, 77
Rama, 284, 293, 339
Rāmānanda, 220, 284, 431
Rāmānuja, 206, 220, 240, 282–84, 287–91, 389, 484
Rāmāyaṇa, 328
Rationalism, 24
Reality, 27–28, 157–61
Ancient Vedanta, 241, 243, 475
Atomism, 105
bipolarity, 28, 220
Buddhism, 85
Conditioned Difference-in-Identity, 265
Dualist Vedanta, 122, 123 127, 134, 157–61
Indivisible Nondualism, 271
Innate Difference-in-Identity, 486
Nondualism, 190, 194–96, 210, 472
Śaiva Orthodoxy, 176
Triadism, 357, 366, 376, 379, 381, 388
Reflectionism (*Pratibimbavāda*), 189, 322–23
Lamp of the Vedanta, 426–27
Wheel of systems, 420–21
Repositories (*sthala*), 395–405, 500, 502–3
Revelation (*śruti*)
Ancient Vedanta, 239–43, 248–49
Conditioned Difference-in-Identity, 262–66
Dualist Vedanta, 122, 125, 128–37, 149, 150, 154, 155, 161–65
Energicism, 407
Energy-Qualified Nondualism, 396, 400, 402
Indivisible Nondualism, 269–74, 277, 279
Ineffable Difference-in-Identity, 337, 344
Innate Difference-in-Identity, 307, 308, 310–12
Logicism, 108, 116, 119, 120
Nondualism, 186, 191, 202, 205–6, 210–12
Pure Nondualism, 318, 321–26, 330
Qualified Nondualism, 285, 290
Ritualism, 84, 85, 90–99
Śaiva Nondualism, 390–93
Śaiva Orthodoxy, 177, 178
Śālika Nātha Miśra, 95–99
Sankhya, 56, 73

Sonic Absolutism, 224–27, 234–37
Triadism, 373–74, 381, 387
Ṛg, 41, 225
Ṛgveda, 54, 244
Ritual
Ancient Vedanta, 247–48
Monist Pastoralism, 493–94
Pure Nondualism, 319
Qualified Nondualism, 295, 296
Ritual Fruit (*phala*), 90–95, 112
Ritualism (*Mīmāṁsā* or *Pūrva Mīmāṁsā*), 29, 51, 84–104, 223, 460–61
Brahman, 84
categories, 460–61
Contrarist school, 85–86
Dualist Vedanta and, 129–32
Evil, 88–89
Expressed Relation theory, 133, 134
Happiness, 88, 101–2, 104
Heaven, 87, 90, 94
Indivisible Nondualism and, 272, 274
injunction, 86–87, 89
injury, 88–89
Jaimini, 86–89
Knowledge, 85, 95–96, 99–104, 460–61
Kumārila Bhaṭṭa, 89–95
Mind, 97–100
Nondualism and, 195, 199
Observance, 84, 86, 88, 89, 104
Occult Virtue, 84, 85, 89–95, 104
Pārtha Sārathi Miśra, 86, 99–104
pragmatism, 86
Pure Nondualism and, 328
Revelation, 84, 85, 90–99
Sacrifice, 84, 87, 89–95, 104
Śālika Nātha Miśra, 95–99
Soul, 92, 93
Vericism and, 85–86
Wheel of systems, 420–21
Word, 85, 87–88, 90, 95–99
words (human), 96–99
Ritualist Aphorisms or *Mimaṁsā Sūtras* (Jaimini), 84
Ritual sex, 360
Rituals on the Incantations of the Goddess or *Devīmantrakalpa*, 176
Rituals on the Mistress of the Worlds or *Bhuvaneśvarīkalpa*, 177
Roman Catholic Church. *See* Christianity
Rousseau, Jean Jacques, 27
Rudra, 394, 399, 407
Rūpa Gosvāmī, 221, 335–39

Śabara, 84, 85
Śabdabrahmavāda. *See* Sonic Absolutism
Sacred Incantation (*gāyatri*), 125
Sacrifice
Ancient Vedanta, 247–48
Destruction and, 94
Fire, 87, 88, 112
Full Moon, 90
Heaven and, 90, 94
Jaimini, 93

Logicism, 112
New Moon, 90, 91
Observance and, 104
Qualified Nondualism, 295
Ritualism, 84, 87, 89–95, 104
Secret, 90
Soma, 90, 101
the Vedas, 88–89
Sadānanda, 472
Sadyojyoti, 167, 435
Saha world, the, 26
Śaiva Nondualism (*Śivādvaita*), 221, 389–94
Action, 393, 394
Bādarāyaṇa, 389
Brahman, 389–92
Causality, 392
Consciousness, 392
Destruction, 389
Energy, 393
Ignorance, 393
Kaṇṭha (Śrī), 389–94, 428, 435
Knowledge, 390–94
Lamp of the Vedanta, 426, 428
Matter, 393
Mirific Power, 392, 393
Qualified Nondualism and, 389
Revelation, 390–93
Śiva, 391–94
Soul, 392
Tradition, 391, 393
Trident Cluster, 434–35
the Vedanta, 389
violence, 390, 392
Wheel of systems, 420, 422
Will, 393, 394
Śaiva Orthodoxy (*Śaiva Siddhānta*), 52, 166–82, 468–71
Action, 167, 170, 470
Aghora Śiva, 167, 168, 179–82
Beasts, 166–70, 176, 180, 468–70
Bhoja Deva, 167–76, 179–82, 468–69
Bond, 166, 168–70, 468, 470
Brahman, 177
categories, 166, 468–71
Causality, 167, 177, 179–82
Consciousness, 168, 176–78, 181
Creation, 169, 468
Destruction, 468
Devotion, 167–68, 470–71
Dualist Pastoralism and, 166
Egoism, 169, 170, 173, 469, 471
emanationism, 166, 167
Energy, 171, 176, 181, 468, 470
Energy-Qualified Nondualism and, 396
Essence, 177, 180
Faculties, 173–74, 469
Five Impure Principles, 166, 170, 173–74, 469
Five Mixed Principles, 166, 170, 172–73
Five Pure Principles, 166–67, 170, 171, 177, 180, 181, 468–70
the Gāyatrī, 176
Gnostic, 167, 168, 468–69
God, 166–69, 179–82

God-Goddess nature, 176–78
Happiness, 176, 188
Instinct, 169–73, 469
Joy, 176–78
karma, 168–71, 175, 468, 469
Knowledge, 167, 170–72, 179–80, 468–70
Kumāra (Śrī), 167, 175–78, 468–69
Liberation, 167–71, 175, 176, 468
masculine-feminine polarity of the universe, 175–78
Master, 166–70, 468, 470
Matter, 166, 170, 470
Meykanta Tevar, 168, 435
Mind, 169, 170, 173, 180
Mirific Power, 168–74, 177–82, 468, 469
Monist Pastoralism and, 166
Necessity, 166, 170, 172, 469
Obscuring Power, 170
OM, 169
Pāñcarātra, 166
Pollution, 168–70, 468, 469
Reality, 176
Revelation, 177, 178
Sankhya and, 166
the Self, 177, 182, 471
Śiva, 166–82, 468, 470
Śiva Principle, 178–81
Sonic Absolutism and, 182
Sorrow, 176
Soul, 166–70, 173, 179, 180, 468, 469
Time, 166, 170, 172, 174, 469, 470
transmigration, 177, 470
transmogrification, 181
Triadism and, 166–68, 367, 470
Trident Cluster, 434–35
Truth, 175
Wheel of systems, 420–21
Will, 167, 170, 471

Śaiva Siddhānta. *See* Śaiva Orthodoxy
Śākta Darśana. *See* Energicism
Śakti, 32, 34, 220
Śaktiviśiṣṭādvaita. *See* Energy-Qualified Nondualism
Śakuntalā, 328
Sales, François de, 315
Śālika Nātha Miśra, 86, 95–99
Salmanticenses, 425
Salvation
Monist Pastoralism, 346, 350, 353–54
Qualified Nondualism, 284
Triadism, 360
Sāma (*Veda*), 41, 225
Śambhu Nātha, 373
Sanandana, 76, 307
Śāṇḍilya, 446–47
Śaṅkara, 186, 188, 196–200
Sankhya, 51, 53–76, 452–56
Ancient Vedanta and, 243
categories, 452–53
Egoism, 53, 54, 59, 65, 67, 74, 452–53
Evolution, 53, 58–59, 61–62, 454–56
Gauḍa Pāda, 55, 64–67
God, 66–67
Indivisible Nondualism and, 268–75, 280

Ineffable Difference-in-Identity and, 344
Instinct, 53, 57–60, 65, 67, 452
Īśvara Kṛṣṇa, 54, 56–70, 452–54
Kapila, 54, 55, 63, 70–76, 431
karma, 75–76
Knowledge, 56, 100
Liberation, 56–57, 63, 70–72, 75
Lotus Pool, 430–31
Matter, 53–58, 62–67, 72–75, 452
Mind, 53, 59
Monist Pastoralism and, 352, 355
Nondualism and, 186, 194
Pure Nondualism and, 326–27, 489
Revelation, 56, 73
Śaiva Orthodoxy and, 166
Sorrow, 68–69, 71
Soul, 53
Spirit, 53–58, 64–67, 72, 76, 452
Triadism and, 366
Vācaspati Miśra, 68–70
Wheel of systems, 420–21
Yoga and, 77–78
Sanskrit, 167, 168, 180, 185, 229, 280–82, 395, 399
peculiarities of, 17–18, 44–45
Śāntirakṣita, 24
Santo Tomás, João de. *See* João de Santo Tomás
Satyakāma Jābāla, 446–47
Scholasticism, 24–25, 123
pluralism and, 31–32
Schopenhauer, Arthur, 25
Science of the Brahman, The, or *Brahmatarka* or *Logic of the Brahman* (q.v.) (Bādarāyaṇa), 134
Secret Sacrifice (*upāṁśu*), 90
Self, the
Ancient Vedanta, 240–44, 252–59, 475
attainment of, 247–48
Buddhism, 27
Continued Difference-in-Identity, 265, 266
Dualist Vedanta, 131, 164
Energy-Qualified Nondualism, 396
Indivisible Nondualism, 269–71, 275, 277–80 478
Innate Difference-in-Identity, 310, 311
Nondualism, 185, 186, 191–93, 198, 200, 202, 205
self-evidence of, 209–13
Pure Nondualism, 316
Qualified Nondualism, 291–94
Śaiva Orthodoxy, 177, 182, 471
Sonic Absolutism, 225
Triadism, 361–64, 381–82, 387
Self-Awareness (*vimarśa*), 357, 360, 370, 371, 381–84, 386, 387
Self-Intuitionism. *See* Yoga
Self-obscuration, 357, 358, 367, 497
Semitic religion, 30, 41
speculative aspect of, 23–24
three branches of, 23

Sentiment (*rasa*), 328–30
Śiva, 32, 125, 135, 220
  Energicism, 407
  Energy-Qualified Nondualism, 396–405, 500
  Indivisible Nondualism, 274–75, 279
  Innate Difference-in-Identity, 308, 313
  Monist Pastoralism, 347–50, 354
  Nondualism, 190
  Pure Nondualism, 325
  Śaiva Nondualism, 391–94
  Śaiva Orthodoxy, 166–82, 468, 470
  Triadism, 357–88, 496
Śivādvaita. See Śaiva Nondualism
Śivāgrayogi, 168
Śivānanda Nātha, 360, 435
Śiva Principle (*Śivatattva*), 170, 178–81, 368, 376, 398, 399, 403
Śivayogi, 395
Skepticism, 27, 30–31
Somānanda, 167, 360, 364–70
Soma Sacrifice, 90, 101
Sonic Absolutism (*Sabdabrahmavāda*), 220, 223–38
  the Absolute, 223, 224
  Bhartṛ Hari, 220, 223–37
  Brahman, 224–26, 235–38
  Consciousness, 227, 234
  Energy, 224
  grammar, 235–36
    greatness of, 225–26
    processing of words, 229–30
  karma, 227
  Knowledge, 224–27, 231, 234, 237
  Liberation, 225, 234–35
  logic, 226–27, 235–36
  OM, 223–25, 237–38
  Pāṇini, 223, 229
  the Phoneme, 224, 225
  Revelation, 224–27, 234–37
  Śaiva Orthodoxy and, 182
  the Self, 225
  Time, 224
  Tradition, 224–27, 235–36
  Truth, 224
  the Vedas, 224–25, 231
  Wheel of systems, 420–21
  Word, 223–37
Sorrow (*duḥkha*)
  Indivisible Nondualism, 269, 276, 278, 280, 281
  Śaiva Orthodoxy, 176
  Sankhya, 68–69, 71
  Triadism, 370
Soul (*ātman*)
  Ancient Vedanta, 241–44, 253, 258, 475, 476
  Atomism, 106
  Brahman, 136–40
  Conditioned Difference-in-Identity, 265
  Dualist Vedanta, 122, 126, 128, 132, 136–40, 149, 150, 154–55
  Energy-Qualified Nondualism, 396, 397, 400, 401
  God and, 136–40, 151, 154–55
  Indivisible Nondualism, 269–70, 274, 275, 278–80

  Ineffable Difference-in-Identity, 492
  Innate Difference-in-Identity, 307, 308, 310, 487
  Logicism, 112, 464–65
  Monist Pastoralism, 352, 493
  Nondualism, 187, 190
  Pure Nondualism, 316, 320–27, 330, 489, 490
  Qualified Nondualism, 292–93, 298, 484, 485
  Ritualism, 92, 93
  Śaiva Nondualism, 392
  Śaiva Orthodoxy, 166–70, 173, 179, 180, 468, 469
  Sankhya, 53
  Triadism, 360–63, 367–68, 380, 382
Specifics (*viśeṣa*), 123, 141–47
  Brahman, 141–43, 145
  Infinity of, 145–47
  proof of, 143–45
Spinoza, Baruch, 28, 39, 219
Spirit (*puruṣa*)
  Energy-Qualified Nondualism, 399
  Indivisible Nondualism, 273, 281, 478
  Ineffable Difference-in-Identity, 343, 492
  Monist Pastoralism, 352
  Nondualism, 186
  Pure Nondualism, 321
  Qualified Nondualism, 293
  Sankhya, 53–58, 64–67, 72, 76, 452
  Yoga, 77, 78, 82, 83
Suárez, Francisco, 24, 39, 123, 359, 417, 425
Sudarśana Sūri, 283, 290–91
Śuddhādvaita. *See* Pure Nondualism
Suhrawardy, Al-, 358
Śuka, 52, 427, 431
Supreme Person (*puruṣottama*), 283, 309, 310, 313, 489
Sureśvara, 189, 427
Suta, 344
Svābhavikabhedābheda. *See* Innate Difference-in-Identity
Svāmī Narāyana, 220, 284
Symbols, 395, 399–405, 500, 502
Symeon the New Theologian, 358
Syncretic Nondualism (*Saṁyuktādvaita*), 189–90
  Lamp of the Vedanta, 426–27
  Wheel of systems, 420–21

Tae Kwon Do, 77
Taittirīya Upaniṣad, 243
Ṭaṅka, 239, 247–49
Tantra, 41–42, 182, 337, 373–78
  Elephant (*Mātaṅga tantra*), 180
  Lion (*Mṛgendra*), 182
  Yoga, 77
Taoism, 29, 32
Temple of Hindu Theology, 411–15
Tillich, Paul, 219, 395
Time, 26
  Dualist Vedanta, 148
  Pure Nondualism, 324, 489
  Śaiva Orthodoxy, 166, 170, 172, 174, 469, 470

Sonic Absolutism, 224
Yoga, 78
Tradition (*smṛti*)
Dualist Vedanta, 154, 155
Energy-Qualified Nondualism, 396, 397
Indivisible Nondualism, 269–74, 278
Ineffable Difference-in-Identity, 344, 345
Innate Difference-in-Identity, 308
Pure Nondualism, 318–19, 325, 328
Śaiva Nondualism, 391, 393
Sonic Absolutism, 224–27, 235–36
Triadism, 373–74, 380
Transformation (*pariṇāma*), 201–5, 225–26
Transmigration
Ineffable Difference-in-Identity, 339
Nondualism, 198
Pure Nondualism, 319, 320, 325
Śaiva Orthodoxy, 177, 470
Triadism, 363
Transmogrification (*vivarta*)
Brahman, 201–6
Nondualism, 187, 201–6
Śaiva Orthodoxy, 181
Treatise on the Dance or *Nāṭyaśāstra* (Bharata), 317
Triadism (*Trika*), 42, 221, 357–88, 496–99
Abhinava Gupta, 167, 358, 360, 368–78, 496–99
Action, 375, 382, 384
Atomism and, 366, 367
Brahman, 367, 371, 372
categories, 496–97
Causality, 377
Christianity and, 358
Consciousness, 357, 360, 364–70, 374–79, 384, 385, 496–97
Creation, 363, 365, 498
Divine Feminine, 357, 360
Divine Way, 359–61, 375–78, 386–87
Egoism, 383, 497
Energic Way, 359–62, 375, 384–86
Energy, 357, 361–72, 375–86, 496–99
Energy-Qualified Nondualism and, 396
Essence, 357, 374, 375, 386
Faculties, 362, 383, 387, 497
Family (of Energies) School, 360, 372, 378
Force, Agitation of, 369–72
Freedom, 357, 360, 370, 371, 374–80
God, 365–71, 376–80, 386, 498–99
Gradation School, 360
Happiness, 378
Identity, 357, 359
Ignorance, 360, 361, 373, 374
Illusionism and, 362
Impulse, 365–67
Individual Way, 359–64, 375
Infinity, 359, 360
Instinct, 366, 383, 385, 497
Jayaratha, 498–99

Joy, 361, 364, 370–72, 375–78, 384–86
Kālīs, 357, 385, 498–99
karma, 363
Knowledge, 360–67, 373–76, 382–86, 496
Kṣema Rāja, 360, 378–80
Liberation, 358, 363, 378, 379, 388
Light, 357, 358, 368–69, 374–77, 381–83, 496
Logicism and, 366, 367
Maheśvarānanda, 360, 381–88
Matter, 366, 382, 497
Mind, 383, 385, 497
Mirific Power, 360–62, 367, 382
Monist Pastoralism and, 347
Nondualism and, 187, 368–69
norms, 373, 376
Null Way, 359, 360, 375–76, 387–88
Pain, 363
Pleasure, 363, 367
Plenitude, 357, 359, 367
Pollution, 386
Qualified Nondualism and, 283
Reality, 357, 366, 376, 379, 381, 388
Revelation, 373–74, 381, 387
ritual sex, 360
Śaiva Orthodoxy and, 166–68, 367, 470
Salvation, 360
Sankhya and, 366
the Self, 361–64, 381–82, 387
Self-Awareness, 357, 360, 370, 371, 381–84, 386, 387
self-obscuration, 357, 358, 367, 497
Śiva, 357–88, 496
Somānanda, 360, 364–70
Sorrow, 370
Soul, 360–63, 367–68, 380, 382
Tradition, 373–74, 380
transmigration, 363
Trident Cluster, 434–35
Truth, 361, 381–88
the Universe, 357, 361, 377, 381
Vasu Gupta, 221, 360–64, 378–79, 435
Vibrancy, 357, 360, 370, 371, 378–81, 387
Wheel of Energies, 360, 361
Wheel of systems, 420, 422
Will, 366, 368, 375, 377, 380, 384–86
Wonder, 357–58, 361, 364
Word, 383
Yoga and, 362, 363, 368, 375, 386, 387
Trident Cluster, 434–36
Trika. See Triadism
Trimūrti, the, 34
Triumph of the Engarlanded Goddess, The, or *Mālinīvijaya,* 374
Truth
Ancient Vedanta, 252–53
Conditioned Difference-in-Identity, 260, 266
Dualist Vedanta, 132
Energy-Qualified Nondualism, 400–1

Indivisible Nondualism, 268, 269
Logicism, 109, 111, 112
Nondualism, 185, 188, 190, 193
Pure Nondualism, 323
Qualified Nondualism, 286–87, 298, 299
Śaiva Orthodoxy, 175
Sonic Absolutism, 224
Triadism, 361, 381–88

Udayana, 105, 108, 112–21, 185
Uddālaka, 27, 54, 105, 316, 317, 417, 446–47
Uddhava, 337, 341, 345
Uddyotakara, 108, 111–12
Umā, 361, 393
Umāpati Śivacārya, 168
Undivided Nondualism (*Purātanādvaita*), 188
Lamp of the Vedanta, 426–27
Wheel of systems, 420–21
Universe, the
Atomism, 105–7
Evolution of, 473–74, 479, 502–3
Pāñcarātra theology, 480–83
masculine-feminine polarity of, 175–78
Nondualism, 189, 472, 473–74
Qualified Nondualism, 283
Triadism, 357, 361, 377, 381

Vācaspati Miśra, 55, 68–70, 80, 154, 215, 427
Vacuism (*Śūnyavāda* or *Mādhyamika darśana*), 185, 189, 395
Lotus of, 418–19
Vādi Rāja, 124, 156
Vaiseśika. See Atomism
Vaiṣṇava Alvars, 282
Vaiṣṇava Vedanta, 220–21, 429–32
Lotus Pool of, 430–32
Vallabha, 221, 284, 315–28, 333, 335, 339, 428, 431, 489
Vamadeva, 246, 439
Vanamāli Miśra, 124, 162–65
Varṣagaṇya, 54
Varuṇa, 446, 448
Vasiṣṭha, 209
Vasubandhu, 26, 28, 84, 419
Vasudeva, 340, 343
Vasu Gupta, 360–64, 378–79, 435
Vātsyāyana, 108–11
Vedanta
Energy-Qualified Nondualism, 396, 397
Indivisible Nondualism, 268, 271–75, 281
Lamp of, 426–28
Pure Nondualism, 318
Śaiva Nondualism, 389
Vedānta Deśika, 284, 299–305
Vedas, the, 29, 41, 42, 85, 86, 119, 130–33, 151, 285–87
Energy-Qualified Nondualism, 396, 397, 404
the impersonal in, 285–86
Innate Difference-in-Identity, 308, 309

Nondualism, 196–99
Observance, 88
pluralism, 31
Pure Nondualism, 318, 319
Sacrifice, 88–89
Sonic Absolutism, 224–25, 231
Word, 87–88, 98–99, 102–4
Vericism (*Prābhākara Mīmāṁsā*), 102–4
Ritualism and, 85–86
Vibrancy (*spanda*), 357, 360, 370, 371, 378–81, 387
Vidyāranya, 472, 473
Vieira, António, 406
Vienna Circle, 223
Vijñāna Bhikṣu, 70, 78, 220, 268–75, 427, 457, 478, 479
Vimalamitra, 419
Violence, 41, 77
Monist Pastoralism, 346, 350
Śaiva Nondualism, 390, 392
Vīra-Śaiva Darśana. See Energy-Qualified Nondualism
Viśiṣṭādvaita. See Qualified Nondualism
Viṣṇu, 32, 34, 151, 154, 220, 274, 394
Dualist Vedanta, 126, 135–36, 150
Energicism, 407
Ineffable Difference-in-Identity, 337, 339, 344, 345
Innate Difference-in-Identity, 307
Nondualism, 197
Pure Nondualism, 321, 325
Qualified Nondualism, 284, 297, 298
Viṣṇudharmottara Purāṇa, 313
Viṣṇu Nārāyaṇa, 124–25, 134–36
Viṣṇu Purāṇa, 274, 345
Viṣṇu Svāmin, 221, 428, 431
Viśvakarmā, 446–47
Vraja land, 335–40, 343
Vṛndāvana, 335, 342, 491
Vṛṣabha, 307
Vyāsa, 78, 79, 125, 135, 153, 197, 272, 273
Pure Nondualism, 318, 325
Yoga, 81–83
Vyāsa Rāmācārya, 124, 157–61
Vyāsa Rāya, 123, 124, 149–61, 186, 213–14

Way of Fullness (*puṣṭi mārga*), 316
Wheel of Energies (*śakticakra*), 360, 361
Wheel of Hindu Systems, 420–22
Will (*icchā*)
Śaiva Nondualism, 393, 394
Śaiva Orthodoxy, 167, 170, 471
Triadism, 366, 368, 375, 377, 380, 384–86
Witness (*sākṣī*), 122, 126–27, 329

Wonder (*camatkāra*), 357–58, 361, 364
Word (*śabda*)
  Ancient Vedanta, 241
  Dualist Vedanta, 122, 126, 133
  Energy-Qualified Nondualism, 397
  Knowledge and, 85, 87, 95–96, 103
  Pure Nondualism, 316
  Ritualism, 85, 87–88, 90, 95–99
  Sonic Absolutism, 223–37
  Triadism, 383
  the Vedas, 87–88, 98–99, 102–4
  Vericism, 102–4
Words (human)
  Dualist Vedanta, 129–30, 133–34
  Knowledge and, 103–4
  processing of, 229–30
  Ritualism, 96–99
  Vericism, 102–4
Works (*Karma*), Era of, 44

Yādava Prakāśa, 427, 431
Yajñadatta, 88
Yājñavalkya, 258, 260, 446, 448
Yajur, 41, 225
Yama, 152
Yāmuna, 220, 282–87, 389, 427, 431
Yang and Yin, 29
Yoga, 28, 41, 51, 77–83, 457–59
  Buddhism and, 77
  Consciousness, 77
  Energy-Qualified Nondualism and, 397, 398
  Indivisible Nondualism and, 268, 271–74
  Ineffable Difference-in-Identity and, 344
  interiority, 29–30
  Karate, 77
  karma, 79–80
  Kempo, 77
  Matter, 77, 78
  Monist Pastoralism and, 348, 355–56
  OM, 80
  Patañjali, 78–83
  Pure Nondualism and, 327
  Sankhya and, 77–78
  Spirit, 77, 78, 82, 83
  Tae Kwon Do, 77
  Tantra, 77
  Time, 78
  Triadism and, 362, 363, 368, 375, 386, 387
  Trident Cluster, 434–35
  Vyāsa, 81–83
  Wheel of systems, 420–21
  Zen, 77
Yudhiṣṭhira, 336

Zagaglia, Giuseppe, 425
Zen, 77